Undergraduate Topics in Science

Undergraduate Topics in Computer Science (UTiCS) delivers high-quality instructional content for undergraduates studying in all areas of computing and information science. From core foundational and theoretical material to final-year topics and applications, UTiCS books take a fresh, concise, and modern approach and are ideal for self-study or for a one- or two-semester course. The texts are all authored by established experts in their fields, reviewed by an international advisory board, and contain numerous examples and problems. Many include fully worked solutions.

For further volumes:
www.springer.com/series/7592

Reinhard Klette

Concise Computer Vision

An Introduction into Theory and Algorithms

 Springer

Reinhard Klette
Computer Science Department
University of Auckland
Auckland, New Zealand

Series Editor
Ian Mackie

ISSN 1863-7310   ISSN 2197-1781 (electronic)
Undergraduate Topics in Computer Science
ISBN 978-1-4471-6319-0   ISBN 978-1-4471-6320-6 (eBook)
DOI 10.1007/978-1-4471-6320-6
Springer London Heidelberg New York Dordrecht

Library of Congress Control Number: 2013958392

Springer is part of Springer Science+Business Media (www.springer.com)

Dedicated to all who have dreams

Computer vision may count the trees, estimate the distance to the islands, but it cannot detect the fantasies the people might have had who visited this bay

Preface

This is a textbook for a third- or fourth-year undergraduate course on Computer vision, which is a discipline in science and engineering.

Subject Area of the Book Computer Vision aims at using cameras for analysing or understanding scenes in the real world. This discipline studies methodological and algorithmic problems as well as topics related to the implementation of designed solutions.

In computer vision we may want to know how far away a building is to a camera, whether a vehicle drives in the middle of its lane, how many people are in a scene, or we even want to recognize a particular person—all to be answered based on recorded images or videos. Areas of application have expanded recently due to a solid progress in computer vision. There are significant advances in camera and computing technologies, but also in theoretical foundations of computer vision methodologies.

In recent years, computer vision became a key technology in many fields. For modern consumer products, see, for example apps for mobile phones, driver-assistance for cars, or user interaction with computer games. In industrial automation, computer vision is routinely used for quality or process control. There are significant contributions for the movie industry (e.g. the use of avatars or the creation of virtual worlds based on recorded images, the enhancement of historic video data, or high-quality presentations of movies). This is just mentioning a few application areas, which all come with particular image or video data, and particular needs to process or analyse those data.

Features of the Book This text book provides a general introduction into basics of computer vision, as potentially of use for many diverse areas of applications. Mathematical subjects play an important role, and the book also discusses algorithms. The book is not addressing particular applications.

Inserts (grey boxes) in the book provide historic context information, references or sources for presented material, and particular hints on mathematical subjects discussed first time at a given location. They are *additional* readings to the baseline material provided.

The book is *not* a guide on current research in computer vision, and it provides only a *very few* references; the reader can locate more easily on the net by searching for keywords of interest. The field of computer vision is actually so vivid, with countless references, such that any attempt would fail to insert in the given limited space a reasonable collection of references. But here is one hint at least: visit homepages.inf.ed.ac.uk/rbf/CVonline/ for a web-based introduction into topics in computer vision.

Target Audiences   This text book provides material for an introductory course at third- or fourth-year level in an Engineering or Science undergraduate programme. Having some prior knowledge in image processing, image analysis, or computer graphics is of benefit, but the first two chapters of this text book also provide a first-time introduction into computational imaging.

Previous Uses of the Material   Parts of the presented materials have been used in my lectures in the Mechatronics and Computer Science programmes at The University of Auckland, New Zealand, at CIMAT Guanajuato, Mexico, at Freiburg and Göttingen University, Germany, at the Technical University Cordoba, Argentina, at the Taiwan National Normal University, Taiwan, and at Wuhan University, China.

The presented material also benefits from four earlier book publications, [R. Klette and P. Zamperoni. Handbook of Image Processing Operators. Wiley, Chichester, 1996], [R. Klette, K. Schlüns, and A. Koschan. Computer Vision. Springer, Singapore, 1998], [R. Klette and A. Rosenfeld. Digital Geometry. Morgan Kaufmann, San Francisco, 2004], and [F. Huang, R. Klette, and K. Scheibe. Panoramic Imaging. Wiley, West Sussex, 2008].

The first two of those four books accompanied computer vision lectures of the author in Germany and New Zealand in the 1990s and early 2000s, and the third one also more recent lectures.

Notes to the Instructor and Suggested Uses   The book contains more material than what can be covered in a one-semester course. An instructor should select according to given context such as prior knowledge of students and research focus in subsequent courses.

Each chapter ends with some exercises, including programming exercises. The book does not favour any particular implementation environment. Using procedures from systems such as OpenCV will typically simplify the solution. Programming exercises are intentionally formulated in a way to offer students a wide range of options for answering them. For example, for Exercise 2.5 in Chap. 2, you can use Java applets to visualize the results (but the text does not ask for it), you can use small- or large-sized images (the text does not specify it), and you can limit cursor movement to a central part of the input image such that the 11×11 square around location p is always completely contained in your image (or you can also cover special cases when moving the cursor also closer to the image border). As a result, every student should come up with her/his individual solution to programming exercises, and creativity in the designed solution should also be honoured.

Supplemental Resources The book is accompanied by supplemental material (data, sources, examples, presentations) on a website. See www.cs.auckland.ac.nz/~rklette/Books/K2014/.

Acknowledgements In alphabetical order of surnames, I am thanking the following colleagues, former or current students, and friends (if I am just mentioning a figure, then I am actually thanking for joint work or contacts about a subject related to that figure):

A-Kn *Ali Al-Sarraf* (Fig. 2.32), *Hernan Badino* (Fig. 9.25), *Anko Börner* (various comments on drafts of the book, and also contributions to Sect. 5.4.2), *Hugo Carlos* (support while writing the book at CIMAT), *Diego Caudillo* (Figs. 1.9, 5.28, and 5.29), *Gilberto Chávez* (Figs. 3.39 and 5.36, top row), *Chia-Yen Chen* (Figs. 6.21 and 7.25), *Kaihua Chen* (Fig. 3.33), *Ting-Yen Chen* (Fig. 5.35, contributions to Sect. 2.4, to Chap. 5, and provision of sources), *Eduardo Destefanis* (contribution to Example 9.1 and Fig. 9.5), *Uwe Franke* (Figs. 3.36, 6.3, and bottom, right, in 9.23), *Stefan Gehrig* (comments on stereo analysis parts and Fig. 9.25), *Roberto Guzmán* (Fig. 5.36, bottom row), *Wang Han* (having his students involved in checking a draft of the book), *Ralf Haeusler* (contributions to Sect. 8.1.5), *Gabriel Hartmann* (Fig. 9.24), *Simon Hermann* (contributions to Sects. 5.4.2 and 8.1.2, Figs. 4.16 and 7.5), *Václav Hlaváč* (suggestions for improving the contents of Chaps. 1 and 2), *Heiko Hirschmüller* (Fig. 7.1), *Wolfgang Huber* (Fig. 4.12, bottom, right), *Fay Huang* (contributions to Chap. 6, in particular to Sect. 6.1.4), *Ruyi Jiang* (contributions to Sect. 9.3.3), *Waqar Khan* (Fig. 7.17), *Ron Kimmel* (presentation suggestions on local operators and optic flow—which I need to keep mainly as a project for a future revision of the text), *Karsten Knoeppel* (contributions to Sect. 9.3.4),

Ko-Sc *Andreas Koschan* (comments on various parts of the book and Fig. 7.18, right), *Vladimir Kovalevsky* (Fig. 2.15), *Peter Kovesi* (contributions to Chaps. 1 and 2 regarding phase congruency, including the permission to reproduce figures), *Walter Kropatsch* (suggestions to Chaps. 2 and 3), *Richard Lewis-Shell* (Fig. 4.12, bottom, left), *Fajie Li* (Exercise 5.9), *Juan Lin* (contributions to Sect. 10.3), *Yizhe Lin* (Fig. 6.19), *Dongwei Liu* (Fig. 2.16), *Yan Liu* (permission to publish Fig. 1.6), *Rocío Lizárraga* (permission to publish Fig. 5.2, bottom row), *Peter Meer* (comments on Sect. 2.4.2), *James Milburn* (contributions to Sect. 4.4). *Pedro Real* (comments on geometric and topologic subjects), *Mahdi Rezaei* (contributions to face detection in Chap. 10, including text and figures, and Exercise 10.2), *Bodo Rosenhahn* (Fig. 7.9, right), *John Rugis* (definition of similarity curvature and Exercises 7.2 and 7.6), *James Russell* (contributions to Sect. 5.1.1), *Jorge Sanchez* (contribution to Example 9.1, Figs. 9.1, right, and 9.5), *Konstantin Schauwecker* (comments on feature detectors and RANSAC plane detection, Figs. 6.10, right, 7.19, 9.9, and 2.23), *Karsten Scheibe* (contributions to Chap. 6, in particular to Sect. 6.1.4), and Fig. 7.1), *Karsten Schlüns* (contributions to Sect. 7.4),

Sh-Z *Bok-Suk Shin* (Latex editing suggestions, comments on various parts of the book, contributions to Sects. 3.4.1 and 5.1.1, and Fig. 9.23 with related comments),

Eric Song (Fig. 5.6, left), *Zijiang Song* (contributions to Chap. 9, in particular to Sect. 9.2.4), *Kathrin Spiller* (contribution to 3D case in Sect. 7.2.2), *Junli Tao* (contributions to pedestrian detection in Chap. 10, including text and figures and Exercise 10.1, and comments about the structure of this chapter), *Akihiko Torii* (contributions to Sect. 6.1.4), *Johan VanHorebeek* (comments on Chap. 10), *Tobi Vaudrey* (contributions to Sect. 2.3.2 and Fig. 4.18, contributions to Sect. 9.3.4, and Exercise 9.6), *Mou Wei* (comments on Chap. 4), *Shou-Kang Wei* (joint work on subjects related to Sect. 6.1.4), *Tiangong Wei* (contributions to Sect. 7.4.3), *Jürgen Wiest* (Fig. 9.1, left), *Yihui Zheng* (contributions to Sect. 5.1.1), *Zezhong Xu* (contributions to Sect. 3.4.1 and Fig. 3.40), *Shenghai Yuan* (comments on Sects. 3.3.1 and 3.3.2), *Qi Zang* (Exercise 5.5, and Figs. 2.21, 5.37, and 10.1), *Yi Zeng* (Fig. 9.15), and *Joviša Žunić* (contributions to Sect. 3.3.2).

The author is, in particular, indebted to *Sandino Morales* (D.F., Mexico) for implementing and testing algorithms, providing many figures, contributions to Chaps. 4 and 8, and for numerous comments about various parts of the book, to *Władysław Skarbek* (Warsaw, Poland) for manifold suggestions for improving the contents, and for contributing Exercises 1.9, 2.10, 2.11, 3.12, 4.11, 5.7, 5.8, and 6.10, and to *Garry Tee* (Auckland, New Zealand) for careful reading, commenting, for parts of Insert 5.9, the footnote on p. 402, and many more valuable hints.

I thank my wife, *Gisela Klette*, for authoring Sect. 3.2.4 about the Euclidean distance transform and critical views on structure and details of the book while the book was written at CIMAT Guanajuato between mid July to beginning of November 2013 during a sabbatical leave from The University of Auckland, New Zealand.

Guanajuato, Mexico   Reinhard Klette
3 November 2013

Contents

Symbols

$\|S\|$	Cardinality of a set S
$\|\mathbf{a}\|_1$	L_1 norm
$\|\mathbf{a}\|_2$	L_2 norm
$\wedge$	Logical 'and'
$\vee$	Logical 'or'
$\cap$	Intersection of sets
$\cup$	Union of sets
$\square$	End of proof
a, b, c	Real numbers
A	Adjacency set
$\mathscr{A}(\cdot)$	Area of a measurable set (as a function)
$\mathbf{a}, \mathbf{b}, \mathbf{c}$	Vectors
$\mathbf{A}, \mathbf{B}, \mathbf{C}$	Matrices
α, β, γ	Angles
b	Base distance of a stereo camera system
$\mathbb{C}$	Set of complex numbers $a + i \cdot b$, with $i = \sqrt{-1}$ and $a, b \in \mathbb{R}$
d	Disparity
d_1	L_1 metric
d_2	L_2 metric, also known as the Euclidean metric
e	Real constant $e = \exp(1) \approx 2.7182818284$
ε	Real number greater than zero
f	Focal length
f, g, h	Functions
$G_{\max}$	Maximum grey level in an image
γ	Curve in a Euclidean space (e.g. a straight line, polyline, or smooth curve)
$\mathbf{H}$	Hessian matrix
i, j, k, l, m, n	Natural numbers; pixel coordinates (i, j) in a window
$I, I(., ., t)$	Image, frame of a sequence, frame at time t
L	Length (as a real number)

$\mathscr{L}(\cdot)$	Length of a rectifiable curve (as a function)
λ	Real number; default: between 0 and 1
n	Natural number
N	Neighbourhood (in the image grid)
N_{cols}, N_{rows}	Number of columns, number of rows
$\mathbb{N}$	Set $\{0, 1, 2, \ldots\}$ of natural numbers
$\mathcal{O}(\cdot)$	Asymptotic upper bound
Ω	Image carrier, set of all $N_{cols} \times N_{rows}$ pixel locations
p, q	Points in $\mathbb{R}^2$, with coordinates x and y
P, Q, R	Points in $\mathbb{R}^3$, with coordinates X, Y, and Z
π	Real constant $\pi = 4 \times \arctan(1) \approx 3.14159265358979$
Π	Polyhedron
r	Radius of a disk or sphere; point in $\mathbb{R}^2$ or $\mathbb{R}^3$
$\mathbb{R}$	Set of real numbers
$\mathbf{R}$	Rotation matrix
ρ	Path with finite number of vertices
s	Point in $\mathbb{R}^2$ or $\mathbb{R}^3$
S	Set
t	Time; point in $\mathbb{R}^2$ or $\mathbb{R}^3$
$\mathbf{t}$	Translation vector
T, τ	Threshold (real number)
u, v	Components of optical flow; vertices or nodes; points in $\mathbb{R}^2$ or $\mathbb{R}^3$
$\mathbf{u}$	Optical flow vector with $\mathbf{u} = (u, v)$
W, W_p	Window in an image, window with reference pixel p
x, y	Real variables; pixel coordinates (x, y) in an image
X, Y, Z	Coordinates in $\mathbb{R}^3$
$\mathbb{Z}$	Set of integers

Image Data

This chapter introduces basic notation and mathematical concepts for describing an image in a regular grid in the spatial domain or in the frequency domain. It also details ways for specifying colour and introduces colour images.

1.1 Images in the Spatial Domain

A (digital) *image* is defined by *integrating* and *sampling* continuous (analog) data in a spatial domain. It consists of a rectangular array of *pixels* (x, y, u), each combining a location $(x, y) \in \mathbb{Z}^2$ and a value u, the *sample* at location (x, y). $\mathbb{Z}$ is the set of all integers. Points $(x, y) \in \mathbb{Z}^2$ form a *regular grid*. In a more formal way, an image I is defined on a rectangular set, the *carrier*

$$\Omega = \left\{ (x, y) : 1 \leq x \leq N_{cols} \wedge 1 \leq y \leq N_{rows} \right\} \subset \mathbb{Z}^2 \qquad (1.1)$$

of I containing the *grid points* or *pixel locations* for $N_{cols} \geq 1$ and $N_{rows} \geq 1$.

We assume a left-hand coordinate system as shown in Fig. 1.1. *Row* y contains grid points $\{(1, y), (2, y), \ldots, (N_{cols}, y)\}$ for $1 \leq y \leq N_{rows}$, and *column* x contains grid points $\{(x, 1), (x, 2), \ldots, (x, N_{rows})\}$ for $1 \leq x \leq N_{cols}$.

This section introduces into the subject of digital imaging by discussing ways to represent and to describe image data in the spatial domain defined by the carrier Ω.

1.1.1 Pixels and Windows

Figure 1.2 illustrates two ways of thinking about geometric representations of pixels, which are samples in a regularly spaced grid.

Grid Cells, Grid Points, and Adjacency Images that we see on a screen are composed of homogeneously shaded square cells. Following this given representation, we may think about a pixel as a tiny shaded square. This is the *grid cell model*. Alternatively, we can also consider each pixel as a grid point labelled with the image value. This *grid point model* was already indicated in Fig. 1.1.

R. Klette, *Concise Computer Vision*, Undergraduate Topics in Computer Science, DOI 10.1007/978-1-4471-6320-6_1, © Springer-Verlag London 2014

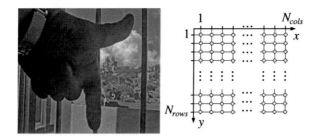

Fig. 1.1 A left-hand coordinate system. The thumb defines the x-axis, and the pointer the y-axis while looking into the palm of the hand. (The image on the *left* also shows a view on the baroque church at Valenciana, always present outside windows while this book was written during a stay of the author at CIMAT Guanajuato)

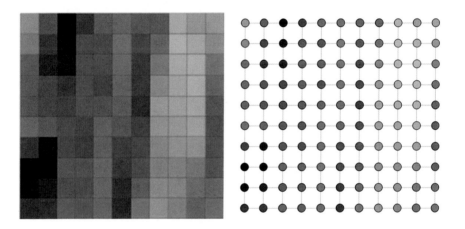

Fig. 1.2 *Left*: When zooming into an image, we see shaded *grid squares*; different shades represent values in a chosen set of image values. *Right*: Image values can also be assumed to be labels at *grid points* being the centres of grid squares

Insert 1.1 (Origin of the Term "Pixel") *The term* pixel *is short for* picture element. *It was introduced in the late* 1960s *by a group at the Jet Propulsion Laboratory in Pasadena, California, that was processing images taken by space vehicles. See* [R.B. Leighton, N.H. Horowitz, A.G. Herriman, A.T. Young, B.A. Smith, M.E. Davies, and C.B. Leovy. Mariner 6 television pictures: First report. *Science*, **165**:684–690, 1969].

Pixels are the "atomic elements" of an image. They do not define particular adjacency relations between pixels per se. In the grid cell model we may assume that pixel locations are adjacent iff they are different and their tiny shaded squares share

Fig. 1.3 A 73×77 window in the image `SanMiguel`. The marked reference pixel location is at $p = (453, 134)$ in the image that shows the main pyramid at Cañada de la Virgin, Mexico

an edge.[1] Alternatively, we can also assume that they are adjacent iff they are different and their tiny shaded squares share at least one point (i.e. an edge or a corner).

Image Windows   A *window* $W_p^{m,n}(I)$ is a subimage of image I of size $m \times n$ positioned with respect to a *reference point* p (i.e., a pixel location). The default is that $m = n$ is an odd number, and p is the centre location in the window. Figure 1.3 shows the window $W_{(453,134)}^{73,77}(\text{SanMiguel})$.

Usually we can simplify the notation to W_p because the image and the size of the window are known by the given context.

1.1.2   Image Values and Basic Statistics

Image values u are taken in a discrete set of possible values. It is also common in computer vision to consider the real interval $[0, 1] \subset \mathbb{R}$ as the range of a scalar image. This is in particular of value if image values are interpolated within performed processes and the data type REAL is used for image values. In this book we use integer image values as a default.

Scalar and Binary Images   A *scalar image* has integer values $u \in \{0, 1, \ldots, 2^a - 1\}$. It is common to identify such scalar values with grey levels, with $0 = \text{black}$ and $2^a - 1 = \text{white}$; all other grey levels are linearly interpolated between black and white. We speak about *grey-level images* in this case. For many years, it was common to use $a = 8$; recently $a = 16$ became the new technological standard. In order to be independent, we use $G_{\max} = 2^a - 1$.

A *binary image* has only two values at its pixels, traditionally denoted by $0 = \text{white}$ and $1 = \text{black}$, meaning black objects on a white background.

---

[1]Read *iff* as "if and only if"; acronym proposed by the mathematician P.R. Halmos (1916–2006).

Fig. 1.4 Original RGB colour image Fountain (*upper left*), showing a square in Guanajuato, and its decomposition into the three contributing channels: *Red* (*upper right*), *Green* (*lower left*), and *Blue* (*lower right*). For example, *red* is shown with high intensity in the *red channel*, but in low intensity in the *green* and *blue channel*

Vector-Valued and RGB Images   A *vector-valued image* has more than one *channel* or *band*, as it is the case for scalar images. Image values $(u_1, \ldots, u_{N_{channels}})$ are vectors of length $N_{channels}$. For example, colour images in the common RGB colour model have three channels, one for the red component, one for the green, and one for the blue component. The values u_i in each channel are in the set $\{0, 1, \ldots, G_{max}\}$; each channel is just a grey-level image. See Fig. 1.4.

Mean   Assume an $N_{cols} \times N_{rows}$ scalar image I. Following basic statistics, we define the *mean* (i.e., the "average grey level") of image I as

$$\mu_I = \frac{1}{N_{cols} \cdot N_{rows}} \sum_{x=1}^{N_{cols}} \sum_{y=1}^{N_{rows}} I(x, y)$$

$$= \frac{1}{|\Omega|} \sum_{(x,y) \in \Omega} I(x, y) \tag{1.2}$$

where $|\Omega| = N_{cols} \cdot N_{rows}$ is the cardinality of the carrier Ω of all pixel locations. We prefer the second way. We use I rather than u in this formula; I is a unique mapping defined on Ω, and with u we just denote individual image values.

Variance and Standard Deviation   The *variance* of image I is defined as

$$\sigma_I^2 = \frac{1}{|\Omega|} \sum_{(x,y)\in\Omega} \left[I(x,y) - \mu_I \right]^2 \tag{1.3}$$

Its root σ_I is the *standard deviation* of image I.

Some well-known formulae from statistics can be applied, such as

$$\sigma_I^2 = \left[\frac{1}{|\Omega|} \sum_{(x,y)\in\Omega} I(x,y)^2 \right] - \mu_I^2 \tag{1.4}$$

Equation (1.4) provides a way that the mean and variance can be calculated by running through a given image I only once. If only using (1.2) and (1.3), then two runs would be required, one for calculating the mean, to be used in a second run when calculating the variance.

Histograms   A *histogram* represents tabulated frequencies, typically by using bars in a graphical diagram. Histograms are used for representing value frequencies of a scalar image, or of one channel or band of a vector-valued image.

Assume a scalar image I with pixels (i, j, u), where $0 \leq u \leq G_{max}$. We define *absolute frequencies* by the count of appearances of a value u in the carrier Ω of all pixel locations, formally defined by

$$H_I(u) = \left| \left\{ (x,y) \in \Omega : I(x,y) = u \right\} \right| \tag{1.5}$$

where $| \cdot |$ denotes the cardinality of a set. *Relative frequencies* between 0 and 1, comparable to the *probability density function* (PDF) of a distribution of discrete random numbers $I(p)$, are denoted by

$$h_I(u) = \frac{H_I(u)}{|\Omega|} \tag{1.6}$$

The values $H_I(0), H_I(1), \ldots, H_I(G_{max})$ define the (absolute) *grey-level histogram* of a scalar image I. See Fig. 1.5 for histograms of an original image and three altered versions of it.

We can compute the mean and variance also based on relative frequencies as follows:

$$\mu_I = \sum_{u=0}^{G_{max}} u \cdot h_I(u) \quad \text{or} \quad \sigma_I^2 = \sum_{u=0}^{G_{max}} [u - \mu_I]^2 \cdot h_I(u) \tag{1.7}$$

This provides a speed-up if the histogram was already calculated.

Absolute and relative *cumulative frequencies* are defined as follows, respectively:

$$C_I(u) = \sum_{v=0}^{u} H_I(v) \quad \text{and} \quad c_I(u) = \sum_{v=0}^{u} h_I(v) \tag{1.8}$$

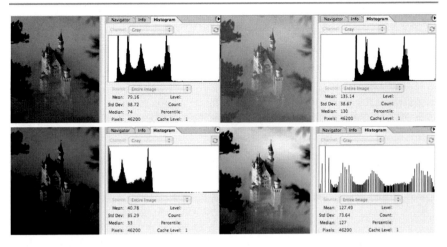

Fig. 1.5 Histograms for the 200×231 image Neuschwanstein. *Upper left*: Original image. *Upper right*: Brighter version. *Lower left*: Darker version. *Lower right*: After histogram equalization (will be defined later)

Those values are shown in *cumulative histograms*. Relative frequencies are comparable to the *probability function* $\Pr[I(p) \leq u]$ of discrete random numbers $I(p)$.

Value Statistics in a Window   Assume a (default) window $W = W_p^{n,n}(I)$, with $n = 2k + 1$ and $p = (x, y)$. Then we have in window coordinates

$$\mu_W = \frac{1}{n^2} \sum_{i=-k}^{+k} \sum_{j=-k}^{+k} I(x+i, y+j) \tag{1.9}$$

See Fig. 1.6. Formulas for the variance, and so forth, can be adapted analogously.

Example 1.1 (Examples of Windows and Histograms) The 489×480 image Yan, shown in Fig. 1.6, contains two marked 104×98 windows, W_1 showing the face, and W_2 containing parts of the bench and of the dress. Figure 1.6 also shows the histograms for both windows on the right.

A 3-dimensional (3D) view of grey levels (here interpreted as being elevations) illustrates the different "degrees of homogeneity" in an image. See Fig. 1.7 for an example. The steep slope from a lower plateau to a higher plateau in Fig. 1.7, left, is a typical illustration of an "edge" in an image.

In image analysis we have to classify windows into categories such as "within a homogeneous region" or "of low contrast", or "showing an edge between two different regions" or "of high contrast". We define the *contrast* $C(I)$ of an image I as the mean absolute difference between pixel values and the mean value at adjacent

Count: 10192	Min: 9
Mean: 133.711	Max: 255
StdDev: 55.391	Mode: 178 (180)

Count: 10192	Min: 11
Mean: 104.637	Max: 254
StdDev: 89.862	Mode: 23 (440)

Fig. 1.6 Examples of two 104×98 windows in image Yan, shown with corresponding histograms on the *right*. *Upper window*: $\mu_{W_1} = 133.7$ and $\sigma_{W_1} = 55.4$. *Lower window*: $\mu_{W_2} = 104.6$ and $\sigma_{W_2} = 89.9$

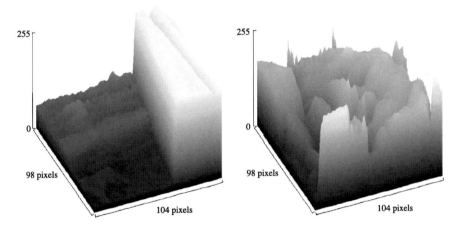

Fig. 1.7 *Left*: A "steep slope from dark to bright". *Right*: An "insignificant" variation. Note the different scales in both 3D views of the two windows in Fig. 1.6

pixels

$$C(I) = \frac{1}{|\Omega|} \sum_{(x,y)\in\Omega} \left| I(x, y) - \mu_{A(x,y)} \right| \tag{1.10}$$

where $\mu_{A(x,y)}$ is the mean value of pixel locations adjacent to pixel location (x, y).

Fig. 1.8 *Left*: Two selected image rows in the intensity channel (i.e. values $(R + G + B)/3$) of image SanMiguel shown in Fig. 1.3. *Right*: Intensity profiles for both selected rows

For another example for using low-level statistics for simple image interpretations, see Fig. 1.4. The mean values of the Red, Green, and Blue channels show that the shown colour image has a more significant Red component (upper right, with a mean of 154) and less defining Green (lower left, with a mean of 140) and Blue (lower right, with a mean of 134) components. This can be verified more in detail by looking at the histograms for these three channels, illustrating a "brighter image" for the Red channel, especially for the region of the house in the centre of the image, and "darker images" for the Green and Blue channels in this region.

1.1.3   Spatial and Temporal Data Measures

The provided basic statistical definitions already allow us to define functions that describe images, such as row by row in a single image or frame by frame for a given sequence of images.

Value Statistics in an Intensity Profile   When considering image data in a new application domain, it is also very informative to visualize *intensity profiles* defined by 1D cuts through the given scalar data arrays.

Figure 1.8 illustrates two intensity profiles along the x-axis of the shown grey-level image. Again, we can use mean, variance, and histograms of such selected $N_{cols} \times 1$ "narrow" windows for obtaining an impression about the distribution of image values.

Spatial or Temporal Value Statistics   Histograms or intensity profiles are examples for *spatial value statistics*. For example, intensity profiles for rows 1 to N_{rows} in one image I define a sequence of discrete functions, which can be compared with the corresponding sequence of another image J.

As another example, assume an image sequence consisting of *frames* I_t for $t = 1, 2, \ldots, T$, all defined on the same carrier Ω. For understanding value distributions, it can be useful to define a scalar *data measure* $\mathscr{D}(t)$ that maps one frame I_t into

Fig. 1.9 *Top*: A plot of two data measures for a sequence of 400 frames. *Bottom*: The same two measures, but after normalizing mean and variance of both measures

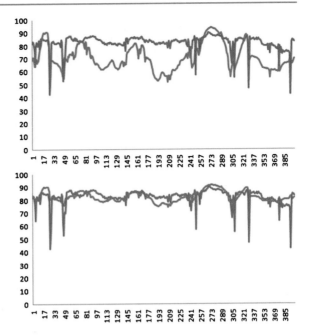

one number and to compare then different data measures for the given discrete time interval $[1, 2, \ldots, T]$, thus supporting *temporal value statistics*.

For example, the contrast as defined in (1.10) defines a data measure $\mathscr{P}(t) = C(I_t)$, the mean as defined in (1.2) defines a data measure $\mathscr{M}(t) = \mu_{I_t}$, and the variance as defined in (1.3) defines a data measure $\mathscr{V}(t) = \sigma_{I_t}^2$.

Figure 1.9, top, illustrates two data measures on a sequence of 400 images. (The used image sequence and the used data measures are not of importance in the given context.) Both measures have their individual range across the image sequence, characterized by mean and variance. For a better comparison, we map both data measures onto functions having identical mean and variance.

Normalization of Two Functions   Let μ_f and σ_f be the mean and standard deviation of a function f. Given are two real-valued functions f and g with the same discrete domain, say defined on arguments $1, 2, \ldots, T$, and non-zero variances. Let

$$\alpha = \frac{\sigma_g}{\sigma_f}\mu_f - \mu_g \quad \text{and} \quad \beta = \frac{\sigma_f}{\sigma_g} \tag{1.11}$$

$$g_{new}(x) = \beta\big(g(x) + \alpha\big) \tag{1.12}$$

As a result, the function g_{new} has the same mean and variance as the function f.

Fig. 1.10 Edges, or visual silhouettes, have been used for thousands of years for showing the "essential information", such as in ancient cave drawings. *Left*: Image `Taroko` showing historic drawings of native people in Taiwan. *Middle*: Segment of image `Aussies` with shadow silhouettes recorded on top of building Q1, Goldcoast, Australia. *Right*: Shopping centre in Shanghai, image `OldStreet`

Distance Between Two Functions   Now we define the distance between two real-valued functions defined on the same discrete domain, say $1, 2, \ldots, T$:

$$d_1(f, g) = \frac{1}{T} \sum_{x=1}^{T} |f(x) - g(x)| \tag{1.13}$$

$$d_2(f, g) = \frac{1}{T} \sqrt{\sum_{x=1}^{T} (f(x) - g(x))^2} \tag{1.14}$$

Both distances are *metrics* thus satisfying the following axioms of a metric:
1. $f = g$ iff $d(f, g) = 0$,
2. $d(f, g) = d(g, f)$ (symmetry), and
3. $d(f, g) \leq d(f, h) + d(h, g)$ for a third function h (triangular inequality).

Structural Similarity of Data Measures   Assume two different spatial or temporal data measures $\mathscr{F}$ and $\mathscr{G}$ on the same domain $1, 2, \ldots, T$. We first map $\mathscr{G}$ into $\mathscr{G}_{new}$ such that both measures have now identical mean and variance and then calculate the distance between $\mathscr{F}$ and $\mathscr{G}_{new}$ using either the L_1- or L_2-metric.

Two measures $\mathscr{F}$ and $\mathscr{G}$ are *structurally similar* iff the resulting distance between $\mathscr{F}$ and $\mathscr{G}_{new}$ is close to zero. Structurally similar measures take their local maxima or minima at about the same arguments.

1.1.4   Step-Edges

Discontinuities in images are features that are often useful for initializing an image analysis procedure. Edges are important information for understanding an image (e.g. for eliminating the influence of varying illumination); by removing "non-edge" data we also simplify the data. See Fig. 1.10 for an illustration of the notion "edge" by three examples.

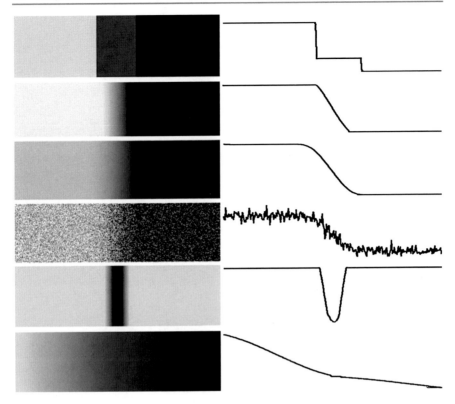

Fig. 1.11 Illustration for the step-edge model. *Left*: Synthetic input images. *Right*: Intensity profiles for the corresponding images on the left. *Top to bottom*: Ideal step-edges, linear edge, smooth edge, noisy edge, thin line, and a discontinuity in shaded region

Discontinuities in images can occur in small windows (e.g. noisy pixels) or define *edges* between image regions of different signal characteristics.

What Is an Edge?   Figure 1.11 illustrates a possible diversity of edges in images by sketches of 1D cuts through the intensity profile of an image, following the *step-edge model*. The step-edge model assumes that edges are defined by changes in local derivatives; the *phase-congruency model* is an alternative choice, and we discuss it in Sect. 1.2.5.

After having noise removal performed, let us assume that image values represent samples of a continuous function $I(x, y)$ defined on the Euclidean plane $\mathbb{R}^2$, which allows partial derivatives of first and second order with respect to x and y. See Fig. 1.12 for recalling properties of such derivatives.

Detecting Step-Edges by First- or Second-Order Derivatives   Figure 1.12 illustrates a noisy smooth edge, which is first mapped into a noise-free smooth edge (of course, that is our optimistic assumption). The first derivative maps intervals where the function is nearly constant onto values close to 0 and represents then an increase

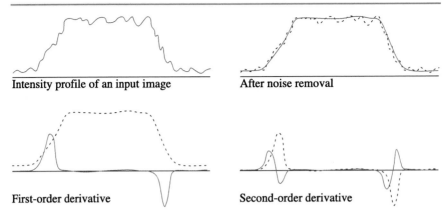

Fig. 1.12 Illustration of an input signal, signal after noise removal, first derivative, and second derivative

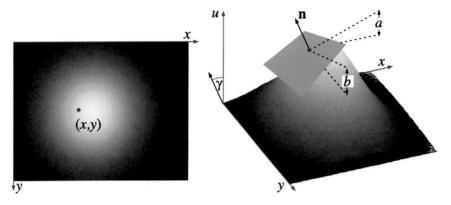

Fig. 1.13 *Left*: Synthetic input image with pixel location (x, y). *Right*: Illustration of tangential plane (in *green*) at pixel $(x, y, I(x, y))$, normal $\mathbf{n} = [a, b, 1]^\top$, which is orthogonal to this plane, and partial derivatives a (in x-direction) and b (in y-direction) in the left-hand Cartesian coordinate system defined by image coordinates x and y and the image-value axis u

or decrease in slope. The second derivative just repeats the same taking the first derivative as its input. Note that "middle" of the smooth edge is at the position of a local maximum or local minimum of the first derivative and also at the position where the second derivative changes its sign; this is called a *zero-crossing*.

Image as a Continuous Surface   Intensity values in image I can be understood as defining a surface having different elevations at pixel locations. See Fig. 1.13. Thus, an image I represents valleys, plateaus, gentle or steep slopes, and so forth in this interpretation. Values of partial derivatives in x- or y-direction correspond to a decrease or increase in altitude, or staying at the same height level. We recall a few notions used in mathematical analysis for describing surfaces based on derivatives.

First-Order Derivatives The *normal* **n** is orthogonal to the *tangential plane* at a pixel $(x, y, I(x, y))$; the tangential plane follows the surface defined by image values $I(x, y)$ on the xy-plane. The normal has an angle γ with the image-value axis.

The *gradient*

$$\nabla I = \mathbf{grad}\, I = \left[\frac{\partial I}{\partial x}, \frac{\partial I}{\partial y} \right]^{\mathsf{T}} \tag{1.15}$$

combines both partial derivatives at a given point $p = (x, y)$. Read ∇I as "nabla I". To be precise, we should write $[\mathbf{grad}\, f](p)$ and so forth, but we leave pixel location p out for easier reading of the formulae.

The *normal*

$$\mathbf{n} = \left[\frac{\partial I}{\partial x}, \frac{\partial I}{\partial y}, +1 \right]^{\mathsf{T}} \tag{1.16}$$

can point either into the positive or negative direction of the u-axis; we decide here for the positive direction and thus $+1$ in the formal definition. The *slope angle*

$$\gamma = \arccos \frac{1}{\|\mathbf{n}\|_2} \tag{1.17}$$

is defined between the u-axis and normal **n**. The first-order derivatives allow us to calculate the *length* (or *magnitude*) of gradient and normal:

$$\|\mathbf{grad}\, I\|_2 = \sqrt{\left(\frac{\partial I}{\partial x} \right)^2 + \left(\frac{\partial I}{\partial y} \right)^2} \quad \text{and} \quad \|\mathbf{n}\|_2 = \sqrt{\left(\frac{\partial I}{\partial x} \right)^2 + \left(\frac{\partial I}{\partial y} \right)^2 + 1} \tag{1.18}$$

Following Fig. 1.12 and the related discussion, we conclude that:

Observation 1.1 *It appears to be meaningful to detect edges at locations where the magnitudes* $\|\mathbf{grad}\, I\|_2$ *or* $\|\mathbf{n}\|_2$ *define a local maximum.*

Second-Order Derivatives Second-order derivatives are combined into either the *Laplacian* of I, given by

$$\triangle I = \nabla^2 I = \frac{\partial^2 I}{\partial x^2} + \frac{\partial^2 I}{\partial y^2} \tag{1.19}$$

or the *quadratic variation* of I, given by[2]

$$\left(\frac{\partial^2 I}{\partial x^2} \right)^2 + 2\left(\frac{\partial^2 I}{\partial x\, \partial y} \right)^2 + \left(\frac{\partial^2 I}{\partial y^2} \right)^2 \tag{1.20}$$

---

[2]To be precise, a function I satisfies the second-order differentiability condition iff $\left(\frac{\partial^2 I}{\partial x \partial y} \right) = \left(\frac{\partial^2 I}{\partial y \partial x} \right)$. We simply assumed in (1.20) that I satisfies this condition.

Fig. 1.14 The grey-level image WuhanU on the *left* is mapped into an edge image (or edge map) in the *middle*, and a coloured edge map on the *right*; a colour key may be used for illustrating directions or strength of edges. The image shows the main administration building of Wuhan University, China

Note that the Laplacian and quadratic variation are scalars and not vectors like the gradient or the normal. Following Fig. 1.12 and the related discussion, we conclude that:

Observation 1.2 *It appears to be meaningful to detect edges at locations where the Laplacian $\triangle I$ or the quadratic variation define a zero-crossing.*

Edge Maps and Ways for Detecting Edges   Operators for detecting "edges" map images into *edge images* or *edge maps*; see Fig. 1.14 for an example. There is no "general edge definition", and there is no "general edge detector".

In the spatial domain, they can be detected by following the step-edge model, see Sects. 2.3.3 and 2.4, or by applying residuals with respect to smoothing, see Sects. 2.3.2 and 2.3.5.

Discontinuities can also be detected in the frequency domain, such as by a high-pass filter as discussed in Sect. 2.1.3, or by applying a phase-congruency model; see Sect. 1.2.5 for the model and Sect. 2.4.3 for an algorithm using this model.

1.2   Images in the Frequency Domain

The *Fourier transform* defines a traditional way for processing signals. This section provides a brief introduction into basics of the Fourier transform and Fourier filtering, thus also explaining the meaning of "high-frequency information" or of "low-frequency information" in an image. The 2D Fourier transform maps an image from its spatial domain into the *frequency domain*, thus providing a totally different (but mathematically equivalent) representation.

1.2.1   Discrete Fourier Transform

The 2D *Discrete Fourier Transform* (DFT) maps an $N_{cols} \times N_{rows}$ scalar image I into a complex-valued Fourier transform $\mathbf{I}$. This is a mapping from the *spatial domain* of images into the *frequency domain* of Fourier transforms.

Insert 1.2 (Fourier and Integral Transforms) *J.B.J. Fourier (1768–1830) was a French mathematician. He analysed series and integrals of functions that are today known by his name.*

The Fourier transform is a prominent example of an integral transform. *It is related to the computationally simpler* cosine transform, *which is used in the baseline JPEG image encoding algorithm.*

Fourier Transform and Fourier Filtering—An Outlook   The analysis or changes of data in the frequency domain provide insights into the given image I. Changes in the frequency domain are *Fourier filter operations*. The inverse 2D DFT then maps the modified Fourier transform back into the modified image.

The whole process is called *Fourier filtering*, and it allows us, for example, to do contrast enhancement, noise removal, or smoothing of images. 1-dimensional (1D) Fourier filtering is commonly used in signal theory (e.g., for audio processing in mobile phones), and 2-dimensional (2D) Fourier filtering of images follows the same principles, just in 2D instead of in 1D.

In the context of the Fourier transform we assume that the image coordinates run from 0 to $N_{cols} - 1$ for x and from 0 to $N_{rows} - 1$ for y; otherwise, we would have to use $x - 1$ and $y - 1$ in all the formulas.

2D Fourier Transform   Formally, the 2D DFT is defined as follows:

$$\mathbf{I}(u, v) = \frac{1}{N_{cols} \cdot N_{rows}} \sum_{x=0}^{N_{cols}-1} \sum_{y=0}^{N_{rows}-1} I(x, y) \cdot \exp\left[-i 2\pi \left(\frac{xu}{N_{cols}} + \frac{yv}{N_{rows}}\right)\right]$$

(1.21)

for *frequencies* $u = 0, 1, \ldots, N_{cols} - 1$ and $v = 0, 1, \ldots, N_{rows} - 1$. The letter $i = \sqrt{-1}$ denotes (here in the context of Fourier transforms only) the *imaginary unit* of complex numbers.[3] For any real α, the *Eulerian formula*

$$\exp(i\alpha) = e^{i\alpha} = \cos\alpha + i \cdot \sin\alpha$$

(1.22)

demonstrates that the Fourier transform is actually a weighted sum of sine and cosine functions, but in the complex plane. If α is outside the interval $[0, 2\pi)$, then it is taken modulo 2π in this formula. The Eulerian number $e = 2.71828\ldots = \exp(1)$.

---

[3]Physicists or electric engineers use j rather than i, in order to distinguish from the intensity i in electricity.

Insert 1.3 (Descartes, Euler, and the Complex Numbers) *R. Descartes (1596–1650), a French scientist with a great influence on modern mathematics (e.g. Cartesian coordinates), still called negative solutions of quadric equations $a \cdot x^2 + b \cdot x + c = 0$ "false" and other solutions (that is, complex numbers) "imaginary". L. Euler (1707–1783), a Swiss mathematician, realized that*

$$e^{i\alpha} = \cos \alpha + i \cdot \sin \alpha$$

for $e = \lim_{n \to \infty}(1 + \frac{1}{n})^n = 2.71828\ldots$. This contributed to the acceptance of complex numbers at the end of the 18th century.

Complex numbers combine real parts and imaginary parts, and those new entities simplified mathematics. For instance, they made it possible to formulate (and later prove) the Fundamental Theorem of Algebra *that every polynomial equation has at least one root. Many problems in calculus, in physics, engineering, and other applications can be solved most conveniently in terms of complex numbers, even in those cases where the imaginary part of the solution is not used.*

1.2.2   Inverse Discrete Fourier Transform

The *inverse 2D DFT* transforms a Fourier transform $\mathbf{I}$ back into the spatial domain:

$$I(x, y) = \sum_{u=0}^{N_{cols}-1} \sum_{v=0}^{N_{rows}-1} \mathbf{I}(u, v) \exp \left[i 2\pi \left(\frac{xu}{N_{cols}} + \frac{yv}{N_{rows}} \right) \right] \qquad (1.23)$$

Note that the powers of the root of unity are here reversed compared to (1.21) (i.e., the minus sign has been replaced by a plus sign).

Variants of Transform Equations   Definitions of DFT and inverse DFT may vary. We can have the plus sign in the DFT and the minus sign in the inverse DFT.

   We have the scaling factor $1/N_{cols} \cdot N_{rows}$ in the 2D DFT and the scaling factor 1 in the inverse transform. Important is that the product of both scaling factors in the DFT and in the inverse DFT equals $1/N_{cols} \cdot N_{rows}$. We could have split $1/N_{cols} \cdot N_{rows}$ into two scaling factors, say, for example, $1/\sqrt{N_{cols} \cdot N_{rows}}$ in both transforms.

Basis Functions   Equation (1.23) shows that we represent the image I now as a weighted sum of basis functions $\exp(i\alpha) = \cos \alpha + i \sin \alpha$ being 2D combinations of cosine and sine functions in the complex plane. Figure 1.15 illustrates five of such basis functions $\sin(u + nv)$ for the imaginary parts b of complex values $a + ib$ represented in the uv frequency domain; for the real part a, we have cosine functions.

   The values $\mathbf{I}(u, v)$ of the Fourier transform of I in (1.23), called the *Fourier coefficients*, are the weights in this sum with respect to the basis functions $\exp(i\alpha)$. For example, point noise or edges require sufficiently large coefficients for high

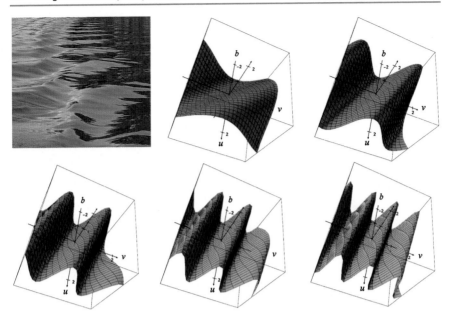

Fig. 1.15 *Top, left*: Waves on water. *Top, middle, to bottom, right*: 2D waves defined by $\sin(u + nv)$, for $n = 1, \ldots, 5$, having decreasing wave length (thus being of higher frequency) for an increase in n

frequency (i.e. short wave length) components, to be properly represented in this weighted sum.

1.2.3 The Complex Plane

We provide a brief discussion of elements, contributing to the DFT definition in (1.21), for supporting a basic understanding of this very fundamental signal transformation.

It is common practice to visualize complex numbers $a + i \cdot b$ as points (a, b) or vectors $[a, b]^\top$ in the plane, called *the complex plane*. See Fig. 1.16.

Calculus of Complex Numbers   Let $z_1 = a_1 + i \cdot b_1$ and $z_2 = a_2 + i \cdot b_2$ be two complex numbers, with $i = \sqrt{-1}$, *real parts* a_1 and a_2, and *imaginary parts* b_1 and b_2. We have that

$$z_1 + z_2 = (a_1 + a_2) + i \cdot (b_1 + b_2) \tag{1.24}$$

and

$$z_1 \cdot z_2 = (a_1 a_2 - b_1 b_2) + i \cdot (a_1 b_2 + a_2 b_1) \tag{1.25}$$

The sum or the product of two complex numbers is again a complex number, and both are invertible (i.e. by a difference or a multiplicative inverse; see z^{-1} below).

Fig. 1.16 A unit circle in the complex plane with all the powers of $W = i2\pi/24$. The figure also shows one complex number $z = a + ib$ having (r, α) as polar coordinates

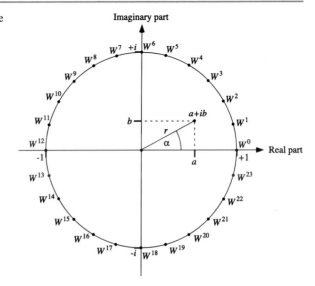

The *norm* of a complex number $z = a + i \cdot b$ coincides with the L_2-length of the vector $[a, b]^\top$ (starting at the origin $[0, 0]^\top$); we have that $\|z\|_2 = \sqrt{a^2 + b^2}$.

The *conjugate* $z^\star$ of a complex number $z = a + i \cdot b$ is the complex number $a - i \cdot b$. We have that $(z^\star)^\star = z$. We also have that $(z_1 \cdot z_2)^\star = z_1^\star \cdot z_2^\star$, and, assuming that $z \neq 0$, $z^{-1} = \|z\|_2^{-2} \cdot z^\star$.

Complex Numbers in Polar Coordinates   A complex number z can also be written in the form $z = r \cdot e^{i\alpha}$, with $r = \|z\|_2$ and α (the *complex argument of z*) is uniquely defined modulo 2π if $z \neq 0$. This maps complex numbers into polar coordinates (r, α).

A rotation of a vector $[c, d]^\top$ [i.e., starting at the origin $[0, 0]^\top$] about an angle α is the vector $[a, b]^\top$, with

$$a + i \cdot b = e^{i\alpha} \cdot (c + i \cdot d) \qquad (1.26)$$

Roots of Unity   The complex number $W_M = \exp[i2\pi/M]$ defines the *M*th *root of unity*; we have $W_M^M = W_M^{2M} = W_M^{3M} = \cdots = 1$. Assume that M is a multiple of 4. Then we have that $W_M^0 = 1 + i \cdot 0$, $W_M^{M/4} = 0 + i \cdot 1$, $W_M^{M/2} = -1 + i \cdot 0$, and $W_M^{3M/4} = 0 + i \cdot (-1)$.

Insert 1.4 (Fast Fourier Transform) *The properties of Mth roots of unity, M a power of 2, supported the design of the original* Fast Fourier Transform *(FFT), a time-efficient implementation of the DFT.*

The design of the FFT has an interesting history, see [J.M. Cooley, P.A. Lewis, P.D. Welch. History of the fast Fourier transform. Proc. IEEE 55 (1967), pp. 1675–1677]. *Origins date back to C.F. Gauss (see Insert* 2.4). *The algorithm became popular by the paper* [J.M. Cooley, J.W. Tukey. An algorithm for the machine calculation of complex Fourier series. Math. Comp. 19 (1965), pp. 297–301].

The FFT algorithm typically performs "in place": the original image is used for initializing the $N_{cols} \times N_{rows}$ *matrix of the real part, and the matrix of the imaginary part is initialized by zero at all positions. Then the 2D FFT replaces all values in both matrices by 2D DFT results.*

Figure 1.16 shows all the powers of the 24th root of unity, $W_{24} = e^{i2\pi/24}$. In this case we have, for example, that $W_{24}^0 = e^0 = 1$, $W_{24}^1 = \cos \frac{\pi}{12} + i \sin \frac{\pi}{12}$, $W_{24}^6 = \cos \frac{\pi}{2} + i \sin \frac{\pi}{2} = i$, $W_{24}^{12} = \cos \pi + i \sin \pi = -1$, and $W_{24}^{18} = \cos \frac{3\pi}{2} + i \sin \frac{3\pi}{2} = -i$.

Equation (1.21) can be simplified by using the notion of roots of unity. It follows that

$$\mathbf{I}(u, v) = \frac{1}{N_{cols} \cdot N_{rows}} \sum_{x=0}^{N_{cols}-1} \sum_{y=0}^{N_{rows}-1} I(x, y) \cdot W_{N_{cols}}^{-xu} \cdot W_{N_{rows}}^{-yv} \qquad (1.27)$$

For any root of unity $W_n = i2\pi/n$, $n \geq 1$, and for any power $m \in \mathbb{Z}$, it follows that

$$\left\| W_n^m \right\|_2 = \left\| e^{i2\pi m/n} \right\|_2 = \sqrt{\cos(2\pi m/n)^2 + \sin(2\pi m/n)^2} = 1 \qquad (1.28)$$

Thus, all those powers are located on the unit circle, as illustrated in Fig. 1.16.

1.2.4   Image Data in the Frequency Domain

The complex values of the 2D Fourier transform are defined in the uv frequency domain. The values for low frequencies u or v (i.e. close to 0) represent long wavelengths of sine or cosine components; values for large frequencies u or v (i.e. away from zero) represent short wavelengths. See Fig. 1.15 for examples for sine waves.

Interpretation of Matrix I   Low frequencies represent long wavelengths and thus homogeneous additive contributions to the input image I. High frequencies represent short wavelengths (and thus local discontinuities in I such as edges or intensity outliers).

Directional patterns in I, for example lines into direction β or $\beta + \pi$, create value distributions in $\mathbf{I}$ in the orthogonal direction (i.e., in direction $\beta + \pi/2$ in the assumed line example).

In images we have the origin at the upper left corner (according to the assumed left-hand coordinate system; see Fig. 1.1). The values in the matrix $\mathbf{I}$ can be repeated periodically in the plane, with periods N_{cols} and N_{rows}. This infinite number

Fig. 1.17 The *shaded area* is the $N_{cols} \times N_{rows}$ area of matrix $\mathbf{I}$, and it is surrounded by eight more copies of $\mathbf{I}$ in this figure. The origins are always at the *upper left corner*. Due to the periodicity, low frequencies are in the shown ellipses and thus in the four corners of the matrix $\mathbf{I}$; the highest frequencies are at the centre of the matrix $\mathbf{I}$

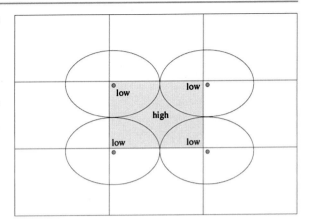

of copies of the matrix $\mathbf{I}$ tessellates the plane in the form of a regular rectangular grid; see Fig. 1.17.

If we want to have the origin (i.e. the low frequencies) in the centre locations of the Fourier transform, then this can be achieved by a permutation of the four quadrants of the matrix. Alternatively (as not difficult to verify mathematically), this shift of $\mathbf{I}$ into a centred position can also be achieved by first multiplying all values $I(x, y)$ by $(-1)^{x+y}$, before performing the 2D DFT.

Three Properties of the DFT   We consider the 2D Fourier transform of an image I. It consists of two $N_{cols} \times N_{rows}$ arrays representing the real (i.e., the as) and the imaginary part (i.e., the bs) of the obtained complex numbers $a + i \cdot b$. Thus, the $N_{cols} \times N_{rows}$ real data of the input image I are now "doubled". But there is an important *symmetry property*:

$$\mathbf{I}(N_{cols} - u, N_{rows} - v) = \mathbf{I}(-u, -v) = \mathbf{I}(u, v)^* \qquad (1.29)$$

(recall: the number on the right is the conjugate complex number). Thus, actually half of the data in both arrays of $\mathbf{I}$ can be directly obtained from the other half. Another property is that

$$\mathbf{I}(0, 0) = \frac{1}{N_{cols} \cdot N_{rows}} \sum_{x=0}^{N_{cols}-1} \sum_{y=0}^{N_{rows}-1} I(x, y) \qquad (1.30)$$

which is the mean of I. Because I has only real values, it follows that the imaginary part of $\mathbf{I}(0, 0)$ is always equal to zero. Originating from applications of the Fourier transform in Electrical Engineering, the mean $\mathbf{I}(0, 0)$ of the signal is known as the *DC component* of I, meaning *direct current*. For any other frequency $(u, v) \neq (0, 0)$, $\mathbf{I}(u, v)$ is called an *AC component* of I, meaning *alternating current*.

As a third property, we mention *Parseval's theorem*

$$\frac{1}{|\Omega|} \sum_{\Omega} |I(x, y)|^2 = \sum_{\Omega} |\mathbf{I}(u, v)|^2 \qquad (1.31)$$

which states identities in total sums of absolute values for the input image I and the Fourier transform $\mathbf{I}$; the placement of the scaling factor $\frac{1}{|\Omega|}$ corresponds to our chosen way of having this scaling factor only in the forward transform.

> **Insert 1.5** (Parseval and Parseval's Theorem) *The French mathematician M.-A. Parseval (1755–1836) is famous for his theorem that the integral of the square of a function is equal to the integral of the square of its transform, which we formulate in* (1.31) *in discrete form, using sums rather than integrals.*

Spectrum and Phase   The L_2-norm, *magnitude* or *amplitude* $\|z\|_2 = r = \sqrt{a^2 + b^2}$, and the complex argument or *phase* $\alpha = \mathrm{atan2}(b, a)$ define complex numbers $z = a + i \cdot b$ in polar coordinates (r, α).[4] The norm receives much attention because it provides a convenient way of representing the complex-valued matrix $\mathbf{I}$ in the form of the *spectrum* $\|\mathbf{I}\|$. (To be precise, we use $\|\mathbf{I}\|(u, v) = \|\mathbf{I}(u, v)\|_2$ for all $N_{cols} \cdot N_{rows}$ frequencies (u, v).)

Typically, when visualizing the spectrum $\|\mathbf{I}\|$ in the form of a grey-level image, it would be just black, just with a bright dot at the origin (representing the mean). This is because all values in $\mathbf{I}$ are typically rather small. For better visibility, the spectrum is normally log-transformed into $\log_{10}(1 + \|\mathbf{I}(u, v)\|_2)$. See Fig. 1.18.

Visualizations of the phase components of $\mathbf{I}$ are not so common; this is actually not corresponding to the importance of phase for representing information present in an image.

The image I in the lower example in Fig. 1.18 has a directional pattern; accordingly, it is rotated by $\pi/2$ in the spectrum. The upper example does not have a dominant direction in I and thus also no dominant direction in the spectrum.

Figure 1.19 illustrates that uniform transforms of the input image, such as adding a constant to each pixel value, histogram equalization, or value inversion do not change the basic value distribution pattern in the spectrum.

Fourier Pairs   An input image and its Fourier transform define a *Fourier pair*. We show some examples of Fourier pairs, expressing in brief form some properties of the Fourier transform:

$$\text{Function } I \Leftrightarrow \text{ its Fourier transform } \mathbf{I}$$

$$I(x, y) \Leftrightarrow \mathbf{I}(u, v)$$

$$I * G(x, y) \Leftrightarrow \mathbf{I} \circ \mathbf{G}(u, v)$$

---

[4]The function atan2 is the arctangent function with two arguments that returns the angle in the range $[0, 2\pi)$ by taking the signs of the arguments into account.

Fig. 1.18 *Left*: Original images Fibers and Straw. *Right*: Centred and log-transformed spectra for those images

$$I(x, y) \cdot (-1)^{x+y} \Leftrightarrow \mathbf{I}\left(u + \frac{N_{cols}}{2}, v + \frac{N_{rows}}{2}\right)$$

$$a \cdot I(x, y) + b \cdot J(x, y) \Leftrightarrow a \cdot \mathbf{I}(u, v) + b \cdot \mathbf{J}(u, v)$$

The first line expresses just a general relationship. The second line says that the Fourier transform of a convolution of I with a filter kernel G equals a point-by-point product of values in the Fourier transforms of I and G; we discuss this important property, known as the *convolution theorem* further below; it is the theoretical basis for Fourier filtering.

The third line expresses the mentioned shift of the Fourier transform into a centred position if the input image is multiplied by a chessboard pattern of $+1$ and -1.

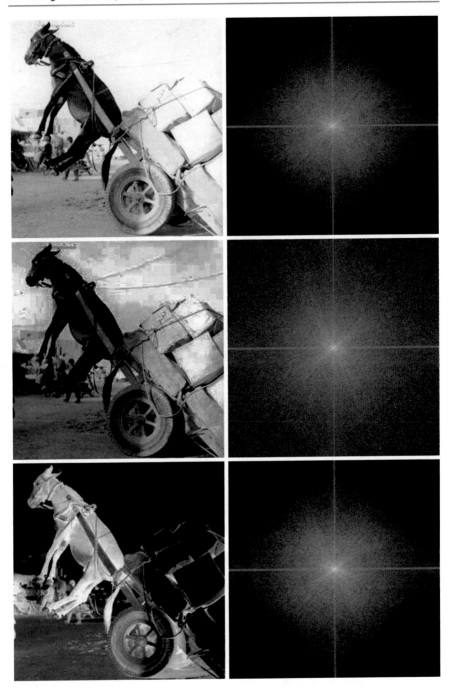

Fig. 1.19 *Left, top to bottom*: Original low-quality jpg-image Donkey (in the public domain), after histogram equalization (showing jpg-artefacts), and in inverted grey levels. *Right*: The corresponding spectra do not show significant changes because the "image structure" remains constant

Fig. 1.20 Simple geometric shapes illustrating that the main directions in an image are rotated by 90° in the spectrum (e.g., a vertical bar also generates a horizontal stripe in its spectrum)

The fourth line is finally the brief expression for the important property that the Fourier transform is a linear transformation. Rotations of main directions are illustrated in Fig. 1.20. The additive behaviour is illustrated in the upper right example in Fig. 1.21.

1.2.5   Phase-Congruency Model for Image Features

By *phase congruency* (or *phase congruence*) we quantify the correspondence of phase values calculated in an image window defined by a reference point p, expressed below by a measure $\mathscr{P}_{ideal\_phase}(p)$.

Local Fourier Transform at Image Features   Equation (1.23) describes the input signal in the frequency domain as a sum of sine and cosine waves. Figure 1.22 illustrates this for a 1D signal: The shown step-curve is the input signal, and it is decomposed in the frequency domain into a set of sine and cosine curves whose addition defines (approximately) the input signal. At the position of the step, all those curves are in the same phase.

When discussing the Fourier transform, we noticed that real-valued images are mapped into a complex-valued Fourier transform and that each complex number $z = a + \sqrt{-1}b$ is defined in polar coordinates by the amplitude $\|z\|_2 = r = \sqrt{a^2 + b^2}$

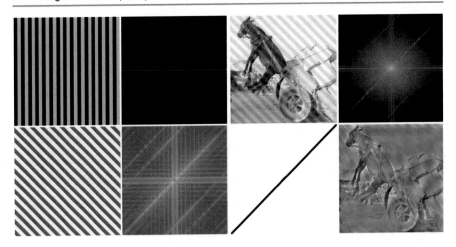

Fig. 1.21 *Top, left:* The ideal wave pattern generates non-negative values only at $v = 0$. *Bottom, left:* The diagonal wave pattern is influenced by the "finite-array effect". *Top, right:* For the overlaid diagonal wave pattern, compare with the DFT spectrum shown in Fig. 1.19. *Bottom, right:* We apply the shown (very simple) mask in the frequency domain that blocks all the values along the black diagonal; the inverse DFT produces the filtered image on the right; the diagonal pattern is nearly removed

Fig. 1.22 1D signal describing a step (in *bold grey*) and frequency components (in shades of *brown* to *orange*) whose addition defines the *blue* signal, which approximates the ideal step

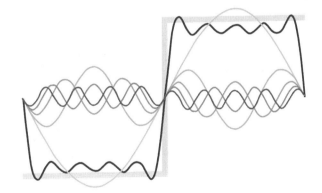

and phase $\alpha = \arctan(b/a)$. We do not use i for the imaginary unit here because we will use it as an index in the sum below. According to (1.30), we have $b = 0$ at the origin in the frequency domain, i.e. the phase $\alpha = 0$ for the DC component.

Consider a *local Fourier transform*, centred at a pixel location $p = (x, y)$ in image I, using a $(2k + 1) \times (2k + 1)$ filter kernel of Fourier basis functions:

$$\mathbf{J}(u, v) = \frac{1}{(2k + 1)^2} \sum_{i=-k}^{k} \sum_{j=-k}^{k} I(x + i, y + j) \cdot W_{2k+1}^{-iu} \cdot W_{2k+1}^{-jv} \qquad (1.32)$$

Fig. 1.23 Addition of four complex numbers represented by polar coordinates (r_h, α_h) in the complex plane

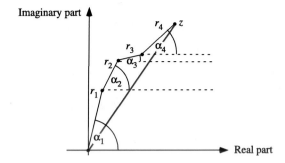

Ignoring the DC component that has the phase zero (and is of no importance for locating an edge), the resulting Fourier transform $\mathbf{J}$ is composed of $n = (2k+1)^2 - 1$ complex numbers z_h, each defined by the amplitude $r_h = \|z_h\|_2$ and the phase α_h, for $1 \leq h \leq n$.

Figure 1.23 illustrates an addition of four complex numbers represented by the amplitudes and phases, resulting in a complex number z. The four complex numbers (r_h, α_h) are roughly *in phase*, meaning that the phase angles α_h do not differ much (i.e. have a small variance only). Such an approximate identity defines a high *phase congruency*, formally defined by the property measure

$$\mathscr{P}_{ideal\_phase}(p) = \frac{\|z\|_2}{\sum_{h=1}^n r_h} \tag{1.33}$$

with z being the sum of all n complex vectors represented by (r_h, α_h). We have that $\mathscr{P}_{ideal\_phase}(p) = 1$ defines perfect congruency, and $\mathscr{P}_{ideal\_phase}(p) = 0$ occurs for perfectly opposing phase angles and amplitudes.

Observation 1.3 *Local phase congruency identifies features in images. Under the phase congruency model, step-edges represent just one narrow class of an infinite range of feature types that can occur. Phase congruency marks lines, corners, "roof edges", and a continuous range of hybrid feature types between lines and steps.*

Insert 1.6 (Origin of the Phase-Congruency Measure) *The measure of phase congruency was proposed in* [M. C. Morrone, J. R. Ross, D. C. Burr, and R. A. Owens. Mach bands are phase dependent. Nature, vol. 324, pp. 250–253, November 1986] *following a study on relations between features in an image and Fourier coefficients.*

See Fig. 1.24 for an example when applying the Kovesi algorithm (reported later in Sect. 2.4.3), which implements the phase-congruency model.

Fig. 1.24 *Left*: Original image AnnieYukiTim. *Right*: Edge map resulting when applying the Kovesi algorithm

1.3 Colour and Colour Images

Perceived colour is not objectively defined. Colour perception varies for people, and it depends on lighting. If there is no light, then there is no colour, such as, for example, inside of a non-transparent body. Colour can be an important component of given image data, and it is valuable for visualizing information by using false colours (e.g., see Fig. 7.5). Human vision can only discriminate a few dozens of grey levels on a screen, but hundreds to thousands of different colours.

This section informs about the diversity of interesting subjects related to the topic "colour" and provides details for the RGB and HSI colour model such that you may use those two when analyzing colour images, or when visualizing data using the colour as an important tool.

1.3.1 Colour Definitions

An "average human" perceives colour in the *visible spectrum* as follows (recall that 1 nm = 1 nanometer = 10^{-9} m):

1. Red (about 625 to 780 nm) and Orange (about 590 to 625 nm) for the long wavelengths of the visible spectrum [the invisible spectrum continues with Infrared (IR)];
2. Yellow (about 565 to 590 nm), Green (about 500 to 565 nm), and Cyan (about 485 to 500 nm) in the middle range of the visible spectrum;
3. Blue (about 440 to 485 nm) for the short wavelengths, for example visible on the sky during the day when the sun is high up, and there is neither air pollution nor clouds (but the light is broken into short wavelengths by the multi-layered atmosphere); and, finally, also
4. Violet (about 380 to 440 nm) for very short wavelengths of the visible spectrum, before it turns into the invisible spectrum with Ultraviolet (UV).

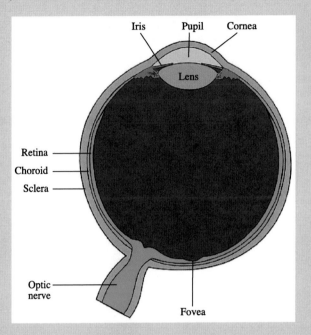

Tristimulus Values   The CIE (*Commission Internationale de l'Eclairage = International Commission on Illumination*) has defined colour standards since the 1930s.

A light source creates an energy distribution $L(\lambda)$ for the visible spectrum for wavelengths $380 \leq \lambda \leq 780$ of monochromatic light. See Fig. 1.25, left, for an example. Such an energy distribution is mapped into three *tristimulus values* X, Y, and Z by integrating a given energy distribution function L weighted by given energy distribution functions $\overline{x}$, $\overline{y}$, and $\overline{z}$ as follows:

$$X = \int_{400}^{700} L(\lambda)\overline{x}(\lambda)\, d\lambda \tag{1.34}$$

$$Y = \int_{400}^{700} L(\lambda)\overline{y}(\lambda)\, d\lambda \tag{1.35}$$

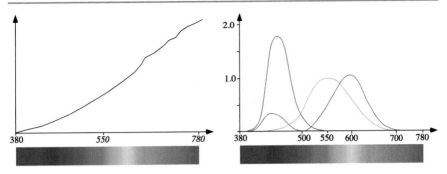

Fig. 1.25 *Left*: Sketch of an energy distribution curve $L(\lambda)$ of an incandescent house lamp, for wavelengths λ between 380 nm and 780 nm for monochromatic light. *Right*: The energy distribution functions $\bar{x}(\lambda)$ (*blue*), $\bar{y}(\lambda)$ (*green*), and $\bar{z}(\lambda)$ (*red*) for defining tristimulus values X, Y, and Z

$$Z = \int_{400}^{700} L(\lambda)\bar{z}(\lambda)\,d\lambda \tag{1.36}$$

The weighting functions $\bar{x}$, $\bar{y}$, and $\bar{z}$ have been defined by the CIE within the visible spectrum. The cut-offs on both ends of those weighting functions do not correspond exactly to human-eye abilities to perceive shorter (down to 380 nm) or larger (up to 810 nm) wavelengths. The three curves have also been scaled such that their integrals are all equal:

$$\int_{400}^{700} \bar{x}(\lambda)\,d\lambda = \int_{400}^{700} \bar{y}(\lambda)\,d\lambda = \int_{400}^{700} \bar{z}(\lambda)\,d\lambda \tag{1.37}$$

For example, the value Y models the brightness (= intensity) or, approximately, the green component of the given distribution L. Its energy distribution curve $\bar{y}$ was derived by modelling the luminosity response of an "average human eye". See Fig. 1.25, right.

The tristimulus values X, Y, and Z define the normalized xy-parameters

$$x = \frac{X}{X+Y+Z} \quad \text{and} \quad y = \frac{Y}{X+Y+Z} \tag{1.38}$$

Assuming that Y is given, we are able to derive X and Z from x and y. Together with $z = Z/(X+Y+Z)$ we would have $x+y+z=1$; thus, we do not need this third value z.

The xy Colour Space of the CIE   Parameters x and y define the 2D *CIE Colour Space*, not representing brightness, "just" the colours. The xy colour space is commonly represented by a chromaticity diagram as shown in Fig. 1.26. It is $0 \le x, y \le 1$. This diagram only shows the *gamut* of human vision, that is, the colours that are visible to the average person; the remaining white parts in the square shown in the diagram are already in the invisible spectrum.

Fig. 1.26 Chromaticity
diagram for the xy CIE
Colour Space

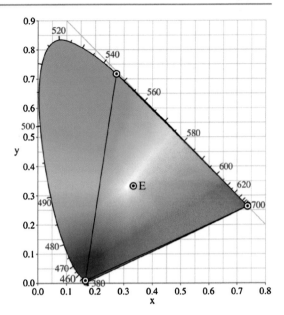

The convex outer curve in the diagram contains monochromatic colours (pure spectral colours). The straight edge at the bottom (i.e. the purple line) contains colours that are not monochromatic. In the interior of the human vision gamut, there are less saturated colours, with white at the centre $E = (0.33, 0.33)$. The triangle displayed is the gamut of the *RGB primaries*, as defined by the CIE by standardized wavelengths of 700 nm for Red, 546.1 nm for Green, and 435.8 nm for Blue; the latter two are monochromatic lines of a mercury vapour discharge.

Insert 1.8 (Different Gamuts of Media) *The* gamut *is the available colour range (such as "perceivable", "printable", or "displayable"). It depends on the used medium. An image on a screen may look very different from a printed copy of the same image because screen and printer have different gamuts. You might see a warning like that in your image-editing system:*

As a rule of thumb, transparent media (such as a TV, a computer screen, or slides) have potentially a larger gamut than printed material. The (very rough!) sketch above just indicates this. For common gamuts (also called

Fig. 1.27 A dot pattern as used in an *Ishihara colour test*, showing a 5 for most of the people, but for some it shows a 2 instead

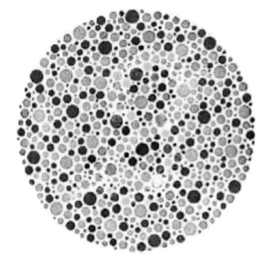

colour spaces), *you may check, for example, for* DCI-P3, Rec. 709, *or* sRGB. *Mapping images from one gamut to another is an important subject in colour image processing.*

1.3.2 Colour Perception, Visual Deficiencies, and Grey Levels

When designing figures for reports, publications, or presentations, it is worthwhile to think about a good choice of a colour scheme, such that all of the audience can see best what is supposed to be visualized.

Red–Green Colour Blindness Two energy distributions $L_1(\lambda)$ and $L_2(\lambda)$ for the visible spectrum may be different curves, but a human H may perceive both as identical colours, formally expressed by

$$L_1 \overset{H}{=} L_2 \tag{1.39}$$

Colour blindness means that some colours cannot be distinguished. In about 99 % of cases this is red–green colour blindness. Total colour blindness is extremely rare (i.e. seeing only shades of grey). Estimates for red–green colour blindness for people of European origin are about 8–12 % for males and about 0.5 % for females.

Normal colour vision sees a 5 revealed in the dot pattern in Fig. 1.27, but an individual with red–green colour blindness sees a 2.

Observation 1.4 *When using red–green colours in a presentation, the above-mentioned percentage of your audience with European origin might not see what you are intending to show.*

Insert 1.9 (Dalton, Ishihara, and the Ishihara Colour Test) *Red–green colour blindness was discovered by the chemist J. Dalton* (1766–1844) *in himself, and it is usually called* Daltonism. *The Japanese ophthalmologist S. Ishihara* (1879–1963) *and his assistant (who was a colour-blind physician) designed test patterns for identifying colour blindness.*

Algebra of Colour Vision   Adding two colours L and C means that we are super-imposing both light spectra $L(\lambda)$ and $C(\lambda)$. Experimental evidence (R.P. Feynman in 1963) has shown that

$$L_1 + C \overset{H}{=} L_2 + C \quad \text{if } L_1 \overset{H}{=} L_2 \tag{1.40}$$

$$aL_1 \overset{H}{=} aL_2 \quad \text{if } L_1 \overset{H}{=} L_2 \text{ and } 0 \leq a \leq 1 \tag{1.41}$$

These equations define (for a test person H) an algebra of colour perception, with general linear combinations $aL + bC$ as elements.

If you are interested in doing related experiments, then be aware that a computer screen uses gamma correction for some $\gamma > 0$. When specifying colour channel values $u = k/2^a$ (e.g. for R, G, and B channels), the presented values on screen are actually equal to u^γ, where $\gamma < 1$ defines the *gamma compression*, and $\gamma > 1$ defines the *gamma expansion*. The perception of changes in colour values will be influenced by the given γ.

Insert 1.10 (Benham Disk and Colour as a Purely Visual Sensation) *A typical colour-based visual illusion is the "Benham disk" (of a nineteenth-century toymaker):*

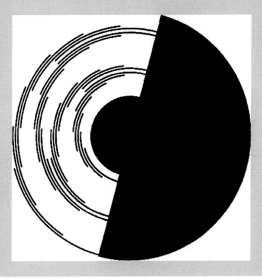

Fig. 1.28 The four primary colours for colour perception

When spinning this disk (at various speeds, clockwise or counter-clockwise) under bright incandescent light or sunlight, different "bands" of colour appear.

An explanation is given on www.exploratorium.edu/snacks/, starting with the words: "There are three types of cones (in the eye). One is most sensitive to red light, one to green light, and one to blue light. Each type of cone has a different latency time, the time it takes to respond to a colour, and a different persistence of response time, the time it keeps responding after the stimulus has been removed."

At the end it reads: "The explanation of the colours produced by Benham's disk is more complicated than the simple explanation outlined above."

Primary Colour Perceptions   Humans perceive colour differently; "colour" is a psychological phenomenon. But there appears to be agreement that Yellow (top row in the colour pyramid in Fig. 1.28), Red (right), Green (left), and Blue (bottom) define the four *primary colour perceptions.*

For avoiding possible green-red misperceptions, there is, for example, the option to use yellow, red, and blue as base colours in presentations.

Grey Levels   Grey levels are not colours; they are described by the *luminance* (the physical intensity) or the *brightness* (the perceived intensity). A uniform scale of *grey levels* or *intensities* is common, such as

$$u_k = k/2^a \quad \text{for } 0 \le k < 2^a \tag{1.42}$$

where $u_0 = 0$ represents black, and $u_{2^a-1} \approx 1$ represents white. We decided in Chap. 1 to represent such intensities by integers $0, 1, \ldots, G_{\max} = 2^a - 1$ rather than by fractions between 0 and 1.

Both squares in Fig. 1.29, top, have the same constant intensity. Human vision perceives the ratio of intensities. Grey value ratios are 5:6 in all the three cases shown in Fig. 1.29, bottom, for a smaller and brighter rectangle in a larger and darker rectangle. It is visually very difficult to discriminate between slightly different very dark grey levels. The human eye has better abilities for noticing different very bright grey levels.

Insert 1.11 (Visual Illusions Originating from Colour) *They can originate from motion, luminance or contrast, geometry, 3D space, cognitive effects, specialized imaginations, and, of course, also from colour; see, for example, www.michaelbach.de/ot/.*

The strength of the illusion of the rotating snake by A. Kitaoka, shown above, depends on contrast, background luminance, and viewing distance. Colour enhances the illusion, but you may also try a grey-level version as well.

1.3.3 Colour Representations

Figure 1.4 shows an RGB colour image and its representation in three scalar channels, one for the Red, one for the Green, and one for the Blue component. The used RGB colour representation model is *additive*: adding to a colour, which means

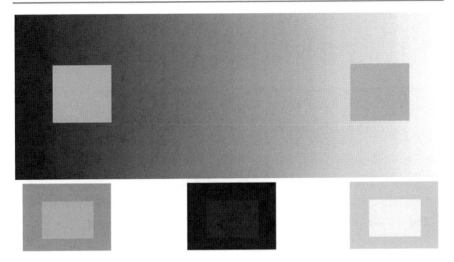

Fig. 1.29 *Top*: Two squares of identical intensity. *Bottom*: Three examples for grey-level ratios of 5 to 6

Fig. 1.30 The RGB cube spanned by the *Red*, *Green*, and *Blue* coordinate axes, illustrating one colour **q** in the cube defined by a value triple (R, G, B)

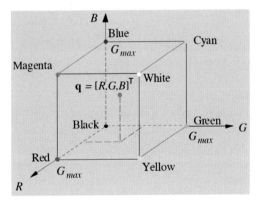

increasing values in its scalar representation, contributes to going towards White. This is the common way for representing colours on a screen. Colour models used for printing are *subtractive*: adding to a colour means adding more ink, which contributes to going towards Black.

The RGB Space   Assume that $0 \leq R, G, B \leq G_{max}$ and consider a multi-channel image I with pixel values $\mathbf{u} = (R, G, B)$. If $G_{max} = 255$, then we have 16,777,216 different colours, such as $\mathbf{u} = (255, 0, 0)$ for Red, $\mathbf{u} = (255, 255, 0)$ for Yellow, and so forth. The set of all possible RGB values defines the *RGB cube*, a common representation of the RGB colour space. See Fig. 1.30.

The diagonal in this cube, from White at $(255, 255, 255)$ to Black at $(0, 0, 0)$, is the location of all grey levels (u, u, u), which are not colours. In general, a point $\mathbf{q} = (R, G, B)$ in this RGB cube defines either a colour or a grey level, where the

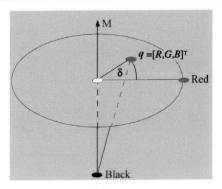

Fig. 1.31 The intensity axis points along the grey-level diagonal in the RGB cube. For the cut with the cube, we identify one colour (here, *Red*) as the reference colour. Now we can describe **q** by the *intensity* (i.e. its mean value), *hue*, which is the angle with respect to the reference colour (*Red* here, and, say, in counter-clockwise order), and *saturation* corresponding to the distance to the intensity axis

mean

$$M = \frac{R+G+B}{3} \tag{1.43}$$

defines the *intensity* of colour or grey level **q**.

The HSI Space   Consider a plane that cuts the RGB cube orthogonally to its grey-level diagonal, with $\mathbf{q} = (R, G, B)$ incident with this plane but not on the diagonal (see also Fig. 1.33). In an abstract sense, we represent the resulting cut by a disk, ignoring the fact that cuts of such a plane with the cube are actually simple polygons. See Fig. 1.31.

For the disk, we fix one colour for reference; this is Red in Fig. 1.31. The location of **q** in the disk is uniquely defined by an angle H (the *hue*) and a scaled distance S (the *saturation*) from the intersecting grey-level diagonal of the RGB cube. Formally, we have

$$H = \begin{cases} \delta & \text{if } B \leq G \\ 2\pi - \delta & \text{if } B > G \end{cases} \quad \text{with} \tag{1.44}$$

$$\delta = \arccos \frac{(R-G)+(R-B)}{2\sqrt{(R-G)^2+(R-B)(G-B)}} \quad \text{in } [0, \pi) \tag{1.45}$$

$$S = 1 - 3 \cdot \frac{\min\{R, G, B\}}{R+G+B} \tag{1.46}$$

Altogether, this defines the *HSI colour model*. We represent intensity by M, to avoid confusion with the use of I for images.

Example 1.2 (RGB and HSI Examples) Grey levels (u, u, u) with $u \neq 0$ have the intensity $M = u$ and the saturation $S = 0$, but the hue H remains undefined because δ is undefined (due to division by zero). In the case of Black $(0, 0, 0)$ we have the intensity $M = 0$, and the saturation and hue remain undefined.

Besides these cases of points in the RGB cube representing non-colours, the transformation of RGB values into HSI values is one-to-one, which means that we can also transform HSI values uniquely back into RGB values. The hue and saturation may represent RGB vectors with respect to an assumed fixed intensity.

Red $(G_{max}, 0, 0)$ has the intensity $M = G_{max}/3$, the hue $H = 0°$ (note: Red was chosen to be the reference colour), and the saturation $S = 1$. We always have $S = 1$ if $R = 0$ or $G = 0$ or $B = 0$.

Green $(0, G_{max}, 0)$ has the intensity $M = G_{max}/3$ and the saturation $S = 1$; we obtain that $\delta = \arccos(-0.5)$, thus $\delta = 2\pi/3$ in $[0, \pi)$ and $H = 2\pi/3$ because $B = 0 \leq G = G_{max}$. Blue $(0, 0, G_{max})$ also leads to $\delta = 2\pi/3$, but $H = 4\pi/3$ because $B = G_{max} > G = 0$.

Assume that we map S and H both linearly into the grey-level set $\{0, 1, \ldots, G_{max}\}$ and visualize the resulting images. Then, for example, the hue value of $(G_{max}, \varepsilon_1, \varepsilon_2)$ can either be about black or white, just for minor changes in ε_1 and ε_2. Why? Fig. 1.32 illustrates this effect at the bottom, left.

Figure 1.32, top, left, shows one of the colour checkers used for testing colour accuracy of a camera, to be used for computer vision applications. There are three rows of very precisely (uniform) coloured squares numbered 1 to 18 and one row of squares showing grey levels. When taking an image of the card, the lighting at this moment will contribute to the recorded image. Assuming monochromatic light, all the grey-level squares should appear equally in the channels for Red (not shown), Green, Blue, and intensity. The bottom, right, image of the saturation channel illustrates that grey levels have the saturation value zero assigned in the program. Of course, there can be no "undefined" cases in a program. Note that the hue value for reference colour Red (Square 15) also "jumps" from white to black, as expected.

Insert 1.12 (Itten and Colour Perception) *J. Itten* (1888–1967, *Switzerland*) *wrote the influential book "The Art of Colour", which deals with contrast, saturation, and hue and how colour affects a person's psychology. In brief, he assigned the following meanings*:

Red: *resting matter, the colour of gravity and opacity.*

Blue: *eternal restless mind, relaxation, and continuous motion.*

Yellow: *fierce and aggressive, thinking, weightless.*

Orange: *brilliant luminance, cheap and brash, energy and fun, an unpopular colour (well, do not say this in The Netherlands).*

Purple: *ancient purple dye was made out of purple sea-snails, and more valuable than gold, only kings were allowed to wear purple; the colour of power, belief, and force, or of death and darkness, of loneliness, but also of devotedness and spiritual love.*

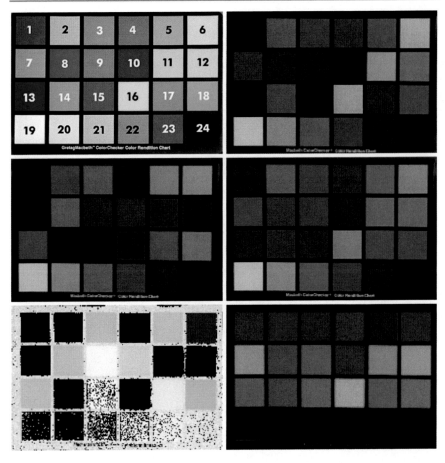

Fig. 1.32 *Top*: Colour checker by Macbeth™ and the channel for *Green*. *Middle*: Channels for *Blue* and intensity values. *Bottom*: Channels visualizing hue and saturation values by means of grey levels

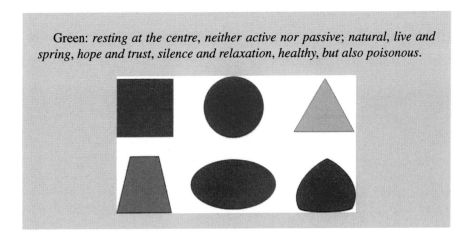

Green: *resting at the centre, neither active nor passive; natural, live and spring, hope and trust, silence and relaxation, healthy, but also poisonous.*

Itten also assigned geometric shapes to colours, illustrated by a few examples above.

We end this brief section about colour with a comment of Leonardo da Vinci (1452–1519); see [The Notebooks of Leonardo da Vinci. Edited by J.P. Richter, 1880]:

Note 273: *The effect of colours in the camera obscura.*
The edges of a colour(ed) object transmitted through a small hole are more conspicuous than the central portions.
The edges of the images, of whatever colour, which are transmitted through a small aperture into a dark chamber, will always be stronger than the middle portion.

Leonardo da Vinci provided a large number of interesting notes on colour in those notebooks.

1.4 Exercises

1.4.1 Programming Exercises

Exercise 1.1 (Basic Acquaintance with Programmed Imaging) Implement a program (e.g., in Java, C++, or Matlab) that does the following:

1. Load a colour (RGB) image I in a lossless data format, such as bmp, png, or tiff, and display it on a screen.
2. Display the histograms of all three colour channels of I.
3. Move the mouse cursor within your image. For the current pixel location p in the image, compute and display
   (a) the *outer border* (see grey box) of the 11×11 square window W_p around pixel p in your image I (i.e., p is the reference point of this window),
   (b) (above this window or in a separate command window) the location p (i.e., its coordinates) of the mouse cursor and the RGB values of your image I at p,
   (c) (below this window or in a separate command window) the intensity value $[R(p) + G(p) + B(p)]/3$ at p, and
   (d) the mean μ_{W_p} and standard deviation σ_{W_p}.
4. Discuss examples of image windows W_p (within your selected input images) where you see "homogeneous distributions of image values", and windows showing "inhomogeneous areas". Try to define your definition of "homogeneous" or "inhomogeneous" in terms of histograms, means, or variances.

The *outer border* of an 11×11 square window is a 13×13 square curve (which could be drawn, e.g., in white) having the recent cursor position at its centre. You are expected that you dynamically update this outer border of the 11×11 window when moving the cursor.

Alternatively, you could show the 11×11 window also in a second frame on a screen. Creative thinking is welcome; a modified solution might be even more elegant than the way suggested in the text. It is also encouraged to look for solutions that are equivalent in performance (same information to the user, similar run time, and so forth).

Insert 1.13 (Why not jpg format?) jpg *is a lossy compression scheme that modifies image values* (*between compressed and uncompressed state*), *and therefore it is not suitable for image analysis in general.* bmp *or* raw *or* tiff *are examples of formats where pixel values will not be altered by some type of compression mechanism. In* jpg *images you can often see an* 8×8 *block structure* (*when zooming in*) *due to low-quality compression.*

Exercise 1.2 (Data Measures on Image Sequences) Define three different data measures $\mathscr{D}_i(t)$, $i = 1, 2, 3$, for analysing image sequences. Your program should do the following:
1. Read as input an image sequence (e.g. in VGA format) of at least 50 frames.
2. Calculate your data measures $\mathscr{D}_i(t)$, $i = 1, 2, 3$, for those frames.
3. Normalize the obtained functions such that all have the same mean and the same variance.
4. Compare the normalized functions by using the L_1-metric.

Discuss the degree of structural similarity between your measures in dependence of the chosen input sequence of images.

Exercise 1.3 (Different Impacts of Amplitudes and Phase in Frequency Space on Resulting Filtered Images) It is assumed that you have access to FFT programs for the 2D DFT and inverse 2D DFT. The task is to study the problem of evaluating information contained in amplitude and phase of the Fourier transforms:
1. Transform images of identical size into the frequency domain. Map the resulting complex numbers into amplitudes and phases. Use the amplitudes of one image and the phases of the other image, and transform the resulting array of complex numbers back into the spatial domain. Who is "winning", i.e. can you see the image contributing the amplitude or the image contributing the phase?
2. Select scalar images showing some type of homogeneous textures; transform these into the frequency domain and modify either the amplitude or the phase of the Fourier transform in a uniform way (for all frequencies), before transforming back into the spatial domain. Which modification causes a more significant change in the image?
3. Do the same operations and tests for a set of images showing faces of human beings.

   Discuss your findings. How do uniform changes (of different degrees), either in amplitude or in phase, alter the information in the given image?

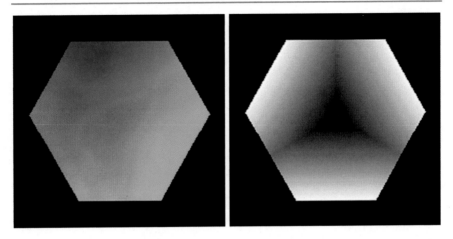

Fig. 1.33 Cuts through the RGB cube at $u = 131$ showing the RGB image I_{131} and saturation values for the same cutting plane

Exercise 1.4 (Approximating the HSI Space by Planar Cuts) Assume that $G_{max} = 255$. We are cutting the RGB cube by a plane Π_u that is orthogonal to the grey-level diagonal and passing through the grey level (u, u, u) for $0 \le u \le 255$. Each cut (i.e., the intersection of Π_u with the RGB cube) is represented by one $N \times N$ image I_u, where the value $\mathbf{u} = (R, G, B)$ at pixel location (x, y) is either defined by the nearest integer-valued RGB triple in the RGB cube (or the mean if there is more than one nearest RGB triple), if this distance is less than $\sqrt{2}$, or equals a default value (say, black) otherwise. Do the following:

1. Implement a program which allows one to show the RGB images I_u, for $u = 0$, $u = 1, \ldots, u = 255$ (e.g., by specifying the value of u in a dialogue or by having a continuously running animation).
2. Also show the (scalar) saturation values instead of RGB values. Figure 1.33 shows the results for $u = 131$.
3. You may either select a fixed value $N > 30$ (size of the image), or you may also allow a user to choose N within a given range.

1.4.2 Non-programming Exercises

Exercise 1.5 Show the correctness of (1.4).

Exercise 1.6 Who was *Fourier*? When was the Fast Fourier Transform designed for the first time? How is the Fourier transform related to optical lens systems?

Exercise 1.7 Assume an $N \times N$ image. Prove that a multiplication by $(-1)^{x+y}$ in the spatial domain causes a shift by $N/2$ (both in row and column direction) in the frequency domain.

Exercise 1.8 In extension of Example 1.2, transform a few more (easy) RGB values manually into corresponding HSI values.

Exercise 1.9 Let (δ, S, M) be the colour representation in the HSI space. Justify the following steps for recovering the RGB components in the following special cases:
- If $\delta \in [0, 2\pi/3]$, then $B = (1 - S)M$.
- If $\delta \in [2\pi/3, 4\pi/3]$, then $R = (1 - S)M$.
- If $\delta \in [4\pi/3, 2\pi]$, then $G = (1 - S)M$.

How can we compute the remaining components in each of the above cases?

Exercise 1.10 In the CIE's RGB colour space (which models human colour perception), the scalars R, G, or B may also be negative. Provide a physical interpretation (obviously, we cannot subtract light from a given spectrum).

Image Processing

2

This chapter introduces basic concepts for mapping an image into an image, typically used for improving image quality or for purposes defined by a more complex context of a computer vision process.

2.1 Point, Local, and Global Operators

When recording image data outdoors (a common case for computer vision), there are often particular challenges compared to indoor recording, such as difficulties with lighting, motion blur, or sudden changes in scenes. Figure 2.1 shows images recorded in a car (for vision-based driver-assistance). An unwanted data is called *noise*. These are three examples of noise in this sense of "unwanted data". In the first case we may aim at transforming the images such that the resulting images are "as taken at uniform illumination". In the second case we could try to do some sharpening for removing the blur. In the third case we may aim at removing the noise.

This section provides time-efficient methods that you may consider for preprocessing your data prior to subsequent image analysis.

2.1.1 Gradation Functions

We transform an image I into an image I_{new} of the same size by mapping a grey level u at pixel location p in I by a *gradation function* g onto a grey level $v = g(u)$ at the same pixel location p in I_{new}. Because the change only depends on value u at location p, we also speak about a *point operator* defined by a gradation function g.

If the goal is that I_{new} satisfies some properties defined in terms of its histogram, then we speak about a *histogram transform*.

R. Klette, *Concise Computer Vision*, Undergraduate Topics in Computer Science, DOI 10.1007/978-1-4471-6320-6_2, © Springer-Verlag London 2014

Fig. 2.1 *Top*: A pair of images SouthLeft and SouthRight taken time-synchronized but of different brightness; see the shown grey-level histograms. *Bottom left*: Blurring caused by rain in image Wiper. *Bottom right*: Noise in a scene Uphill recorded at night

Histogram Equalization   We transform a scalar image I such that all grey levels appear equally often in the transformed image I_{new}. The goal is to achieve that

$$H_{I_{new}}(u) = \text{const} = \frac{N_{cols} N_{rows}}{G_{max} + 1} \tag{2.1}$$

for all $u \in \{0, 1, \dots, G_{max}\}$.

Unfortunately, this is not possible in general, due to the constraint that identical values in I can only map on the same value in I_{new}. For example, a binary image I cannot be mapped onto a histogram-equalized grey-level image I_{new} (even in the case if we would have a continuous binary image; but having digital images also contributes to excluding perfect equalization). The following transform is thus just an approximate solution towards the ideal goal.

Given is an $N_{cols} \times N_{rows}$ scalar image I with absolute frequencies $H_I(u)$ for $0 \le u \le G_{max}$. We transform I into an image I_{new} of the same size by mapping intensities u in I by the following gradation function g onto new intensities $v = g(u)$ in I_{new}:

$$g(u) = c_I(u) \cdot G_{max} \tag{2.2}$$

Fig. 2.2 *Left*: Input image `RagingBull` (in the public domain) with histogram. *Right*: The same image after histogram equalization

Fig. 2.3 Graph of the gradation function for linear scaling, defined by being incident with points $(u_{\min}, 0)$ and $(u_{\max}, G_{\max})$

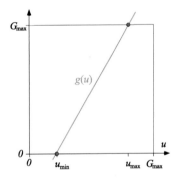

where c_I is the relative cumulative frequency function. Figure 2.2 illustrates such a *histogram equalization*.

It is not difficult to show the equalization property for the histogram transform, defined by (2.2), using the property that the cumulative relative frequency c_I is an increasing function. The relative histogram $h_I(u)$ corresponds to an estimate of a density function, $c_I(u)$ to an estimate of a probability distribution function, and $h_{I_{new}}(u)$ to an estimate of the uniform density function.

Linear Scaling   Assume that an image I has positive histogram values in a limited interval only. The goal is that all values used in I are spread linearly onto the whole scale from 0 to $G_{\max}$. Let $u_{\min} = \min\{I(x, y) : (x, y) \in \Omega\}$, $u_{\max} = \max\{I(x, y) : (x, y) \in \Omega\}$, and

$$a = -u_{\min} \quad \text{and} \quad b = \frac{G_{\max}}{u_{\max} - u_{\min}} \tag{2.3}$$

$$g(u) = b(u + a) \tag{2.4}$$

As a result, pixels having the value $u_{\min}$ in the image I now have the value 0 in the resulting image I_{new}, and pixels having the value $u_{\max}$ in the image I now have the value $G_{\max}$ in I_{new}. This is illustrated in Fig. 2.3. This figure can also serve as an illustration when discussing the correctness of the histogram transform defined by (2.4).

Conditional Scaling As another example of a use of a gradation function, we want to map an image J into an image J_{new}, such that it has the same mean and the same variance as an already given image I. For this *conditional scaling*, let

$$a = \mu_J \cdot \frac{\sigma_I}{\sigma_J} - \mu_I \quad \text{and} \quad b = \frac{\sigma_J}{\sigma_I} \tag{2.5}$$

$$g(u) = b(u + a) \tag{2.6}$$

Now we map the grey level u at pixel p in J onto the new value $v = g(u)$ at the same pixel p in J_{new}. It is not difficult to show that $\mu_{J_{new}} = \mu_I$ and $\sigma_{J_{new}} = \sigma_I$. The performed normalization is the same as in (1.12), where we normalized data measures.

2.1.2 Local Operators

For a given $N_{cols} \times N_{rows}$ image I, we consider sliding windows W_p, each of size $(2k + 1) \times (2k + 1)$, where the reference point p is always at the centre of the window. The reference point moves into all possible pixel locations of I and so moves the window over the image. At these locations we perform a *local operation*; the result of the operation defines the new value at p. Thus, the input image I is transformed into a new image J.

Two Examples: Local Mean and Maximum For example, the local operation can be the *local mean*, $J(p) = \mu_{W_p(I)}$, with

$$\mu_{W_p(I)} = \frac{1}{(2k + 1)^2} \cdot \sum_{i=-k}^{+k} \sum_{j=-k}^{+k} I(x + i, y + j) \tag{2.7}$$

for $p = (x, y)$.

As another example, the local operation can be the calculation of the *local maximum*

$$J(p) = \max\{I(x + i, y + j) : -k \le i \le k \wedge -k \le j \le k\} \tag{2.8}$$

for $p = (x, y)$. See Fig. 2.4 for an example.

Windows centred at p and not completely contained in I, require a special "border-pixel strategy"; there is no general proposal for such a strategy. One option is to consider the same local operation just for a smaller window, which is possible for the two examples of local operations given above.

Fig. 2.4 *Top, left*: Original image Set1Seq1 with $N_{cols} = 640$. *Top, right*: Local maximum for $k = 3$. *Bottom, left*: Local minimum for $k = 5$. *Bottom, right*: Local operator using the 3×3 filter kernel shown in the middle of Fig. 2.5

w_{11}	w_{12}	w_{13}	
w_{21}	w_{22}	w_{23}	/S
w_{31}	w_{32}	w_{33}	

1	0	-1	
2	0	-2	/9
1	0	-1	

1	1	1	
1	1	1	/9
1	1	1	

Fig. 2.5 *Left*: General representation for a 3×3 filter kernel. *Middle*: Filter kernel illustrated in Fig. 2.4, bottom, right, approximating a derivative in x-direction. *Right*: The filter kernel of a 3×3 box filter

Linear Operators and Convolution A *linear local operator* is defined by a *convolution* of an image I at $p = (x, y)$ with a *filter kernel* W,

$$J(p) = I * W(p) = \frac{1}{S} \sum_{i=-k}^{+k} \sum_{j=-k}^{+k} w_{i,j} \cdot I(x+i, y+j) \qquad (2.9)$$

with weights $w_{i,j} \in \mathbb{R}$ and a *scaling factor* $S > 0$. The arguments in (2.9) go out of Ω if p is close to the border of this image carrier. A theorem says that then you apply a modulo rule conceptually equivalent to a 2D periodic copying of the image I on Ω into the grid $\mathbb{Z}^2$.

The array of $(2k + 1) \times (2k + 1)$ weights and scaling factor S define the filter kernel W. It is common to visualize filter kernels W of linear local operators as shown in Fig. 2.5.

Equation (2.7) is an example of such a linear local operator, known as a *box filter*. Here we have all weights equal to 1, and $S = (2k + 1)^2$ is the sum of all those weights.

General View on Local Operators   We summarize the properties of *local operators*:

1. Operations are limited to windows, typically of square and odd size $(2k + 1) \times (2k + 1)$; of course, with respect to *isotropy* (i.e. rotation invariance), approximately circular windows should be preferred instead, but rectangular windows are easier to use.
2. The window moves through the given image following a selected scan order (typically aiming at a complete scan, having any pixel at the reference position of the window at some stage).
3. There is no general rule how to deal with pixels close to the border of the image (where the window is not completely in the image anymore), but they should be processed as well.
4. The operation in the window should be the same at all locations, identifying the purpose of the local operator.
5. The results can either be used to replace values in place at the reference points in the input image I, defining a *sequential local operator* where new values propagate like a "wave" over the original values (windows of the local operator then contain the original data and already-processed pixel values), or resulting values are written into a second array, leaving the original image unaltered this way, defining a *parallel local operator*, so called due to the potential of implementing this kind of a local operator on specialized parallel hardware.

In case of $k = 0$ (i.e., the window is just a single pixel), we speak about a *point operator*. If k grows so that the whole picture is covered by the window, then it turns into a *global operator*. The 2D Fourier transform of an image is an example for a global transform.

Insert 2.1 (Zamperoni) *There is immense diversity of published proposals for image processing operators due to the diversity of image data and particular tasks in applications. For example, the book* [R. Klette and P. Zamperoni. Handbook of Image Processing Operators. Wiley, Chichester, 1996] *details many of the usual point, local, and global operators.*

The memory of Piero Zamperoni (1939–1998), *an outstanding educator in pattern recognition, is honoured by the IAPR by issuing the Piero Zamperoni Best Student Paper Award at their biennial ICPR conferences.*

2.1.3 Fourier Filtering

The inverse 2D DFT (see (1.23)) transforms a Fourier transform $\mathbf{I}$ back from the frequency domain into the spatial domain. The inverse 2D DFT will lead to a real-valued function I as long as $\mathbf{I}$ satisfies the symmetry property of (1.29). Thus, any change in the frequency domain is constrained by this.

Fourier Filtering   The inverse 2D DFT can be read as follows: the complex numbers $\mathbf{I}(u, v)$ are the Fourier coefficients of I, defined for different frequencies u and v. Each Fourier coefficient is multiplied with a combination of sine and cosine functions (see the Eulerian formula (1.22)), and the sum of all those combinations forms the image I. In short, the image I is represented by basis functions being powers of roots of unity in the complex plane, and the Fourier coefficients specify this basis function representation.

This means that if we modify one of the Fourier coefficients (and its symmetric coefficient due to the constraint imposed by the symmetry property) before applying the inverse 2D DFT, then we obtain a modified function I.

For a linear transform of the image I, there are two options:

1. We modify the image data by a linear convolution

$$J(x, y) = (I * G)(x, y) = \sum_{i=0}^{N_{cols}-1} \sum_{j=0}^{N_{rows}-1} I(i, j) \cdot G(x - i, y - j) \qquad (2.10)$$

in the spatial domain, where G is the filter kernel (also called the *convolution function*). Function J is the *filtered image*.

2. We modify the 2D DFT $\mathbf{I}$ of I by multiplying the values in $\mathbf{I}$, position by position, with the corresponding complex numbers in $\mathbf{G}$ [i.e., $\mathbf{I}(u, v) \cdot \mathbf{G}(u, v)$]. We denote this operation by $\mathbf{I} \circ \mathbf{G}$ (not to be confused with matrix multiplication). The resulting complex array is transformed by the inverse 2D DFT into the modified image J.

Interestingly, both options lead to identical results assuming that $\mathbf{G}$ is the 2D DFT of G, due to the *convolution theorem*:

$$I * G \text{ equals the inverse 2D DFT of } \mathbf{I} \circ \mathbf{G} \qquad (2.11)$$

Thus, either a convolution in the spatial domain or a position-by-position multiplication in the frequency domain produce identical filtered images. However, in the convolution case we miss the opportunity to design frequency-dependent filter functions in the frequency domain.

Steps of Fourier Filtering   Given is an image I and a complex-valued filter function $\mathbf{G}$ (which is satisfying the symmetry property of (1.29)) in the frequency domain. Apply an FFT program for doing the following; if required for the applied FFT program, first map the image I into a larger $2^n \times 2^n$ array:

1. Transform the image I into the frequency domain, into the complex-valued $\mathbf{I}$ by using the FFT program.
2. Multiply the complex-valued $\mathbf{I}$, element by element, with the complex-valued filter function $\mathbf{G}$.
3. Transform the result back into the spatial domain by using the FFT program for the inverse DFT.

The filter function $\mathbf{G}$ can be obtained as the Fourier transform of a filter kernel G in the spatial domain. It is common procedure to design filter functions $\mathbf{G}$ directly in the frequency domain.

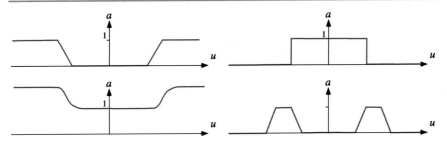

Fig. 2.6 1D profiles of rotation-symmetric filter functions. *Top*: A linear high-pass filter and an ideal low-pass filter. *Bottom*: An exponential high-emphasis filter and a linear band-pass filter

Example 2.1 The *box filter* is a linear convolution in the spatial domain. Its filter kernel is defined by the weights $G(x, y) = 1/a$ for (x, y) in a $(2k + 1) \times (2k + 1)$ window, centred at the origin $(0, 0)$, with $a = (2k + 1)^2$. Outside of this window we have that $G(x, y) = 0$.

The 2D DFT of this function G has amplitudes close to 1 for low frequencies, with a steep decrease in amplitudes towards zero for higher frequencies.

The Fourier transform **G** of Example 2.1 is a typical *low-pass filter*: low frequencies are "allowed to pass" (because multiplied with values of amplitudes close to 1), but higher frequencies are "drastically reduced" (because multiplied with values of amplitude close to 0).

Design of Filter Functions   The frequency domain is well suited for the design of filter functions. See Fig. 2.6. We may decide for a *high-pass filter* (e.g., for edge detection, or for visualizing details and for suppressing low frequencies), a *high-emphasis filter* (e.g., for enhancing contrast), a *band-pass filter* (for allowing only a certain range of frequencies "to pass"), or a filter that eliminates or enhances selected frequencies (under proper consideration of the symmetry constraint). The impact of a low-pass filter is a reduction of outliers and of contrast, i.e. a smoothing effect.

Attributes "linear", "exponential", or "ideal" of a filter function specify the way how the transition is defined from large amplitudes of the filter to low amplitudes. See Fig. 2.6 for examples of transitions. Low-pass and band-pass filtering of an image is illustrated in Fig. 2.7.

Besides the flexibility in designing filter functions, the availability of time-efficient 2D FFT algorithms is also an important argument for using a DFT-based filter instead of a global convolution. Local convolutions are normally more efficiently performed in the spatial domain by a local operator.

2.2   Three Procedural Components

This section introduces three procedural components that are commonly used in image processing programs, such as for local operators, but also when implementing particular image analysis or computer vision procedures.

Fig. 2.7 *Upper row, left*: Intensity channel of image Emma, shown also in colour in Fig. 2.9. *Upper row, right*: Its spectrum, centred and with log-transform. *Lower row, left*: An ideal low-pass filtered *Emma*, showing a typical smoothing effect. *Lower row, right*: An exponential-band-pass filtered *Emma*, already showing more higher frequencies than lower frequencies

2.2.1 Integral Images

The calculation of an *integral image* I_{int} for a given image I is a common preprocessing step for speeding up operations on I which involve rectangular windows (e.g. for feature detection). "Integration" means adding small units together. In this case, the small units are the pixel values. For a pixel $p = (x, y)$, the *integral value*

$$I_{int}(p) = \sum_{1 \le i \le x \wedge 1 \le j \le y} I(i, j) \qquad (2.12)$$

is the sum of all the values $I(i, j)$ at pixel locations $q = (i, j)$ that are neither below p nor right of p. See Fig. 2.8, left.

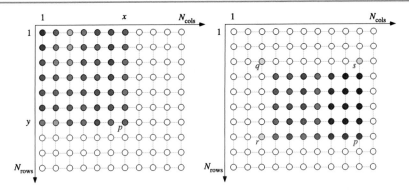

Fig. 2.8 *Left*: At $I_{int}(x, y)$ we have the sum of all the shown pixel values. *Right*: If an algorithm requires to use the sum of all pixel values in the shown rectangular window, then we only need to combine the values of the integral image in the four corners p, q, r, and t; see the text for the formula

> **Insert 2.2** (The Introduction of Integral Images into Computer Vision) *Integral images have been introduced in the Computer Graphics literature in* [F.C. Crow. Summed-area tables for texture mapping. Computer Graphics, vol. 18, pp. 207–212, 1984] *and then popularized by* [J.P. Lewis. Fast template matching. In Proc. Vision Interface, pp. 120–123, 1995] *and* [P. Viola and M. Jones. Robust real-time object detection. Int. J. Computer Vision, pp. 137–154, 2001] *in the Computer Vision literature.*

Now consider a rectangular window W in an image defining four pixels p, q, r, and s, as illustrated in Fig. 2.8, right, with q, r, and s just one pixel away from W. The sum S_W of all pixel values in W is now simply defined by

$$S_W = I_{int}(p) - I_{int}(r) - I_{int}(s) + I_{int}(q) \qquad (2.13)$$

We only have to perform one addition and two subtractions, independent upon the size of the rectangular window W. This will later (in this book) prove to be very handy for classifying objects shown in images.

Example 2.2 (Number of Operations with or Without Integral Image) Assume that we calculate the sum in an $n \times m$ window by using (2.13). We have three arithmetic operations, no matter what are the values of m or n.

Without an integral image, just by adding all the $m \cdot n$ numbers in the window, we have $m \cdot n - 1$ arithmetic operations.

If we also count the addressing arithmetic operations, for the sequential sliding window in the integral image, they are reduced to four ++ increments if we keep the addresses for pixels p, q, r, and s in address registers.

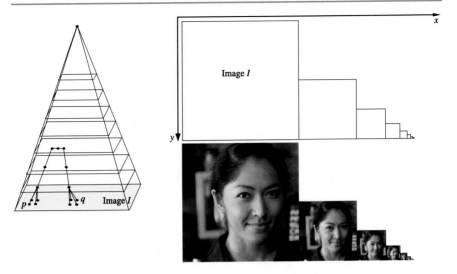

Fig. 2.9 Illustrations of picture pyramids. *Left*: A regular pyramid is the assumed model behind subsequent size reductions. *Left, top*: Sketch of pairwise disjoint arrays. *Left, bottom*: Example of layers for image Emma

Observation 2.1 *After one preprocessing step for generating the integral image, any subsequent step, requiring to know the sum of pixel values in a rectangular window, only needs constant time, no matter what is the size of the window.*

2.2.2 Regular Image Pyramids

A pyramid is a common data structure used for representing one input image I at different sizes. See Fig. 2.9. The original image is the base layer of the pyramid. Images of reduced sizes are considered to be subsequent layers in the pyramid.

Use of Scaling Factor 2 If scaling down by factor 2, as illustrated in Fig. 2.9, then all additional levels of the pyramid require less than one third of the space of the original image, according to the geometric series

$$1 + \frac{1}{2 \cdot 2} + \frac{1}{2^2 \cdot 2^2} + \frac{1}{2^3 \cdot 2^3} + \cdots < \frac{4}{3} \tag{2.14}$$

When reducing the size from one layer to the next layer of the pyramid, bottom-up, the mean was calculated for 2×2 pixels for generating the corresponding single pixel at the next layer. For avoiding spatial aliasing, it is also recommended to perform some *Gauss smoothing* (to be explained in the following section) prior to taking those means.

By creating a new pixel r in Layer $n + 1$ of the pyramid, defined by (say) four pixels p_1, p_2, p_3, and p_4 at Layer n, we create new adjacencies (p_1, r), (p_2, r), (p_3, r), and (p_4, r), additionally to (say) 4-adjacency in Layer n, as illustrated in

Fig. 2.9, right. For going via adjacent pixels from pixel location p to pixel location q in image I, we now also have the option to go first up in the pyramid to some level, then a few steps sideward in this level, and again down to q. In general, this supports shorter connecting paths than only using 4-adjacency in the input image I.

Example 2.3 (Longest Path in a Regular Pyramid of Scaling Factor 2) Assume an image I of size $2^n \times 2^n$ and a regular pyramid on top of this image created by using scaling factor 2.

For the longest path between two pixel locations, we consider p and q being diagonal corners in I. Using 4-adjacency in I, their distance to each other is $2^n - 1$ steps towards one side, and again $2^n - 1$ steps towards another side, no matter in which order we do those steps. Thus, the longest path in I, not using the pyramid, equals

$$2^{n+1} - 2 \tag{2.15}$$

This reduces to a path of length $2n$ when also using the adjacencies defined by the pyramid.

Observation 2.2 *Adjacencies in a pyramid reduce distances between pixels in an image significantly; this can be used when there is a need to send a "message" from one pixel to others.*

Pyramids can also be used for starting a computer vision procedure at first at one selected level in the data structure, and results are then refined by propagating them down in the pyramid to layers of higher resolution. We will discuss examples at some places in the book.

2.2.3 Scan Orders

The basic control structure of an image analysis program (not only for local operators, also, e.g. for component labelling) typically specifies a scan order for visiting all or some of the pixels.

Standard Scan Order and Variants Figure 2.10 illustrates not only the standard scan order, but also others that might be of interest under particular circumstances. Spiral or meander scans offer the opportunity that prior calculations are used at the next location of the sliding window, because only $2k + 1$ pixels enter the window, replacing $2k + 1$ "leaving" pixels.

Insert 2.3 (Hilbert, Peano, and Euclid) *In 1891, D. Hilbert (1862–1943), the major German mathematician, defined a curve filling completely the unit square, following Jordan's initial definition of a curve. A finite number of repetitions of this construction, as illustrated in Fig. 2.11, leads to a Hilbert scan*

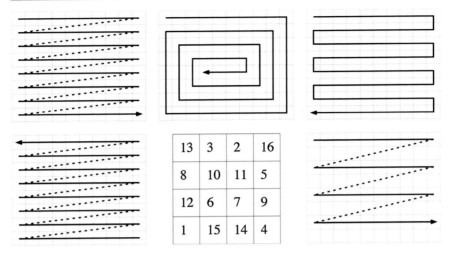

Fig. 2.10 Scan orders: standard (*upper left*), inward spiral (*upper middle*), meander (*upper right*), reverse standard (*lower left*), magic square (*lower middle*), and selective standard (as used in interlaced scanning), e.g. every second row (*lower right*)

in a grid of size $2^n \times 2^n$, not to be confused with the original curve defined by Hilbert in the Euclidean space. Hilbert's curve is a variant of a curve defined in 1890 by the Italian mathematician G. Peano (1858–1932) for the same purpose.

Euclid of Alexandria (about −300) was a Greek mathematician, known for his Elements, which was the standard work in Geometry until the 19th century.

A *magic square scan* (Fig. 2.10, bottom, middle, shows a simple 4×4 example) generates a pseudo-random access to pixels; in a *magic square*, numbers add up to the same sum in each row, in each column, and in forward and backward main diagonals. A *Hilbert scan* is another option to go towards pseudo-random access (or output, e.g. for generating a picture on a screen). See Fig. 2.11.

Hilbert Scan   Fig. 2.11 specifies the Hilbert scan in a way that we enter the image at its north–west corner, and we leave it at its north–east corner. Let us denote the four corners of a $2^n \times 2^n$ picture by a, b, c, d, starting at the north–west corner and in clock-wise order. We assume a Hilbert scan $H_n(a, d, c, b)$, where we start at corner a, continue then with corner d, proceed to corner c, and terminate then at corner b.

$H_1(a, b, c, d)$ is a scan of a 2×2 image, where we just visit in the order a, b, c, d as shown.

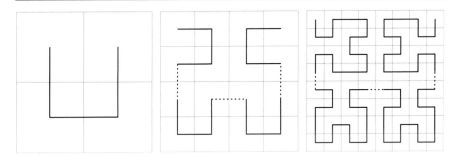

Fig. 2.11 Hilbert scans for 2×2, 4×4, or 8×8 images illustrating the recursive extension to larger images of size $2^n \times 2^n$

$H_{n+1}(a, d, c, b)$ is a scan where we start at the north–west corner; we perform $H_n(a, b, c, d)$, followed by one step down, then $H_n(a, d, c, b)$, followed by one step to the right, then (again) $H_n(a, d, c, b)$, followed by one step up, and finally $H_n(c, d, a, b)$, which takes us to the north–east corner of the $2^{n+1} \times 2^{n+1}$ image.

2.3 Classes of Local Operators

Local intensity patterns in one image can be considered to be "fairly" independent if they are at some distance to each other within the carrier Ω. Local operators make good use of this and are time-efficient and easy to implement on usual sequential and parallel hardware. Thus, not surprisingly, there is a large diversity of proposed local operators for different purposes. This section illustrates this diversity by only providing a few "popular" examples for four classes of local operators.

2.3.1 Smoothing

Image *smoothing* aims at eliminating "outliers" in image values considered to be noise in a given context.

Box Filter   The $(2k + 1) \times (2k + 1)$ box filter, performing the local mean calculation as already defined in (2.7), is a simple option for image smoothing. It removes outliers, but it also reduces significantly the contrast $C(I)$ of an image I. Often it is sufficient to use just a 3×3 or 5×5 filter kernel. The local mean for larger kernel sizes can be conveniently calculated by using the integral image I_{int} of input image I.

Median Operator   The *median* of $2n + 1$ values is the value that would appear in sorted order at position $n + 1$. For example, 4 is the median of the set $\{4, 7, 3, 1, 8, 7, 4, 5, 2, 3, 8\}$ because 4 is in position 6 in the sorted sequence $1, 2, 3, 3, 4, 4, 5, 7, 7, 8, 8$.

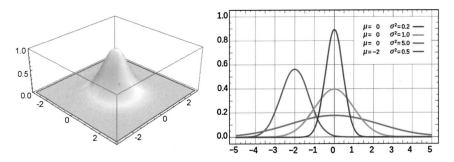

Fig. 2.12 *Left*: The 2D Gauss function for expected values $\mu_x = \mu_y = 0$. *Right*: Four examples of 1D Gauss functions for different expected values and different variances

The $(2k+1) \times (2k+1)$ median operator maps the median of a $(2k+1) \times (2k+1)$ window to the reference pixel p. It achieves the removal of outliers with only an insignificant change in image contrast $C(I)$.

Insert 2.4 *C.F. Gauss (1777–1855), a brilliant German mathematician working at Göttingen university, very well described in a novel "Measuring the World" by D. Kehlmann (original publication in German in 2005).*

Gauss Filter   The Gauss filter is a local convolution with a filter kernel defined by samples of the 2D *Gauss function*. This function is the product of two 1D Gauss functions defined as follows:

$$
\begin{aligned}
G_{\sigma, \mu_x, \mu_y}(x, y) &= \frac{1}{2\pi\sigma^2} \exp\left(-\frac{(x - \mu_x)^2 + (y - \mu_y)^2}{2\sigma^2} \right) \\
&= \frac{1}{2\pi\sigma^2} \cdot e^{-\frac{(x - \mu_x)^2}{2\sigma^2}} \cdot e^{-\frac{(y - \mu_y)^2}{2\sigma^2}}
\end{aligned}
\tag{2.16}
$$

where (μ_x, μ_y) combines the expected values for x- and y-components, σ is the standard deviation (σ^2 is the variance), which is also called the *radius* of this function, and e is the Euler number.

The Gauss function is named after C.F. Gauss (see Insert 2.4). The Euler number is named after L. Euler; see Insert 1.3 and 1.22 for the *Eulerian formula*. Figure 2.12 illustrates the Gauss function. The standard deviation σ is also called the *scale*.

Observation 2.3 *The second line in* (2.16) *shows that a 2D Gauss filter can be realized by two subsequent 1D Gauss filters, one in horizontal and one in vertical direction.*

Fig. 2.13 Filter kernel for
Gaussian smoothing defined
by $k = 2$ and $s = 2$ (i.e.
$\sigma = 1$)

1	4	7	4	1
4	16	26	16	4
7	26	41	26	7
4	16	26	16	4
1	4	7	4	1

/273

Centred Gauss Function   By assuming a centred Gauss function (i.e. with zero
means $\mu_x = \mu_y = 0$, as in Fig. 2.12, left), (2.16) simplifies to

$$G_\sigma(x, y) = \frac{1}{2\pi\sigma^2} \exp\left(-\frac{x^2 + y^2}{2\sigma^2}\right) = \frac{1}{\pi s} \cdot e^{-\frac{x^2}{2\sigma^2}} \cdot e^{-\frac{y^2}{2\sigma^2}} \qquad (2.17)$$

Such a centred Gauss function is now sampled at $(2k + 1) \times (2k + 1)$ locations,
with the window's reference pixel at the origin $(0, 0)$. This defines an important
filter kernel for a local operator, parameterized by $\sigma > 0$ and $k \geq 1$. We will later
use it for defining *differences of Gaussians* (DoGs) and the *scale space*.

Figure 2.13 shows a sampled filter kernel for $\sigma = 1$. Following the *three-sigma
rule* in statistics, G_σ is sampled by a kernel of size $6\sigma - 1$.

For an input image I, let

$$L(x, y, \sigma) = [I * G_\sigma](x, y) \qquad (2.18)$$

be a local convolution with function G_σ with $\sigma > 0$. For implementation, we sample
G_σ symmetrically to the origin at $w \times w$ grid positions for defining the filter kernel,
where w is the nearest odd integer to $6\sigma - 1$.

Gaussian Scale Space   For a scaling factor $a > 1$, we can step from the smoothed
image $L(x, y, \sigma)$ to $L(x, y, a\sigma)$. By using repeatedly scales $a^n \cdot \sigma$, for an initial
scale σ and $n = 0, 1, \ldots, m$, we create a set of subsequent *layers* of a *Gaussian
scale space*. See Fig. 2.14 for an example.

In this book, the layers in a scale space are all of identical size $N_{cols} \times N_{rows}$. For
implementation efficiency, some authors suggested to reduce this size by a factor
of 2 for any doubling of the used scale σ, thus creating *octaves* of blurred images.
The blurred images in one octave remain at constant size until the next doubling of
σ occurs, and the size is then again reduced by factor of 2. This is an implementation
detail, and we do not use octaves in the discussion of scale spaces in this book.

Sigma Filter   This filter is just an example of a simple but often useful local
operator for noise removal. For an example of a result, see Fig. 2.15. Again, we
discuss this local operator for $(2k + 1) \times (2k + 1)$ windows $W_p(I)$ with $k \geq 1$. We
use a parameter $\sigma > 0$, considered to be an approximation of the image acquisition
noise of image I (for example, σ equals about 50 if $G_{max} = 255$). Suggesting a
parallel local operator, resulting values are forming a new picture J as follows:

Fig. 2.14 Smoothed versions of the image Set1Seq1 (shown in Fig. 2.4, upper left) for $\sigma = 0.5$, $\sigma = 1$, $\sigma = 2$, $\sigma = 4$, $\sigma = 8$, and $\sigma = 16$, defining six layers of the Gaussian scale space

1. Calculate the histogram of window $W_p(I)$.
2. Calculate the mean μ of all values in the interval $[I(p) - \sigma, I(p) + \sigma]$.
3. Let $J(p) = \mu$.

   In some cases, camera producers specify parameters for the expected noise of their CCD or CMOS sensor elements. The parameter σ could then be taken as 1.5 times the noise amplitude. Note that

$$\mu = \frac{1}{S} \cdot \sum_{u=I(p)-\sigma}^{I(p)+\sigma} u \cdot H(u) \qquad (2.19)$$

where $H(u)$ denotes the histogram value of u for window $W_p(I)$ and scaling factor $S = H(I(p) - \sigma) + \cdots + H(I(p) + \sigma)$.

   Figure 2.15 illustrates the effects of a box filter, the median filter, and the sigma filter on a small image.

Fig. 2.15 Illustration of noise removal. *Upper left*: 128×128 input image with added uniform noise (± 15). *Upper right*: 3×3 box filter. *Lower left*: 3×3 sigma-filter with $\sigma = 30$. *Lower right*: 3×3 median filter

2.3.2   Sharpening

Sharpening aims at producing an enhanced image J by increasing the contrast of the given image I along edges, without adding too much noise within homogeneous regions in the image.

Unsharp Masking   This local operator first produces a residual $R(p) = I(p) - S(p)$ with respect to a smoothed version $S(p)$ of $I(p)$. This residual is then added to the given image I:

$$J(p) = I(p) + \lambda\big[I(p) - S(p)\big]$$
$$= [1 + \lambda]I(p) - \lambda S(p) \qquad (2.20)$$

Fig. 2.16 Illustration of unsharp masking with $k = 3$ and $\lambda = 1.5$ in (2.20). *Upper left*: 512×512 blurred input image `Altar` (of the baroque altar in the church at Valenciana, Guanajuato). *Upper right*: Use of a median operator. *Lower left*: Use of a Gauss filter with $\sigma = 1$. *Lower right*: Use of a sigma filter with $\sigma = 25$

where $\lambda > 0$ is a scaling factor. Basically, any of the smoothing operators of Sect. 2.3.1 may be tried to produce the smoothed version $S(p)$. See Fig. 2.16 for three examples.

The size parameter k (i.e. the "radius") of those operators controls the spatial distribution of the smoothing effect, and the parameter λ controls the influence of the correction signal $[I(p) - S(p)]$ on the final output. Thus, k and λ are the usual interactive control parameters for unsharp masking.

According to the second equation (2.20), the process is also qualitatively described by the equation

$$J(p) = I(p) - \lambda' S(p) \qquad (2.21)$$

(for some $\lambda' > 0$), which saves some computing time. Instead of applying unsharp masking uniformly in the whole image I, we can also add some kind of local adaptivity, for example such that changes in homogeneous regions are suppressed.

2.3.3 Basic Edge Detectors

We describe simple edge detectors that follow the step-edge model, either by approximating first-order derivatives or by approximating second-order derivatives.

Discrete Derivatives   The derivative of a unary function f in the continuous case is defined by the convergence of difference quotients where a nonzero offset ε approaches 0:

$$\frac{\mathrm{d}f}{\mathrm{d}x}(x) = f'(x) = \lim_{\varepsilon \to 0} \frac{f(x+\varepsilon) - f(x)}{\varepsilon} \qquad (2.22)$$

The function f is differentiable at x if there is a limit for these difference quotients. In the case of functions with two arguments, we have partial derivatives, such as

$$\frac{\partial f}{\partial y}(x, y) = f_y(x, y) = \lim_{\varepsilon \to 0} \frac{f(x, y+\varepsilon) - f(x, y)}{\varepsilon} \qquad (2.23)$$

with respect to y, and analogously with respect to x.

However, in the discrete grid we are limited by a smallest distance $\varepsilon = 1$ between pixel locations. Instead of just reducing the derivative in (2.23) to a difference quotient for $\varepsilon = 1$, we can also go for a symmetric representation taking the difference $\varepsilon = 1$ in both directions. The simplest symmetric difference quotient with respect to y is then as follows:

$$\begin{aligned} I_y(x, y) &= \frac{I(x, y+\varepsilon) - I(x, y-\varepsilon)}{2\varepsilon} \\ &= \frac{I(x, y+1) - I(x, y-1)}{2} \end{aligned} \qquad (2.24)$$

where we decide for a symmetric difference for better balance. We cannot use any smaller ε without doing some subpixel-kind of interpolations.

Equation (2.24) defines a very noise-sensitive approximation of the first derivative. Let $I_x(x, y)$ be the corresponding simple approximation of $\frac{\partial I}{\partial x}(x, y)$. The resulting approximated magnitude of the gradient is then given by

$$\sqrt{I_x(x, y)^2 + I_y(x, y)^2} \approx \|\mathbf{grad}\, I(x, y)\|_2 \qquad (2.25)$$

This value combines results of two linear local operators, one with a filter kernel representing I_x and one for I_y, shown in Fig. 2.17. The scaling factor 2 is in this case not the sum of the given weights in the kernel; the sum of the weights is zero. This corresponds to the fact that the derivative of a constant function equals zero.

Fig. 2.17 Filter kernels for differences as defined in (2.24)

0	0	0
−1	0	1
0	0	0

/2

0	−1	0
0	0	0
0	1	0

/2

Fig. 2.18 Filter kernels for the Sobel operator

−1	0	1
−2	0	2
−1	0	1

/1

−1	−2	−1
0	0	0
1	2	1

/1

The result of a convolution with one of those kernels can be negative. Thus, I_x and I_y are not images in the sense that we also have negative values here, and also rational numbers, not only integer values in $\{0, 1, \ldots, G_{max}\}$. It is common to visualize discrete derivatives such a I_x and I_y by showing rounded integer values of $|I_x|$ and $|I_y|$.

> **Insert 2.5** (Origin of the Sobel Operator) *The Sobel operator was published in* [I.E. Sobel. Camera models and machine perception. Stanford, Stanford Univ. Press, 1970, pp. 277–284].

Sobel Operator The *Sobel operator* approximates the two partial derivatives of image I by using the filter kernels shown in Fig. 2.18. The convolution with the filter kernel approximating a derivative in the x-direction is shown in Fig. 2.4, bottom, right.

These two masks are discrete versions of simple Gaussian convolutions along rows or columns followed by derivative estimates described by masks in Fig. 2.17. For example,

$$\begin{bmatrix} -1 & 0 & 1 \\ -2 & 0 & 2 \\ -1 & 0 & 1 \end{bmatrix} = \begin{bmatrix} 1 \\ 2 \\ 1 \end{bmatrix} \begin{bmatrix} -1 & 0 & 1 \end{bmatrix} \tag{2.26}$$

The two masks in Fig. 2.18 define two local convolutions that calculate approximations S_x and S_y of the partial derivatives. The value of the Sobel operator at pixel location (x, y) equals

$$|S_x(x, y)| + |S_y(x, y)| \approx \|\mathbf{grad}\, I(x, y)\|_1 \tag{2.27}$$

This value is shown as grey level in the edge map defined by the Sobel operator. Of course, this can also be followed by a detection of local maximum of the values of the Sobel operator; this extension explains why the Sobel operator is also called an *edge detector*.

Insert 2.6 (Origin of the Canny Operator) *This operator was published in* [J. Canny. A computational approach to edge detection. IEEE Trans. Pattern Analysis Machine Intelligence, vol. 8, pp. 679–698, 1986].

Canny Operator   The *Canny operator* maps a scalar image into a binary edge map of "thin" (i.e. having the width of one pixel only) edge segments. The output is not uniquely defined; it depends on two thresholds T_{low} and T_{high} with $0 < T_{low} < T_{high} < G_{max}$, not counting a fixed scale used for Gaussian smoothing.

Let I be already the smoothed input image, after applying a convolution with a Gauss function G_σ of scale $\sigma > 0$, for example $1 \le \sigma \le 2$.

We apply now a basic gradient estimator such as the Sobel operator, which provides, for any $p \in \Omega$, simple estimates for the partial derivatives I_x and I_y, allowing one to have estimates $g(p)$ for the magnitude $\|\mathbf{grad}\, I(p)\|_2$ of the gradient and estimates $\theta(p)$ for its direction atan2(I_y, I_x). The estimates $\theta(p)$ are rounded to multiples of $\pi/4$ by taking $(\theta(p) + \pi/8)$ modulo $\pi/4$.

In a step of *non-maxima suppression* it is tested whether a value $g(p)$ is maximal in the (now rounded) direction $\theta(p)$. For example, if $\theta(p) = \pi/2$, i.e. the gradient direction at $p = (x, y)$ is downward, then $g(p)$ is compared against $g(x, y - 1)$ and $g(x, y + 1)$, the values above and below of p. If $g(p)$ is not larger than the values at both of those adjacent pixels, then $g(p)$ becomes 0.

In a final step of *edge following*, the paths of pixel locations p with $g(p) > T_{low}$ are traced, and pixels on such a path are marked as being edge pixels. Such a trace is initialized by a location p with $g(p) \ge T_{high}$.

When scanning Ω, say with a standard scan, left-to-right, top-down, and arriving at a (not yet marked) pixel p with $g(p) \ge T_{high}$, then

1. mark p as an edge pixel,
2. while there is a pixel location q in the 8-adjacency set of p with $g(q) > T_{low}$, mark this as being an edge pixel,
3. call q now p and go back to Step 2,
4. search for the next start pixel p until the end of Ω is reached.

By using two thresholds, this algorithm applies *hysteresis*: The following pixel q may not be as good as having a value above T_{high}, but it had at least one predecessor on the same path with a value above T_{high}; thus, this "positive" history is used to support the decision at q, and we also accept $g(q) > T_{low}$ for continuation.

Insert 2.7 (Laplace) *P.S. Marquis de Laplace (1749–1827) was a French applied mathematician and theoretical physicist.*

Laplacian   Following the step-edge model, edges are also identified with zero-crossings of second-order derivatives. Common (simple) discrete approximations of the Laplacian of an image I are defined by the filter kernels shown in Fig. 2.19.

Fig. 2.19 Three masks for approximate calculations of the Laplacian

0	1	0
1	-4	1
0	1	0

1

1	1	1
1	-8	1
1	1	1

1

-1	2	-1
2	-4	2
-1	2	-1

1

In the following example we derive the filter kernel given on the left as an example for operator discretization.

Example 2.4 For deriving the first mask in Fig. 2.19, assume that we map I into a matrix of first-order difference quotients

$$I_y(x, y) = \frac{I(x, y + 0.5) - I(x, y - 0.5)}{1}$$
$$= I(x, y + 0.5) - I(x, y - 0.5)$$

and then again into a matrix of second-order difference quotients

$$I_{yy}(x, y) = I_y(x, y + 0.5) - I_y(x, y - 0.5)$$
$$= \left[I(x, y + 1) - I(x, y) \right] - \left[I(x, y) - I(x, y - 1) \right]$$
$$= I(x, y + 1) + I(x, y - 1) - 2 \cdot I(x, y)$$

We do the same for approximating I_{xx} and add both difference quotients. This defines an approximation of $\nabla^2 I = \Delta I$, which coincides with the first mask in Fig. 2.19. Figure 2.20 illustrates a row profile of an image after applying this approximate Laplacian.

2.3.4 Basic Corner Detectors

A *corner* in an image I is given at a pixel p where two edges of different directions intersect; edges can be defined by the step-edge or the phase congruency model. See Fig. 2.21 for a general meaning of "corners" in images and Fig. 2.22 for an illustration of three corners when zooming into an image.

> **Insert 2.8** (Hesse and the Hessian Matrix) *The Hessian matrix is named after L.O. Hesse (1811–1874), a German mathematician.*

Corner Detection Using the Hessian Matrix Following the definition of a corner above, it is characterized by high curvature of intensity values. Accordingly, it can be identified by the eigenvalues λ_1 and λ_2 (see Insert 2.9) of the *Hessian matrix*

$$\mathbf{H}(p) = \begin{bmatrix} I_{xx}(p) & I_{xy}(p) \\ I_{xy}(p) & I_{yy}(p) \end{bmatrix} \tag{2.28}$$

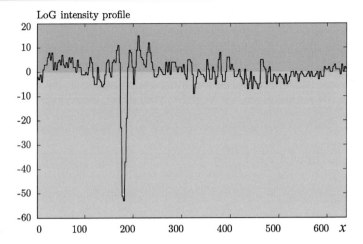

Fig. 2.20 Value profile of a row (close to the middle) in the resulting array when applying the Laplacian to a smoothed version of the image Set1Seq1 (see Fig. 2.4, upper left) using scale $s = 2$. The steep global minimum appears between branches of a shrub

Fig. 2.21 Detected corners provide important information for localizing and understanding shapes in 3D scenes

at pixel location p. If the magnitude of both eigenvalues is "large", then we are at a corner; one large and one small eigenvalue identifies a step edge, and two small eigenvalues identify a low-contrast region.

Insert 2.9 (Trace of a Matrix, Determinant, and Eigenvalues) *The trace* $\mathrm{Tr}(\mathbf{A})$ *of an* $n \times n$ *matrix* $\mathbf{A} = (a_{ij})$ *is the sum* $\sum_{i=1}^{n} a_{ii}$ *of its (main) diagonal elements. The determinant of a* 2×2 *matrix* $\mathbf{A} = (a_{ij})$ *is given by*

$$\det(\mathbf{A}) = a_{11}a_{22} - a_{12}a_{21}$$

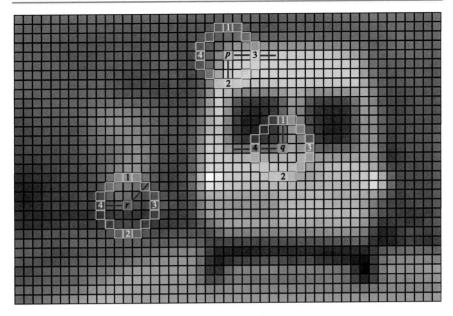

Fig. 2.22 Pixels p, q, and r are at intersections of edges; directions of those edges are indicated by the shown *blue lines*. The shown discrete circles (of 16 pixels) are used in the discussion of the FAST corner detector. Small window of image Set1Seq1

The determinant of a 3×3 matrix $\mathbf{A} = (a_{ij})$ is given by

$$\det(\mathbf{A}) = a_{11}a_{22}a_{33} + a_{12}a_{23}a_{31} + a_{13}a_{21}a_{32} - a_{13}a_{22}a_{31} - a_{12}a_{21}a_{33} - a_{11}a_{23}a_{32}$$

The eigenvalues of an $n \times n$ matrix $\mathbf{A}$ are the n solutions of its characteristic polynomial $\det(\mathbf{A} - \lambda\mathbf{I}) = 0$, where $\mathbf{I}$ is the $n \times n$ identity matrix, and det denotes the determinant.

Eigenvalues are real numbers for a real-valued matrix $\mathbf{A}$. They can be used for modelling stability of solutions of a linear equational system defined by a matrix $\mathbf{A}$.

The determinant of a square matrix is equal to the product of its eigenvalues, and the trace is equal to the sum of its eigenvalues.

Corner Detector by Harris and Stephens   This corner detection method is known as the *Harris detector*. Rather than considering the Hessian of the original image I (i.e. second-order derivatives), we use the first-order derivatives of the smoothed version $L(., ., \sigma)$, as defined in (2.18), for some $\sigma > 0$. Let

$$\mathbf{G}(p, \sigma) = \begin{bmatrix} L_x^2(p, \sigma) & L_x(p, \sigma)L_y(p, \sigma) \\ L_x(p, \sigma)L_y(p, \sigma) & L_y^2(p, \sigma) \end{bmatrix} \qquad (2.29)$$

at pixel location p. The eigenvalues λ_1 and λ_2 of the matrix $\mathbf{G}$ represent changes in the intensities in orthogonal directions in the image I. Instead of calculating those eigenvalues, we consider the *cornerness measure*

$$\mathcal{H}(p, \sigma, a) = \det(\mathbf{G}) - a \cdot \text{Tr}(\mathbf{G}) \tag{2.30}$$

for a small parameter $a > 0$ (e.g. $a = 1/25$). Due to the general properties of eigenvalues, we have that

$$\mathcal{H}(p, \sigma, \lambda) = \lambda_1 \lambda_2 - a \cdot (\lambda_1 + \lambda_1) \tag{2.31}$$

If we have one large and one small eigenvalue (such as on a step edge), then having also the trace in (2.30) ensures that the resulting value $\mathcal{H}(p, \sigma, a)$ remains reasonably small.

The cornerness measure $\mathcal{H}$ was proposed in 1988 as a more time-efficient way in comparison to a calculation and analysis of eigenvalues. For results, see Fig. 2.23, left.

Insert 2.10 (Origin of the Harris Detector) *This method was published in* [C. Harris and M. Stephens. A combined corner and edge detector. In Proc. Alvey Vision Conference, pp. 147–151, 1988].

FAST   Time constraints in today's embedded vision (i.e. in "small" independent systems such as micro-robots or cameras in mini-multi-copters), define time-efficiency as an ongoing task. *Features from an accelerated segment test* FAST identify a corner by considering image values on a digital circle around the given pixel location p; see Fig. 2.22 for 16 image values on a circle of radius $\rho = 3$.

Cornerness test: The value at the centre pixel needs to be darker (or brighter) compared to more than 8 (say, 11 for really identifying a corner and not just an irregular pixel on an otherwise straight edge) subsequent pixels on this circle and "similar" to the values of the remaining pixels on the circle.

For results, see Fig. 2.23, right.

Time Efficiency   For being time efficient, we first compare the value at the centre pixel against the values at locations 1, 2, 3, and 4 in this order (see Fig. 2.22); only in cases where it still appears to be possible that the centre pixel passes the cornerness test, we continue with testing more pixels on the circle, such as between locations 1, 2, 3, and 4. The original FAST paper proposes to learn a decision tree for time optimization. The FAST detector in `OpenCV` (and also the one in `libCVD`) applies SIMD instructions for concurrent comparisons, which is faster then the use of the originally proposed decision tree.

Non-maxima Suppression   FAST also applies non-maxima suppression for keeping numbers of detected corners reasonably small. For example, for a detected corner, we can calculate the maximum difference T between the value at the centre

Fig. 2.23 Window of image Set1Seq1. *Left*: Detected corners using the Harris detector. *Right*: Corners detected by FAST

pixel and values on the discrete circle being classified as "darker" or "brighter" such that we still detect this corner. Non-maxima suppression deletes then in the order of differences T.

Insert 2.11 (Origin of FAST) *The paper* [E. Rosten and T. Drummond. Machine learning for high-speed corner detection. In Proc. European Conf. Computer Vision, vol. 1, pp. 430–443, 2006] *defined FAST as a corner detector.*

2.3.5   Removal of Illumination Artefacts

Illumination artefacts such as differing exposures, shadows, reflections, or vignetting pose problems for computer vision algorithms. See Fig. 2.24 for examples.

Failure of Intensity Constancy Assumption   Computer vision algorithms often rely on the *intensity constancy assumption* (ICA) that there is no change in the appearance of objects according to illumination between subsequent or time-synchronized recorded images. This assumption is actually violated when using real-world images, due to shadows, reflections, differing exposures, sensor noise, and so forth.

There are at least three different ways to deal with this problem. (1) We can transform input images such that illumination artefacts are reduced (e.g. mapping images into a uniform illumination model by removing shadows); there are proposals for this way but the success is still limited. (2) We can also attempt to enhance computer vision algorithms so that they do not rely on ICA, and examples for this option are discussed later in this book. (3) We can map input images into images containing still the "relevant" information for subsequent computer vision algorithms, without aiming at keeping those images visually equivalent to the original data, but at removing the impacts of varying illumination.

Fig. 2.24 Example images from real-world scenes (*black pixels* at borders are caused by image rectification, to be discussed later in the book). The pair of images NorthLeft and NorthRight in the *top row* show illumination differences between time-synchronized cameras when the exposures are bad. The *bottom-left image* LightAndTrees shows an example where trees can cause bad shadow effects. The *bottom-right image* MainRoad shows a night scene where head-lights cause large bright spots on the image

We discuss two methods for the third option. A first approach could be to use either histogram equalization or conditional scaling as defined before. Those methods map the whole image uniformly onto a normalized image, normalized with respect to a uniform grey-level histogram or constant mean and standard deviation, respectively. But those uniform transforms are not able to deal with the non-global nature of illumination artefacts.

For example, in vision-based driver assistance systems, there can be the "dancing light" from sunlight through trees, creating local illumination artefacts. See the bottom-left image in Fig. 2.24.

Using Edge Maps Local derivatives do not change when increasing image values by an additive constant. Local derivatives, gradients, or edge maps can be used to derive image representations that are less impacted by lighting variations.

For example, we may simply use Sobel edge maps as input for subsequent computer vision algorithms rather than the original image data. See Fig. 2.25 on the

Fig. 2.25 Original image `Set2Seq1` (*left*) has its residual image (*middle*), computed using TVL$_2$ (not discussed in this textbook) for smoothing, and the Sobel edge map (*right*) shown

right. The Sobel edge map is not a binary image, and also not modified due to particular heuristics (as it is the case for many other edge operators), just the "raw edge data".

> **Insert 2.12** (Video Test Data for Computer Vision on the Net) *The shown synthetic image in Fig. 2.25 is taken from Set 2 of EISATS, available online at www.mi.auckland.ac.nz/EISATS. There are various test data available on the net for comparing computer vision algorithms on recorded image sequences. For current challenges, see also www.cvlibs.net/datasets/kitti/, the KITTI Vision Benchmark Suite, and the Heidelberg Robust Vision Challenge at ECCV 2012, see hci.iwr.uni-heidelberg.de/Static/challenge2012/.*

Another Use of Residuals with Respect to Smoothing   Let I be an original image, assumed to have an additive decomposition

$$I(p) = S(p) + R(p) \tag{2.32}$$

for all pixel positions p, S denotes the smooth component of image I (as above when specifying sharpening), and R is again the residual image with respect to the smoothing operation which produced image S. The decomposition expressed in (2.32) is also referred to as the *structure-texture decomposition*, where the structure refers to the smooth component, and the texture to the residual.

The residual image is the difference between an input image and a smoothed version of itself. Values in the residual image can also be negative, and it might be useful to rescale it into the common range of $\{0, 1, \ldots, G_{\max}\}$, for example when visualizing a residual image. Figure 2.25 shows an example of a residual image R with respect to smoothing when using a TV-L^2 operator (not explained in this textbook).

A smoothing filter can be processed in multiple iterations, using the following scheme:

$$S^{(0)} = I$$

$$S^{(n)} = S(S^{(n-1)}) \quad \text{for } n > 0 \tag{2.33}$$

$$R^{(n)} = I - S^{(n)}$$

The iteration number n defines the applied residual filter. When a 3×3 box filter is used iteratively n times, then it is approximately identical to a Gauss filter of radius $n + 1$.

The appropriateness of different concepts needs to be tested for given classes of input images. The iteration scheme (2.33) is useful for such tests.

2.4   Advanced Edge Detectors

This section discusses step-edge detectors that combine multiple approaches into one algorithm, such as combining edge-detection with pre- or post-processing into one optimized procedure. We also address the phase-congruency model for defining edges by discussing the Kovesi operator.

2.4.1   LoG and DoG, and Their Scale Spaces

The *Laplacian of Gaussian* (LoG) and the *difference of Gaussians* (DoG) are very important basic image transforms, as we will see later at several places in the book.

Insert 2.13 (Origin of the LoG Edge Detector) *The origin of the Laplacian of Gaussian (LoG) edge detector is the publication* [D. Marr and E. Hildreth. Theory of edge detection. Proc. Royal Society London, Series B, Biological Sciences, vol. 207, pp. 187–217, 1980]. *For this reason, it is also known as* the Marr–Hildreth algorithm.

LoG Edge Detector   Applying the Laplacian for a Gauss-filtered image can be done in one step of convolution, based on the theorem

$$\nabla^2(G_\sigma * I) = I * \nabla^2 G_\sigma \tag{2.34}$$

where $*$ denotes the convolution of two functions, and I is assumed (for showing this theorem) to be twice differentiable. The theorem follows directly when applying twice the following *general rule of convolutions*:

$$D(F * H) = D(F) * H = F * D(H) \tag{2.35}$$

Fig. 2.26 The 2D Gauss function is rotationally symmetric with respect to the origin $(0, 0)$; it suffices that we show cuts through the function graph of G and its subsequent derivatives

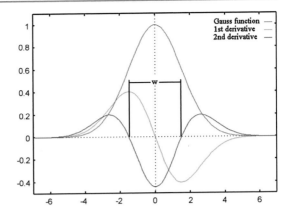

where D denotes a derivative, and F and H are differentiable functions. We have:

Observation 2.4 *For calculating the Laplacian of a Gauss-filtered image, we only have to perform one convolution with* $\nabla^2 G_\sigma$.

The filter kernel for $\nabla^2 G_\sigma$ is not limited to be a 3×3 kernel as shown in Fig. 2.19. Because the Gauss function is given as a continuous function, we can actually calculate the exact Laplacian of this function. For the first partial derivative with respect to x, we obtain that

$$\frac{\partial G_\sigma}{\partial x}(x, y) = -\frac{x}{2\pi \sigma^4} e^{-(x^2+y^2)/2\sigma^2} \tag{2.36}$$

and the corresponding result for the first partial derivative with respect to y. We repeat the derivative for x and y and obtain the LoG as follows:

$$\nabla^2 G_\sigma(x, y) = \frac{1}{2\pi \sigma^4} \left(\frac{x^2 + y^2 - 2\sigma^2}{\sigma^2} \right) e^{-(x^2+y^2)/2\sigma^2} \tag{2.37}$$

See Fig. 2.26. The LoG is also known as the *Mexican hat function*. In fact, it is an "inverted Mexican hat". The zero-crossings define the edges.

Advice on Sampling the LoG Kernel Now we sample this Laplacian into a $(2k + 1) \times (2k + 1)$ filter kernel for an appropriate value of k. But what is an appropriate value for k? We start with estimating the standard deviation σ for the given class of input images, and an appropriate value of k follows from this.

The parameter w is defined by zero-crossings of $\nabla^2 G_\sigma(x, y)$; see Fig. 2.26. Consider $\nabla^2 G_\sigma(x, y) = 0$ and, for example, $y = 0$. We obtain that we have both zero-crossings defined by $x^2 = 2\sigma^2$, namely at $x_1 = -\sqrt{2}\sigma$ and at $x_2 = +\sqrt{2}\sigma$. Thus, we have that

$$w = |x_1 - x_2| = 2\sqrt{2}\sigma \tag{2.38}$$

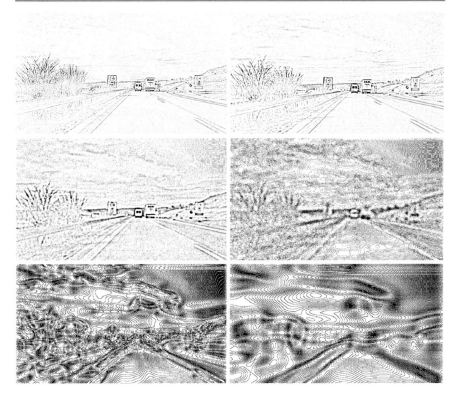

Fig. 2.27 Laplacians of the images shown in Fig. 2.13, representing six layers in the LoG scale space of the image `Set1Seq1`

For representing the Mexican hat function properly by samples, it is proposed to use a window size of $3w \times 3w = 6\sqrt{2}\sigma \times 6\sqrt{2}\sigma$. In conclusion we have that

$$2k + 1 \times 2k + 1 = \text{ceil}(6\sqrt{2}\sigma) \times \text{ceil}(6\sqrt{2}\sigma) \qquad (2.39)$$

where ceil denotes the ceiling function (i.e. the smallest integer equal to or larger than the argument).

The value of σ needs to be estimated for the given image data. Smoothing a digital image with a very "narrow" (i.e. $\sigma < 1$) Gauss function does not make much sense. So, let us consider $\sigma \geq 1$. The smallest kernel (for $\sigma = 1$, thus $3w = 8.485\ldots$) will be of size 9×9 (i.e., $k = 4$). For given images, it is of interest to compare results for $k = 4, 5, 6, \ldots$.

LoG Scale Space   Figure 2.13 shows six layers of the Gaussian scale space for the image `Set1Seq1`. We calculate the Laplacians of those six layers and show the resulting images (i.e. the absolute values of results) in Fig. 2.27; linear scaling was applied to all the images for making the intensity patterns visible. This is an example of a *LoG scale space*. As in a Gaussian scale space, each layer is defined by the scale σ, the used standard deviation in the Gauss function, and we can generate subsequent layers when starting at an initial scale σ and using subsequent scales $a^n \cdot \sigma$ for $a > 1$ and $n = 0, 1, \ldots, m$.

Difference of Gaussians (DoG)   The *difference of Gaussians* (DoG) operator is a common approximation of the LoG operator, justified by reduced run time. Equation (2.17) defined a centred (i.e. zero-mean) Gauss function G_σ.

The DoG is defined by an initial scale σ and a scaling factor $a > 1$ as follows:

$$D_{\sigma,a}(x, y) = L(x, y, \sigma) - L(x, y, a\sigma) \tag{2.40}$$

It is the difference between a blurred copy of image I and an even more blurred copy of I. As for LoG, edges (following the step-edge model) are detected at zero-crossings.

Regarding a relation between LoG and DoG, we have that

$$\nabla^2 G_\sigma(x, y) \approx \frac{G_{a\sigma}(x, y) - G_\sigma(x, y)}{(a - 1)\sigma^2} \tag{2.41}$$

with $a = 1.6$ as a recommended parameter for approximation. Due to this approximate identity, DoGs are used in general as time-efficient approximations of LoGs.

DoG Scale Space   Different scales σ produce layers $D_{\sigma,a}$ in the *DoG scale space*. See Fig. 2.28 for a comparison of three layers in LoG and DoG scale space, using scaling factor $a = 1.6$.

Insert 2.14 (Origins of Scale Space Studies) *Multi-scale image representations are a well-developed theory in computer vision, with manifold applications. Following the LoG studies by Marr and Hildreth (see Insert 2.13), P.J. Burt introduced Gaussian pyramids while working in A. Rosenfeld's group at College Park*; see [P. J. Burt. Fast filter transform for image processing. Computer Graphics Image Processing, vol. 16, pp. 20–51, 1981].

See also [J.L. Crowley. A representation for visual information. Carnegie-Mellon University, Robotics Institute, CMU-RI-TR-82-07, 1981] *and* [A.P. Witkin. Scale-space filtering. In Proc. Int. Joint Conf. Artificial Intelligence, pp. 1019–1022, 1983] *for early publications on Gaussian pyramids, typically created in increments by factor $a = 2$, and resulting blurred images of varying size were called octaves.*

Arbitrary scaling factors $a > 1$ were later introduced into scale-space theory; see, for example, [T. Lindeberg. Scale-Space Theory in Computer Vision. Kluwer Academic Publishers, 1994] *and* [J.L. Crowley and A.C. Sanderson. Multiple resolution representation and probabilistic matching of 2-D grey-scale shape. IEEE Trans. Pattern Analysis Machine Intelligence, vol. 9, pp. 113–121, 1987].

Fig. 2.28 LoG (*left*) and DoG (*right*) layers of image Set1Seq1 are generated for $\sigma = 0.5$ and $a_n = 1.6^n$ for $n = 0, \ldots, 5$, and the figure shows results for $n = 1$, $n = 3$, and $n = 5$

2.4.2 Embedded Confidence

A *confidence measure* is quantified information derived from calculated data, to be used for deciding about the existence of a particular feature; if the calculated data match the underlying model of the feature detector reasonably well, then this should correspond to high values of the measure.

> **Insert 2.15** (Origin of the Meer–Georgescu Algorithm) *This algorithm has been published in* [P. Meer and B. Georgescu. Edge detection with embedded confidence. IEEE Trans. Pattern Analysis Machine Intelligence, vol. 23, pp. 1351–1365, 2001].

The Meer–Georgescu Algorithm The *Meer–Georgescu algorithm* detects edges while applying a confidence measure based on the assumption of the validity of the step-edge model.

1: **for** every pixel p in image I **do**
2:     estimate gradient magnitude $g(p)$ and edge direction $\theta(p)$;
3:     compute the confidence measure $\eta(p)$;
4: **end for**
5: **for** every pixel p in image I **do**
6:     determine value $\rho(p)$ in the cumulative distribution of gradient magnitudes;
7: **end for**
8: generate the $\rho\eta$ diagram for image I;
9: perform non-maxima suppression;
10: perform hysteresis thresholding;

Fig. 2.29 Meer–Georgescu algorithm for edge detection

Four parameters are considered in this method. For an estimated gradient vector $\mathbf{g}(p) = \nabla I(x, y)$ at a pixel location $p = (x, y)$, these are the estimated gradient magnitude $g(p) = \|\mathbf{g}(p)\|_2$, the estimated gradient direction $\theta(p)$, an edge confidence value $\eta(p)$, and the percentile ρ_k of the cumulative gradient magnitude distribution. We specify those values below, to be used in the Meer–Georgescu algorithm shown in Fig. 2.29.

Insert 2.16 (Transpose of a Matrix) *The transpose $\mathbf{W}^\top$ of a matrix $\mathbf{W}$ is obtained by mirroring elements about the main diagonal, and $\mathbf{W}^\top = \mathbf{W}$ if $\mathbf{W}$ is symmetric with respect to the main diagonal.*

Let $\mathbf{A}$ be a matrix representation of the $(2k + 1) \times (2k + 1)$ window centred at the current pixel location p in input image I. Let

$$\mathbf{W} = \mathbf{sd}^\top \tag{2.42}$$

be a $(2k + 1) \times (2k + 1)$ matrix of weights, obtained as the product of two vectors $\mathbf{d} = [d_1, \ldots, d_{2k+1}]$ and $\mathbf{s} = [s_1, \ldots, s_{2k+1}]$, where
1. both are unit vectors in the L_1-norm, i.e. $|d_1| + \cdots + |d_{2k+1}| = 1$ and $|s_1| + \cdots + |s_{2k+1}| = 1$,
2. $\mathbf{d}$ is an asymmetric vector, i.e. $d_1 = -d_{2k+1}$, $d_2 = -d_{2k}$, $\ldots$, $d_{k+1} = 0$, which represents differentiation of one row of matrix $\mathbf{A}$, and
3. $\mathbf{s}$ is a symmetric vector, i.e. $s_1 = s_{2k+1} \leq s_2 = s_{2k} \leq \cdots \leq s_{k+1}$, which represents smoothing in one column of a matrix $\mathbf{A}$.
For example, asymmetric $\mathbf{d} = [-0.125, -0.25, 0, 0.25, 0.125]^\top$ and symmetric $\mathbf{s} = [0.0625, 0.25, 0.375, 0.25, 0.0625]^\top$ define a 5×5 matrix $\mathbf{W}$.
Let $\mathbf{a}_i$ be the ith row of Matrix $\mathbf{A}$. By using

$$d_1 = \text{Tr}(\mathbf{WA}) = \text{Tr}(\mathbf{sd}^\top \mathbf{A}) \tag{2.43}$$

$$d_2 = \text{Tr}(\mathbf{W}^\top \mathbf{A}) = \mathbf{s}^\top \mathbf{Ad} = \sum_{i=1}^{2k+1} s_i (\mathbf{d}^\top \mathbf{a}_i) \tag{2.44}$$

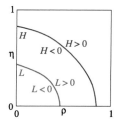 

Fig. 2.30 *Left*: Illustration of curves L and H in a $\rho\eta$ diagram; each separates the square into points with positive L or H, or negative L or H signs. For a (ρ, η) point on a curve, we have $L(\rho, \eta) = 0$ or $H(\rho, \eta) = 0$. *Right*: A 3×3 neighbourhood of pixel location p and virtual neighbours q_1 and q_2 in estimated gradient direction

we obtain the first two parameters used in the algorithm:

$$g(p) = \sqrt{d_1^2 + d_2^2} \quad \text{and} \quad \theta(p) = \arctan\left(\frac{d_1}{d_2}\right) \tag{2.45}$$

Let $\mathbf{A}_{ideal}$ be a $(2k+1) \times (2k+1)$ matrix representing a template of an ideal step edge having the gradient direction $\theta(p)$. The value $\eta(p) = |\text{Tr}(\mathbf{A}_{ideal}^{\top}\mathbf{A})|$ specifies the used confidence measure. The values in $\mathbf{A}$ and $\mathbf{A}_{ideal}$ are normalized such that $0 \leq \eta(p) \leq 1$, with $\eta(p) = 1$ in case of a perfect match with the ideal step edge.

Let $g_{[1]} < \cdots < g_{[k]} < \cdots < g_{[N]}$ be the ordered list of distinct (rounded) gradient-magnitudes in image I, with cumulative distribution values (i.e. probabilities)

$$\rho_k = \text{Prob}[g \leq g_{[k]}] \tag{2.46}$$

for $1 \leq k \leq N$. For a given pixel in I, assume that $g_{[k]}$ is the closest real to its edge magnitude $g(p)$; then we have the percentile $\rho(p) = \rho_k$.

Altogether, for each pixel p, we have a percentile $\rho(p)$ and a confidence $\eta(p)$ between 0 and 1. These values $\rho(p)$ and $\eta(p)$ for any pixel in I define a 2D $\rho\eta$-diagram for image I. See Fig. 2.30, left.

We consider curves in the $\rho\theta$ space given in implicit form, such as $L(\rho, \theta) = 0$. For example, this can be just a vertical line passing the square, or an elliptical arc. Figure 2.30, left, illustrates two curves L and H. Such a curve separates the square into points having positive or negative signs with respect to the curve and into the set of points where the curve equals zero. Now we have all the tools together for describing the decision process.

Non-maxima Suppression   For the current pixel p, determine virtual neighbours q_1 and q_2 in estimated gradient direction (see Fig. 2.30, right) and their ρ and η values by interpolation using values at adjacent pixel locations.

A pixel location p describes with respect to a curve X in $\rho\theta$ space a *maximum* if both virtual neighbours q_1 and q_2 have a negative sign for X. We suppress non-maxima in Step 9 of the algorithm by using a selected curve X for this step; the remaining pixels are the candidates for the edge map.

Fig. 2.31 Resultant images when using the Meer–Georgescu algorithm for a larger (*left*) or smaller (*right*) filter kernel defined by parameter k. Compare with Fig. 2.32, where the same input image `Set1Seq1` has been used (shown in Fig. 2.4, top, left)

Hysteresis Thresholding *Hysteresis thresholding* is a general technique to decide in a process based on previously obtained results. In this algorithm, hysteresis thresholding in Step 10 is based on having two curves L and H in the $\rho\theta$ space, called the two *hysteresis thresholds*; see Fig. 2.30, left. Those curves are also allowed to intersect in general.

We pass through all pixels in I in Step 9. At pixel p we have values ρ and θ. It stays on the edge map if *(a)* $L(\rho, \eta) > 0$ and $H(\rho, \eta) \geq 0$ or *(b)* it is adjacent to a pixel in the edge map and satisfies $L(\rho, \eta) \cdot H(\rho, \eta) < 0$. The second condition *(b)* describes the hysteresis thresholding process; it is applied recursively.

This edge detection method can be a Canny operator if the two hysteresis thresholds are vertical lines, and a confidence-only detector if the two lines are horizontal. Figure 2.31 illustrates images resulting from an application of the Meer-Georgescu algorithm.

2.4.3 The Kovesi Algorithm

Figure 2.32 illustrates results of four different edge detectors on the same night-vision image, recorded for vision-based driver assistance purposes. The two edge maps on the top are derived from phase congruency; the two at the bottom by applying the step-edge model.

Differences between step-edge operators and phase-based operators are even better visible for a simple synthetic input image as in Fig. 2.33. Following its underlying model, a gradient-based operator such as the Canny operator identifies edge pixels defined by maxima of gradient magnitudes, resulting in double responses around the sphere and a confused torus boundary in Fig. 2.34, left. We present the algorithm used for generating the result in Fig. 2.34, right.

Gabor Wavelets For a local analysis of frequency components, it is convenient not to use wave patterns that run uniformly through the whole $(2k + 1) \times (2k + 1)$ window (as illustrated in Fig. 1.15) but rather *wavelets*, such as *Gabor wavelets*, which are sine or cosine waves modulated by a Gauss function of some scale σ and

Fig. 2.32 The phase-congruency model versus the step-edge model on the image Set1Seq1, shown in Fig. 2.4, top, left. *Upper row*: Results of the *Kovesi operator*, which is based on the phase-congruency model, using program phasecongmono.m (see link in Insert 2.18) on the *left* and the next most recent code phasecong3.m on the *right*, both with default parameters. *Lower left*: The Sobel operator follows the step-edge model, using OpenCV's Sobel() with *x* order 1, *y* order 0, and aperture 3. *Lower right*: The Canny operator is another implementation for the step-edge model using Canny() with minimum threshold 150 and maximum threshold 200

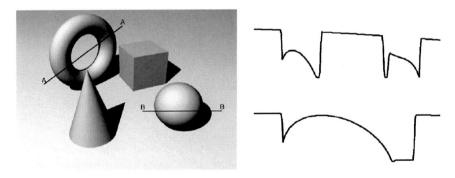

Fig. 2.33 *Left*: Synthetic input image. *Right:* Intensity profiles along Section A–A (*top*) and Section B–B (*bottom*)

thus of decreasing amplitudes around a centre point. See Fig. 2.35. The image in the middle shows *stripes* that are orthogonal to a defining rotation angle θ.

There are *odd* and *even* Gabor wavelets. An odd wavelet is generated from a sine wave, thus having the value 0 at the origin. An even wavelet is generated from a cosine wave, thus having its maximum at the origin.

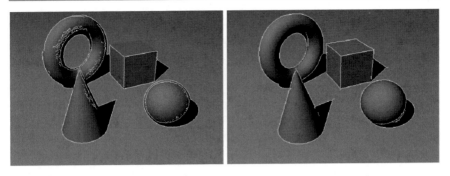

Fig. 2.34 *Left*: Edges detected by the Canny operator. *Right:* Edges detected by the Kovesi algorithm

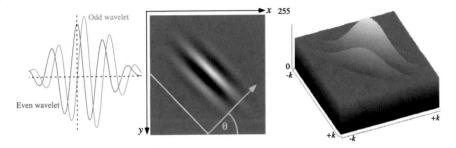

Fig. 2.35 *Left*: Two 1D cuts through an odd and an even Gabor wavelet. *Middle*: A grey-level representation of a square Gabor wavelet in a window of size $(2k + 1) \times (2k + 1)$ with direction θ, with its 3D surface plot (*right*)

Insert 2.17 (Gabor) *The Hungarian born D. Gabor (1900–1979) was an electrical engineer and physicist. He worked in Great Britain and received in 1971 the Nobel Prize in Physics for inventing holography.*

For a formal definition of Gabor wavelets, we first recall the definition of the Gauss function:

$$G_\sigma(x, y) = \frac{1}{2\pi\sigma^2} \exp\left(-\frac{x^2 + y^2}{2\sigma^2}\right) \tag{2.47}$$

Furthermore, we map the coordinates x and y in the image into rotated coordinates

$$u = x\cos\theta + y\sin\theta \tag{2.48}$$

$$v = -x\sin\theta + y\cos\theta \tag{2.49}$$

where θ is orthogonal to the stripes in the Gabor wavelets; see Fig. 2.35, middle. Now consider also a phase-offset $\psi \geq 0$, wavelength $\lambda > 0$ of the sinusoidal factor, and a spatial aspect ratio $\gamma > 0$. Then, altogether,

$$g_{even}(x, y) = G_\sigma(u, \gamma v) \cdot \cos\left(2\pi\frac{u}{\lambda} + \psi\right) \tag{2.50}$$

$$g_{odd}(x, y) = G_\sigma(u, \gamma v) \cdot \sin\left(2\pi\frac{u}{\lambda} + \psi\right) \tag{2.51}$$

define one *Gabor pair* where sine and cosine functions are modulated by the same Gauss function. The pair can also be combined into one complex number using

$$g_{pair}(x, y) = g_{even}(x, y) + \sqrt{-1} \cdot g_{odd}(x, y)$$

$$= G_\sigma(u, \gamma v) \cdot \exp\left(2\pi\frac{u}{\lambda} + \psi\right) \tag{2.52}$$

Insert 2.18 (Origin of the Kovesi Algorithm) *This algorithm has been published in* [P.D. Kovesi. A dimensionless measure of edge significance from phase congruency calculated via wavelets. In Proc. New Zealand Conf. Image Vision Computing, pp. 87–94, 1993]. *See also sources provided on www.csse.uwa.edu.au/~pk/Research/ MatlabFns/index.html#phasecong. The program is very fast and routinely applied to images of size* 2000 × 2000 *or more; it applies actually log-Gabor wavelets instead of Gabor wavelets for better operator response and for better time efficiency.*

Preparing for the Algorithm   The Kovesi algorithm applies a set of n square Gabor pairs, centred at the current pixel location $p = (x, y)$. Figure 2.36 illustrates such a set for $n = 40$ by illustrating only one function (say, the odd wavelet) for each pair; the Kovesi algorithm uses 24 pairs as default.

The convolution with each Gabor pair defines one complex number. The obtained n complex numbers have amplitude r_h and phase α_h.

Equation (1.33) defines an ideal phase congruency measure. For cases where the sum $\sum_{h=1}^{n} r_h$ becomes very small, it is convenient to add a small positive number ε to the denominator, such as $\varepsilon = 0.01$. There is also noise in the image, typically uniform. Let $T > 0$ be the sum of all noise responses over all AC components (which can be estimated for given images). Assuming constant noise, we simply subtract the noise component and have

$$\mathscr{P}_{phase}(p) = \frac{\text{pos}(\|z\|_2 - T)}{\sum_{h=1}^{n} r_h + \varepsilon} \tag{2.53}$$

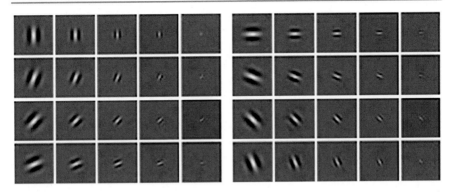

Fig. 2.36 Illustration of a set of Gabor functions to be used for detecting phase congruency at a pixel location

where the function pos returns the argument if positive and 0 otherwise. We have that

$$0 \le \mathscr{P}_{phase}(p) \le 1 \qquad (2.54)$$

Select m_1 uniformly distributed directions $\theta_1, \ldots, \theta_{m_1}$ and m_2 scales $s_1, \ldots, s_{m_2}$ (for example, $m_1 = 6$ and $m_2 = 4$). For specifying the set of $m_1 \cdot m_2$ Gabor wavelets, select the smallest scale (e.g. equal to 3) and a scaling factor between successive scales (say, equal to 2.1). The convolution with those Gabor wavelets can be done more time-efficiently in the frequency domain than in the spatial domain. If in the spatial domain, then the size $(2k + 1) \times (2k + 1)$ of the convolution kernel should be such that $2k + 1$ is about three times the wavelength of the filter.

Processing at One Pixel   Now we have all together for analysing phase congruency at the given pixel location $p = (x, y)$:

1. Apply at p the set of convolution masks of $n = m_1 \cdot m_2$ Gabor pairs producing n complex numbers (r_h, α_h).
2. Calculate the phase congruency measures $\mathscr{P}_i(p)$, $1 \le i \le m_1$, as defined in (2.53), but by only using the m_2 complex numbers (r_h, α_h) defined for direction θ_i by m_2 scales.
3. Calculate the directional components X_i and Y_i for $1 \le i \le m_1$ by

$$[X_i, Y_i]^\top = \mathscr{P}_i(p) \cdot \left[\sin(\theta_i), \cos(\theta_i) \right]^\top \qquad (2.55)$$

4. For the resulting *covariance matrix* of directional components,

$$\begin{bmatrix} \sum_{i=1}^{m_1} X_i^2 & \sum_{i=1}^{m_1} X_i Y_i \\ \sum_{i=1}^{m_1} X_i Y_i & \sum_{i=1}^{m_1} Y_i^2 \end{bmatrix} \qquad (2.56)$$

calculate the eigenvalues λ_1 and λ_2; let $\lambda_1 \ge \lambda_2$. (This matrix corresponds to the 2×2 Hessian matrix of second-order derivatives; for L.O. Hesse, see Insert 2.8.)

Fig. 2.37 Colour-coded
results when classifying
detected feature points in a
scale between "Step" and
"Line", using the colour key
shown on the *right*. For the
original image, see Fig. 2.33,
left

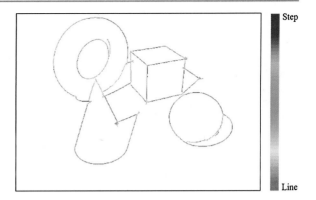

The magnitude of λ_1 indicates the significance of a local feature (an edge, corner,
or another local feature); if λ_2 is also of large magnitude, then we have a corner; the
principle axis corresponds with the direction of the local feature.

Detection of Edge Pixels   After applying the procedure above for all $p \in \Omega$, we
have an array of λ_1 values, called the *raw result* of the algorithm. All values below
a chosen cut-off threshold (say, 0.5) can be ignored.

We perform non-maxima suppression in this array (possibly combined with hysteresis thresholding, similar to the Meer–Georgescu algorithm), i.e. set to zero all
values that do not define a local maximum in their (say) 8-neighbourhood.

All the pixels having non-zero values after the non-maxima suppression are the
identified edge pixels.

Besides technical parameters which can be kept constant for all processed images
(e.g. the chosen Gabor pairs, parameter ε for eliminating instability of the denominator, or the cut-off threshold), the algorithm only depends on the parameter T used
in (2.53), and even this parameter can be estimated from the expected noise in the
processed images.

Equation (2.53) gives a measure $\mathcal{P}(p)$ that is proportional to the cosine of the
phase deviation angles, which gives a "soft" response.

Given that $\mathcal{P}(p)$ represents a weighted sum of the cosines of the phase deviation
angles, taking the arc cosine gives us a weighted sum of the phase deviation angles.
A suggested revision of the phase deviation measure is then given by

$$\mathcal{P}_{rev}(p) = \text{pos}\big(1 - \arccos(\mathcal{P}(p))\big) \qquad (2.57)$$

with function pos as defined above.

Classification into Edge or Line Pixels   Having two eigenvalues as results for
each pixel, these two values can also be used for classifying a detected feature. See
Fig. 2.37 for an example.

2.5   Exercises

2.5.1   Programming Exercises

Exercise 2.1 (Variations of Histogram Equalization) The book [R. Klette and P. Zamperoni: *Handbook of Image Processing Operators*. Wiley, Chichester, 1996] discusses variations of histogram transforms, in particular variations of histogram equalization

$$g_{equal}^{(r)}(u) = \frac{G_{\max}}{Q} \sum_{w=0}^{u} h_I(w)^r \quad \text{with } Q = \sum_{w=0}^{G_{\max}} h_I(w)^r$$

Use noisy (scalar) input pictures (of your choice) and apply the sigma filter prior to histogram equalization. Verify by your own experiments the following statements:

A stronger or weaker equalization can be obtained by adjusting the exponent $r \geq 0$. The resultant histogram is uniformly (as good as possible) distributed for $r = 1$. For $r > 1$, sparse grey values of the original picture will occur more often than in the equalized picture. For $r = 0$, we have about (not exactly!) the identical transform. A weaker equalization in comparison to $r = 1$ is obtained for $r < 1$.

Visualize results by using *2D histograms* where one axis is defined by r and the other axis, as usual, by grey levels; show those 2D histograms either by means of a 2D grey-level image or as a 3D surface plot.

Exercise 2.2 (Developing an Edge Detector by Combining Different Strategies) Within an edge detector we can apply one or several of the following strategies:
1. An edge pixel should define a local maximum when applying an operator (such as the Sobel operator) that approximates the magnitude of the gradient ∇I.
2. After applying the LoG filter, the resulting arrays of positive and negative values need to be analysed with respect to zero-crossings (i.e. pixel locations p where the LoG result is about zero, and there are both positive and negative LoG values at locations adjacent to p).
3. The discussed operators are modelled with respect to derivatives in x- or y-directions only. The consideration of directional derivatives is a further option; for example, derivatives in directions of multiples of $45°$.
4. More heuristics can be applied for edge detection: an edge pixel should be adjacent to other edge pixels.
5. Finally, when having a sequences of edge pixels, then we are interested in extracting "thin arcs" rather than having "thick edges".

The task in this programming exercise is to design your own edge detector that combines at least two different strategies as listed above. For example, verify the presence of edge pixels by tests using both first-order and second-order derivatives. As a second example, apply a first-order derivative operator together with a test for adjacent edge pixels. As a third example, extend a first-order derivative operator by directional derivatives in more than just two directions. Go for one of those three examples or design your own combination of strategies.

Exercise 2.3 (Amplitudes and Phases of Local Fourier Transforms) Define two $(2k + 1) \times (2k + 1)$ local operators, one for amplitudes and one for phases, mapping an input image I into the *amplitude image* $\mathcal{M}$ and *phase image* $\mathcal{P}$ defined as follows:

Perform the 2D DFT on the current $(2k + 1) \times (2k + 1)$ input window, centred at pixel location p. For the resulting $(2k + 1)^2 - 1$ complex-valued AC coefficients, calculate a value $\mathcal{M}(p)$ representing the percentage of amplitudes at high-frequency locations compared to the total sum of all $(2k + 1)^2 - 1$ amplitudes and the phase-congruency measure $\mathcal{P}(p)$ as defined in (2.53).

Visualize $\mathcal{M}$ and $\mathcal{P}(p)$ as grey-level images and compare with edges in the input image I. For doing so, select an edge operator, thresholds for edge map, amplitude image, and phase image and quantify the numbers of pixels being in the thresholded edge and amplitude image versus numbers of pixels being in the thresholded edge and phase image.

Exercise 2.4 (Residual Images with Respect to Smoothing) Use a 3×3 box filter recursively (up to 30 iterations) for generating residual images with respect to smoothing. Compare with residual images when smoothing with a Gauss filter of size $(2k + 1) \times (2k + 1)$ for $k = 1, \ldots, 15$. Discuss the general relationship between recursively repeated box filters and a Gauss filter of the corresponding radius. Actually, what is the corresponding radius?

2.5.2   Non-programming Exercises

Exercise 2.5 Linear local operators are those that can be defined by a convolution. Classify the following whether they are linear operators or not: box, median, histogram equalization, sigma filter, Gauss filter, and LoG.

Exercise 2.6 Equalization of colour pictures is an interesting area of research. Discuss why the following approach is expected to be imperfect: do histogram equalization for all three colour (e.g. RGB) channels separately; use the resulting scalar pictures as colour channels for the resulting image.

Exercise 2.7 Prove that conditional scaling correctly generated an image J that has the mean and variance identical to those corresponding values of the image I used for normalization.

Exercise 2.8 Specify exactly how the integral image can be used for minimizing run time for a box filter of large kernel size.

Exercise 2.9 Following Example 2.4, what could be a filter kernel for the quadratic variation (instead of the one derived for the Laplace operator)?

Exercise 2.10 Prove that Sobel masks are of the form $\mathbf{ds}^\top$ and $\mathbf{sd}^\top$ for 3D vectors $\mathbf{s}$ and $\mathbf{d}$ that satisfy the assumptions of the Meer–Georgescu algorithm for edge detection.

Exercise 2.11 The sigma filter replaces $I(p)$ by $J(p)$ as defined in (2.19). The procedure uses the histogram $H(u)$ computed for values u in the window $W_p(I)$ that belong to the interval $[I(p) - \sigma, I(p) + \sigma]$. Alternatively, a direct computation can be applied:

$$J(p) = \frac{\sum_{q \in Z_{p,\sigma}} I(q)}{|Z_{p,\sigma}|} \tag{2.58}$$

where $Z_{p,\sigma} = \{q \in W_p(I) : I(p) - \sigma \leq I(q) \leq I(p) + \sigma\}$. Analyse possible advantages of this approach for small windows.

Exercise 2.12 Sketch (as in Fig. 2.6) filter curves in the frequency domain that might be called an "exponential low-emphasis filter" and "ideal band-pass filter".

Image Analysis

3

This chapter provides topologic and geometric basics for analysing image regions, as well as two common ways for analysing distributions of image values. It also discusses line and circle detection as examples for identifying particular patterns in an image.

3.1 Basic Image Topology

In Sect. 1.1.1 it was stated that pixels do not define a particular adjacency relation between them per se. It is our model that specifies a chosen adjacency relation. The selected adjacency relation has later significant impacts on defined image regions, to be used for deriving properties in an image analysis context. See Fig. 3.1.

This section is a brief introduction into *digital topology* as needed for understanding basic concepts such as an "image region" or "border of an image region", also highlighting particular issues in a digital image that do not occur in the Euclidean plane.

> **Insert 3.1** (Topology and Listing) *Topology can informally be described as being "rubber-sheet geometry". We are interested in understanding the numbers of components of sets, adjacencies between such components, numbers of holes in sets, and similar properties that do not depend on measurements in a space equipped with coordinates.*
>
> *The* Descartes–Euler theorem $\alpha_0 - \alpha_1 + \alpha_2 = 2$ *is often identified as the origin of* topology, *where* α_2, α_1, *and* α_0 *are the numbers of faces, edges, and vertices of a convex polyhedron.* (A convex *polyhedron* is a nonempty bounded set that is an intersection of finitely many half-spaces.) *For Euler and Descartes, see Insert* 1.3.

R. Klette, *Concise Computer Vision*, Undergraduate Topics in Computer Science,
DOI 10.1007/978-1-4471-6320-6_3, © Springer-Verlag London 2014

Fig. 3.1 *Left*: The number of black regions does not depend on a chosen adjacency relation. *Right*: In the Euclidean topology, the number of black regions depends on whether two adjacent black squares are actually connected by the black corner point between both or not

> *J.B. Listing* (1802–1882) *was the first to use the word "topology" in his correspondence, beginning in* 1837. *He defined: "Topological properties are those which are related not to quantity or content, but to spatial order and position."*

3.1.1   4- and 8-Adjacency for Binary Images

Assumed pixel adjacency (or pixel neighbourhood) defines connectedness in an image and thus regions of pairwise connected pixels.

Pixel Adjacency   Assuming *4-adjacency*, each pixel location $p = (x, y)$ is adjacent to pixel locations in the set

$$A_4(p) = p + A_4 = \big\{(x + 1, y), (x - 1, y), (x, y + 1), (x, y - 1)\big\} \qquad (3.1)$$

for the *4-adjacency set* $A_4 = \{(1, 0), (-1, 0), (0, 1), (0, -1)\}$. The graphs in Figs. 1.1 and 1.2 illustrate 4-adjacency. This type of adjacency corresponds to edge-adjacency when considering each pixel as a shaded tiny square (i.e. the grid cell model). Assuming *8-adjacency*, each grid point $p = (x, y)$ is adjacent to pixel locations in the set

$$A_8(p) = p + A_8 = \big\{(x + 1, y + 1), (x + 1, y - 1), (x - 1, y + 1), (x - 1, y - 1),$$
$$(x + 1, y), (x - 1, y), (x, y + 1), (x, y - 1)\big\} \qquad (3.2)$$

for the *8-adjacency set* $A_8 = \{(1, 1), (1, -1), (-1, 1), (-1, -1)\} \cup A_4$. This also introduces diagonal edges that are not shown in the graphs in Figs. 1.1 and 1.2. Figure 3.3, left, illustrates 8-adjacency for the shown black pixels. This type of adjacency corresponds to edge- or corner-adjacency in the grid cell model.

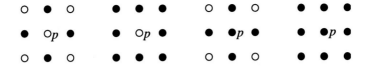

Fig. 3.2 *Left:* 4-adjacency set and 8-adjacency set of p. *Right:* 4-neighbourhood and 8-neighbourhood of p

Pixel Neighbourhoods A *neighbourhood* of a pixel p contains the pixel p itself and some adjacent pixels. For example, the *4-neighbourhood* of p equals $A_4(p) \cup \{p\}$, and the *8-neighbourhood* of p equals $A_8(p) \cup \{p\}$. See Fig. 3.2.

Insert 3.2 (Adjacency, Connectedness, and Planarity in Graph Theory) *An (undirected) graph $G = [N, E]$ is defined by a set N of nodes and a set E of edges; each edge connects two nodes. The graph G is finite if N is finite.*

Two nodes are adjacent if there is an edge between them. A path is a sequence of nodes, where each node in the sequence is adjacent to its predecessor.

A set $S \subseteq N$ of nodes is connected iff there is a path in S from any node in S to any node in S. Maximal connected subsets of a graph are called components.

A planar graph can be drawn on the plane in such a way that its edges intersect only at their endpoints (i.e. nodes). Let α_1 be the number of edges, and α_0 be the number of nodes of a graph. For a planar graph with $\alpha_0 \geq 3$, we have that $\alpha_1 \leq 3\alpha_0 - 6$; if there are no cycles of length 3 in the graph, then it is even $\alpha_1 \leq 2\alpha_0 - 4$.

Euler's formula states that for a finite planar and connected graph, $\alpha_2 - \alpha_1 + \alpha_0 = 2$, where α_2 denotes the number of faces of the planar graph.

Pixel Connectedness The following *transitive closure* of the adjacency relation defines *connectedness*. Let $S \subseteq \Omega$:

1. A pixel is connected to itself.
2. Adjacent pixels in S are connected.
3. If pixel $p \in S$ is connected to pixel $q \in S$, and pixel $q \in S$ is adjacent to pixel $r \in S$, then p is also connected to r (in S).

Depending on the chosen adjacency, we thus have either *4-connectedness* or *8-connectedness* of subsets of Ω.

Regions Maximal connected sets of pixels define *regions*, also called *components*. The black pixels in Fig. 3.3, left, define one 8-region and eight 4-regions (isolated pixels); the figure contains two white 4-regions and only one white 8-region.

Figure 3.4, left, provides a more general example. Assume that the task is to count "particles" in an image represented (after some image processing) by black pixels. The chosen adjacency relation defines your result, not the input image!

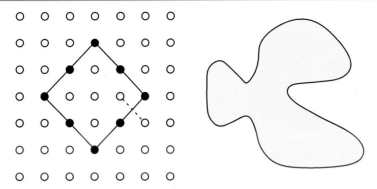

Fig. 3.3 *Left*: Assume 4-adjacency: The disconnected black pixels separate a connected "inner region" from a connected "outer region". Assume 8-adjacency: The black pixels are connected (as illustrated by the inserted edges), but all the white pixels remain connected (see the dashed edge as an example). *Right*: A simple curve in the Euclidean plane always separates interior (the shaded region) from exterior

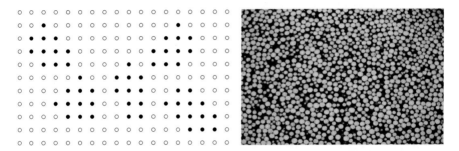

Fig. 3.4 *Left*: Assuming 4-adjacency for black pixels, we count five "particles" in this binary image; assuming 8-adjacency, the count is three. *Right*: Illustration of an application where such a count is relevant

Insert 3.3 (Jordan) *C. Jordan (1838–1922), a French mathematician, contributed to many areas in mathematics. For example, he showed that the centre of a tree is either a single node or a pair of adjacent nodes. He is especially known for his definitions and characterizations of curves in the plane.*

Dual Adjacencies in Binary Images Figure 3.3 illustrates the consequences when deciding for one particular type of adjacency by drawing a comparison with the geometry in the Euclidean plane $\mathbb{R}^2$. $\mathbb{R}$ is the set of all real numbers. A *simple curve*, also known as a *Jordan curve*, always separates an inner region, called the *interior*, from an outer region, called the *exterior*. This appears to be obvious, in correspondence with our intuition, but a mathematical proof of this property, known as the *Jordan–Brouwer theorem*, is actually difficult. What is the corresponding theorem for images based on connectedness?

Insert 3.4 (Rosenfeld and the Origin of Dual Adjacencies) *Figure* 3.3, *left, was used in* [A. Rosenfeld and J.L. Pfaltz. Sequential operations in digital picture processing. *J. ACM*, **13**:471–494, 1966] *for showing that one uniformly applied adjacency relation leads to topological 'issues'. The authors wrote:*

> *"The 'paradox' of (Fig. 3.3, left,) can be (expressed) as follows: If the 'curve' is connected ('gapless') it does not disconnect its interior from its exterior; if it is totally disconnected it does disconnect them. This is of course not a mathematical paradox but it is unsatisfying intuitively; nevertheless, connectivity is still a useful concept. It should be noted that if a digitized picture is defined as an array of hexagonal, rather than square, elements, the paradox disappears".*

Commenting on this publication, R.O. Duda, P.E. Hart, and J.H. Munson proposed (in an unpublished technical report in 1967) *the dual use of* 4- *and* 8-*connectedness for black and white pixels.*

A. Rosenfeld (1931–2004) *is known for many pioneering contributions to computer vision. The Azriel Rosenfeld Life-Time Achievement Award was established at ICCV* 2007 *in Rio de Janeiro to honour outstanding researchers who are recognized as making significant contributions to the field of Computer Vision over longtime careers.*

Figure 3.3, left, contains one 8-region forming a *simple digital curve*. But this curve does not separate two white 8-regions. Assuming 4-adjacency, then we have isolated pixels, thus no simple curve, and thus there should be no separation. But, we do have two separated 4-regions. Thus, using the same adjacency relation for both black and white pixels leads to a topological result that does not correspond to the Jordan–Brouwer theorem in the Euclidean plane and thus not to our intuition when detecting a simple curve in an image. The straightforward solution is:

Observation 3.1 *The dual use of types of adjacency for white or black pixels, for example 4-adjacency for white pixels and 8-adjacency for black pixels, ensures that simple digital curves separate inner and outer regions. Such a dual use results in a planar adjacency graph for the given binary image.*

Insert 3.5 (Two Separation Theorems) *Let ϕ be a parameterized continuous path $\phi : [a, b] \rightarrow \mathbb{R}^2$ such that $a \neq b$, $\phi(a) = \phi(b)$, and let $\phi(s) \neq \phi(t)$ for all s, t ($a \leq s < t < b$). Following C. Jordan* (1893), *a Jordan curve in the plane is a set*

$$\gamma = \left\{ (x, y) : \phi(t) = (x, y) \wedge a \leq t \leq b \right\}$$

An open set M is called topologically connected *if it is not the union of two disjoint nonempty open subsets of M.*

Theorem 3.1 (C. Jordan, 1887; O. Veblen, 1905) *Let γ be a Jordan curve in the Euclidean plane. The open set $\mathbb{R}^2 \setminus \gamma$ consists of two disjoint topologically connected open sets with the common frontier γ.*

This theorem was first stated by C. Jordan in 1887, but his proof was incorrect. The first correct proof was given by O. Veblen in 1905.
   Two sets $S_1, S_2 \subseteq \mathbb{R}^n$ are homeomorphic *if there is a one-to-one continuous mapping Φ such that $\Phi(S_1) = S_2$, and Φ^{-1} is also continuous [with $\Phi^{-1}(S_2) = S_1$].*
   L.E.J. Brouwer generalized in 1912 the definition of a Jordan curve. A Jordan manifold in $\mathbb{R}^n$ ($n \geq 2$) is the homeomorphic image of the frontier of the n-dimensional unit ball.

Theorem 3.2 (L.E.J. Brouwer, 1911) *A Jordan manifold separates $\mathbb{R}^n$ into two connected subsets and coincides with the frontier of each of these subsets.*

3.1.2   Topologically Sound Pixel Adjacency

The dual use of 4- or 8-adjacency avoids the described topological problems for binary images. For multi-level images (i.e. more than two different image values), we can either decide that we ignore topological issues as illustrated by Fig. 3.3 (and assume just 4- or 8-adjacency for all pixels, knowing that this will cause topological problems sometimes), or we apply a topologically sound adjacency approach, which comes with additional computational costs.

If your imaging application requires to be topologically sound at pixel adjacency level, or you are interested in the raised mathematical problem, then this is your subsection. Figure 3.5 illustrates the raised mathematical problem: how to provide a sound mathematical model for dealing with topology in multi-level images?

For the chessboard-type pattern in Fig. 3.1, right, we assume that it is defined in the Euclidean (i.e., continuous) plane, and we have to specify whether the corners of squares are either black or white. *Topology* is the mathematical theory for modelling such decisions.

Insert 3.6 (Euclidean Topology) *We briefly recall some basics of the Euclidean topology. Consider the Euclidean metric d_2 in the n-dimensional (nD) Euclidean space $\mathbb{R}^n$ ($n = 1, 2, 3$ is sufficient for our purpose). Let $\varepsilon > 0$. The*

Fig. 3.5 Is the black line crossing "on top" of the grey line? How many grey components? How many black components? How many white components?

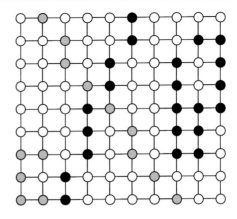

set

$$U_\varepsilon(p) = \big\{ q : q \in \mathbb{R}^n \wedge d_2(p,q) < \varepsilon \big\}$$

is the (open) ε-neighbourhood of $p \in \mathbb{R}^n$, also called the (open) ε-ball centred at p, or unit ball if $\varepsilon = 1$.

Let $S \subseteq \mathbb{R}^n$. The set S is called open if, for any point $p \in S$, there is a positive ε such that $U_\varepsilon(p) \subseteq S$. A set $S \subseteq \mathbb{R}^n$ is called closed if the complement $\overline{S} = \mathbb{R}^n \setminus S$ is an open set. The class of all open subsets of $\mathbb{R}^n$ defines the nD Euclidean topology.

Let $S \subseteq \mathbb{R}^n$. The maximum open set S° contained in S is called the interior *of S, and the minimum closed set $S^\bullet$, containing S, is called the* closure *of S.*

It follows that a set is open iff it equals its interior; a set is closed iff it equals its closure. The difference set $\delta S = S^\bullet \setminus S^\circ$ is the boundary *or* frontier *of S.*

Examples*: Consider $n = 1$. For two reals $a < b$, the interval $[a,b] = \{x : a \leq x \leq b\}$ is closed, and the interval $(a,b) = \{x : a < x < b\}$ is open. The frontier of $[a,b]$, $(a,b]$, $[a,b)$, or (a,b) equals $\{a,b\}$.*

A straight line $y = Ax + B$ in 2D space also contains open or closed segments. For example, $\{(x,y) : a < x < b \wedge y = Ax + B\}$ is an open segment. The singleton $\{p\}$ is closed for $p \in \mathbb{R}^2$. The frontier of a square can be partitioned into four (closed) vertices and four open line segments.

A set in $\mathbb{R}^n$ is compact *iff it is closed and bounded; it has an* interior *and a* frontier. *After removing its frontier, it would become* open. *See Fig. 3.6 for an illustration of a set in the plane.*

We can consider all black squares in a chessboard-type pattern to be closed; then we have only one connected black region. We can consider all black squares to be

Fig. 3.6 The *dashed line* illustrates the open interiors, and the *solid line* illustrates the frontier. Of course, in the continuous plane there are no gaps between interior and frontier; this is just a rough sketch

Fig. 3.7 Components for "black > grey > white"

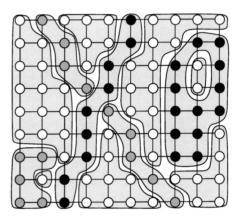

open; then we have only one connected white region. The important point is: Which pixel "owns" the corner where all four pixels meet?

Observation 3.2 *We have to define a preference which grey-level pixels should be closed or open in relation to another grey level; considering closed pixels as being "more important", we need to define an order of importance.*

Consider the example in Fig. 3.5 and assume that "black > grey > white" for the order of importance. If four pixels meet at one corner (as shown in Fig. 3.6) and there is any black pixel in the set of four, then the corner is also black. If there is no black pixel in the set of four, then a grey pixel would "win" against white pixels. Applying this order of importance, we have two black components, three grey components, and seven white components. See Fig. 3.7.

Under the assumption of "white > grey > black", we would have one white component, two grey components, and five black components for Fig. 3.5.

Fig. 3.8 Three 2-by-2 pixel
arrays defining each
"flip-flop" case

The order of importance defines the *key* for this way of adjacency definition; thus, we call it *K-adjacency*. A simple general rule for a scalar image is that the order of importance follows the order of grey levels, either in increasing or in decreasing order. For a vector-valued image, it is possible to take an order by vector magnitudes followed by lexicographic order (in cases of identical magnitudes). Defining K-adjacencies based on such orders of importance solves the raised mathematical problem (due to a partition of the plane in the sense of Euclidean topology), and the analysis in the image thus follows the expected topological rules.

We need to access those orders actually only in cases where two pixel locations, being diagonally positioned in a 2×2 pixel array, have an identical value, which is different from the two other values in this 2×2 pixel array. This defines a *flip-flop case*. Figure 3.8 illustrates three flip-flop cases.

The number of such flip-flop cases is small in recorded images; see four examples of grey-level images in Fig. 3.9. Despite those small numbers, the impact of those few flip-flop cases on the shape or number of connected regions (defined by identical image values) in an image is often significant.

Observation 3.3 *K-adjacency creates a planar adjacency graph for a given image and ensures that simple digital curves separate inner and outer regions.*

Back to the case of binary images: If we assume that "white > black", then K-adjacency means that we have 8-adjacency for white pixels, and 4-adjacency for black pixels, and "black > white" defines the swapped assignment.

3.1.3   Border Tracing

When arriving via a scanline at an object, we like to trace its border such that the object region is always on the right or always on the left. See Fig. 3.10.

According to the defined pixel adjacency, at a current pixel we have to test all the adjacent pixels in a defined order such that we keep to our strategy (i.e. object region either always on the right or always on the left).

The adjacency used might be 4-, 8-, or K-adjacency, or any other adjacency of your choice. At every pixel location p we have a local circular order $\xi(p) = \langle q_1, \ldots, q_n \rangle$, which lists all adjacent pixels in $A(p)$ exactly once. In case of K-adjacency, the number n of adjacent pixels can vary from pixel to pixel. We trace a border and generate the sequence of pixels $p_0, p_1, \ldots, p_i$ on this border.

Assume that we arrive at $p_{i+1} \in A(p_i)$. Let q_1 be the pixel next to pixel p_i in the local circular order of p_{i+1}. We test whether q_1 is in the object; if "yes", then we have $p_{i+2} = q_1$ and continue at p_{i+2}; if "not", then we test the next pixel q_2 in the local circular order $\xi(p_{i+1})$ of p_{i+1}, and so forth.

Fig. 3.9 These images are of size 2014 × 1426 (they contain 2,872,964 pixels) and have $G_{max} = 255$. For the image Tomte on the *upper left*, the percentage of flip-flop cases is 0.38 % compared to the total number of pixels. In the images PobleEspanyol, Rangitoto, and Kiri on the *upper right*, *lower left*, and *lower right*, respectively, the percentages of flip-flop cases are 0.22 %, 0.5 %, and 0.38 %, respectively

Fig. 3.10 Illustration of two scanlines that arrive for the first time (assuming a standard scan: *top–down, left* to *right*) at objects of interest (lights). At this moment a tracing procedure starts for going around on the border of the object

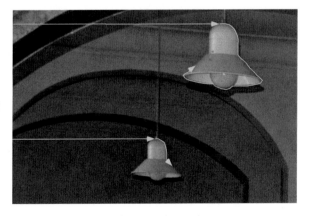

Not any local circular order of an adjacency set is applicable. Clockwise or counter-clockwise orders of adjacent pixels are the possible options.

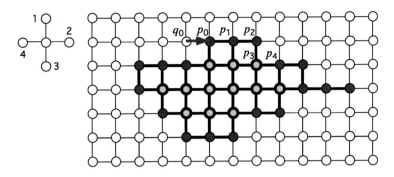

Fig. 3.11 *Left*: Used local circular order. *Right*: Arrival at an object when going from q_0 to p_0

1: Let $(q_0, p_0) = (q, p)$, $i = 0$, and $k = 1$;
2: Let q_1 be the pixel which follows q_0 in $\xi(p_0)$;
3: **while** $(q_k, p_i) \neq (q_0, p_0)$ **do**
4:     **while** q_k in the object **do**
5:         Let $i := i + 1$ and $p_i := q_k$;
6:         Let q_1 be the pixel which follows p_{i-1} in $\xi(p_i)$ and $k = 1$;
7:     **end while**
8:     Let $k = k + 1$ and go to pixel q_k in $\xi(p_i)$;
9: **end while**
10: The calculated border cycle is $\langle p_0, p_1, \ldots, p_i \rangle$;

Fig. 3.12 Voss algorithm

Example 3.1 We consider tracing for 4-adjacency. See the example in Fig. 3.11.

We arrive at the object via edge (q, p); let $(q_0, p_0) := (q, p)$ and assume the local circular order for 4-adjacency as shown. We take the next pixel position in $\xi(p_0)$, which is the pixel position right of p_0: this is in the object, and it is the next pixel p_1 on the border.

We stop if we test again the initial edge; but this would be in direction (p, q), opposite to the arrival direction (q, p). Arriving at the same pixel again is not yet a stop.

General Border-Tracing Algorithm by Voss Given is an image with a defined adjacency relation and an initial edge (q, p) such that we arrive at p for the first time at an object border not yet traced so far. Note: We do not say "first time at an object" because one object may have one outer and several inner borders. The algorithm is provided in Fig. 3.12.

An object O may have holes, acting as objects again (possibly again with holes). Holes generate *inner border cycles* for object O in this case; see the following example. The provided tracing algorithm is also fine for calculating inner borders. The local circular orders remain always the same, only defined by adjacent object or non-object pixels.

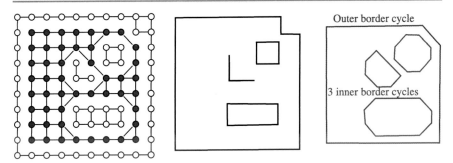

Fig. 3.13 *Left*: Object for "white < black". *Middle*: All border cycles of the non-object pixels. *Right*: All border cycles of the object

Example 3.2 We illustrate all border-tracing results for a binary image. See Fig. 3.13. Here we apply the dual adjacency for binary images defined by the key "white < black". In the figure there is one object with three holes. We notice the correct topologic duality of connectedness and separation. The set of all border cycles of the non-object pixels subdivides the plane and the set of all border cycles of the object. Both subdivisions are topologically equivalent by describing one set with three holes in both cases.

> **Insert 3.7** (Voss) *Klaus Voss* (1937–2008) *described the given general border-tracing algorithm in his book* [K. Voss. Discrete Images, Objects, and Functions in Z^n. Springer, Berlin, 1993]. *He contributed to many areas of theoretical foundations of image analysis and computer vision.*

3.2   Geometric 2D Shape Analysis

This section discusses the measurement of three basic properties, length, area, and curvature in 2D images. By measuring we leave topology and enter the area of *geometry*. The section also presents the Euclidean distance transform.

Images are given at some geometric resolution, specified by the size $N_{cols} \times N_{rows}$. An increase in geometric resolution should lead to an increase in accuracy for measured properties. For example, measuring the perimeter of an object in an image of size $1{,}000 \times 600$ should provide (potentially) a more accurate value than measuring the perimeter for the same object in an image of size 500×300. Spending more on technically improved equipment should pay off with better results.

3.2.1   Area

A triangle $\Pi = \langle p, q, r \rangle$, where $p = (x_1, y_1)$, $q = (x_2, y_2)$, and $r = (x_3, y_3)$, has the area

$$\mathscr{A}(T) = \frac{1}{2} \cdot \left| D(p, q, r) \right| \tag{3.3}$$

where $D(p, q, r)$ is the *determinant*

$$\begin{vmatrix} x_1 & y_1 & 1 \\ x_2 & y_2 & 1 \\ x_3 & y_3 & 1 \end{vmatrix} = x_1 y_2 + x_3 y_1 + x_2 y_3 - x_3 y_2 - x_2 y_1 - x_1 y_3 \tag{3.4}$$

The value $D(p, q, r)$ can be positive or negative; the sign of $D(p, q, r)$ identifies the orientation of the ordered triple (p, q, r).

The area of a simple polygon $\Pi = \langle p_1, p_2, \ldots, p_n \rangle$ in the Euclidean plane, with $p_i = (x_i, y_i)$ for $i = 1, 2, \ldots, n$, is equal to

$$\mathscr{A}(\Pi) = \frac{1}{2} \left| \sum_{i=1}^{n} x_i (y_{i+1} - y_{i-1}) \right| \tag{3.5}$$

for $y_0 = y_n$ and $y_{n+1} = y_1$. In general, the area of a compact set R in $\mathbb{R}^2$ equals

$$\mathscr{A}(R) = \int_R dx \, dy \tag{3.6}$$

How to measure the area of a region in an image?

Figure 3.14 illustrates an experiment. We generate a simple polygon in a grid of size 512×512 and subsample it in images of reduced resolution. The original polygon Π has the area 102,742.5 and perimeter 4,040.7966... in the 512×512 grid.

For the *perimeter* of the generated polygons, we count the number of cell edges on the frontier of the polygon times the length of an edge for the given image resolution. For the 512×512 image, we assume the edge length to be 1, for the 128×128 image, the edge length to be 4, and so forth.

For the *area* of the generated polygons, we count the number of pixels (i.e. grid cells) in the polygon times the square of the edge length.

The *relative deviation* is the absolute difference between the property values for the subsampled polygon and original polygon Π, divided by the property value for Π.

Figure 3.15 summarizes the errors of those measurements by showing the relative deviations. It clearly shows that the measured perimeter for the subsampled polygons is not converging towards the true value; the relative deviations are even increasing!

Regarding the measurement of the area of a region in an image, since the times of Gauss, it is known that the number of grid points in a convex set S estimates the area of S accurately. Thus, not surprisingly, the measured area shows the convergence towards the true area as the image size increases.

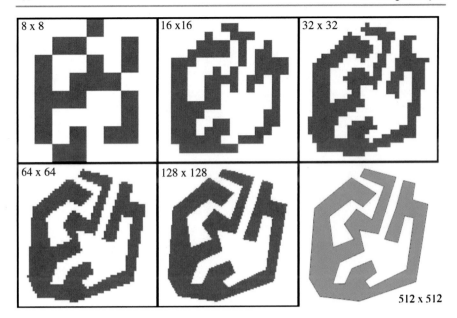

Fig. 3.14 Different digitizations of a simple polygon Π using grids of size 8×8 to 128×128; the original polygon was drawn on a grid of resolution 512×512. All images are shown in the grid cell model

Fig. 3.15 Relative deviations of the area and perimeter of subsampled polygons relatively to the true value in the 512×512 grid

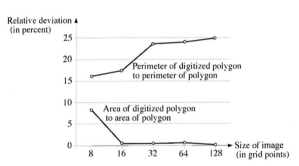

Observation 3.4 *The number of grid points in a region is a reliable estimator for the area of the shown object.*

The experimental data for the method used for estimating the perimeter show that there are "surprises" on the way.

3.2.2   Length

We start with the definition of length for the Euclidean plane. Length is measured for arcs (e.g. line segments or segments of a circle).

Fig. 3.16 A polygonal approximation of an arc defined by points $\phi(t_i)$ on the arc

Assume that we have a parameterized one-to-one representation $\phi(t)$ of an arc γ, starting with $\phi(c)$ and ending at $\phi(d)$ for $c < d$. Values $t_0 = c < t_1 < \cdots < t_n = d$ define a polygonal approximation of this arc; see Fig. 3.16.

A polygonal approximation has a defined length (i.e. the sum of lengths of all line segments on this polygonal path). The limits of lengths of such polygonal approximations, as n tends to infinity (i.e. as line segments become smaller and smaller), define the length of γ.

Insert 3.8 (Jordan Arcs) *The general mathematical definition of an arc is as follows: A Jordan arc γ is defined by a subinterval $[c, d]$ of a Jordan curve (or simple curve)*

$$\{(x, y) : \phi(t) = (x, y) \wedge a \leq t \leq b\}$$

with $a \leq c < d \leq b$, $\phi(t_1) \neq \phi(t_2)$ for $t_1 \neq t_2$, except $t_1 = a$ and $t_2 = b$.
  A rectifiable Jordan arc γ has a bounded arc length as follows:

$$\mathscr{L}(\gamma) = \sup_{n \geq 1 \wedge c = t_0 < \cdots < t_n = d} \sum_{i=1}^{n} d_e\big(\phi(t_i), \phi(t_{i-1})\big) < \infty$$

See Fig. 3.16. In 1883, Jordan proposed the following definition of a curve:

$$\gamma = \{(x, y) : x = \alpha(t) \wedge y = \beta(t) \wedge a \leq t \leq b\}$$

G. Peano showed in 1890 that this allows a curve that fills the whole unit square. The Peano curve is not differentiable at any point in $[0, 1]$. Thus, Jordan's 1883 definition is used for arc length calculation:

$$\mathscr{L}(\gamma) = \int_a^b \sqrt{\left(\frac{d\alpha(t)}{dt}\right)^2 + \left(\frac{d\beta(t)}{dt}\right)^2}\, dt$$

(assuming differentiable functions α and β).

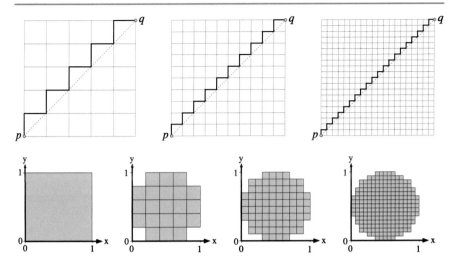

Fig. 3.17 *Top*: Approximations of the diagonal in a square by 4-paths for different grid resolutions. *Bottom*: Digitizations of a unit disk for different grid resolutions

The "Staircase Effect"   Assume a diagonal pq in a square with sides of length a. The length of the diagonal is equal to $a\sqrt{2}$. Consider a 4-path approximating the diagonal as shown in Fig. 3.17, top (i.e. for different grid resolutions). The length of these 4-paths is always equal to $2a$, whatever grid resolution will be chosen.

As a second example, consider the frontiers of digitized disks as shown in Fig. 3.17, bottom. Independent of grid resolution, the length of these frontiers is always equal to 4.

Observation 3.5 *The use of the length of a 4-path for estimating the length of a digital arc can lead to errors of* 41.4 % *(compared to original arcs in the continuous pre-image), without any chance to reduce these errors in some cases by using higher grid resolution. This method is not recommended for length measurements in image analysis.*

Use of Weighted Edges   Assume that we are using the length of an 8-path for length measurements. We use the *weight* $\sqrt{2}$ for diagonal edges and just 1 as before for edges parallel to one of the coordinate axes. (A line or line segment in the Euclidean plane is *isothetic* iff it is parallel to one of the two Cartesian coordinate axes.)

We consider the line segment pq in Fig. 3.18 with slope 22.5° and a length of $5\sqrt{5}/2$.

The length of $\rho(pq)$ is $3 + 2\sqrt{2}$ for a grid with edges of length 1 (shown on the left) and $(5 + 5\sqrt{2})/2$ for *any* grid with edges of length $1/2^n$ ($n \geq 1$). This shows that the length of those 8-paths does not converge to $5\sqrt{5}/2$ as the length of grid edges goes to zero.

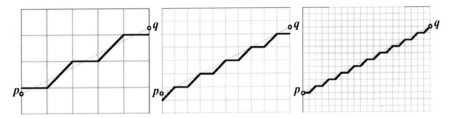

Fig. 3.18 Approximation of line segment pq by 8-paths for different grid resolutions

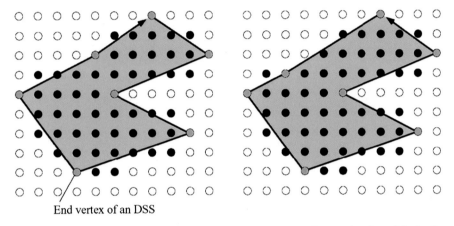

End vertex of an DSS

Fig. 3.19 Clockwise (*left*) and counterclockwise (*right*) polygonal approximation of the border of a region by calculating maximum-length DSSs in subsequent order

Observation 3.6 *For 8-paths we have a situation similar as for the use of 4-paths, but here only with errors of up to 7.9 ... % (when digitizing arcs of known length), without any chance to reduce these errors in some cases by using higher grid resolution.*

This upper bound for magnitudes of errors might be acceptable in some applications. The use of weighted edges (including diagonal edges) for length estimation is certainly acceptable for low image resolution or relatively short digital arcs.

Polygonal Simplification of Borders   What is a certified accurate way for measuring length? We go back to the scheme illustrated in Fig. 3.16. If segmenting an arc into maximum-length *digital straight segments* (DSSs), as illustrated in Fig. 3.19, then the sum of lengths of those straight segments converges to the true length of a digitized arc, provided that we have the budget to acquire equipment with finer and finer grid resolution.

Fig. 3.20 The Frenet frame
at $p = \gamma(t)$, also showing
length $l = \mathcal{L}(t)$

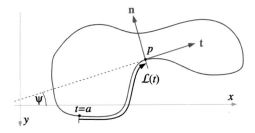

Insert 3.9 (Digital Geometry) *Publications in digital geometry provide further details on "How to calculate DSSs?" and other algorithmic problems related to calculations in the image grid. For example, see the monograph* [R. Klette and A. Rosenfeld. Digital Geometry. Morgan Kaufmann, San Francisco, 2004].

3.2.3 Curvature

A Jordan curve is called *smooth* if it is continuously differentiable. A polygon is not smooth at *singular points* (i.e. its vertices). Curvature can be defined only at non-singular points of a curve.

Curvature as Rate of Change of Tangential Angle   Assume an arc γ in the Euclidean plane that is a segment of a smooth Jordan curve. Thus, we have a tangent $\mathbf{t}(p)$ defined at any point p on γ. This tangent describes an angle ψ with the positive x-axis, called the *slope angle*. See Fig. 3.20.

Insert 3.10 (Frenet Frame and Frenet) *To define curvature it is convenient to use the* Frenet frame, *which is a pair of orthogonal coordinate axes (see Fig. 3.20) with origin at a point $p = \gamma(t)$ on the curve, named after the French mathematician J.F. Frenet (1816–1900). One axis is defined by the* tangent vector

$$\mathbf{t}(t) = \left[\cos\psi(t), \sin\psi(t)\right]^{\top}$$

where ψ is the slope angle *between the tangent and the positive x-axis. The other axis is defined by the* normal vector

$$\mathbf{n}(t) = [-\sin\psi(t), \cos\psi(t)[^{\top}$$

While p is sliding along γ, the angle ψ will change. The rate of change in ψ (with respect to the movement of p on γ) is one way to define *curvature* $\kappa_{tan}(p)$ along γ.

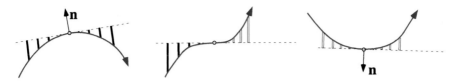

Fig. 3.21 Three tangents (*dashed lines*). The curvature is positive on the *left*, has a zero crossing in the *middle*, and is negative on the *right*

Let $l = \mathscr{L}(t)$ be the arc length between the starting point $\gamma(a)$ and general point $p = \gamma(t)$. A curvature definition has to be independent of the *speed* (or rate of evolution)

$$v(t) = \frac{d\mathscr{L}(t)}{dt} \tag{3.7}$$

of the parameterization of γ. Curvature is now formally defined by

$$\kappa_{tan}(t) = \frac{d\psi(t)}{dl} \tag{3.8}$$

at a point $\gamma(t) = (x(t), y(t))$ of a smooth Jordan curve γ.

The rate of change can be positive or negative, and zero at points of inflection. If positive at p, then p is a *concave point*, and if negative at p, then p is a *convex point*. See Fig. 3.21.

As Fig. 3.21 shows, the situation at p can be approximated by measuring the distances between γ and the tangent to γ at p along equidistant lines perpendicular to the tangent. In Fig. 3.21, positive distances are represented by bold line segments and negative distances by "hollow" line segments. The area between the curve and the tangent line can be approximated by summing these distances; it is positive on the left, negative on the right, and zero in the middle where the positive and negative distances cancel.

For example, assume that γ is a straight line. Then the tangent coincides with γ at any point p, and there is no rate of change at all, i.e. there is curvature zero for all points on γ. Assume that γ is a circle. Then we already know that there is a constant rate of change in slope angle; assuming uniform speed, it follows that this constant is the inverse of the radius of this circle.

Curvature as Radius of Osculating Circle Another option for analysing curvature is by means of osculating circles; see Fig. 3.22. The osculating circle at a point p of γ is the largest circle tangent to γ at p on the concave side. Assume that the osculating circle at p has radius r. Then γ has the curvature $\kappa_{osc}(p) = 1/r$ at p. In the case of a straight line, r is infinity, and the curvature equals zero. It holds that

$$\kappa_{osc}(p) = |\kappa_{tan}(p)| \tag{3.9}$$

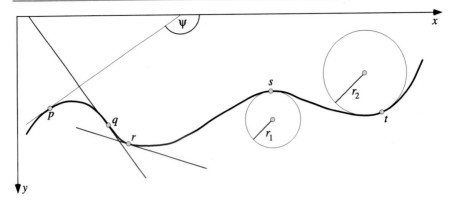

Fig. 3.22 Illustration of curvature defined either by rate of change (*left*) or radius of osculating circle (*right*). Points p, q, and r illustrate curvature by rate of change in the slope angle ψ. Assume that points move from *left* to *right*. Then p has a positive curvature, zero curvature at a point of inflection q, and negative curvature at r. Points s and t illustrate curvature by their osculating circles. The curvature at s equals $1/r_1$, and at t it is $1/r_2$

Fig. 3.23 Illustration for the use of $k = 3$ when estimating the curvature at p_i

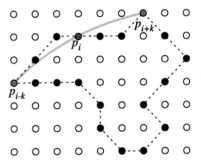

Curvature of a Parameterized Arc   There is a third option for defining curvature in the Euclidean plane. Assume a parametric representation $\gamma(t) = (x(t), y(t))$, which is Jordan's first proposal for defining a curve. Then it follows that

$$\kappa_{tan}(t) = \frac{\dot{x}(t) \cdot \ddot{y}(t) - \dot{y}(t) \cdot \ddot{x}(t)}{[\dot{x}(t)^2 + \dot{y}(t)^2]^{1.5}} \tag{3.10}$$

where

$$\dot{x}(t) = \frac{dx(t)}{dt}, \qquad \dot{y}(t) = \frac{dy(t)}{dt}, \qquad \ddot{x}(t) = \frac{d^2x(t)}{dt^2}, \qquad \ddot{y}(t) = \frac{d^2y(t)}{dt^2} \tag{3.11}$$

Algorithms for estimating curvature of digital curves in images are a subject of digital geometry. Typically, they follow the rate-of-change model, rather than the osculating circle model, and only a few attempt to digitize (3.10).

Example 3.3 (An Option for Estimating Curvature of a Digital Curve) Actually, (3.10) can be followed very easily. Assume that a given digital curve $\langle p_1, \ldots, p_m \rangle$, where $p_j = (x_j, y_j)$ for $1 \leq j \leq m$, is sampled along a parameterized curve $\gamma(t) = (x(t), y(t))$, where $t \in [0, m]$. At point p_i we assume that $\gamma(i) = p_i$. The functions $x(t)$ and $y(t)$ are locally interpolated by second-order polynomials

$$x(t) = a_0 + a_1 t + a_2 t^2 \tag{3.12}$$

$$y(t) = b_0 + b_1 t + b_2 t^2 \tag{3.13}$$

and curvature is calculated using (3.10). Let $x(0) = x_i$, $x(1) = x_{i-k}$, and $x(2) = x_{i+k}$ with integer parameter $k \geq 1$, and analogously for $y(t)$. See Fig. 3.23. The curvature at p_i is then defined by

$$\kappa_i = \frac{2(a_1 b_2 - b_1 a_2)}{[a_1^2 + b_1^2]^{1.5}} \tag{3.14}$$

The use of a constant $k > 1$ can be replaced by locally adaptive solutions.

3.2.4 Distance Transform (by Gisela Klette)

The *distance transform* labels each object pixel (say, defined by $I(p) > 0$) with the Euclidean distance between its location and the nearest non-object pixel location (defined by $I(p) = 0$). For simplicity, we can say that the distance transform determines for *all* pixel locations $p \in \Omega$ the distance value

$$D(p) = \min_{q \in \Omega} \{ d_2(p, q) : I(q) = 0 \} \tag{3.15}$$

where $d_2(p, q_k)$ denotes the Euclidean distance. It follows that $D(p) = 0$ for all non-object pixels.

Insert 3.11 (Origins of the Distance Transform) [A. Rosenfeld and J.L. Pfaltz. Distance functions on digital pictures. Pattern Recognition, vol. 1, pp. 33–61] *is the pioneering paper not only for defining distance transforms in images, but also for an efficient 2-pass algorithm; A. Rosenfeld and J. Pfaltz used grid metrics rather than the Euclidean metric and proposed the alternative use of 4- and 8-adjacency for approximating Euclidean distances. This approximation improves by chamfering as defined in* [G. Borgefors: Chamfering—a fast method for obtaining approximations of the Euclidean distance in N dimensions. In Proc. Scand. Conf. Image Analysis, pp. 250–255, 1983].

The papers [T. Saito and J. Toriwaki. New algorithms for Euclidean distance transformation of an *n*-dimensional digitized picture with applications. Pattern Recognition, vol. 27, pp. 1551–1565, 1994] *and* [T. Hirata. A unified linear-time algorithm for computing distance maps. Information Processing Letters, vol. 58, pp. 129–133, 1996] *applied the Euclidean metric and introduced a new algorithm using the lower envelopes of families of parabolas.*

Maximal Circles in the Image Grid   Let $S \subset \Omega$ be the set of all object pixel locations, and $B = \Omega \setminus S$ be the set of all non-object pixel locations. The distance transform satisfies the following properties:

1. $D(p)$ represents the radius of the largest disk centred at p and totally contained in S.
2. If there is only one non-object pixel location $q \in B$ with $D(p) = d_2(p, q)$, then there are two cases:
   (a) There exists a pixel location $p' \in S$ such that the disk centred at p' totally contains the disk centred at p, or
   (b) there exist pixel locations $p' \in S$ and $q' \in B$ such that $d_2(p, q) = d_2(p', q')$ and p is 4-adjacent to p'.
3. If there are two (or more) non-object pixel locations $q, q' \in B$ such that $D(p) = d_2(p, q) = d_2(p, q')$, then the disk centred at p is a maximal disk in S; the point p is called *symmetric* in this case.

   In Case 2(b), the pixel locations p and p' are both centres of maximal discs, and they are 4-adjacent to each other.

   Figure 3.24, top, shows a rectangle with a subset of maximal disks. At least two non-object pixel locations have the same distance to one of the centres of those disks. The middle row shows maximal disks where two centres are 4-adjacent to each other and there is only one non-object pixel location with distance r (radius of the disk) for each disk. Figure 3.24, bottom, shows a disk B that has only one non-object pixel location at distance r to its centre and is contained in the maximal disk A.

Distance and Row–Column Component Map   The *distance map* is a 2D array of the same size as the original image that stores the results $D(p)$ at locations $p \in \Omega$.

Let a shortest distance $D(p)$ be defined by the distance $d_2(p, q)$ with $p = (x_p, y_p)$ and $q = (x_q, y_q)$. Then we have that

$$D(p) = \sqrt{(x_p - x_q)^2 + (y_p - y_q)^2} \tag{3.16}$$

By knowing $\Delta x = x_p - x_q$ and $\Delta y = y_p - y_q$ we also know $D(p)$, but just the distance value $D(p)$ does not tell us the signed *row component* Δx and the signed *column component* Δy. Thus, instead of the distance map, we might also be interested in the *row–column component map*: At $p \in \Omega$ we store the tuple $(\Delta x, \Delta y)$ that defines $D(p)$.

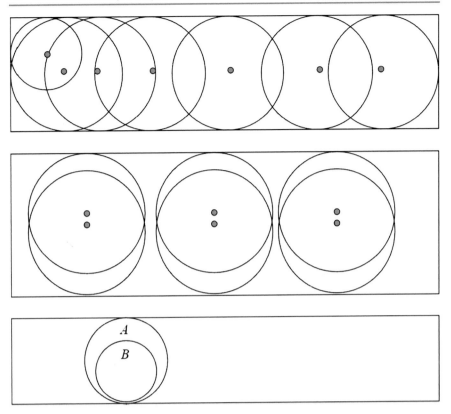

Fig. 3.24 *Top*: A set of maximal disks. *Middle*: Symmetric points as defined in Case 2(b). *Bottom*: Illustration of Case 2(a)

Squared Euclidean Distance Transform (SEDT)   It is common to compute squares $D(p)^2$ of Euclidean distances for saving time. We explain the principles of one algorithm that delivers accurate SEDT maps in linear time, where many authors have contributed to improvements over time.

The algorithm starts with integer operations to compute the SEDT to the nearest non-object point for one dimension in two row scans. Then it operates in the continuous plane $\mathbb{R}^2$ by computing the lower envelope of a family of parabolas for each column. The algorithm identifies the parabolas that contribute segments to the lower envelope and calculates the endpoints of those segments. The squared Euclidean distance values are calculated in an additional column scan using the formulas of the parabolas identified in the previous step.

We explain the algorithm for the 2D case in detail and also highlight that all computations can be done independently for each dimension; thus, the approach can be followed for arbitrary dimensions.

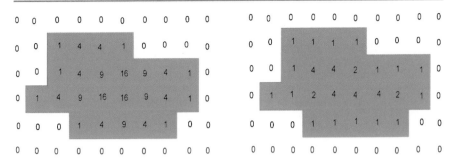

Fig. 3.25 The zeros are all the non-object pixels. The numbers are squared Euclidean distances. *Left*: Intermediate results after the initial row scans. *Right*: Final results after column scans

Distances in a Row   The initial step is a calculation of the distance from a pixel in an object to the nearest non-object pixel in the same row:

$$f_1(x, y) = f_1(x - 1, y) + 1 \quad \text{if } I(x, y) > 0 \tag{3.17}$$

$$f_1(x, y) = 0 \quad \text{if } I(x, y) = 0 \tag{3.18}$$

$$f_2(x, y) = \min\{f_1(x, y), f_2(x + 1, y) + 1\} \quad \text{if } f_1(x, y) \neq 0 \tag{3.19}$$

$$f_2(x, y) = 0 \quad \text{if } f_1(x, y) = 0 \tag{3.20}$$

Here, $f_1(x, y)$ determines the distance between the pixel location $p(x, y)$ and nearest non-object pixel location q on the left, and f_2 replaces f_1 if the distance to the nearest non-object pixel location on the right is shorter.

The result is a matrix that stores integer values $(f_2(x, y))^2$ in each pixel location. See Fig. 3.25, left, for an example.

We express $f_2(x, y)$ for a fixed row y as follows:

$$f_2(x, y) = \min_{i=1,\dots,N_{cols}} \{|x - i| : I(i, y) = 0\} \tag{3.21}$$

The example in Fig. 3.25, left, shows the results for the 1D SEDT after computing $[f_2(x, y)]^2$ row by row for $1 \leq y \leq N_{rows}$.

Distances in a Column   If there are only two non-object pixel locations, then, for given $p = (x, y)$, we need to know which of the two non-object pixel locations (x, y_1) or (x, y_2) is closer. We compare

$$\left[\left(f_2(x, y_1) \right)^2 + (y - y_1)^2 \right] < \left[\left(f_2(x, y_2) \right)^2 + (y - y_2)^2 \right] \tag{3.22}$$

The function $f_3(x, y)$ determines values for the 2D SEDT, column by column, considering x to be fixed, for all $1 \leq y \leq N_{rows}$:

$$f_3(x, y) = \min_{j=1,\dots,N_{rows}} \{ \left(f_2(x, j) \right)^2 + (y - j)^2 \} \tag{3.23}$$

Fig. 3.26 Family of parabolas for column $[0, 4, 9, 16, 4, 0]$ in Fig. 3.25, left

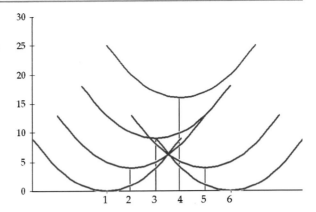

We discuss a geometric interpretation that illustrates the basic idea for designing a time-efficient solution.

Lower Envelopes For a fixed column (e.g., for $x = 5$, let $f_2(5, y) = g(y)$) and a fixed row (e.g. $y = 3$), consider the equation

$$\gamma_3(j) = \big(g(3)\big)^2 + (3 - j)^2 \tag{3.24}$$

with $j = 1, \ldots, N_{rows}$. We continue to refer to Fig. 3.25; the assumed values represent the third parabola in Fig. 3.26.

For $1 \le y \le N_{rows}$, altogether we consider a family of N_{rows} parabolas; see Fig. 3.26. This is one parabola for each row and a family of N_{rows} parabolas per column. The horizontal axis represents the row number y, and the vertical axis represents $\gamma_y(j)$, with the local minima at $y = j$ and $\gamma_y(j) = (g(y))$.

The *lower envelope* of the family of parabolas corresponds to the minimum calculation in (3.23). Efficient SEDT algorithms calculate the lower envelope of the family of parabolas and then assign the height (i.e. the vertical distance to the abscissa) of the lower envelope to the point with coordinates (x, y). The computation of the lower envelope of the family of parabolas is the main part of the SEDT algorithm.

Observation 3.7 *The concept of envelope calculation reduces the quadratic time complexity of a naive EDT algorithm to linear time as envelopes can be computed incrementally.*

Example 3.4 (Calculation of Sections) The example in Fig. 3.26 shows a family of six parabolas. The lower envelope consists of two curve segments.

The first segment starts at $(1, 0)$ and ends at the intersection of the first and last parabolas. The second segment begins at this intersection and ends at $(6, 0)$. The projections of the segments on the horizontal axis are called *sections*.

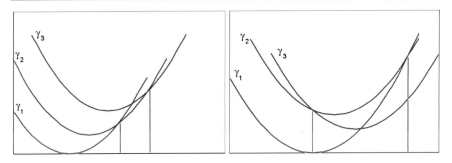

Fig. 3.27 *Left*: Sketch for $y_s(\gamma_2, \gamma_3) > y_s(\gamma_1, \gamma_2)$. *Right*: Sketch for $y_s(\gamma_2, \gamma_3) < y_s(\gamma_1, \gamma_2)$

In this simple example, the interval $[1, 6]$ is partitioned into two sections. Only two of the six parabolas contribute to the lower envelope of the family. For calculating $f_3(y)$ (x is fixed), we need the start and end for each section, and the index of the associated parabola.

This can be done in two more column scans; one scan from the top to the bottom that identifies the parabola segments of the lower envelope together with their associated sections, and a second scan that calculates the values for $f_3(y)$.

Preparing for the Calculation of the Lower Envelope   The determination of the lower envelope is done by a sequential process of computing the lower envelope of the first k parabolas. We calculate the intersection between two parabolas. Let y_s be the abscissa of the intersection, and let $y_1 < y_2$. The equation for the intersection $y_s = y_s(\gamma_1, \gamma_2)$ of any two parabolas γ_1 and γ_2 is given by

$$\left[g(y_1)\right]^2 + (y_s - y_1)^2 = \left[g(y_2)\right]^2 + (y_s - y_2)^2 \tag{3.25}$$

From this we obtain that

$$y_s = y_2 + \frac{[g(y_2)]^2 - [g(y_1)]^2 - (y_2 - y_1)^2}{2(y_2 - y_1)} \tag{3.26}$$

We apply (3.26) in the SEDT algorithm for the first column scan, where we compute the lower envelope of parabolas per column. We store the information in a stack.

Only parabolas that contribute to the lower envelope stay in the stack, and all the others are eliminated from the stack. This results in a straightforward algorithm; see also the sketch in Fig. 3.27.

The Calculation of the Lower Envelope   Each stack item stores a pair of real values (b, e) for the begin and end of the section of a parabola, which contributes to the lower envelope. (b_t, e_t) belongs to the top parabola of the stack, and (b_f, e_f) is the pair associated with the subsequent parabola in the sequential process.

The first item stores the start and end of the section for the first parabola. It is initialized by $(1, N_{rows})$; the lower envelope would consist of one segment between $(1, N_{rows})$ if all the following parabolas have no intersections with the first one.

The parabolas are ordered according to their y-values in the image. For each sequential step, we evaluate the intersection for the top item of the stack representing γ_t, and the next following parabola γ_f. There are three possible cases:

1. $y_s(\gamma_t, \gamma_f) > N_{rows}$: γ_f does not contribute to the lower envelope, do not change the stack, take the following parabola;
2. $y_s(\gamma_t, \gamma_f) \leq b_t$: Remove γ_t from the stack, evaluate the intersection of the new top item with γ_f (see Fig. 3.27, right); if the stack is empty, then add the item for γ_f to the stack;
3. $y_s(\gamma_t, \gamma_f) > b_t$: Adjust γ_t with $e_t = y_s(\gamma_t, \gamma_f)$, add the item for γ_f to the stack with $b_f = e_t, e_f = n$ (see Fig. 3.27, left).

The procedure continues until the last parabola has been evaluated with the top item of the stack. At the end, only sections of the lower envelope are registered in the stack, and they are used for calculating the values for $f_3(x, y)$ in an additional scan.

Example 3.5 (Lower Envelope) For our simple example (see Fig. 3.26), the lower envelope consists of γ_1 starting at $b_1 = 1$ and ending at $e_1 = 3.5$ and of γ_6 starting at $b_2 = 3.5$ and ending at $e_2 = 6$. Now we just compute the values for

$$\gamma_1(j) = \big(g(1)\big)^2 + (1 - j)^2 \quad \text{for } j = 1, 2, 3 \tag{3.27}$$

and

$$\gamma_6(j) = \big(g(6)\big)^2 + (6 - j)^2 \quad \text{for } j = 4, 5, 6 \tag{3.28}$$

Variations of this principal approach can reduce the number of computations.

Preprocessing and Time Complexity   In a preprocessing step, we can eliminate all the parabolas with $g(y) > (N_{rows} - 1)/2$ that have no segment in the lower envelope. In our simple example (see Fig. 3.26), the parabolas $\gamma_3(j)$ with $g(3) = 3 > 2.5$ and $\gamma_4(j)$ with $g(4) = 4 > 2.5$ would be eliminated before starting with computations of intersections for the lower envelop.

The SEDT algorithm works in linear time. Computations for each dimension are done independently. The resulting squared minimal distance for one dimension is an integer value for each grid point, which will be used for the computation in the next dimension.

Arbitrary Dimensions   The 2D SEDT can be expressed as follows:

$$D(x, y) = \min_{i=1,\dots,N_{cols} \wedge j=1,\dots,N_{rows}} \big\{(x - i)^2 + (y - j)^2\big\} \tag{3.29}$$

Because i does not depend on j, we can reformulate into

$$D(x, y) = \min_{j=1,\dots,N_{rows}} \Big\{ \min_{i=1,\dots,N_{cols}} \big\{(x - i)^2 + (y - j)^2\big\} \Big\} \tag{3.30}$$

The minimum calculation in (3.30), $\min((x - i)^2) = g(j)^2$, corresponds to the row scans in the first part of the SEDT algorithm. We can rewrite the equation for fixed x and derive the equation for the second dimension:

$$D(x, y) = \min_{j=1,\dots,N_{rows}} \left\{ g(j)^2 + (y - j)^2 \right\} \qquad (3.31)$$

The minimum calculation in (3.31) corresponds to the column scans.

Let p be a 3D point at location (x, y, k) for $k = 1, \dots, N_{layer}$, and $h(k)^2$ be the result of the minimum computation in (3.31) for fixed pairs x, y. Then we have also an equation for the third dimension:

$$D(x, y, z) = \min_{k=1,\dots,N_{layer}} \left\{ h(k)^2 + (z - k)^2 \right\} \qquad (3.32)$$

This can be continued for further dimensions.

3.3   Image Value Analysis

Besides geometric analysis of image contents, we are also interested in describing the given signal, i.e. the distribution of image values. We continue with assuming a scalar input image I.

This section describes co-occurrence matrices and data measures defined on those matrices, and moments of regions or image windows.

3.3.1   Co-occurrence Matrices and Measures

Basic statistics (mean, variance, grey-level histogram) provide measures summarizing individual pixel values. Co-occurrence studies the distribution of values in dependence upon values at adjacent pixels. Such co-occurrence results are represented in the *co-occurrence matrix* **C**.

Assume an input image I and an adjacency set A. For example, in case of 4-adjacency we have the adjacency set $A_4 = \{(0, 1), (1, 0), (0, -1), (-1, 0)\}$, defining $A_4(p) = A_4 + p$ for any pixel location p. As before, we denote by Ω the set of all $N_{cols} \times N_{rows}$ pixel locations. We define the $(G_{max} + 1) \times (G_{max} + 1)$ co-occurrence matrix $\mathbf{C}_I$ for image I and image values u and v in $\{0, 1, \dots, G_{max}\}$ as follows:

$$\mathbf{C}_I(u, v) = \sum_{p \in \Omega} \sum_{q \in A \wedge p+q \in \Omega} \begin{cases} 1 & \text{if } I(p) = u \text{ and } I(p + q) = v \\ 0 & \text{otherwise} \end{cases} \qquad (3.33)$$

The adjacency set can also be non-symmetric, for example $A = \{(0, 1), (1, 0)\}$. Figure 3.28 illustrates the adjacency set $A = \{(0, 1)\}$. The figure shows three examples for increasing a counter value in the co-occurrence matrix. For example, at $(x, y) = (3, 2)$ we have the value $u = 2$ and $v = 1$ one row down. Accordingly, the counter at $(u, v) = (2, 1)$ increases by one.

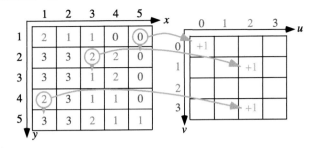

Fig. 3.28 We have a small 5×5 image on the left, with $G_{max} = 3$, and generate its 4×4 co-occurrence matrix on the right. The adjacency set $A = \{(0, 1)\}$ only contains one off-set, meaning that we have to look from a pixel location one row down. At $(x, y) = (5, 1)$ we have the value $u = 0$ and $v = 0$ one row down. Accordingly, the counter at $(u, v) = (0, 0)$ increases by one

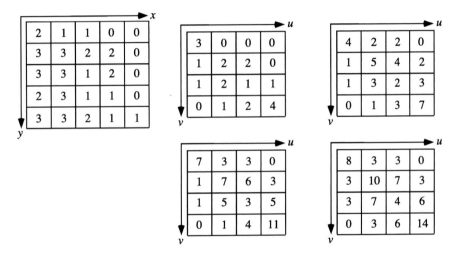

Fig. 3.29 *Top, left*: Input image I; x goes from 1 to $N_{cols} = 5$, and y goes from 1 to $N_{rows} = 5$. *Top, middle*: Co-occurrence matrix $\mathbf{C}_1$ for adjacency set A_1; u and v go from 0 to $G_{max} = 3$. *Top, right*: Co-occurrence matrix $\mathbf{C}_2$ for adjacency set A_2. *Bottom, middle*: Co-occurrence matrix $\mathbf{C}_3$ for adjacency set A_3. *Bottom, right*: Co-occurrence matrix $\mathbf{C}_4$ for adjacency set A_4

Example 3.6 (Examples of four Co-Occurrence Matrices) We consider a small 5×5 image I (see Fig. 3.29, left), $G_{max} = 3$, and four different adjacency sets: first, $A_1 = \{(0, 1)\}$, then $A_2 = \{(0, 1), (1, 0)\}$, then $A_3 = \{(0, 1), (1, 0), (0, -1)\}$, and finally the usual adjacency set A_4. These simple data should allow you to follow the calculations easily.

Figure 3.29, middle, and Fig. 3.29, right, show the corresponding four co-occurrence matrices.

We provide a few examples for the performed calculations. We start with A_1. At first we have $(u, v) = (0, 0)$. We have to count how often there is a case that $I(x, y) = 0$ and $I(x, y + 1) = 0$ in I, i.e. a zero at a pixel and also a zero at the pixel below. This occurs three times. Accordingly, we have $\mathbf{C}_1(0, 0) = 3$ for A_1. One more example: Consider $(u, v) = (3, 1)$. It never happens that a 3 is on top of a 1, thus we have $\mathbf{C}_1(3, 1) = 0$.

Now also two examples for A_2. A_1 is a subset of A_2, thus we have that $\mathbf{C}_1(u, v) \leq \mathbf{C}_2(u, v)$ for any pair (u, v) of image values. In case of $(u, v) = (0, 0)$, besides the case "$I(x, y) = 0$ and $I(x, y + 1) = 0$" we have also to count how often there is a zero at (x, y) and also a zero at $(x + 1, y)$. There is one case. Thus, we have that $\mathbf{C}_2(0, 0) = 3 + 1 = 4$. A final example: $(u, v) = (2, 1)$. For $q = (0, 1)$, we count two cases. For $q = (1, 0)$, we also count two cases, and thus $\mathbf{C}_2(2, 1) = 2 + 2 = 4$.

The sums of all entries in one of those co-occurrence matrices are 20 times the number of elements in the adjacency set. The final matrix (for A_4) is symmetric because A_4 is symmetric.

The example illustrates two general properties of those co-occurrence matrices:
1. Each element q in the adjacency set adds either $N_{cols} \cdot (N_{rows} - 1)$ or $(N_{cols} - 1) \cdot N_{rows}$ to the total sum of entries in the co-occurrence matrix, depending on whether it is directed in row or column direction.
2. A symmetric adjacency set produces a symmetric co-occurrence matrix.

Those co-occurrence matrices are used to define *co-occurrence-based measures* to quantify information in an image I. Note that noise in an image is still considered to be information when using these measures. We provide here two of such measures:

$$M_{hom}(I) = \sum_{u,v \in \{0,1,\ldots,G_{max}\}} \frac{\mathbf{C}_I(u, v)}{1 + |u - v|} \quad \text{(Homogeneity measure)} \quad (3.34)$$

$$M_{uni}(I) = \sum_{u,v \in \{0,1,\ldots,G_{max}\}} \mathbf{C}_I(u, v)^2 \quad \text{(Uniformity measure)} \quad (3.35)$$

Informally speaking, a high homogeneity or uniformity indicates that the image I has more "untextured" areas.

Measures can also be defined by comparing the sum of all entries on or close to the main diagonal of the co-occurrence matrix to the sum of all entries in the remaining cells of the co-occurrence matrix.

Insert 3.12 (Co-Occurrence Measures) *The book* [R.M. Haralick and L.G. Shapiro. Computer and Robot Vision (vol. 1), Reading, MA, Addison-Wesley, 1992] *contains further co-occurrence measures and a detailed discussion of their meaning when analysing images.*

3.3.2 Moment-Based Region Analysis

Assume a region $S \subset \Omega$ of pixel locations in an image I. This region may represent an "object", such as illustrated in Fig. 3.30.

Fig. 3.30 Main axes and centroids for detected fish regions

We assume again a scalar image I. The *moments* of a region S in the image I are defined by

$$m_{a,b}(S) = \sum_{(x,y) \in S} x^a y^b \cdot I(x, y) \qquad (3.36)$$

for non-negative integers a and b. The sum $a + b$ defines the *order* of the moment. There is only one moment

$$m_{0,0}(S) = \sum_{(x,y) \in S} I(x, y) \qquad (3.37)$$

of order zero. If $I(x, y) = 1$ in S, then $m_{0,0}(S) = \mathscr{A}(S)$, the area of S. The moments of order 1,

$$m_{1,0}(S) = \sum_{(x,y) \in S} x \cdot I(x, y) \quad \text{and} \quad m_{0,1}(S) = \sum_{(x,y) \in S} y \cdot I(x, y) \qquad (3.38)$$

define the *centroid* (x_S, y_S) of S as follows:

$$x_S = \frac{m_{1,0}(S)}{m_{0,0}(S)} \quad \text{and} \quad y_S = \frac{m_{0,1}(S)}{m_{0,0}(S)} \qquad (3.39)$$

Note that the centroid depends on the values of I over S, not just on the shape of S.

The *central moments* of region S in image I are defined by

$$\mu_{a,b}(S) = \sum_{(x,y) \in S} (x - x_S)^a (y - y_S)^b \cdot I(x, y) \qquad (3.40)$$

for non-negative integers a and b. The central moments provide a way to characterize regions S by features that are invariant with respect to any linear transform.

We only provide two examples here for such features. *Main axes* as shown in Fig. 3.30 are defined by an angle $\theta(S)$ (modulo π) with the positive x-axis and by being incident with the centroid. It holds that

$$\tan\big(2 \cdot \theta(S)\big) = \frac{2\mu_{1,1}(S)}{\mu_{2,0}(S) - \mu_{0,2}(S)} \tag{3.41}$$

Furthermore, the *eccentricity* $\varepsilon(S)$ of a region S is defined by

$$\varepsilon(S) = \frac{[\mu_{2,0}(S) - \mu_{0,2}(S)]^2 - 4\mu_{1,1}(S)^2}{[\mu_{2,0}(S) + \mu_{0,2}(S)]^2} \tag{3.42}$$

and characterizes the ratio of the main axis to the orthogonal axis of S. The eccentricity equals zero (in the ideal case) if S is a rotationally symmetric disk; then we have that $\mu_{2,0}(S) = \mu_{0,2}(S)$. A line segment has eccentricity one in the ideal case (and close to one when measured in an image). Rotational symmetric sets with the centroid at the origin also satisfy that $m_{1,1}(S) = 0$.

Example 3.7 (Accuracy of Recorded Marks) In computer vision we have cases that a special mark on a surface (e.g. a drawn cross or circle) needs to be accurately localized in a captured image I. There is a standard two-step procedure for doing so:
1. Detect the region S of pixels which is considered to be the image of the mark.
2. Calculate the centroid of the region S also using the values of I in S, defined by (3.39).
In this way, the position of the mark in I is determined with subpixel accuracy.

Example 3.8 (Achieving Rotation Invariance for Analysing a Region) When deriving features for an image region, it is often desirable to have *isotropic* features (i.e. invariant with respect to rotation). Moments support a four-step procedure for doing so:
1. Detect the region S of pixels which needs to be analysed.
2. Calculate the main axis, as defined by (3.41).
3. Rotate S so that its main axis coincides with the x-axis (or any other chosen fixed axis). In cases of $\mu_{1,1}(S) = 0$ or $\mu_{2,0} = \mu_{0,2}$ (i.e. rotation-symmetric shapes), no rotation is needed.
4. Calculate the isotropic features for the direction-normalized set as obtained after rotation.
Note that rotation in the grid causes minor deviations in values in a region S, and also its shape will vary a little due to limitations defined by the grid.

Insert 3.13 (Moments and Object Classification) *The paper* [M.K. Hu. Visual pattern recognition by moment invariants. IRE Trans. Info. Theory, vol. IT-8, pp. 179–187, 1962] *was pioneering in the field of linear-transformation invariant object characterizations by moments. Hu's set of moment descriptors was not really* *practicable at the time of publication, due to existing limitations in computing power at that time, but are standard features today for object classifications. Simply check for "Hu moments" on the net, and you will find them.*

3.4 Detection of Lines and Circles

Lines or circles appear in images as 'noisy objects', and their identification is an example for how to identify patterns in an image.

This section provides a detailed guide for detecting line segments and an outline for detecting circles.

3.4.1 Lines

Real-world images often show straight lines, such as edges of buildings, lane borders (see Fig. 3.31), or power poles. An accurate localization of those lines is of help for interpreting the real world.

An edge detector is first used to map a given image into a binary edge map. Then, all remaining edge pixels need to be analysed whether there is any subset that forms "reasonably" a line segment. There is noise involved, and the line detector needs to be robust with respect to some noise.

How to describe a line, visible in an $N_{cols} \times N_{rows}$ image? The obvious answer is by the following equation:

$$y = ax + b \qquad (3.43)$$

This equation is illustrated for the blue line segment in Fig. 3.32, left.

Original Hough Transform The *original Hough transform* proposed for describing line segments in *ab* parameter space; see Fig. 3.32, right. Pixel positions p, q, and r in the image are mapped into three lines in the parameter space. Three lines, shown in Red, Green, and Blue in the image, correspond to the three shown points (in corresponding colours) in the parameter space.

Assuming $y = a_1 x + b_1$ for the blue segment, it intersects the y-axis at b_1. The points $p = (x_p, y_p)$ and $q = (x_q, y_q)$ on the blue line describe the lines $b = -x_p a + y_p$ and $b = -x_q a + y_q$ in the parameter space, respectively. For example, points on $b = -x_p a + y_p$ describe *all* lines in the image that are incident with p in *any* direction (except the vertical line with $a = \infty$). Thus, the lines $b = -x_p a + y_p$ and $b = -x_q a + y_q$ intersect in the *ab* parameter space at a point (a_1, b_1) defined by the parameters a_1 and b_1 of the blue line.

Fig. 3.31 Lane borders and their approximation by detected line segments

The figure illustrates more examples. The red, blue, and green points in the ab space define the red, blue, and green lines in the image plane. If n points in the image would be perfectly on one line γ, then the generated n straight lines in the parameter space would intersect exactly at the parameter pair (a_γ, b_γ) of this line γ.

In images, line patterns are not perfect; they are noisy. A set of n pixels in the image that are all "nearly" on the same straight line γ define the set of n lines in the ab parameter space that all intersect "nearly" at the parameter point (a_γ, b_γ) of γ. The idea is to detect such clusters of intersection points of straight lines in the parameter space for detecting the line γ in the image.

A nice idea, but it does not work. Why? Because the parameters a and b are not bounded for an $N_{cols} \times N_{rows}$ image. We would need to analyse an infinite parameter space for detecting clusters.

Insert 3.14 (Origin of the Hough transform) *The original Hough transform was published in* [P.V.C. Hough. Methods and means for recognizing complex patterns. U.S. Patent 3.069.654, 1962].

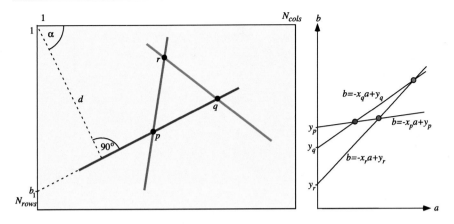

Fig. 3.32 *Left*: Three line segments in an image. The *blue segment* intersects the y-axis at b_1. The *blue segment* is in distance d to the origin, also defining the angle α with the positive x-axis. Which values b, d, and α for the *red* and *green segment*? *Right*: ab parameter space

Parameter Space Proposed by Duda and Hart Instead of representing straight lines in the common form of (3.43), we use a straight-line parameterization by d and α, already illustrated in Fig. 3.32, left, for the blue line:

$$d = x \cdot \cos\alpha + y \cdot \sin\alpha \tag{3.44}$$

Besides that, we follow the ideas of the original Hough transform. This allows us to have a bounded parameter space. The angular parameter α is in the interval $[0, 2\pi)$, and the distance d is in the interval $[0, d_{\max}]$, with

$$d_{\max} = \sqrt{N_{cols}^2 + N_{rows}^2} \tag{3.45}$$

Proceeding this way is known as the *standard Hough transform*. A point in the image generates now a sin/cos-curve in the $d\alpha$ parameter space, also known as *Houghspace*.

Insert 3.15 (Radon) *The straight-line representation in* (3.44) *was intro-duced in* [J. Radon. Über die Bestimmung von Funktionen durch ihre Integralwerte längs gewisser Mannigfaltigkeiten. Berichte Sächsische Akademie der Wissenschaften. Math.-Phys. Kl., 69:262–267, 1917] *when defining a transformation in a continuous space, today known as the Radon transform. The Radon transform is an es-sential theoretical basis for techniques used in Computer Tomography. The (historically earlier) Radon transform is a generalization of the Hough trans-form.*

Fig. 3.33 *Top, right*: Hough space for detected edge points (*bottom, left*) of the original input image (*top, left*). An analysis of the Hough space leads to three line segments (shown *bottom, right*)

Figure 3.33 illustrates an application of the standard Hough transform. The original input image (from a sequence on EISATS) is shown top, left. The edge map (bottom, left) is generated with the Canny operator (see Sect. 2.3.3). Top, right, shows a view into the $d\alpha$ Hough space after inserting the sin/cos-curves for all the detected edge pixels in the input image. There are three clusters (i.e. regions in Hough space where many sin/cos-curves intersect). Accordingly, three lines are detected in the input image.

Hough Space as Discrete Accumulator Array   For implementing the Hough space, it is digitized into an array, using subsequent intervals for d and α for defining a finite number of cells in Hough space. For example, d can be digitized into subsequent intervals $[0, 1), [1, 2), [2, 3), \ldots$ and α into intervals defined by increments of one degree. This defines the *accumulator array*.

When starting with a new edge map, the *counters* in all cells of the accumulator array are set to be zero. When inserting a new sin/cos curve into the accumulator array, all those counters are incremented by one where the curve intersects a cell. At the end of the process, a counter in the accumulator array is equal to the total number of sin/cos curves that were passing through its cell. Figure 3.33 shows zero counters as 'white', and 'red' for non-zero counters, the darker the larger is the counter.

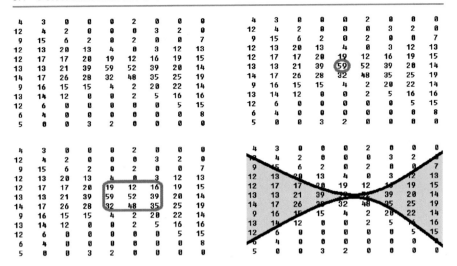

Fig. 3.34 *Top, left*: Counter values in a *dα* space. *Top, right*: Peak defined by local maximum. *Bottom, left*: A 3 × 3 window of counter values with a maximal sum; the peak may be defined by the centroid of this window. *Bottom, right*: The butterfly of a peak

It is expected to identify lines in the given image by *peaks* in the values of the accumulator array, being defined (in some way) as centres of 'dark regions'.

The standard Hough transform identifies peaks at selected local maxima of counter values. As a consequence, parameters of detected lines are at an accuracy as defined by the chosen size of intervals when digitizing the Hough space. We say that parameters are of *cell accuracy* and not yet at *subcell accuracy*. Selecting smaller intervals is one way for improving the cell accuracy (and increasing the computation time), and calculating the centroid in a window of maximal total sum of contained counter values is another option to achieve subcell accuracy. See Fig. 3.34, top, right, and bottom, left.

Improving Accuracy and Reducing Computation Time   The counter values around a peak do resemble the shape of a *butterfly*; see Fig. 3.34, bottom, right. The butterfly of a peak can be approximated by second-order curves from both sides. This provides a way for defining the peak with subcell accuracy.

For the standard Hough transform, as illustrated by Fig. 3.32, the description of straight lines is with respect to the origin of the xy image coordinate system. Consider a move of this reference point into the centre of the image. See Fig. 3.35. The straight line equations change into

$$d = \left(x - \frac{N_{cols}}{2}\right) \cdot \cos\alpha + \left(y - \frac{N_{rows}}{2}\right) \cdot \sin\alpha \qquad (3.46)$$

The value $d_{\max}$ in $d\alpha$ space reduces to

$$d_{\max} = \frac{1}{2}\sqrt{N_{cols}^2 + N_{rows}^2} \qquad (3.47)$$

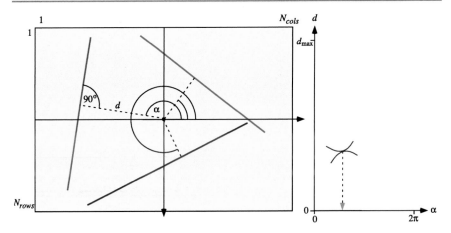

Fig. 3.35 *Left*: Centred coordinate system for representing lines in the image. *Right*: The image shows $d_{\max}$ for the maximum possible value for d and a sketch of a butterfly for one line

This not only halves the size of the accumulator array and thus also the computation; it also improves the shape of the butterflies, as experimental evaluations show. The shape of the butterflies becomes "less elongated", thus supporting a better detection of peaks.

The result in Fig. 3.33 was calculated using the standard Hough transform. The results shown in Fig. 3.31 were obtained by using the centred representation of lines and an approximation of butterflies by second-order curves for detecting peaks at subcell accuracy.

Multiple Line Segments in One Image   A butterfly is detected by using an $m \times n$ search window in the Hough space; for example, $m = n = 11$. If peaks are separated, then there is no problem. The existence of multiple lines in an image I may also lead to overlays of multiple butterflies in the Hough space. In such a case, typically, only one wing of a butterfly overlaps with another butterfly. This destroys the symmetry of the butterfly.

After detecting a peak at (d, α), for not disturbing subsequent peak detection, we select pixels in the image (close to the detected line) and do the inverse process to the insertion of those pixels into the accumulator array: now we decrease counters when the corresponding sin/cos curve intersects cells.

After eliminating the effects of a found peak in the Hough space, the next peak is detected by continuing the search with the $m \times n$ search window.

Endpoints of Line Segments   So far we only discussed the detection of one line, not of a segment of a line defined also by two endpoints. A commonly used method for detecting the endpoints was published by M. Atiquzzaman and M.W. Akhtar in 1994. In general, the endpoints can be detected by tracing the detected line in the image and analysing potentially contributing edge pixels close to the line; alternatively, the endpoints can also be detected in the Hough space.

Fig. 3.36 Input example for detecting stop signs. Their borders form circles with diameters within some expected interval

3.4.2 Circles

The idea of Hough transforms can be generalized: for geometric objects of interest, consider a parameterization that supports a bounded accumulator array. Insert pixels into this array and detect peaks. We illustrate this generalization for circles. For example, see Fig. 3.36 for an application where circle detection is very important. Stop signs are nearly circular.

In this case, a straightforward parameterization of circles is fine for having a bounded accumulator array. We describe a circle by a centre point (x_c, y_c) and radius r. This defines a 3D Hough space.

Consider a pixel location $p = (x, y)$ in an image I. For a start, it may be incident with a circle of radius $r = 0$, being the pixel itself. This defines the point $(x, y, 0)$ in the Hough space, the starting point of the surface of a straight circular cone. Now assume that the pixel location $p = (x, y)$ is incident with circles of radius $r_0 > 0$. The centre points of those circles define a circle of radius r_0 around $p = (x, y)$. See Fig. 3.37, left. This circle is incident with the surface of the straight circular cone defined by (x, y) in the Hough space. To be precise, it is the intersection of this surface with the plane $r = r_0$ in the xyr Hough space.

For the radius r of circular borders in an image, we have an estimate for a possible range $r_0 \leq r \leq r_1$. The size of the images always defines an upper bound. Thus, the 3D Hough space for detecting circles reduces to a "layer" of thickness $r_1 - r_0$ over Ω. Thus, we do have a bounded Hough space.

This Hough space is discretized into 3D cells, defining a 3D accumulator array. At the beginning of a detection process, all counters in the accumulator array are set back to zero. When inserting a pixel location (x, y) into the accumulator array, all counters of the 3D cells that are intersected by the surface of the cone of pixel location (x, y) increase by one.

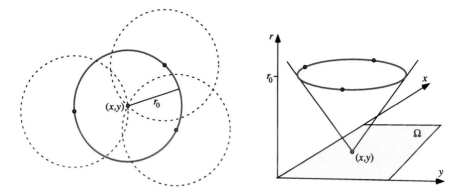

Fig. 3.37 *Left*: Pixel location (x, y) and location of all centre points of circles of radius $r_0 > 0$ around pixel (x, y). *Right*: A pixel location (x, y) defines the surface of a right circular cone in the Hough space

For example, when inserting three non-collinear pixel locations into the 3D Hough space, we generate three surfaces of right circular cones. We know that three non-collinear points determine uniquely a circle in the plane. Thus, all the three surfaces will intersect in one point only, defining the parameters of the uniquely specified circle.

As in case of line detection, now we need to detect peaks in the 3D accumulator array. Multiple circles in a given image usually do not create much interference in the 3D accumulator array, and there is also no "endpoint problem" as in case of line detection.

3.5   Exercises

3.5.1   Programming Exercises

Exercise 3.1 (Identification and Analysis of Components in a Binary Image)   Allow the input of any scalar image I. Apply a defined threshold T, $1 \leq T \leq G_{max}$, for generating a binary image by the following *thresholding* operation:

$$J(x, y) = \begin{cases} 0 & \text{if } I(x, y) < T \\ 1 & \text{otherwise} \end{cases} \tag{3.48}$$

For the resulting binary image J, allow the following two options for a user dialogue:
1. (Counting components) If the user selects this option, then it is possible to use either the key "black < white" or "white < black" for counting the number of black components in the binary image J.
2. (Geometric features of a selected component) When a user selects this option and clicks on one black component, then the area, the perimeter, and the diameter of the component are calculated. For this exercise, it is sufficient to calculate the

Fig. 3.38 Removal of artifacts with a diameter of at most T

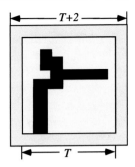

perimeter as the length of the 8-path describing the border of the component (i.e. the output of border tracing when assuming 8-adjacency). The *perimeter* of a component is the maximum distance between any two pixels in this component. (Thus, the perimeter is defined by two pixels on the border of the component.)

Optional, small components with an area below a given threshold may be deleted prior to Options 1 and 2, and the selected components (in Option 2) may be coloured to avoid repeated selection.

Exercise 3.2 (Deletion of Components with a Diameter Below a Given Threshold, and Histograms of Features) Generate binary images as described in Exercise 3.1. Before further processing, delete all black components having a diameter below a given threshold T.

Apply the following procedure, illustrated by Fig. 3.38, for doing so: Have one $T \times T$ window inside of a $(T+2) \times (T+2)$ window. If the number of black pixels in the small window equals the number of black pixels in the larger window (i.e. there are no black pixels in the difference set), as illustrated in Fig. 3.38, then set all pixels in the small window to zero (i.e. white).

For all the remaining components S in the generated binary image, calculate the area $\mathscr{A}(S)$, the perimeter $\mathscr{P}(S)$, and the *shape factor*

$$\mathscr{F}(S) = \frac{\mathscr{P}(S)^2}{2\pi \cdot \mathscr{A}(S)} \tag{3.49}$$

Display histograms showing the distributions of those three features for the remaining components in the generated binary image.

Insert 3.16 (Shape Factor and Isoperimetric Inequality) *The* isoperimetric in-equality *in 2D, known since ancient times, states that for any planar set that has a well-defined area $\mathscr{A}$ and perimeter $\mathscr{P}$, we have that*

$$\frac{\mathscr{P}^2}{4\pi \cdot \mathscr{A}} \geq 1 \tag{3.50}$$

It follows that among all such sets that have the same perimeter, the disk has the largest area. The expression on the left-hand side of (3.50) *is also known as the* isoperimetric deficit *of the set; it measures how much the set differs from a disk. The first proof for the ancient isoperimetric problem was published in* 1882.

Citation from [R. Klette and A. Rosenfeld. Digital Geometry. Morgan Kaufmann, San Francisco, 2004].

Exercise 3.3 (Evaluation of Co-Occurrence Measures) Use as input scalar images I of reasonable size (at least 256×256). Apply recursively the 3×3 box filter or the 3×3 local median operator to an input image and produce smoothed and residual images $S^{(n)}$ and $R^{(n)}$ with respect to these two smoothing or noise-removal operations for $n = 0, \ldots, 30$. See (2.33).

Calculate the co-occurrence matrices for I and images $S^{(n)}$ and $R^{(n)}$. Let T be the total sum of all entries in the co-occurrence matrix of I.

Calculate the homogeneity and the uniformity measures for images $S^{(n)}$ and $R^{(n)}$, and scale the obtained values by dividing by T, thus only having normalized values in the interval $[0, 1]$.

Plot those scaled homogeneity and uniformity results as functions of $n = 0, \ldots, 30$ for both used smoothing operators.

Discuss differences or similarities of results for input images I showing different intensity distributions, such as uniformly illuminated indoor images or outdoor images showing lighting artifacts.

Exercise 3.4 (Features of Components Using Moments) Generate binary images as described in Exercise 3.1. Before further processing, delete all black artifacts, for example by deleting all components having a diameter below a given threshold T or all components having an area below a given threshold.

Provide a user interface that the remaining components can be selected (by clicking) one by one, calculate for each selected component its centroid, main axis, and eccentricity and visualize those values in some way for the selected component. For visualizing eccentricity, you may draw, for example, an ellipse of corresponding eccentricity or just show a bar at the selected component whose height corresponds to the value of eccentricity. For centroid and main axis, do similar as illustrated in Fig. 3.30.

Exercise 3.5 (Directional Normalization of Images) Capture freehand (i.e. no tripod or other means for levelling) still images in an environment showing many vertical and horizontal edges.

Identify such "near-vertical" and "near-horizontal" edges by lines using the Hough transform and a criterion for rejecting slopes neither "nearly vertical" nor "nearly horizontal". Calculate from all the identified vertical and horizontal lines a

Fig. 3.39 Captured (*left*) and normalized (*right*) image

rotation angle for the given image such that the mean directions of horizontal and vertical lines become isothetic (i.e. parallel to the image's coordinate axes). See Fig. 3.39 for an example.

This is one (certainly not the simplest) way for normalizing images with respect to recorded environments.

Exercise 3.6 (Generation of Noisy Line Segments and Hough Transform) Write a program for generating noisy line segments as illustrated in Fig. 3.40. The program needs to support different densities of generated points and different numbers, lengths, and directions of generated noisy line segments.

Apply your line-detection program (you may decide to write it yourself) based on the Hough transform for detecting these line segments, including their endpoints. Compare the results with the true data used when generating the line segments. Increase the noise and discuss the robustness of your line-detection program.

Exercise 3.7 (Lane Border Detection) Have a second person in a car (besides the driver) for recording video data while driving on a well-marked highway. Detect the lane borders in all frames of the recorded video of at least 200 frames length:

1. Detect the edge pixels in each frame using your favourite edge detector.
2. Detect the straight lines in your edge maps. Simply project the detected edges into the image, starting at the bottom row up to about two thirds into the image, as done in Figs. 3.31 and 3.33, bottom, right. No need to identify the endpoints of line segments.
3. Generate a video (e.g. avi or other codec) from your generated labelled lane borders.

Optionally, you may consider using line tracking for making the detection process more efficient.

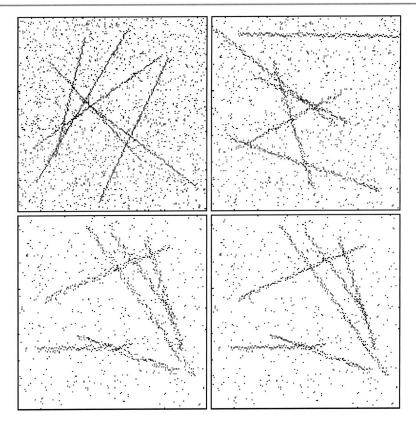

Fig. 3.40 Noisy line segments

3.5.2   Non-programming Exercises

Exercise 3.8 Consider the following *6-adjacency* in images for a pixel location $p = (x, y)$: In an even row (i.e. y is even) use

$$A_6^{even} = A_4 \cup \{(x + 1, y + 1), (x + 1, y - 1)\}$$

and in an odd row use

$$A_6^{odd} = A_4 \cup \{(x - 1, y + 1), (x - 1, y - 1)\}$$

Now consider Fig. 3.3, left, and discuss the result. Now consider a chess-board type of binary input image. What is the result?

Exercise 3.9 K-adjacency requires a test about ownership of the central corner of a 2×2 pixel configuration in some cases. Specify the condition when such a test becomes necessary. For example, if all four pixels have identical values, no test is needed; and if three pixels have identical values, no test is needed either.

Fig. 3.41 Scene of the first Tour de France in 1903 (copyright expired)

Exercise 3.10 What will happen if you use the local circular order

in the Voss algorithm, rather than the local circular order used for Fig. 3.11?

Exercise 3.11 Discuss similarities and differences for the eccentricity measure and the shape factor. Use examples of binary shapes in your discussion.

Exercise 3.12 Explain how image gradient information can be used to enhance accuracy and speed of circle detection using the concept of the Hough transform.

Exercise 3.13 Design a Hough transform method for detecting parabolas, for example as present in an image as shown in Fig. 3.41.

Dense Motion Analysis

4

This chapter discusses the optical flow, a standard representation in computer vision for dense motion. Every pixel is labelled by a motion vector, indicating the change in image data from time t to time $t + 1$. Sparse motion analysis (also known as *tracking*) will be a subject in Chap. 9.

4.1   3D Motion and 2D Optical Flow

Assume a sequence of images (or video frames) with time difference δt between two subsequent images. For example, we have $\delta t = 1/30$ s in case of image recording at 30 Hz (hertz), also abbreviated by 30 fps (frames per second). Let $I(\cdot, \cdot, t)$ denote the recorded frame at time slot t, having values $I(x, y, t)$ at pixel locations (x, y).

> **Insert 4.1** (Hertz) *H. Hertz (1857–1894) was a German physicist working on electromagnetism.*

This section provides basics for motion analysis in image sequences.

4.1.1   Local Displacement Versus Optical Flow

A 3D point $P = (X, Y, Z)$ is projected at time $t \cdot \delta t$ into a pixel location $p = (x, y)$ in the image $I(\cdot, \cdot, t)$; see Fig. 4.1. The camera has *focal length* f, a *projection centre* O, and looks along the *optical axis*, represented as the Z-axis, into the 3D space. This ideal camera model defines the *central projection* into the xy image plane; we discuss camera models in more detail later in Chap. 6.

2D Motion   Assume a linear 3D movement of P between $t \cdot \delta t$ and $(t + 1) \cdot \delta t$ with *velocity* (i.e., speed and direction) $\mathbf{v} = (v_X, v_Y, v_Z)^\top$, defining a 3D *motion* $\mathbf{v} \cdot \delta t$ starting at $P = (X, Y, Z)$ and ending at $(X + v_X \cdot \delta t, Y + v_Y \cdot \delta t, Z + v_Z \cdot \delta t)$.

R. Klette, *Concise Computer Vision*, Undergraduate Topics in Computer Science, DOI 10.1007/978-1-4471-6320-6_4, © Springer-Verlag London 2014

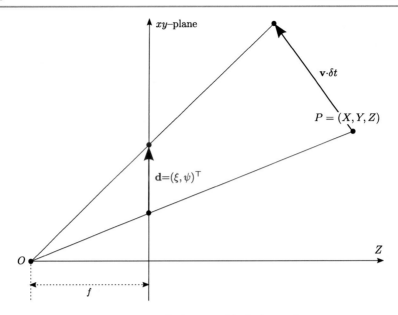

Fig. 4.1 Projection of velocity **v** into a displacement **d** in the image plane

The vector $\mathbf{d} = (\xi, \psi)^{\top}$ is the projection of this 3D motion of point P between the images $I(\cdot, \cdot, t)$ and $I(\cdot, \cdot, t + 1)$. This 2D motion is a geometrically defined local displacement of the pixel originally at p assuming that we know the 3D motion.

The visible displacement in 2D is the *optical flow* $\mathbf{u} = (u, v)^{\top}$; it starts at pixel location $p = (x, y)$ and ends at pixel location $p = (x + u, y + v)$, and it is often not identical to the actual local displacement. *Optical flow calculation* aims at estimating the 2D motion.

Figure 4.2 illustrates the difference between the 2D motion and optical flow. A dense motion analysis algorithm should turn the upward optical flow $\mathbf{u}$ into the actual 2D motion $\mathbf{d}$.

As another example, a "textured" object, which is fixed (with respect to the Earth, called *static* in the following), and a moving light source (e.g. the Sun) generate an optical flow. Here we have no object motion, thus no 2D motion, but an optical flow.

Vector Fields We like to understand the motion of 3D objects by analysing projections of many their surface points $P = (X, Y, Z)$. The results should be consistent with object movements or with the shape of moving rigid objects.

2D motion vectors form a *vector field*. See Fig. 4.3 for an example, illustrating a rotating rectangle (around a fixpoint) in a plane parallel to the image plane.

A rigid body simplifies the analysis of 2D motion vector fields, but even then those vector fields are not easy to read. As a graphical exercise, you may generate visualizations of 2D motion vector fields for simple 3D shapes such as a cube or other simple polyhedra. It is difficult to infer the shape of the polyhedron when just looking at the motion field.

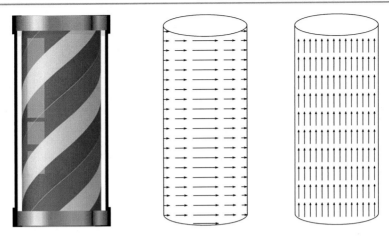

Fig. 4.2 *Left*: In case of a rotating barber's pole we have 2D motion to the right. *Middle*: A sketch of the 2D motion (without scaling vectors). *Right*: A sketch of optical flow, which is 'somehow' upward

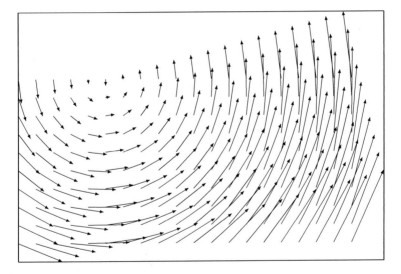

Fig. 4.3 A vector field showing the rotation of a rectangle. Motion vectors start at the position at time t and end at the position of the rotated start point at time $t + 1$

A computed motion vector field is *dense* if it contains motion vectors at (nearly) all pixel locations; otherwise, it is *sparse*.

See Fig. 4.4 for a colour key for visualizing optical flow vectors. The hue of the shown colour represents the direction of movement, and its saturation the magnitude of the motion.

Fig. 4.4 A colour key for visualizing an optical flow. The colour represents a direction of a vector (assumed to start at the centre of the disk), and the saturation corresponds to the magnitude of the vector, with White for "no motion" at all

Figure 4.5 shows an example (two input frames and colour-coded results). Motion colours clearly identify the bicyclist; pixels in this area move distinctively different to other pixels nearby. The result can be improved by adding further algorithmic design ideas to the basic Horn–Schunck algorithm.

4.1.2   Aperture Problem and Gradient Flow

By analysing projected images, we observe a limited area of visible motion, defined by the aperture of the camera, or by the algorithm used for motion analysis. Such an algorithm checks, in general, only a limited neighbourhood of a pixel for deriving a conclusion.

The Aperture Problem   Recall a situation in a train waiting for departure, looking out of the window, and believing that your train started to move, but it was actually the train on the next track that was moving. An aperture problem is caused by a limited view on a dynamic scene. The aperture problem adds further uncertainties to motion estimation.

Figure 4.6 illustrates a situation where an algorithm processes an image and "sees" around the current pixel only the sketched circular area and nothing else. We may conclude that there is an upward move; the diagonal motion component is not apparent in the circular window.

For a real-world example, see Fig. 4.7. A car drives around a roundabout, to the left and away from the camera. We only see a limited aperture. If we even only see the inner rectangles, then we may conclude an upward shift.

However, possibly there is actually something else happening, for example, the car may not move by itself, but is carried on a trailer, or, maybe, the images show some kind of mobile screen driven around on a truck. Increasing the aperture will help, but it remains that we possibly have incomplete information.

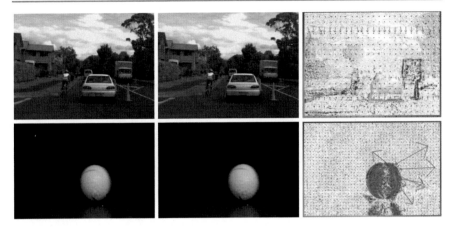

Fig. 4.5 *Top, left, and middle*: Two subsequent frames of video sequence `bicyclist`, taken at 25 fps. *Top, right*: The colour-coded motion field calculated with the basic Horn–Schunck algorithm. Additionally to the colour key, there are also some sparse (magnified) vectors illustrated as redundant information, but for better visual interpretation of the flow field. *Bottom, left, and middle*: Two subsequent frames of video sequence `tennisball`. *Bottom, right*: The colour-coded motion field calculated with the basic Horn–Schunck algorithm

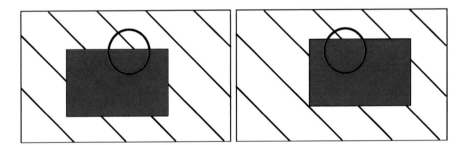

Fig. 4.6 Seeing only both circular windows at time t (*left*) and time $t + 1$ (*right*), we conclude an upward shift and miss the shift diagonally towards the *upper right corner*

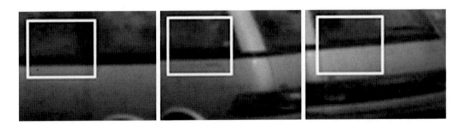

Fig. 4.7 Three images taken at times t, $t + 1$, and $t + 2$. For the *inner rectangles*, we may conclude an upward translation with a minor rotation, but the three images clearly indicate a motion of this car to the *left*

Fig. 4.8 Illustration of a gradient flow. The true 2D motion **d** goes diagonally up, but the identified motion is the projection of **d** onto the gradient vector

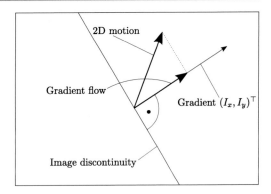

Gradient Flow   Due to the aperture problem, a local method typically detects a *gradient flow*, which is the projection of the true 2D motion onto the gradient at the given pixel. The 2D gradient with respect to coordinates x and y,

$$\nabla_{x,y} I = \left[I_x(x, y, t), I_y(x, y, t) \right]^{\top} \tag{4.1}$$

is orthogonal to the straight image discontinuity (an edge) as illustrated in Fig. 4.8, assuming that the image intensities decrease from the region on the left to the region on the right. Recall that I_x and I_y in (4.1) denote the partial derivatives of the frame $I(\cdot, \cdot, t)$ with respect to x and y, respectively.

The result may improve (i.e. going more towards the true 2D motion) by taking the values at adjacent pixels into account. For example, an object corner may support the calculation of the correct 2D motion.

4.2 The Horn–Schunck Algorithm

We would like to define a relationship between the values in the frames $I(\cdot, \cdot, t)$ and $I(\cdot, \cdot, t + 1)$. A straightforward start is to consider a first-order *Taylor expansion* of the function $I(\cdot, \cdot, t + 1)$.

Insert 4.2 (Taylor and the 1D Taylor Expansion of a Function) *B. Taylor (1685–1731) was an English mathematician. A Taylor expansion is often used in applied physics or engineering. Recall that the difference quotient*

$$\frac{\phi(x) - \phi(x_0)}{x - x_0} = \frac{\phi(x_0 + \delta x) - \phi(x_0)}{\delta x}$$

of a function ϕ converges (assuming that ϕ is continuously differentiable) into the differential quotient

$$\frac{d\phi(x_0)}{dx}$$

as $\delta x \to 0$. For small values of δx, we have a first-order Taylor expansion

$$\phi(x_0 + \delta x) = \phi(x_0) + \delta x \cdot \frac{d\phi(x_0)}{dx} + e$$

where the error e equals zero if ϕ is linear in $[x_0, x_0 + \delta x]$. See the figure below.

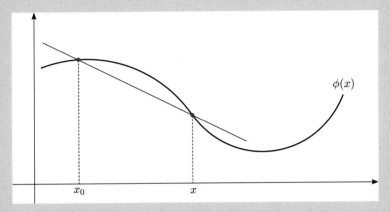

In generalization of this first-order approximation step, the 1D Taylor expansion *is as follows*:

$$\phi(x_0 + \delta x) = \sum_{i=0,1,2,\ldots} \frac{1}{i!} \cdot \delta x^i \cdot \frac{d^i \phi(x_0)}{d^i x}$$

with $0! = 1$, $i! = 1 \cdot 2 \cdot 3 \cdot \cdots \cdot i$ for $i \geq 1$, d^i is the ith derivative, provided that ϕ has continuous derivatives of all required orders.

This section describes in detail about the pioneering Horn–Schunck algorithm. The discussed mathematical methodology in this section is still used today as a guide for designing optical flow algorithms. The section also informs how to evaluate the performance of optical flow algorithms in general.

4.2.1   Preparing for the Algorithm

In our case of a tertiary function $I(\cdot, \cdot, \cdot)$, we apply a first-order 3D Taylor expansion and obtain the following:

$$I(x + \delta x, y + \delta y, t + \delta t)$$
$$= I(x, y, t) + \delta x \cdot \frac{\partial I}{\partial x}(x, y, t) + \delta y \cdot \frac{\partial I}{\partial y}(x, y, t) + \delta t \cdot \frac{\partial I}{\partial t}(x, y, t) + e \quad (4.2)$$

where the term e represents all the second- and higher-order derivatives in the Taylor expansion. As usual in physics and engineering, we assume that $e = 0$, meaning that we assume that our function $I(\cdot, \cdot, \cdot)$ behaves nearly like a linear function for *small* values of δx, δy, and δt.

As the value δt, we take the time difference between the subsequent frames $I(\cdot, \cdot, t)$ and $I(\cdot, \cdot, t+1)$. With δx and δy we like to model the motion of one pixel at time slot t into another location at time slot $t + 1$. Using the intensity constancy assumption (ICA)

$$I(x + \delta x, y + \delta y, t + \delta t) = I(x, y, t) \tag{4.3}$$

before and after the motion, we have that

$$0 = \delta x \cdot \frac{\partial I}{\partial x}(x, y, t) + \delta y \cdot \frac{\partial I}{\partial y}(x, y, t) + \delta t \cdot \frac{\partial I}{\partial t}(x, y, t) \tag{4.4}$$

We divide by δt and obtain the following:

$$0 = \frac{\delta x}{\delta t} \cdot \frac{\partial I}{\partial x}(x, y, t) + \frac{\delta y}{\delta t} \cdot \frac{\partial I}{\partial y}(x, y, t) + \frac{\partial I}{\partial t}(x, y, t) \tag{4.5}$$

The changes in x- and y-coordinates during δt represent the optical flow $\mathbf{u}(x, y, t) = (u(x, y, t), v(x, y, t))^\top$ we are interested to calculate:

$$0 = u(x, y, t) \cdot \frac{\partial I}{\partial x}(x, y, t) + v(x, y, t) \cdot \frac{\partial I}{\partial y}(x, y, t) + \frac{\partial I}{\partial t}(x, y, t) \tag{4.6}$$

Equation (4.6) is known as the *optical flow equation* or the *Horn–Schunck* (HS) *Constraint*.

Insert 4.3 (Origin of the Horn–Schunck Algorithm) *The algorithm was published in* [B.K.P. Horn and B.G. Schunck. Determining optic flow. Artificial Intelligence, vol. 17, pp. 185–203, 1981] *as a pioneering work for estimating an optical flow.*

The derivation of the final algorithm comes with some lengthy formulas and calculations. You will be surprised how simple the final result looks and how easy the algorithm can be implemented if not trying to add any additional optimization strategies. If you are not curious about how the algorithm was derived, then you may go straight to its presentation in Sect. 4.2.2.

Observation 4.1 *Equation* (4.6) *was derived by considering small steps only and the intensity constancy assumption. Logically, these assumptions define the constraints for the final algorithm.*

The uv Velocity Space   We express (4.6) in short form as follows by ignoring the coordinates (x, y, t):

$$-I_t = u \cdot I_x + v \cdot I_y = \mathbf{u} \cdot \nabla_{x,y} I \qquad (4.7)$$

Here, notation I_x and I_y is short for the partial derivatives (as used above) with respect to x- or y-coordinates, respectively, and I_t for the one with respect to t. The scalar $\mathbf{u} \cdot \nabla_{x,y} I$ is the *dot product* of the optical flow vector times the gradient vector (i.e. partial derivatives only with respect to x and y, not for t).

Insert 4.4 (Inner or Dot Vector Product)   *Consider two vectors* $\mathbf{a} = (a_1, a_2, \ldots, a_n)^\top$ *and* $\mathbf{b} = (b_1, b_2, \ldots, b_n)^\top$ *in the Euclidean space* $\mathbb{R}^n$. *The dot product, also called the inner product, of both vectors is defined as*

$$\mathbf{a} \cdot \mathbf{b} = a_1 b_1 + a_2 b_2 + \cdots + a_n b_n$$

It satisfies the property

$$\mathbf{a} \cdot \mathbf{b} = \|\mathbf{a}\|_2 \cdot \|\mathbf{b}\|_2 \cdot \cos \alpha$$

where $\|\mathbf{a}\|_2$ *and* $\|\mathbf{b}\|_2$ *are the magnitudes of both vectors, for example*

$$\|\mathbf{a}\|_2 = \sqrt{a_1^2 + a_2^2 + \cdots + a_n^2}$$

and α *is the angle between both vectors, with* $0 \le \alpha \le \pi$.

I_x, I_y and I_t play the role of parameters in (4.7). They are estimated in the given frames by discrete approximations of derivatives (e.g., Sobel values S_x and S_y for I_x and I_y). Optic flow components u and v are the unknowns in (4.7). Thus, this equation defines a straight line in the *uv velocity space*. See Fig. 4.9.

By (4.7) we know that the optical flow (u, v) for the considered pixel (x, y, t) is a point on this straight line, but we do not know yet which one.

Optical Flow Calculation as a Labelling Problem   Low-level computer vision is often characterized by the task to assign to each pixel a *label l* out of a set of possible labels L. For example, the set L can be a discrete set of identifiers of image segments (see Chap. 5) or a discrete set of disparity values for stereo matching (see Chap. 8). Here we have to deal with labels $(u, v) \in \mathbb{R}^2$ in a 2D continuous space.

Labels are assigned to all the pixels in Ω by a *labelling function*

$$f : \Omega \to L \qquad (4.8)$$

Solving a labelling problem means to identify a labelling f that approximates somehow a given optimum.

Fig. 4.9 The *straight line* $-I_t = u \cdot I_x + v \cdot I_y$ in the uv velocity space. The point Q is discussed in Example 4.1

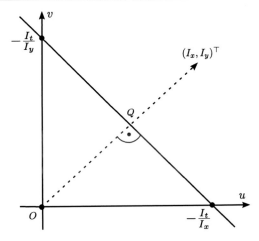

First Constraint   Let f be a labelling function that assigns a label (u, v) to each pixel $p \in \Omega$ in an image $I(\cdot, \cdot, t)$. Due to (4.7), we are interested in a solution f that minimizes the *data error*, also called the *data energy*,

$$E_{data}(f) = \sum_{\Omega} [u \cdot I_x + v \cdot I_y + I_t]^2 \tag{4.9}$$

with $u \cdot I_x + v \cdot I_y + I_t = 0$ in the ideal case for pixels $p \in \Omega$ in the image $I(\cdot, \cdot, t)$.

Second Constraint—Spatial Motion Constancy   Additionally to (4.7), we formulate a second constraint for solutions (u, v), hoping that this leads to a unique solution on the straight line $-I_t = u \cdot I_x + v \cdot I_y$. There are many different options for formulating such a second constraint.

We assume motion constancy within pixel neighbourhoods at time t, which means that adjacent pixels in $I(\cdot, \cdot, t)$ have about the same optical flow vectors. For a function that is nearly constant in local neighbourhoods, its first derivatives will be close to zero. Thus, motion constancy can be formulated as a *smoothness constraint* that the sum of the squares of first-order derivatives needs to be minimized for all pixels $p \in \Omega$ in $I(\cdot, \cdot, t)$. Again, we keep it short without writing arguments (x, y, t).

Let f be the labelling function again that assigns a label (u, v) to each pixel $p \in \Omega$ in $I(\cdot, \cdot, t)$. The *smoothness error*, also called the *smoothness energy*, is defined as

$$E_{smooth}(f) = \sum_{\Omega} \left(\frac{\partial u}{\partial x} \right)^2 + \left(\frac{\partial u}{\partial y} \right)^2 + \left(\frac{\partial v}{\partial x} \right)^2 + \left(\frac{\partial v}{\partial y} \right)^2 \tag{4.10}$$

The Optimization Problem   We like to calculate a labelling function f that minimizes the combined error or energy

$$E_{total}(f) = E_{data}(f) + \lambda \cdot E_{smooth}(f) \tag{4.11}$$

where $\lambda > 0$ is a weight. In general, we take $\lambda < 1$ for avoiding strong smoothing. The selected parameter will depend on application and relevant image data.

We search for an optimum f in the set of all possible labellings, which defines a *total variation* (TV). The used smoothing error term applies squared penalties in the L_2 sense. Altogether, this defines a TVL$_2$ optimization problem. A value of $\lambda > 1$ would give smoothness a higher weight than the Horn–Schunck constraint (i.e., the data term), and this is not recommended. A value such as $\lambda = 0.1$ is often a good initial guess, allowing smoothness a relatively small impact only.

Insert 4.5 (Least-Square Error Optimization) *Least-square error (LSE) optimization follows the following standard scheme:*
1. *Define an error or energy function.*
2. *Calculate the derivatives of this function with respect to all unknown parameters.*
3. *Set the derivatives equal to zero and solve this equation system with respect to the unknowns. The result defines a stationary point, which can only be a local minimum, a saddle point, or a local maximum.*

We perform LSE optimization. The error function has been defined in (4.11). The only possible stationary point is a minimum of the error function.

The unknowns are all the u and v values at all $N_{cols} \times N_{rows}$ pixel positions; that means we have to specify $2N_{cols}N_{rows}$ partial derivatives of the LSE function.

For a formal simplification, we exclude t from the following formulas. The frames $I(\cdot, \cdot, t)$, with adjacent frames $I(\cdot, \cdot, t - 1)$ and $I(\cdot, \cdot, t + 1)$, are fixed for the following considerations. Instead of writing $I(x, y, t)$, we simply use $I(x, y)$ in the following.

For formal simplicity, we assume that all pixels have all their four 4-adjacent pixels also in the image. We approximate the derivatives in the smoothness-error term by simple asymmetric differences and have

$$E_{smooth}(f) = \sum_{x,y}(u_{x+1,y} - u_{xy})^2 + (u_{x,y+1} - u_{xy})^2$$

$$+ (v_{x+1,y} - v_{xy})^2 + (v_{x,y+1} - v_{xy})^2 \qquad (4.12)$$

Asymmetric differences are actually a biased choice, and symmetric differences should perform better (such as $u_{x+1,y} - u_{x-1,y}$ and so forth), but we stay with presenting the original Horn–Schunck algorithm.

We have the following partial derivatives of $E_{data}(u, v)$:

$$\frac{\partial E_{data}}{\partial u_{xy}}(u, v) = 2\big[I_x(x, y)u_{xy} + I_y(x, y)v_{xy} + I_t(x, y)\big]I_x(x, y) \qquad (4.13)$$

and

$$\frac{\partial E_{data}}{\partial v_{xy}}(u, v) = 2\big[I_x(x, y)u_{xy} + I_y(x, y)v_{xy} + I_t(x, y)\big]I_y(x, y) \qquad (4.14)$$

The partial derivatives of $E_{smooth}(u, v)$ are equal to

$$\frac{\partial E_{smooth}}{\partial u_{xy}}(u, v) = -2\big[(u_{x+1,y} - u_{xy}) + (u_{x,y+1} - u_{xy})\big]$$

$$+ 2\big[(u_{xy} - u_{x-1,y}) + (u_{xy} - u_{x,y-1})\big]$$

$$= 2\big[(u_{xy} - u_{x+1,y}) + (u_{xy} - u_{x,y+1})$$

$$+ (u_{xy} - u_{x-1,y}) + (u_{xy} - u_{x,y-1})\big] \qquad (4.15)$$

These are the only terms containing the unknown u_{xy}. We simplify this expression and obtain

$$\frac{1}{4} \cdot \frac{\partial E_{smooth}}{\partial u_{xy}}(u, v) = 2\left[u_{xy} - \left[\frac{1}{4}(u_{i+1,j} + u_{x,y+1} + u_{i-1,j} + u_{x,y-1})\right]\right] \qquad (4.16)$$

Using $\bar{u}_{xy}$ for the mean value of 4-adjacent pixels, we have that

$$\frac{1}{4}\frac{\partial E_{smooth}}{\partial u_{xy}}(u, v) = 2[u_{xy} - \bar{u}_{xy}] \qquad (4.17)$$

$$\frac{1}{4}\frac{\partial E_{smooth}}{\partial v_{xy}}(u, v) = 2[v_{xy} - \bar{v}_{xy}] \qquad (4.18)$$

Equation (4.18) follows analogously to the provided calculations.

Altogether, using λ instead of $\lambda/4$, after setting derivatives equal to zero, we arrive at the equation system

$$0 = \lambda[u_{xy} - \bar{u}_{xy}]$$

$$+ \big[I_x(x, y)u_{xy} + I_y(x, y)v_{xy} + I_t(x, y)\big]I_x(x, y) \qquad (4.19)$$

$$0 = \lambda[v_{xy} - \bar{v}_{xy}]$$

$$+ \big[I_x(x, y)u_{xy} + I_y(x, y)v_{xy} + I_t(x, y)\big]I_y(x, y) \qquad (4.20)$$

This is a discrete scheme for minimizing equation (4.11). This is a linear equational system for $2N_{cols}N_{rows}$ unknowns u_{xy} and v_{xy}. The values of I_x, I_y, and I_t are estimated based on given image data.

Iterative Solution Scheme   This equation system also contains the means $\bar{u}_{xy}$ and $\bar{v}_{xy}$, which are calculated based on the values of those unknowns. The dependency between the unknowns u_{xy} and v_{xy} and means $\bar{u}_{xy}$ and $\bar{v}_{xy}$ within those equations is actually of benefit. This allows us to define an *iterative scheme* (an example of a *Jacobi method*; for C.G.J. Jacobi, see Insert 5.9), starting with some initial values:

1. *Initialization step:* We initialize the values u_{xy}^0 and v_{xy}^0.
2. *Iteration Step 0:* Calculate the means $\bar{u}_{xy}^0$ and $\bar{v}_{xy}^0$ using the initial values and calculate the values u_{xy}^1 and v_{xy}^1.
3. *Iteration Step n:* Use the values u_{xy}^n and v_{xy}^n to compute the means $\bar{u}_{xy}^n$ and $\bar{v}_{xy}^n$; use those data to calculate the values u_{xy}^{n+1} and v_{xy}^{n+1}.

Proceed for $n \geq 1$ until a stop criterion is satisfied.

We skip the details of solving the equation system defined by (4.19) and (4.20). This is a standard linear algebra. The solution is as follows:

$$u_{xy}^{n+1} = \bar{u}_{xy}^n - I_x(x,y) \cdot \frac{I_x(x,y)\bar{u}_{xy}^n + I_y(x,y)\bar{v}_{xy}^n + I_t(x,y)}{\lambda^2 + I_x^2(x,y) + I_y^2(x,y)} \qquad (4.21)$$

$$v_{xy}^{n+1} = \bar{v}_{xy}^n - I_y(x,y) \cdot \frac{I_x(x,y)\bar{u}_{xy}^n + I_y(x,y)\bar{v}_{xy}^n + I_t(x,y)}{\lambda^2 + I_x^2(x,y) + I_y^2(x,y)} \qquad (4.22)$$

Now we are ready to discuss the algorithm.

4.2.2 The Algorithm

The given solutions and the discussed iteration scheme allows us to calculate the values u_{xy}^n and v_{xy}^n at iteration step n for all pixel positions (x,y) in the image $I(\cdot,\cdot,t)$. At least one adjacent image $I(\cdot,\cdot,t-1)$ or $I(\cdot,\cdot,t+1)$ is needed for estimating the I_t values.

Let

$$\alpha(x,y,n) = \frac{I_x(x,y)\bar{u}_{xy}^n + I_y(x,y)\bar{v}_{xy}^n + I_t(x,y)}{\lambda^2 + I_x^2(x,y) + I_y^2(x,y)} \qquad (4.23)$$

The algorithm is shown in Fig. 4.10. $\bar{u}$ and $\bar{v}$ denote the means of 4-adjacent pixels. We use "odd" and "even" arrays for u- and v-values: at the beginning (iteration step $n = 0$) we initialize in the even arrays. In iteration $n = 1$ we calculate the values in the odd arrays, and so forth, always in alternation. The threshold T is for the stop criterion, the maximum number of iterations.

Initialization with value 0 at all positions of u_{xy} and v_{xy} was suggested in the original Horn–Schunck algorithm. This allows us to have non-zero values u_{xy}^1 and v_{xy}^1, as long as $I_x(x,y) \cdot I_t(x,y)$ and $I_y(x,y) \cdot I_t(x,y)$ are not equal to zero at all pixel locations. (Of course, in such a case we would not have any optical flow; the initialization 0 would be correct).

The original Horn–Schunck algorithm used the following asymmetric approximations for I_x, I_y, and I_t:

```
 1: for y = 1 to N_rows do
 2:    for x = 1 to N_cols do
 3:        Compute I_x(x, y), I_y(x, y), and I_t(x, y) ;
 4:        Initialize u(x, y) and v(x, y) (in even arrays);
 5:    end for
 6: end for
 7: Select weight factor λ; select T > 1; set n = 1;
 8: while n ≤ T do
 9:    for y = 1 to N_rows do
10:        for x = 1 to N_cols {in alternation for even or odd arrays} do
11:            Compute α(x, y, n);
12:            Compute u(x, y) = ū − α(x, y, n) · I_x(x, y, t) ;
13:            Compute v(x, y) = v̄ − α(x, y, n) · I_y(x, y, t) ;
14:        end for
15:    end for
16:    n := n + 1;
17: end while
```

Fig. 4.10 Horn–Schunck algorithm

$$I_x(x, y, t) = \frac{1}{4}\big[I(x+1, y, t) + I(x+1, y, t+1)$$
$$+ I(x+1, y+1, t) + I(x+1, y+1, t+1)\big]$$
$$- \frac{1}{4}\big[I(x, y, t) + I(x, y, t+1) + I(x, y+1, t) + I(x, y+1, t+1)\big]$$
$$(4.24)$$

$$I_y(x, y, t) = \frac{1}{4}\big[I(x, y+1, t) + I(x, y+1, t+1)$$
$$+ I(x+1, y+1, t) + I(x+1, y+1, t+1)\big]$$
$$- \frac{1}{4}\big[I(x, y, t) + I(x, y, t+1) + I(x+1, y, t) + I(x+1, y, t+1)\big]$$
$$(4.25)$$

$$I_t(x, y, t) = \frac{1}{4}\big[I(x, y, t+1) + I(x, y+1, t+1)$$
$$+ I(x+1, y, t+1) + I(x+1, y+1, t+1)\big]$$
$$- \frac{1}{4}\big[I(x, y, t) + I(x, y+1, t) + I(x+1, y, t) + I(x+1, y+1, t)\big]$$
$$(4.26)$$

Figure 4.11 illustrates these local approximations by the corresponding convolution masks. Note that showing those masks is much more efficient for understanding the used approximations I_x, I_y, and I_t.

The algorithm requires only a pair of subsequent images as input. There are many alternatives for modifying this algorithm. Figure 4.12 shows the results for the original Horn–Schunck algorithm.

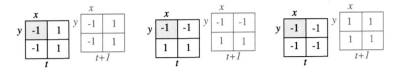

Fig. 4.11 Masks for approximations of partial derivatives I_x, I_y, and I_t (*left* to *right*) as suggested by Horn and Schunck

Fig. 4.12 *Top*: Two subsequent frames of the "Hamburg taxi sequence", published in 1983 for testing optical flow algorithms. *Bottom*: Visualization of the results of the Horn–Schunck algorithm. *Bottom, left*: Use of a colour key in 1995, Otago University, Dunedin, for representing direction and magnitude of calculated optical flow vectors (different to the colour key shown in Fig. 4.4: *Black* is here for "no motion"). *Bottom, right*: Illustration of flow vectors (known as a *needle map*) in a sub-sampled window of the whole image

Example 4.1 (Gradient Flow)   The unknown optical flow $\mathbf{u} = [u, v]^\top$ at pixel $p = (x, y)$ in the image $I(\cdot, \cdot, t)$, relative to the image $I(\cdot, \cdot, t + 1)$, can be any vector starting at the origin O in Fig. 4.9 and ending at a point somewhere on that straight line. This uncertainty is obvious by the aperture problem.

For initialization, you may select a point on the straight line, which is defined by the optical flow equation in the uv velocity space, instead of simply taking 0 for initialization. For example, you may choose the point that is closest to the origin as Q; see Fig. 4.9.

The straight line $I_t = u \cdot I_x + v \cdot I_y$ intersects the u- and v-axes at the points $(-I_t/I_x, 0)$ and $(0, -I_t/I_y)$, respectively. Thus, the vector

$$[-I_t/I_x, 0]^\top - [0, -I_t/I_y]^\top = [-I_t/I_x, I_t/I_y]^\top \qquad (4.27)$$

is parallel to this straight line.

Let $\mathbf{a}$ be the vector from O to Q; we have the dot product (for the dot product, see Insert 4.4 and note that $\cos \frac{\pi}{2} = 0$)

$$\mathbf{a} \cdot [-I_t/I_x, I_t/I_y]^\top = 0 \qquad (4.28)$$

From this equation and $\mathbf{a} = [a_x, a_y]^\top$ it follows that

$$a_x \cdot (-I_t/I_x) + a_y \cdot (I_t/I_y) = 0 \qquad (4.29)$$

and

$$I_t(a_x \cdot I_y) = I_t(a_y \cdot I_x) \qquad (4.30)$$

Assuming a change (i.e., $I_t \neq 0$) at the considered pixel location $p = (x, y)$, it follows that $a_x I_y = a_y I_x$ and

$$\mathbf{a} = c \cdot \mathbf{g}^\circ \qquad (4.31)$$

for some constant $c \neq 0$, where $\mathbf{g}^\circ$ is the unit vector of the gradient $\mathbf{g} = [I_x, I_y]^\top$. Thus, $\mathbf{a}$ is a multiple of the gradient $\mathbf{g}$, as indicated in Fig. 4.9.[1]

Insert 4.6 (Unit Vector) *Consider a vector $\mathbf{a} = [a_1, a_2, \ldots, a_n]^\top$. The magnitude of the vector equals $\|\mathbf{a}\|_2 = \sqrt{a_1^2 + a_2^2 + \cdots + a_n^2}$. The unit vector*

$$\mathbf{a}^\circ = \frac{\mathbf{a}}{\|\mathbf{a}\|_2}$$

is of magnitude one and specifies the direction of a vector $\mathbf{a}$. The product $\mathbf{a}^\circ \cdot \mathbf{a}^\circ$ equals $\|\mathbf{a}^\circ\|_2 \cdot \|\mathbf{a}^\circ\|_2 \cdot \cos 0 = 1$.

---

[1]We could skip (4.28) to (4.30) as the vector $\mathbf{a}$ is orthogonal to the line by definition: it joins the origin with its orthogonal projection on the line (the property of the nearest point). Being orthogonal to the line, it must be parallel to the gradient vector.

The vector $\mathbf{a}$ satisfies the optical flow equation $\mathbf{u} \cdot \mathbf{g} = -I_t$. It follows that

$$c \cdot \mathbf{g}^\circ \cdot \mathbf{g} = c \cdot \|\mathbf{g}\|_2 = -I_t \qquad (4.32)$$

Thus, we have c and altogether

$$\mathbf{a} = -\frac{I_t}{\|\mathbf{g}\|_2}\mathbf{g}^\circ \qquad (4.33)$$

We can use the point Q, as defined by vector $\mathbf{a}$, for initializing the u and v arrays prior to the iteration. That means we start with the *gradient flow*, as represented by $\mathbf{a}$. The algorithm may move away from the gradient flow in subsequent iterations due to the influence of values in the neighbourhood of the considered pixel location.

For approximating I_x, I_y, and I_t, you may also try a very simple (e.g. two-pixel) approximation. The algorithm is robust—but results are erroneous, often mainly due to the intensity constancy assumption (ICA), but there is also a questionable impact of the smoothness constraint (e.g. at motion discontinuities in the considered frames) and, of course, the aperture problem. The number T of iterations can be kept fairly small (say, $T = 7$) because there are typically no real improvements later on.

A *pyramidal Horn–Schunck algorithm* uses image pyramids as discussed in Sect. 2.2.2. Processing starts at a selected level (of lower resolution) images. The obtained results are used for initializing optical flow values at a lower level (of higher resolution). This can be repeated until the full resolution level of the original frames is reached.

4.3   Lucas–Kanade Algorithm

The optical flow equation specifies a straight line $u \cdot I_x + v \cdot I_y + I_t = 0$ in the uv velocity space for each pixel $p \in \Omega$. Consider all straight lines defined by all pixels in a local neighbourhood. Assuming that they are not parallel, but defined by about the same 2D motion, they intersect somehow close to the true 2D motion. See Fig. 4.13.

Insert 4.7 (Origin of the Lucas–Kanade Optical Flow algorithm) *The algorithm was published in* [B. D. Lucas and T. Kanade. An iterative image registration technique with an application to stereo vision. Proc. Imaging Understanding Workshop, pp. 121–130, 1981], *shortly after the Horn–Schunck algorithm.*

This section describes a pioneering optical flow algorithm for which the underlying mathematics is much easier to explain than for the Horn–Schunck algorithm. It serves here as an illustration of an alternative way for detecting motion.

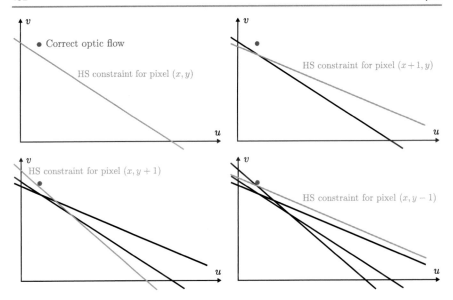

Fig. 4.13 Taking more and more pixels in a local neighbourhood into account by analysing intersection points of lines defined by the optical flow equations for those pixels

4.3.1   Linear Least-Squares Solution

The Lucas–Kanade optical flow algorithm applies a linear least-squares method for analysing the intersections of more than two straight lines.

> **Insert 4.8** (Method of Least Squares) *This method applies in cases of overdetermined equational systems. The task is to find a solution that minimizes the sum of squared errors (called residuals) caused by this solution for each of the equations.*
>
> *For example, we only have n unknowns but m > n linear equations for those; in this case we use a linear least-squares method.*

We start with having only two straight lines (i.e. pixel location p_1 and one adjacent location p_2). Assume that 2D motion at both adjacent pixels p_1 and p_2 is identical and equals $\mathbf{u}$. Also assume that we have two different unit gradients $\mathbf{g}_1^\circ$ and $\mathbf{g}_2^\circ$ at those two pixels.

Consider the optical flow equation $\mathbf{u}^\top \cdot \mathbf{g}^\circ = -\frac{I_t}{\|\mathbf{g}\|_2}$ at both pixels (in the formulation as introduced in Example 4.1). We have two equations in two unknowns u and v for $\mathbf{u} = (u, v)^\top$:

$$\mathbf{u}^\top \cdot \mathbf{g}_1^\circ(p_1) = -\frac{I_t}{\|\mathbf{g}\|_2}(p_1) \tag{4.34}$$

Fig. 4.14 Simple case when considering only two pixels

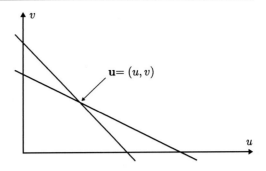

$$\mathbf{u}^{\top} \cdot \mathbf{g}_2^{\circ}(p_2) = -\frac{I_t}{\|\mathbf{g}\|_2}(p_2) \qquad (4.35)$$

Using b_i on the right-hand side, this can also be written in the form of a linear equation system with two unknowns u and v:

$$u g_{x1} + v g_{y1} = b_1 \qquad (4.36)$$

$$u g_{x2} + v g_{y2} = b_2 \qquad (4.37)$$

for unit vectors $\mathbf{g}_1^{\circ} = [g_{x1}, g_{y1}]^{\top}$ and $\mathbf{g}_2^{\circ} = [g_{x2}, g_{y2}]^{\top}$. We write these equations in matrix form:

$$\begin{bmatrix} g_{x1} & g_{y1} \\ g_{x2} & g_{y2} \end{bmatrix} \begin{bmatrix} u \\ v \end{bmatrix} = \begin{bmatrix} b_1 \\ b_2 \end{bmatrix} \qquad (4.38)$$

We can solve this system if the matrix on the left is invertible (i.e. non-singular):

$$\begin{bmatrix} u \\ v \end{bmatrix} = \begin{bmatrix} g_{x1} & g_{y1} \\ g_{x2} & g_{y2} \end{bmatrix}^{-1} \cdot \begin{bmatrix} b_1 \\ b_2 \end{bmatrix} \qquad (4.39)$$

This is the case where we do not have an overdetermined equational system. We have the intersection of two lines defined by the optical flow equations for p_1 and p_2; see Fig. 4.14.

There are errors involved when estimating I_x, I_y, and I_t, and image data are noisy anyway, so it is best to solve for **u** in the least-squares sense by considering a neighbourhood of $k > 2$ pixels, thus having an overdetermined equation system. The neighbourhood should be not too large because we assume that all pixels in this neighbourhood have the same 2D motion **u**. This leads to the overdetermined linear equation system

$$\begin{bmatrix} g_{x1} & g_{y1} \\ g_{x2} & g_{y2} \\ \vdots & \vdots \\ g_{xk} & g_{yk} \end{bmatrix} \begin{bmatrix} u \\ v \end{bmatrix} = \begin{bmatrix} b_1 \\ b_2 \\ \vdots \\ b_k \end{bmatrix} \qquad (4.40)$$

which we write as

$$\underbrace{\mathbf{G}}_{k\times 2}\ \underbrace{\mathbf{u}}_{2\times 1} = \underbrace{\mathbf{B}}_{k\times 1} \qquad (4.41)$$

This system can be solved for $k \geq 2$ in the least-square error sense as follows. First, we make the system square:

$$\mathbf{G}^\top \mathbf{G} \mathbf{u} = \mathbf{G}^\top \mathbf{B} \qquad (4.42)$$

Second, we solve it in the least-square error sense:

$$\mathbf{u} = \left(\mathbf{G}^\top \mathbf{G}\right)^{-1} \mathbf{G}^\top \mathbf{B} \qquad (4.43)$$

Done. $\mathbf{G}^\top \mathbf{G}$ is a 2×2 matrix, while $\mathbf{G}^\top \mathbf{B}$ is a 2×1 matrix. For example, if

$$\mathbf{G}^\top \mathbf{G} = \begin{bmatrix} a & b \\ c & d \end{bmatrix} \qquad (4.44)$$

then

$$\left(\mathbf{G}^\top \mathbf{G}\right)^{-1} = \frac{1}{ad - bc} \begin{bmatrix} d & -b \\ -c & a \end{bmatrix} \qquad (4.45)$$

The rest is simple matrix multiplication.

4.3.2   Original Algorithm and Algorithm with Weights

Compared to the Horn–Schunck algorithm, the mathematics here was pretty simple. We discuss the original algorithm and a variant of it.

Original Lucas–Kanade Optical Flow Algorithm   The basic algorithm is as follows:
1. Decide for a local neighbourhood of k pixels and apply this uniformly in each frame.
2. At frame t, estimate I_x, I_y, and I_t.
3. For each pixel location p in Frame t, obtain the equation system (4.40) and solve it in the least-squares sense as defined in (4.43).
   It might be of benefit to estimate the used derivatives on smoothed images, for example with a Gaussian filter with a small standard deviation such as $\sigma = 1.5$.

Weights for Contributing Pixels   We weight all the k contributing pixels by positive weights w_i for $i = 1, \ldots, k$. In general, the *current pixel* has the maximum weight, and all the adjacent pixels (contributing to those k pixels) have smaller weights. Let $\mathbf{W} = \text{diag}[w_1, \ldots, w_k]$ be the $k \times k$ diagonal matrix of those weights. A diagonal matrix satisfies

$$\mathbf{W}^\top \mathbf{W} = \mathbf{W}\mathbf{W} = \mathbf{W}^2 \qquad (4.46)$$

The task is now to solve the equation

$$\mathbf{WGu} = \mathbf{WB} \qquad (4.47)$$

instead of (4.41) before; the right-hand sides need to be weighted in the same way as the left-hand sides. The solution is derived in steps of matrix manipulations as follows:

$$(\mathbf{WG})^\top \mathbf{WGu} = (\mathbf{WG})^\top \mathbf{WB} \qquad (4.48)$$

$$\mathbf{G}^\top \mathbf{W}^\top \mathbf{WGu} = \mathbf{G}^\top \mathbf{W}^\top \mathbf{WB} \qquad (4.49)$$

$$\mathbf{G}^\top \mathbf{WWGu} = \mathbf{G}^\top \mathbf{WWB} \qquad (4.50)$$

$$\mathbf{G}^\top \mathbf{W}^2 \mathbf{Gu} = \mathbf{G}^\top \mathbf{W}^2 \mathbf{B} \qquad (4.51)$$

and thus

$$\mathbf{u} = \left[\mathbf{G}^\top \mathbf{W}^2 \mathbf{G} \right]^{-1} \mathbf{G}^\top \mathbf{W}^2 \mathbf{B} \qquad (4.52)$$

The meaning of those transforms is that we again have a 2×2 matrix $\mathbf{G}^\top \mathbf{W}^2 \mathbf{G}$, for which we can use the inverse for calculating $\mathbf{u}$ at the current pixel.

Compared to the original algorithm, we only need to change Step 3 into the following:

3. For each pixel location p in Frame t, obtain the equation system (4.47) and solve it in the least-squares sense as defined in (4.52).

Figure 4.15 illustrates results for the original Lucas–Kanade algorithm for a 5×5 neighbourhood. When solving by using (4.43), we only accept solutions for cases where the eigenvalues (see Insert 2.9) of the matrix $\mathbf{G}^\top \mathbf{G}$ are greater than a chosen threshold. By doing so we filter out "noisy" results.

The matrix $\mathbf{G}^T \mathbf{G}$ is a 2×2 (symmetric positive definite) matrix; it has two eigenvalues λ_1 and λ_2. Let $0 \leq \lambda_1 \leq \lambda_2$. Assume a threshold $T > 0$. We "accept" the solution provided by (4.43) if $\lambda_1 \geq T$. This leads to a sparse optical flow field as illustrated in Fig. 4.15. Note that those few shown vectors appear to be close to the true displacement in general.

4.4   The BBPW Algorithm

The *BBPW algorithm* extends the Horn–Schunck algorithm in an attempt to improve the results, especially with regards to large displacements, and also attempts to overcome limitations defined by ICA. Furthermore, the use of squares in optimization allows outliers to have a significant impact; thus, an L_1 optimization approach is used (approximately) instead of the L_2 optimization approach of the Horn–Schunck algorithm.

Fig. 4.15 We refer to the same two subsequent frames of a recorded image sequence as shown in Fig. 4.5. The optical flow calculated with original Lucas–Kanade algorithm; $k = 25$ for a 5×5 neighbourhood

> **Insert 4.9** (Origin of the BBPW Algorithm) *This algorithm was published in* [T. Brox, A. Bruhn, N. Papenberg, and J. Weickert. High accuracy optical flow estimation based on a theory for warping. In Proc. European Conf. Computer Vision, vol. 4, pp. 25–36, 2004].

This section describes the assumptions made, explains the energy function used, and provides a brief information about the basic theory used in the algorithm; a detailed presentation of this algorithm is beyond the scope of this textbook. The section illustrates the progress in the field of optical flow algorithms since the year when the Horn–Schunck and Lucas–Kanade algorithms have been published.

4.4.1   Used Assumptions and Energy Function

The intensity constancy assumption (ICA) is in the considered context formally represented by $I(x, y, t) = I(x + u, y + v, t + 1)$, with u and v being the translations in x- and y-directions, respectively, during a δt time interval. Linearized, this became the *Horn–Schunck constraint* $I_x u + I_y u + I_t = 0$. Intensity constancy is not true for outdoor scenarios; as a result, Horn–Schunck or Lucas–Kanade algorithms often work poorly for pixel changes over, say, five to ten pixels (i.e. for 2D motion vectors that are not "short" in the sense of the only used linear term of the Taylor expansion).

Gradient Constancy   The assumption of *constancy of intensity gradients over displacements* (GCA) is represented as

$$\nabla_{x,y} I(x, y, t) = \nabla_{x,y} I(x + u, y + v, t + 1) \tag{4.53}$$

where $\nabla_{x,y}$ is limited, as before, to the derivatives in the x- and y-directions only; it does not include the temporal derivative. As already discussed in Chap. 1, gradient information is considered to be fairly robust against intensity changes.

Smoothness Assumption   Using only ICA and GCA does not provide sufficient information for having optical flow uniquely identified; we need to involve adjacent pixels and also to introduce some consistency into the calculated flow vector field.

Care needs to be taken at object boundaries. Motion discontinuities should not be fully excluded; piecewise smoothing appears as an option for avoiding the flow vectors from outside an object affect the flow field within the object, and vice versa.

A first Draft of an Energy Formula   In the following draft of the error or energy function we still follow the ICA (but without going to the Horn–Schunck constraint, thus also avoiding the approximation in the Taylor expansion), but combined with the GCA. We consider pixel locations (x, y, t) in the frame $I(\cdot, \cdot, t)$, optical flow vectors $\mathbf{w} = (u, v, 1)^\top$, which also contain the third component for going from an image plane at time t to the plane at time $t + 1$, and use the gradient $\nabla = (\partial_x, \partial_y, \partial_t)$ in the 3D space. Equation (4.9) turns now into

$$E_{data}(f) = \sum_\Omega \Big(\big[I(x + u, y + v, t + 1) - I(x, y, t) \big]^2$$

$$+ \lambda_1 \cdot \big[\nabla_{x,y} I(x + u, y + v, t + 1) - \nabla_{x,y} I(x, y, t) \big]^2 \Big) \tag{4.54}$$

where $\lambda_1 > 0$ is some weight to be specified. For the smoothness term, we basically stay with (4.10), but now for spatio-temporal gradients in the 3D space and in the formulation

$$E_{smooth}(f) = \sum_\Omega \big[\|\nabla u\|_2^2 + \|\nabla v\|_2^2 \big] \tag{4.55}$$

Altogether, the task would be to identify a labelling function f that assigns optical flow u and v to each pixel in $I(\cdot, \cdot, t)$ such that the sum

$$E_{total}(f) = E_{data}(f) + \lambda_2 \cdot E_{smooth}(f) \tag{4.56}$$

is minimized for some weight $\lambda_2 > 0$. As in (4.11), (4.56) still uses quadratic penalizers in the L_2 sense, thus defining a TVL2 optimization problem. Outliers are given too much weight in this scheme for estimating optic flow.

Regularized L_1 Total Variation   A move away from L_2-optimization towards L_1-optimization is by using the function

$$\Psi(s^2) = \sqrt{s^2 + \varepsilon} \approx |s| \tag{4.57}$$

rather than $|s|$ itself in the energy function. This leads to a more robust energy function where we still may consider continuous derivatives at $s = 0$, even for a small positive constant ε. The constant ε can be, for example, equal 10^{-6} (i.e., a very small value). There are no continuous derivatives for $|s|$ at $s = 0$, but we need those for applying an error-minimization scheme.

The function $\Psi(s^2) = \sqrt{s^2 + \varepsilon}$, an increasing concave function, is applied over the error-function terms in (4.54) and (4.55) to reduce the influence of outliers. This defines a *regularized total-variation term* in the L_1 sense. We obtain the energy terms

$$E_{data}(f) = \sum_{\Omega} \Psi \left(\left[I(x+u, y+v, t+1) - I(x, y, t) \right]^2 \right.$$

$$\left. + \lambda_1 \cdot \left[\nabla_{x,y} I(x+u, y+v, t+1) - \nabla_{x,y} I(x, y, t) \right]^2 \right) \quad (4.58)$$

and

$$E_{smooth}(f) = \sum_{\Omega} \Psi \left((\nabla u)^2 + (\nabla v)^2 \right) \quad (4.59)$$

The way for obtaining the total energy remains as specified by (4.56).

4.4.2 Outline of the Algorithm

We have to find a labelling f that minimizes the error function E_{total} as defined in (4.56), using the error terms of (4.58) and (4.59).

Minimizing a nonlinear function such as E_{total} is a difficult problem. When searching for the global minimum, a minimization algorithm could become trapped in a local minimum.

Insert 4.10 (Lagrange and the Euler–Lagrange Equations) *J.-L. Lagrange (1736–1813) was an Italian mathematician. Euler (see Insert 1.3), and Lagrange developed a general way for finding a function f that minimizes a given energy functional E(f). Assuming that f is not just a unary function, the provided solution is a system of differential equations.*

Euler–Lagrange Equations   Let Ψ' be the derivative of Ψ with respect to its only argument. The *divergence* div denotes the sum of derivatives, in our case below the sum of three partial derivatives, being the components of

$$\nabla u = \left[\frac{\partial u}{\partial x}, \frac{\partial u}{\partial y}, \frac{\partial u}{\partial t} \right]^{\top} \quad (4.60)$$

A minimizing labelling function f for the functional $E_{total}(f)$ has to satisfy the following *Euler–Lagrange equations*. We do not provide details about the derivation of those equations using total-variation calculus and just state the resulting equations:

$$\Psi'\left(I_t^2 + \lambda_1\left(I_{xt}^2 + I_{yt}^2\right)\right) \cdot \left(I_x I_t + \lambda_1\left(I_{xx}I_{xt} + I_{xy}I_{yt}\right)\right)$$
$$- \lambda_2 \cdot \mathrm{div}\left(\Psi'\left(\|\nabla u\|^2 + \|\nabla v\|^2\right)\nabla u\right) = 0 \qquad (4.61)$$

$$\Psi'\left(I_t^2 + \lambda_1\left(I_{xt}^2 + I_{yt}^2\right)\right) \cdot \left(I_y I_t + \lambda_1\left(I_{yy}I_{yt} + I_{xy}I_{xt}\right)\right)$$
$$- \lambda_2 \cdot \mathrm{div}\left(\Psi'\left(\|\nabla u\|^2 + \|\nabla v\|^2\right)\nabla v\right) = 0 \qquad (4.62)$$

As before, I_x, I_y, and I_t are the derivatives of $I(\cdot, \cdot, t)$ with respect to pixel coordinates or time, and I_{xx}, I_{xy}, and so forth are 2nd-order derivatives. All those derivatives can be considered to be constants, to be calculated based on approximations in the sequence of frames. Thus, both equations are of the form

$$c_1 - \lambda_2 \cdot \mathrm{div}\left(\Psi'\left(\|\nabla u\|^2 + \|\nabla v\|^2\right)\nabla u\right) = 0 \qquad (4.63)$$

$$c_2 - \lambda_2 \cdot \mathrm{div}\left(\Psi'\left(\|\nabla u\|^2 + \|\nabla v\|^2\right)\nabla v\right) = 0 \qquad (4.64)$$

The solution of these equations for u and v at any pixel $p \in \Omega$ can be supported by using a pyramidal approach.

Pyramidal Algorithm   It is efficient to use down-sampled copies of the processed frames in an image pyramid (see Sect. 2.2.2) for estimating flow vectors first and then use the results in higher-resolution copies for further refinement. This also supports the identification of long flow vectors. See Fig. 4.16 for an example for a pyramidal implementation of the BBPW algorithm. We use the same colour key as introduced by Fig. 4.4.

4.5   Performance Evaluation of Optical Flow Results

The Horn–Schunck algorithm was a pioneering proposal for calculating optical flow; many other algorithms have been designed till today. Motion analysis is still a very challenging subject in computer vision research.

This section informs briefly about (comparative) performance evaluation techniques for optical flows.

4.5.1   Test Strategies

The Horn–Schunck algorithm is in general moving away from a gradient flow. The following simple example (which allows even manual verification) shows that this is not happening if pixel neighbourhoods do not allow computation of a correct motion.

Fig. 4.16 Visualization of calculated optical flow using a pyramidal BBPW algorithm. *Top*: For frames shown in Fig. 4.5. *Bottom*: For a frame in the sequence queenStreet

Example 4.2 (A Simple Input Example) Assume a 16×16 image I_1 as shown in Fig. 4.17, with $G_{\max} = 7$. It contains a vertical linear edge; the gradient at edge pixels points to the left.

The image I_2 is generated by one of the three motions sketched on the left: (A) is a one-pixel shift $(0,1)$ to the right, (B) is a diagonal shift $(1,1)$, and (C) a one-pixel shift $(-1, 0)$ upward. For simplicity, we assume that additional values (i.e. which are "moving in") on the left are zero and at the bottom identical to the given column values.

This simple example allows you to calculate manually values as produced by the Horn–Schunck algorithm, say in the first three iterations only [(4.22) and (4.22)], using zero as initialization, and simple two-pixel approximation schemes for I_x, I_y, and I_t.

Performance Evaluation of Optic Flow Algorithms For evaluating an optical flow algorithm on real-world image sequences, there are different options, such as the following:

1. Assuming that we have high-speed image sequence recording (say, with more than 100 Hz), it might be possible to use alternating frames for *prediction-error analysis*: estimate optical flow for Frames t and $t + 2$, calculate a virtual image for

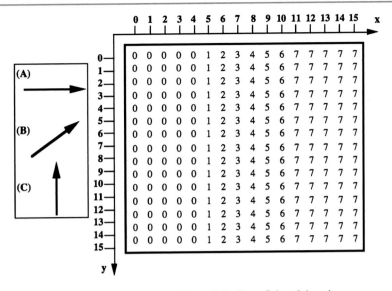

Fig. 4.17 A simple input for a manual experience of the Horn–Schunck iteration

$t + 1$ by interpolating along the calculated flow vectors, and compare the virtual image (e.g. use *normalized cross-correlation*; see insert) with Frame $t + 1$.

2. If there is ground truth available about the actual 2D motion (e.g. such as on the website vision.middlebury.edu/ at Middlebury College for short sequences, or in Set 2 on EISATS for sequences of 100 frames or more), the evaluation of optical flow results may be based on *error measures* (see below) by comparing true (well, modulo measurement errors when generating the ground truth) and estimated vectors.

3. There is also the option to compare results of multiple methods, for understanding which methods generate similar results and which methods differ in their results.

4. A method can be evaluated on real-world data by introducing incrementally different degrees of various kinds of noise into the input data for understanding robustness in results. Noise might be, for example, intensity variations, Gaussian noise, or blurring.

5. Known scene geometry and approximately known camera motion can be used to compare the results with expected flow fields. For example, the camera may move steadily towards a wall.

Insert 4.11 (Normalized Cross-Correlation) *Assume two images I and J of identical size. The normalized cross-correlation (NCC) compares both images and provides one scalar response:*

$$M_{NCC}(I, J) = \frac{1}{|\Omega|} \sum_{(x,y) \in \Omega} \frac{[I(x, y) - \mu_I][J(x, y) - \mu_J]}{\sigma_I \sigma_J}$$

μ_I and μ_J denote the means, and σ_I and σ_J the standard deviations of I and J, respectively. The larger $M_{NCC}(I, J)$, the more similar both images are.

Due to normalizing with respect to mean and variance, the images I and J may differ in these two values and can be still very similar. This is in particular of interest when comparing images that do not follow the ICA, which can happen for two subsequently recorded frames in an image sequence.

The NCC can also be used to compare a small image (the template) with image windows of the same size of the template in a larger image. OpenCV provides several methods for this kind of template matching, also including variants of normalized cross-correlation.

4.5.2 Error Measures for Available Ground Truth

Ground truth for motion analysis is difficult to obtain, especially for real-world sequences. Synthesized sequences are an alternative option. Physics-based image rendering can lead to "fairly realistic" synthetic image sequences, even with an option to study behaviour of optical flow algorithms for varying parameters (something that cannot be done for recorded real-world sequences).

Insert 4.12 (Ground Truth) *Images recorded in an airplane are often used to estimate distances on the ground, or even for 3D reconstruction of whole landscapes or cities. For evaluating results, it was common practice to identify landmarks on the ground, such as corners of buildings, and to measure distances or positions of those landmarks. This was the ground truth, to be compared with the values calculated based on the images recorded in an airplane.*

The term is now in general use for denoting measured data, considered to be fairly accurate, thus useful for evaluating algorithms supposed to provide the same data.

Figure 4.18 illustrates provided ground truth for a synthetic image sequence (of 100 frames) and results of a pyramidal Horn–Schunck algorithm. Additionally to the used colour key, we also show sparse vectors in the ground-truth image and result image. This is redundant information (and similar to a needle map, as shown in Fig. 4.12) but helps a viewer to understand occurring motions. Also, the coloured frame around the visualized flow vectors shows colour values corresponding to all the possible directions.

Fig. 4.18 *Top*: Two input images (Frame 1, Set2Seq1, and Frame 2 from the first sequence of Set 2 of EISATS). *Bottom, left*: Ground truth as provided for this sequence, using a colour key for visualizing local displacements. *Bottom, right*: Result of a pyramidal Horn–Schunck algorithm

Error Measures in the Presence of Ground Truth We have the calculated flow $\mathbf{u} = (u, v)$ and flow $\mathbf{u}^\star = (u^\star, v^\star)$ provided as a ground truth. The L_2 *endpoint error*

$$E_{ep2}\left(\mathbf{u}, \mathbf{u}^\star\right) = \sqrt{\left(u - u^\star\right)^2 + \left(v - v^\star\right)^2}$$

or the L_1 *endpoint error*

$$E_{ep1}\left(\mathbf{u}, \mathbf{u}^\star\right) = |u - u^\star| + |v - v^\star|$$

compare both vectors in 2D space.

The *angular error* between spatio-temporal directions of the estimated flow and ground truth at a pixel location p (not included in the formula) is as follows:

$$E_{ang}\left(\mathbf{u}, \mathbf{u}^\star\right) = \arccos\left(\frac{\mathbf{u}^\top \cdot \mathbf{u}^\star}{|\mathbf{u}|\, |\mathbf{u}^\star|}\right) \tag{4.65}$$

where $\mathbf{u} = (u, v, 1)$ is the estimated optical flow, but now extended by one coordinate (the 1 corresponds to the distance between images recorded at time slots t and $t + 1$) into the 3D space, and $\mathbf{u}^\star = (u_t, v_t, 1)$ is the flow provided as a ground truth, also extended into the 3D space. This error measure evaluates accuracy in both direction and magnitude in the 3D space.

Such error measures are applied to all pixels in a frame, which allows us to calculate the *mean angular error*, the *mean L_2 endpoint error*, and so forth, also with their standard deviations.

4.6 Exercises

4.6.1 Programming Exercises

Exercise 4.1 (Variations of the Horn–Schunck Algorithm) Implement the Horn–Schunck algorithm for optical flow calculation. Of course, there are already programs available for free use, but implement your own version.

Test the algorithm on pairs of images showing a scene with only minor differences in between; motion should be limited to distances of 5–6 pixels at most.

Use both mentioned strategies for initialization of u- and v-values (i.e. just 0 or the closest point Q to the origin O in the velocity space; see Example 4.1). Use also two different approximation schemes for I_x, I_y, and I_t. Discuss the impacts of those different options on your flow results.

After each iteration step $n + 1$, calculate the mean of all changes in u- and v-values compared to the previous step n. Display those changes over the number of iterations. Do you have monotonically decreasing values? Would it be possible to use a threshold for those changes for defining a stop criterion for the algorithm?

Discuss how many iterations you consider as being sufficient for your input sequences and how this is influenced by the used initialization scheme and the selected approximation schemes for I_x, I_y, and I_t.

Finally, compare with the results simply obtained by using (4.33). With this equation you calculate the gradient flow, without using any smoothness constraint for taking adjacent values into account.

Exercise 4.2 (Variations of the Lucas–Kanade Algorithm) Implement the Lucas–Kanade algorithm for optical flow calculation. Of course, there are already programs available for free use, but implement your own version.

Test the algorithm on pairs of images showing a scene with only minor differences in between; motion should be limited to distances of 5–6 pixels at most.

Decide for an approximation scheme for I_x, I_y, and I_t and implement the following variants:

1. Use a 3×3 neighbourhood without weights.
2. Use a 5×5 neighbourhood without weights.
3. Use a 5×5 neighbourhood with weights sampled from a Gauss function.

Discuss your findings (e.g. regarding accuracy, differences in results, computation time) for the used real-world test data.

Exercise 4.3 (Performance Evaluation for Optical Flow Algorithms Available in OpenCV) Use the error measures of endpoint error and angular error for evaluating optical flow algorithms as available in OpenCV on image sequences (of at least 100 frames each) with available ground truth:

1. Use synthetic sequences as, for example, available in Set 2 on EISATS.
2. Use real-world sequences as, for example, available on the KITTI Benchmark Suite.

For a comparison, run the algorithms on challenging input sequences (without ground truth; thus, just for visual inspection) as, for example, made available for the Heidelberg Robust Vision Challenge at ECCV 2012. Summarize your findings in a report.

Exercise 4.4 (Optical Flow Algorithms on Residual Images with Respect to Smoothing) Run optical flow algorithms as available in OpenCV on real-world image sequences (of at least 100 frames each) for comparing

- the results on the original sequences with
- the results on sequences calculated as the residuals with respect to smoothing the original sequences.

Use different iteration steps for generating the residual images. For example, apply a 3×3 box filter for smoothing and do the recursion to up to $n = 30$. Which number of iterations can you recommend for the used test sequences?

Exercise 4.5 (Tests for Known Geometry or Motion) Select your optical flow algorithm of choice and test it on recorded sequences using the following recording scenarios:

1. Slide the recording camera orthogonally to a static scene such that calculated motion fields can be studied with respect to camera translation.
2. Move the recording camera towards a textured wall, for example in a vehicle, or mounted on a robot, such that calculated motion fields can be studied with respect to the expected circular 2D motion.
3. Record a metronome with a moving pendulum (you may also use sequences from Set 8 of EISATS).

Recorded sequences need to be of length 100 frames at least.

Try to optimize the parameters of your algorithm for these two kinds of input sequences.

4.6.2 Non-programming Exercises

Exercise 4.6 Calculate the coefficients of the Taylor expansion of the function

$$I(x, y, t) = 2x^2 + xy^2 + xyt + 5t^3$$

up to the 3rd-order derivatives.

Exercise 4.7 Verify (4.13), (4.14), and (4.15).

Exercise 4.8 An initialization by zero in the Horn–Schunck algorithm would not be possible if the resulting initial u- and v-values would also be zero. Verify that this is not happening in general (i.e. if there exists motion) at the start of the iteration of this algorithm.

Exercise 4.9 Use the provided Example 4.2 for manual calculations of the first three iterations of the Horn–Schunck algorithm, using zero as initialization, and simple two-pixel approximation schemes for I_x, I_y, and I_t.

Exercise 4.10 Verify (4.45).

Exercise 4.11 For the Lucas–Kanade algorithm, show that the matrix inversion in (4.43) fails if the image gradients in the selected neighbourhood are parallel to each other. Is this possible to happen for real image data? Check a linear algebra book about how to tackle such singularities in order to get a least-square solution.

Image Segmentation

5

In this chapter we explain special approaches for image binarization and segmentation of still images or video frames, in the latter case with attention to ensuring temporal consistency. We discuss mean-shift segmentation in detail. We also provide a general view on image segmentation as (another) labelling example in computer vision, introduce segmentation this way from an abstract point of view, and discuss belief-propagation solutions for this labelling framework.

Image segmentation partitions an image into regions, called *segments*, for defined purposes of further image analysis, improved efficiency of image compression, or just for visualization effects. See Fig. 5.1. Mathematically, we *partition* the carrier Ω into a finite number of segments S_i, $i = 1, \ldots, n$, such that

1. $S_i \neq \emptyset$ for all $i \in \{1, \ldots, n\}$
2. $\bigcup_{i=1}^{n} S_i = \Omega$
3. $S_i \cap S_j = \emptyset$ for all $i, j \in \{1, \ldots, n\}$ with $i \neq j$

Image segmentation creates *segments* of connected pixels by analysing some similarity criteria, possibly supported by detecting pixels that show some dissimilarity with adjacent pixels. Dissimilarity creates *borders* between segments; see Sect. 2.4.1. Ideally, both approaches might support each other. Unfortunately, edges rarely describe simple curves circumscribing a segment; they are typically just arcs. It is a challenge to map such arcs into simple curves.

Segmentation aims at identifying "meaningful" segments that can be used for describing the contents of an image, such as a segment for "background", segments for "objects", or particular object categories (e.g. "eye", "mouth", or "hair", as illustrated by Fig. 5.2, bottom, middle, and right; zooming-in helps to see the different degrees of segmentation in this figure).

5.1 Basic Examples of Image Segmentation

Figure 5.3 illustrates an application of image analysis where the initial step, image segmentation, can be reduced to binarization, aiming at creating black image regions defining *objects* (being foot prints in this application), and white image re-

R. Klette, *Concise Computer Vision*, Undergraduate Topics in Computer Science, DOI 10.1007/978-1-4471-6320-6_5, © Springer-Verlag London 2014

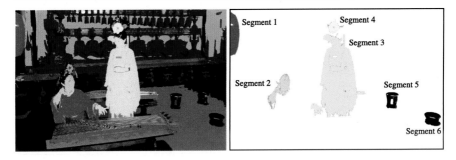

Fig. 5.1 *Left*: The image Yan partitioned into segments. *Right*: Six segments of this partition

Fig. 5.2 *Top*: The image AnnieYukiTim (*left*) mapped into a (nearly binary) image defined by Winnemöller stylization. Connected dark or bright regions define segments. *Bottom*: Segmentation of the image Rocio (*left*) by mean-shift for radii $r = 12$ (*middle*) and $r = 24$ (*right*), see text for explanations, showing a window only

gions defining segments of the *background*.[1] Monochrome patterns of footprints of small animals are collected on inked tracking cards, with no need to understand intensity variations within dark (inked) regions. The whole image analysis procedure aims at automatically identifying the specie that created a given footprint pattern.

---

[1]Figure from [B.-S. Shin, J. Russell, Y. Zheng, and R. Klette. Improved segmentation for footprint recognition of small mammals. In Proc. IVCNZ, an ACM publication, Nov. 2012].

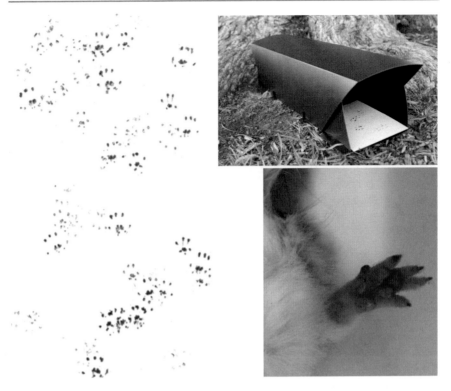

Fig. 5.3 The image RattusRattus collected in New Zealand for environmental surveillance, to be segmented into object and non-object pixels. *Left*: An Example of footprints on a tracking card. *Right, top*: The tracking tunnel for collecting footprints. *Right, bottom*: A foot of a ship rat (Rattus rattus)

This section explains basic examples of image segmentation procedures, namely one adaptive binarization method, one image stylization method where simple post-processing also leads to binarization, and concepts for growing segments based on selected seed pixels.

5.1.1   Image Binarization

Image binarization applies often just one global threshold T for mapping a scalar image I into a binary image

$$J(x, y) = \begin{cases} 0 & \text{if } I(x, y) < T \\ 1 & \text{otherwise} \end{cases} \qquad (5.1)$$

The global threshold can be identified by an optimization strategy aiming at creating "large" connected regions and at reducing the number of small-sized regions, called *artifacts*.

1: Compute histogram H_I for $u = 0, \ldots, G_{max}$;
2: Let T_0 be the increment for potential thresholds; $u = T_0$; $T = u$; and $S_{max} = 0$;
3: **while** $u < G_{max}$ **do**
4:       Compute $c_I(u)$ and $\mu_i(u)$ for $i = 1, 2$;
5:       Compute $\sigma_b^2(u) = c_I(u)[1 - c_I(u)][\mu_i(u) - \mu_2(u)]^2$;
6:       **if** $\sigma_b^2(u) > S_{max}$ **then**
7:            $S_{max} = \sigma_b^2(u)$ and $T = u$;
8:       **end if**
9:       Set $u = u + T_0$
10: **end while**

Fig. 5.4 Otsu's algorithm. Histogram values are used for updating in Step 4. Step 5 is defined by (5.2)

Insert 5.1 (Origin of Otsu Binarization) *This binarization algorithm has been published in* [N. Otsu. A threshold selection method from grey-level histograms. IEEE Trans. Systems Man Cybernetics, vol. 9, pp. 62–66, 1979] .

Otsu Binarization   The method uses the grey-value histogram of the given image I as input and aims at providing the best threshold in the sense that the "overlap" between two classes, sets of object and background pixels, is minimized (i.e. by finding the "best balance").

Otsu's algorithm selects a threshold that maximizes the *between-class variance* σ_b^2 defined as a regular variance computed for class means. In case of two classes, the formula is especially simple:

$$\sigma_b^2 = P_1(\mu_1 - \mu)^2 + P_2(\mu_2 - \mu)^2 = P_1 P_2 (\mu_1 - \mu_2)^2 \qquad (5.2)$$

where P_1 and P_2 denote the class probabilities.

A chosen threshold u , $0 < u < G_{max}$, defines "dark" object pixels with $I(p) \leq u$ and "bright" background pixels with $u < I(p)$. Let $\mu_i(u)$, $i = 1, 2$, be the means of object and background classes. Let c_I be the relative cumulative histogram of an image I as defined in (1.8). The probabilities P_1 and P_2 are approximated by $c_I(u)$ and $1 - c_I(u)$, respectively; they are the total numbers of pixels in each class divided by the cardinality $|\Omega|$.

Otsu's algorithm is given in Fig. 5.4; it simply tests all the selected candidates for an optimum threshold T.

Figure 5.5 shows results when binarizing a window in an image of footprints as shown in Fig. 5.3. Object regions have holes if thresholds are too low, and regions merge if thresholds are too high. Otsu's method generates the threshold $T = 162$.

Winnemöller Stylization   Section 2.4 explained the difference of Gaussians (DoG) edge detector. We provide here an extension of this edge detector for non-photorealistic rendering (NPR) of taken photos. The described *Winnemöller styliza-tion* defines basically image binarization.

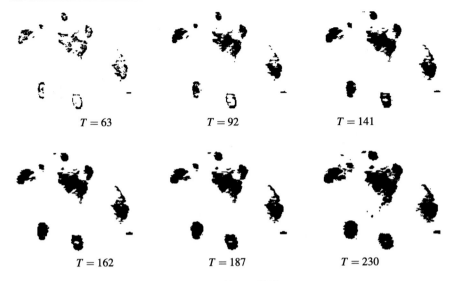

$T = 63$ $T = 92$ $T = 141$

$T = 162$ $T = 187$ $T = 230$

Fig. 5.5 Examples for different thresholds $T \in \{0, \ldots, 255\}$

Insert 5.2 (Origin of Winnemöller Stylization) *This binarization algorithm has been published in* [H. Winnemöller. XDoG: Advanced image stylization with extended difference-of-Gaussians. In Proc. ACM Symp. Non-Photorealistic Animation Rendering, pp. 147–155, 2011] .

We recall (2.40) defining the DoG, but by having $L(x, y, \sigma)$ on the left-hand side:

$$L(x, y, \sigma) = L(x, y, a\sigma) + D_{\sigma,a}(x, y) \qquad (5.3)$$

Here, σ is the scale, and $a > 1$ a scaling factor. Thus, $D_{\sigma,a}(x, y)$ provides those high-frequency components to be added to $L(x, y, a\sigma)$ for obtaining a less-smoothed image $L(x, y, \sigma)$.

The DoG approach is taken one step further by considering

$$D_{\sigma,a,\tau}(x, y) = L(x, y, \sigma) - \tau \cdot L(x, y, a\sigma)$$
$$= (1 - \tau) \cdot L(x, y, \sigma) + \tau \cdot D_{\sigma,a}(x, y) \qquad (5.4)$$

The parameter τ controls the sensitivity of the edge detector. Smaller values of τ mean that edges become "less important" with the benefit that less noise is detected. This modified DoG is then used for defining

$$E_{\sigma,a,\tau}^{\varepsilon,\phi}(x, y) = \begin{cases} 0 & \text{if } D_{\sigma,a,\tau}(x, y) > \varepsilon \\ \tanh(\phi \cdot (D_{\sigma,a,\tau}(x, y) - \varepsilon)) & \text{otherwise} \end{cases} \qquad (5.5)$$

Fig. 5.6 *Left*: The input image `MissionBay`. *Right*: The result of the Winnemöller binarization

Resulting real values are linearly mapped into the range $\{0, 1, \ldots, G_{max}\}$, thus defining an image $E_{\sigma,a,\tau}^{\varepsilon,\phi}$. This image is the result of the Winnemöller stylization algorithm. The function tanh is monotonously increasing for arguments between 0 and 1, with values in the interval $[0, 1)$.

The parameter ε defines thresholding; the use of tanh and ϕ contributes to a softening of this thresholding; by increasing ϕ we sharpen the thresholding.

For an example of Winnemöller stylization, see Fig. 5.2, top, right. Another example is shown in Fig. 5.6, right.

The values in the image $E_{\sigma,a,\tau}^{\varepsilon,\phi}$ are typically either close to 0 (i.e. Black) or close to G_{max} (i.e. White), with only a relatively small number of pixels having values in-between. Thus, a threshold T at about $G_{max}/2$ and (3.48) produce a binary image (with a visually nearly unnoticeable difference to stylized images as in Fig. 5.2, top, right, or in Fig. 5.6, right), if needed for image analysis or visualization purposes.

5.1.2 Segmentation by Seed Growing

For segment generation in grey-level or colour images, we may start at one *seed pixel* $(x, y, I(x, y))$ and add recursively adjacent pixels that satisfy a "similarity criterion" with pixels contained in the so-far grown region around the seed pixel. This can be repeated until all the pixels in an image are contained in one of the generated segments.

An important question is: How to make this process independent upon the selected seed pixels, such that the image data define the resulting segmentation and not the chosen sequence of seed pixels?

Insert 5.3 (Equivalence Relation and Equivalence Classes) *Let R be a binary relation defined on a set S. The notations aRb, $(a, b) \in R$, and $a \in R(b)$ are all equivalent; they denote that an element $a \in S$ is in relation R to $b \in S$. For example, consider 4-adjacency A_4 on Ω; then $p \in A_4(q)$ denotes that the*

*pixel location $p \in \Omega$ is 4-adjacent to the pixel location $q \in \Omega$, and we can
also express this by $p A_4 q$ or $(p, q) \in A_4$.*

A relation R is called an equivalence relation on S iff it satisfies the following three properties on S:

1. *For any $a \in S$, we have that $a R a$ (i.e. R is reflexive on S).*
2. *For any $a, b \in S$, if $a R b$, then also $b R a$ (i.e. R is symmetric on S).*
3. *For any $a, b, c \in S$, if $a R b$ and $b R c$, then also $a R c$ (i.e. R is transitive on S).*

For example, A_4 is not an equivalence relation on Ω; it is symmetric but not reflexive and also not transitive: from $p A_4 q$ and $q A_4 p$ it does not follow that we also have $p A_4 p$. With $N_4 = A_4(p) \cup \{p\}$ we still do not have an equivalence relation; here we have reflexivity $p N_4 p$ and symmetry but no transitivity.

The relation C_4 of 4-connectedness in a binary image I with $p C_4 q$ iff there is a path $p = p_0, p_1, \ldots, p_n = q$ such that $p_i \in N_4(p_{i-1})$ and $I(p_i) = I(p_{i-1})$ for $i = 1, \ldots, n$ is an equivalence relation; here we also have transitivity.

Let R be an equivalence relation on S. Then, for any $a \in S$, $R(a)$ defines an equivalence class of S. If $b \in R(a)$, then $R(b) = R(a)$. The set of all equivalence classes of S partitions S into pairwise-disjoint non-empty sets.

Equivalence Relation on Pixel Features   For an image I, we have or calculate feature vectors $\mathbf{u}(p)$ at pixel locations p. For example, for a colour image I, we already have the RGB vector. For a grey-level image, we can calculate the gradient vectors ∇I at p and the local mean or variance at p for forming vector $\mathbf{u}(p)$. The grey-level alone at pixel location p is a 1D feature vector.

Let $\equiv$ be an equivalence relation on the set of feature vectors $\mathbf{u}$, partitioning all the possible feature vectors into equivalence classes.

Segments Defined by an Equivalence Relation for Features   Two pixel positions p and q are *I-equivalent* iff $\mathbf{u}(p) \equiv \mathbf{u}(q)$. This defines an equivalence relation on the carrier Ω, in dependency of the given image I. The I-equivalence classes $C \subseteq \Omega$ for this relation are not yet the segments of I with respect to relation $\equiv$. Identity of features at p and q does not yet mean that p and q are in the same segment.

Let $C_{\mathbf{u}}$ be the set of all $p \in \Omega$ such that $I(p) \equiv \mathbf{u}$. Each I-equivalence class $C_{\mathbf{u}}$ is a union of (say, 4-, 8-, or K-connected) regions, and these regions are the *segments*.

Observation 5.1   *The outcome of segmentation by seed growing does not depend on selected seed pixels as long as seed growing follows an equivalence relation defined for image features.*

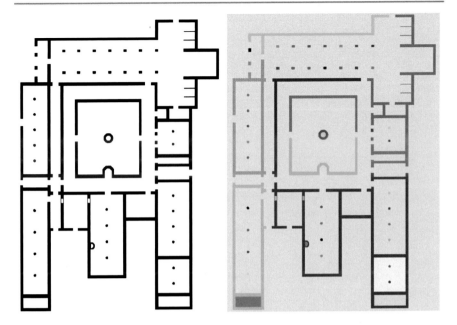

Fig. 5.7 *Left:* An architectural plan Monastry of the monastery at Bebenhausen (Tübingen, Germany). How many black or white segments? *Right:* All black segments are labelled uniquely by colour values, and all white segments uniquely by grey levels

Example 5.1 (Labelling of Segments) We want to label each resulting segment (i.e. all pixels in this segment) by one unique label. The set of labels can be, for example, a set of numbers or (for visualization) a set of colours. To keep the input image I unaltered, we write the labels into an array of the same size as I.

Figure 5.7 shows on the left a binary image. We take the image values 0 or 1 as our image features, and the value identity is the equivalence relation on the feature set $\{0, 1\}$. There are two I-equivalence classes.

In the given binary image Monastry it does not matter whether we use 4-, 8-, or K-adjacency; the two I-equivalence classes C_1 and C_0 split in each case into the same segments, labelled by different colours or grey levels, respectively, on the right of Fig. 5.7.

Recursive Segment Labelling   We describe an algorithm for assigning the same label to all the pixels in one segment. Let A be the chosen adjacency relation for pixel locations.

Assume that we are at a pixel location p in an image that has not yet been labelled as a member of any segment. We select p as our next seed pixel for initiating a new segment.

Let l_k be a label from the set of possible labels that has not yet been used in I for labelling a segment. A recursive labelling procedure is shown in Fig. 5.8.

Fig. 5.8 A recursive labelling procedure starting at a seed pixel p having a feature vector $\mathbf{u} = \mathbf{u}(p)$, and assigning a label l_k that has not yet been assigned before to pixels in input image I

1: label p with l_k;
2: put p into stack;
3: **while** stack is not empty **do**
4:    pop r out of stack;
5:    **for** $q \in A(r)$ and $\mathbf{u}(q) \equiv \mathbf{u}$ and q not yet labelled **do**
6:       label q with l_k ;
7:       put q into stack;
8:    **end for**
9: **end while**

In this recursive labelling algorithm it may happen that the used stack needs to be as large as about half of the total number of pixels in the given image. Of course, such cases are very unlikely to happen.

After labelling the segment that contains p, we can continue with scanning the image for unlabelled pixels until all the pixels have been labelled.

Example 5.2 (Depth-First Visit of Pixels) Assume binary images with the key "white < black" for K-adjacency (i.e. 4-adjacency for white pixels and 8-adjacency for black pixels). Figure 5.9, left, shows the first 21 visits in this white segment.

The order shown on the right is used for visiting adjacent pixels when the algorithm is used for labelling a segment of white pixels. It would be a clockwise or counter-clockwise order of 8-adjacent pixels when labelling a segment of black pixels.

Example 5.3 (Dependency on Seed Point if not Using an Equivalence Relation) Consider the following seed growing procedure, defined by a parameter $\tau > 0$:
1. We select a seed point p_{seed} in a grey-level or colour image having brightness $B(p_{seed})$. At the beginning, the current segment only contains p_{seed}.
2. In an iteration process, we merge any pixel q to the current segment that is 8-adjacent to a pixel in the current segment, not yet labelled, and has an intensity $B(q)$ satisfying $|B(q) - B(p_{seed})| \leq \tau$.
3. We stop if there is no further not yet labelled pixel q, 8-adjacent to the current segment, which still can be merged.

The used merge criterion in this procedure is not defined by an equivalence relation on the set of brightness values. Accordingly, generated segments depend upon the chosen seed pixel. See Fig. 5.10 for an example.

For explaining the effect, consider a 1×8 image $[0, 1, 2, 3, 4, 5, 6, 7]$, $\tau = 2$, $p_{seed} = 3$, with $B(3) = 2$. This seed produces a region $[0, 1, 2, 3, 4]$. The pixel $p = 4$ is in this region with $B(4) = 3$, and it creates the region $[1, 2, 3, 4, 5]$ if taken as a seed.

The dependency of the seed pixel can be removed by partitioning the range $\{0, \ldots, G_{max}\}$ into intervals $V_0 = \{0, \ldots, \tau\}$, $V_1 = \{\tau + 1, \ldots, 2\tau\}$, $\ldots$, $V_m = \{m\tau + 1, \ldots, G_{max}\}$. When selecting a seed pixel p, the brightness $B(p)$ selects now the interval V_k if $B(p) \in V_k$. Then we only merge the pixels q that have values $B(q)$ in the same interval V_k. This specifies an equivalence relation on the set of

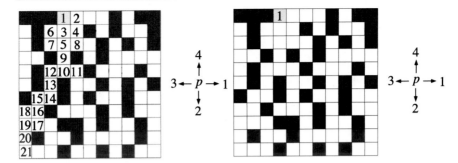

Fig. 5.9 *Left*: The numbers show the order in which the pixels are labelled, assuming a standard scan of the grid (i.e., *left* to *right*, *top* to *bottom*). *Right*: Which order would result if the `stack` in the fill-algorithm in Fig. 5.8 is replaced by a first-in-first-out queue?

Fig. 5.10 Seed growing results for the image `Aussies`, shown in Fig. 1.10, based on the intensity difference τ to a seed pixel. *Left*: Growing a region starting at the shown seed point with $\tau = 15$. *Right*: Also using $\tau = 15$, but a different seed point, which is in the segment produced before

brightness values. The resulting segmentation is independent from the choice of the seed pixel in a segment.

The proposed partition scheme (i.e. disjoint intervals) of the range of feature values can also be adapted for multi-dimensional feature vectors **u**.

Segmentation by Clustering   We briefly mention that, alternatively to seed growing, we can also select multiple seed pixels at the beginning and cluster all pixels in parallel (i.e. considering all the seed pixels at the same time) in the image by assigning them to the "most similar" seed pixel. Chosen seed pixels can be updated during the process such that each new seed pixel shifts into the centroid of the segment produced so far. Such techniques depend typically on the selected seed pixels. See also Exercise 5.9.

5.2   Mean-Shift Segmentation

Mean-shift is a variant of an iterative steepest-ascent method to seek stationary points (i.e. *peaks*) in a density function, which is applicable in many areas of multi-dimensional data analysis, not just in computer vision. This section presents variants of mean-shift algorithms for image segmentation. In this case, the "density function" is the distribution of values in the given image.

Insert 5.4 (Origin of the Mean-Shift Algorithm) *Mean-shift analysis of density functions has been introduced in* [K. Fukunaga and L. D. Hostetler. The estimation of the gradient of a density function, with applications in pattern recognition. IEEE Trans. Information Theory, vol. 21, pp. 32–40, 1975]. *It was shown that the* mean-shift algorithm *converges to local maxima in density functions* (*which correspond to local maxima in values of image channels*).

Mean-shift procedures became popular in computer vision due to the following two papers: [Y. Cheng. Mean shift, mode seeking, and clustering. IEEE Trans. Pattern Analysis Machine Intelligence, vol. 17, pp. 790–799, 1995] *and* [D. Comaniciu and P. Meer. Mean shift: A robust approach toward feature space analysis. IEEE Trans. Pattern Analysis Machine Intelligence, vol. 24, pp. 603–619, 2002]. *Following those two papers, many variants of mean-shift algorithms have been published for computer vision or data analysis in general.*

An implementation of a mean-shift algorithm is available in OpenCV *via the* meanShift *method.*

5.2.1   Examples and Preparation

A grey-level image defines only a 1D feature space by its scalar values. For a better explanation of mean-shift ideas, assume that we have an n-channel image for segmentation, with $n \geq 1$. For example, there are $n = 3$ channels for a colour image I, $n = 2$ gradient channels

$$\nabla I(p) = \mathbf{grad}\, I(p) = \left[\frac{\partial I}{\partial x}(p), \frac{\partial I}{\partial y}(p) \right]^{\top} \qquad (5.6)$$

in case of a scalar image I, $n = 2$ channels (mean, standard deviation) in case of a scalar image I (see Fig. 5.11 for an example), or $n = 4$ channels for a scalar image I if combining gradient channels with mean and standard deviation channels. In general, we can add channels representing local properties at a pixel location p.

Means for nD Feature Spaces   The formula in (3.39) for calculating the mean or centroid (x_S, y_S) of a subset S generalizes for features $\mathbf{u} = (u_1, \dots, u_n)$ to

$$u_{i,S} = \frac{m_{0,\dots,0,1,0,\dots,0}(S)}{m_{00\dots0}(S)} \quad \text{for } i \in \{1, \dots, n\} \qquad (5.7)$$

Fig. 5.11 *Left*: The grey-level image `Odense` with $G_{\max} = 255$. *Right*: Visualization of a 2D feature space (i.e. a 2D histogram) for this image defined by the mean and standard deviation in 3×3 pixel neighbourhoods. The bar on the right is the used colour key for shown frequencies

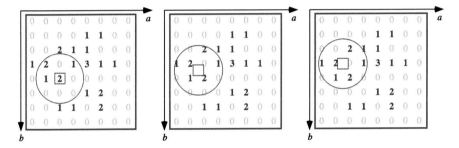

Fig. 5.12 Distribution of 25 calculated local image properties $\mathbf{u} = (a, b)$ in an ab feature space, an initial position of a window (*left*), and its two subsequent moves by mean-shift (*left to right*)

where the moments $m_{0,\dots,0,1,0,\dots,0}(S)$ (with the 1 in the ith position) and $m_{00\dots0}(S)$ (with n zeros) are as defined in (3.36), with using multiplicities of feature vectors as weights instead of image values.

Basic Ideas of Mean-Shift   Assume that we have a 5×5 image I (not shown here) with two channel values a and b, with $0 \le a, b \le 7$. Figure 5.12 illustrates an example of a distribution of 25 feature pairs in the ab feature space (i.e. this is *not* the image plane but a *2D histogram* of image values). Numbers 1, 2, or 3 are the *multiplicities* of occurring feature pairs.

We select a pair $(2, 4)$ as an initial mean with multiplicity 2 (i.e. two pixels in the assumed 5×5 images have $(2, 4)$ as a feature value).

We calculate the mean of a set S defined by radius (say) $r = 1.6$ around $(2, 4)$. This new mean is slightly to the left and up of the previous mean.

We move the circular window defining the current set S such that its centre is now at the new mean. At this location, a new mean $\mathbf{u}_S = (u_{1,S}, u_{2,S})$ for this set S is now slightly up again compared to the previous mean.

Fig. 5.13 Mean-shift moves uphill into the direction of the steepest gradient, here illustrated by five starting points all moving up to the same peak (in general, a local maximum, but here the global maximum),

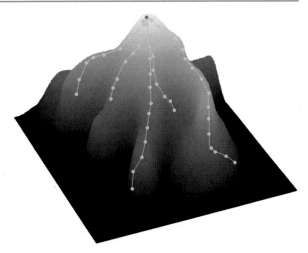

The iteration stops if the distance between the current and the next mean is below a given positive threshold τ (e.g. $\tau = 0.1$); the mean $\mathbf{u}_S$ becomes the *final mean*.

As a result, all pixels in the image having the feature value $(2, 4)$ are *assigned* to this final mean $\mathbf{u}_S$.

We repeat the procedure by starting at other feature pairs. They all define a final mean. The final means being very close to each other can be clustered. The pixels having feature values that are assigned to final means in the same cluster are all value-equivalent; this equivalence class splits into a number of regions (segments).

Mean-Shift Is a Steepest-Ascent Method   Consider feature space multiplicities as being elevations. The shifting window moves up the hill (by following the mean) and has its reference point finally (roughly) at a local *peak*, defining a final mean.

Figure 5.12 is too small for showing this properly; see Fig. 5.13 for a 3D visualization of steepest ascent.

The method depends on two parameters r and τ defining the "region of influence" and the stop criterion, respectively.

Observation 5.2 *Subsequent mean-shift operations of a window move a feature vector towards a local peak in the data distribution of feature vectors, thus implementing a steepest-ascent method by following the local gradient uphill.*

Local Peak Versus Global Mode   For a given set of data, its (global) *mode* is the value that occurs most often in this set. For example, the mode of the set $\{12, 15, 12, 11, 13, 15, 11, 15\}$ is 15. A set of data may have several modes; any value that occurs most often is one mode. For example, the set $\{12, 15, 12, 11, 13, 10, 11, 14\}$ is *bimodal* because there are two modes, 12 and 11. The set $\{16, 15, 12, 17, 13, 10, 11, 14\}$ has no mode because all the values appear equally often. For defining a mode, the data in the set do not need to be numbers; they can be colours, names, or anything else.

A local peak (i.e. a local maximum of density) is not a global mode in general. Modes of the set of feature vectors define global peaks.

When considering density functions, some publications call a local peak also "a mode", but we will not do so for avoiding confusion with the more common mode definition as stated above.

5.2.2 Mean-Shift Model

This subsection presents the mathematics behind the mean-shift algorithm. If you are just interested in the algorithm, then you may skip this subsection and proceed to Sect. 5.2.3.

nD Kernel Function and 1D Profile   Figure 5.12 illustrated the use of a circular window for a uniform inclusion of all feature vectors in this window into the calculation of the new mean. Equation (5.7) is the calculation of the mean in such a case.

For generalizing the calculation of the local mean, we consider the use of a rotation-symmetric nD *kernel function*

$$K(\mathbf{u}) = c_k \cdot k\big(\|\mathbf{u}\|_2^2\big) \tag{5.8}$$

defined at feature points $\mathbf{u}$ in an n-dimensional feature space. It is generated by a 1D *profile* k and a constant c_k such that

$$\int_{\mathbb{R}^n} K(\mathbf{u}) \, d\mathbf{u} = 1 \tag{5.9}$$

The constant c_k normalizes the integration to 1.

The kernel K defines *weights*, similar to local convolutions in images (see Sect. 2.1.2). But now we apply the kernel in feature space. Figure 5.14 illustrates four examples of profiles $k(a)$ for $a \in \mathbb{R}$. The *Epanechnikov function* is defined as follows:

$$k(a) = \frac{3}{4}\big(1 - a^2\big) \quad \text{for } -1 < a < 1 \tag{5.10}$$

and $k(a) = 0$ elsewhere.

Insert 5.5 (Origin of the Epanechnikov function) *This function was published in* [V.A. Epanechnikov. Nonparametric estimation of a multidimensional probability density. Theory Probab. Appl., vol. 14, pp. 153–158, 1969].

Density Estimator   Let $r > 0$ be a parameter defining the *radius* of the kernel (e.g. the standard deviation σ for the Gauss function). We have m feature vectors $\mathbf{u}_i$, $1 \le i \le m$, in $\mathbb{R}^n$; for a given image I, it is $m = N_{cols} \cdot N_{rows}$. For any feature

Fig. 5.14 Profiles of four different kernel functions: triangle, Epanechnikov, uniform, and Gaussian

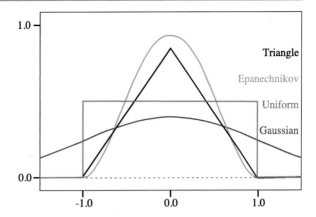

vector $\mathbf{u} \in \mathbb{R}^n$,

$$f_k(\mathbf{u}) = \frac{1}{mr^n} \sum_{i=1}^{m} K\left(\frac{1}{r} \cdot (\mathbf{u} - \mathbf{u}_i)\right) \tag{5.11}$$

$$= \frac{c_k}{mr^n} \sum_{i=1}^{m} k\left(\frac{1}{r^2} \cdot \|\mathbf{u} - \mathbf{u}_i\|_2^2\right) \tag{5.12}$$

defines a *density estimator* at vector $\mathbf{u}$, using a kernel function K.

Gradient Calculation For determining the mean-shift vector, we have to calculate the derivative $\mathbf{grad}\, f_k(\mathbf{u})$ of $f_k(\mathbf{u})$. (See our discussion of images as continuous surfaces and the meaning of gradients, e.g. when discussing Fig. 1.13.)
We differentiate

$$k\left(\frac{1}{r^2} \cdot \|\mathbf{u} - \mathbf{u}_i\|_2^2\right) \tag{5.13}$$

by taking the derivative

$$\frac{2}{r^2}(\mathbf{u} - \mathbf{u}_i) \tag{5.14}$$

of the inner function times the derivative

$$k'\left(\frac{1}{r^2} \|\mathbf{u} - \mathbf{u}_i\|_2^2\right) \tag{5.15}$$

of the outer function; the function k' is the derivative of the profile k.
Local peaks in feature space are at locations $\mathbf{u}$ where

$$0 = \mathbf{grad}\, f_k(\mathbf{u}) = \frac{2c_k}{mr^{n+2}} \sum_{i=1}^{m} (\mathbf{u} - \mathbf{u}_i) k'\left(\frac{1}{r^2} \|\mathbf{u} - \mathbf{u}_i\|_2^2\right) \tag{5.16}$$

$$= \frac{2c_k}{mr^{n+2}} \sum_{i=1}^{m} (\mathbf{u} - \mathbf{u}_i) k'(\mathscr{X}_i^{(r)})$$

using

$$\mathscr{X}_i^{(r)} = \frac{1}{r^2} \|\mathbf{u} - \mathbf{u}_i\|_2^2 \tag{5.17}$$

for abbreviation.

We like to transform the gradient as given in (5.16) such that we can understand the mean-shift vector when moving from any given feature vector $\mathbf{u}$ to the next mean, towards a local peak.

We first introduce the function $g(a) = -k'(a)$. The minus sign allows us to change $(\mathbf{u} - \mathbf{u}_i)$ into $(\mathbf{u}_i - \mathbf{u})$. From (5.16) we obtain the following:

$$\mathbf{grad}\, f_k(\mathbf{u}) = \frac{2c_k}{mr^{n+2}} \sum_{i=1}^{m} (\mathbf{u}_i - \mathbf{u}) \cdot g(\mathscr{X}_i^{(r)})$$

$$= \frac{2c_k}{mr^{n+2}} \left(\sum_{i=1}^{m} [\mathbf{u}_i \cdot g(\mathscr{X}_i^{(r)})] - \mathbf{u} \cdot \sum_{i=1}^{m} g(\mathscr{X}_i^{(r)}) \right)$$

$$= \frac{2c_k}{r^2 c_g} \left[\frac{c_g}{mr^n} \cdot \sum_{i=1}^{m} g(\mathscr{X}_i^{(r)}) \right] \left[\frac{\sum_{i=1}^{m} \mathbf{u}_i \cdot g(\mathscr{X}_i^{(r)})}{\sum_{i=1}^{m} g(\mathscr{X}_i^{(r)})} - \mathbf{u} \right]$$

$$= A \cdot B \cdot C \tag{5.18}$$

The factor A in $(5.18)^2$ is a constant. The factor B is the density estimate f_g in the feature space for a function g, as (5.12) defined the density estimate f_k for a function k. The constant c_g normalizes the integral in the feature space to 1 if we apply f_g as weight.

Mean-Shift Vector as a Scaled Gradient Vector   The factor C in (5.18) is the *mean-shift vector*, which starts at vector $\mathbf{u}$ to a new location in the feature space. We denote it by

$$m_g(\mathbf{u}) = \frac{\sum_{i=1}^{m} \mathbf{u}_i \cdot g(\mathscr{X}_i^{(r)})}{\sum_{i=1}^{m} g(\mathscr{X}_i^{(r)})} - \mathbf{u} \tag{5.19}$$

Altogether we have that

$$\mathbf{grad}\, f_k(\mathbf{u}) = \frac{2c_k}{r^2 c_g} \cdot f_g(\mathbf{u}) \cdot m_g(\mathbf{u}) \tag{5.20}$$

---

[2]See Fig. 10.11 in the book [G. Bradski and A. Kaehler. *Learning OpenCV*. O'Reilly, Beijing, 2008] for a graphical illustration of this equation. Mean-shift is there not discussed for clustering in feature space but for tracking in pixel domain.

or

$$m_g(\mathbf{u}) = \frac{r^2 c_g}{2 c_k \cdot f_g(\mathbf{u})} \cdot \mathbf{grad}\, f_k(\mathbf{u}) \tag{5.21}$$

This is a proof of Observation 5.2: Mean-shift proceeds in the direction of gradient $\mathbf{grad}\, f_k(\mathbf{u})$. By proceeding this way we go towards a feature vector $\mathbf{u_0}$ with $\mathbf{grad}\, f_k(\mathbf{u_0}) = 0$, as stated in (5.16).

5.2.3 Algorithms and Time Optimization

Mean-shift provides reasonable-quality segmentation results, but it has high computational costs if done accurately. By means of a simple example we sketch a mean-shift algorithm, which uses linear algebra (i.e. matrix operations). This algorithm does not apply any run-time optimizations and is here only given for illustrating a brief and general algorithm.

Example 5.4 (Mean-Shift Using Linear Algebra) We use the 2D feature space illustrated in Fig. 5.12 as input. This feature space represents the data

$$\{(5, 2), (6, 2), (3, 3), (3, 3), (4, 3),$$
$$(5, 3), (1, 4), (2, 4), (2, 4), (4, 4),$$
$$(5, 4), (5, 4), (5, 4), (6, 4), (7, 4),$$
$$(2, 5), (3, 5), (3, 5), (5, 6), (6, 6),$$
$$(6, 6), (3, 7), (4, 7), (6, 7), (6, 7)\}$$

assuming integer values a and b starting at 1. We present those data in a form of a *data matrix* as follows:

$$\mathbf{D} = \begin{bmatrix} 5\,6\,3\,3\,4\,5\,1\,2\,2\,4\,5\,5\,5\,6\,7\,2\,3\,3\,5\,6\,6\,3\,4\,6\,6 \\ 2\,2\,3\,3\,3\,3\,4\,4\,4\,4\,4\,4\,4\,4\,5\,5\,5\,6\,6\,6\,7\,7\,7\,7 \end{bmatrix}$$

A mean-shift procedure starts with selecting a feature pair as an initial mean. We take one of the two pairs $(3, 5)$, as already illustrated in Fig. 5.12, and create a *mean matrix* $\mathbf{M}$ which has $(3, 5)$ in all of its columns:

$$\mathbf{M} = \begin{bmatrix} 3\,3\,3\,3\,3\,3\,3\,3\,3\,3\,3\,3\,3\,3\,3\,3\,3\,3\,3\,3\,3\,3\,3\,3\,3 \\ 5\,5\,5\,5\,5\,5\,5\,5\,5\,5\,5\,5\,5\,5\,5\,5\,5\,5\,5\,5\,5\,5\,5\,5\,5 \end{bmatrix}$$

We calculate squared Euclidean distances between columns in matrix $\mathbf{M}$ and columns in matrix $\mathbf{D}$ by taking the squares of all differences $\mathbf{D} - \mathbf{M}$. We obtain the (squared) *Euclidean distance matrix*

$$\mathbf{E} = \begin{bmatrix} 4\,9\,0\,0\,1\,4\,4\,1\,1\,1\,4\,4\,4\,9\,16\,1\,0\,0\,4\,9\,9\,0\,1\,9\,9 \\ 9\,9\,4\,4\,4\,4\,1\,1\,1\,1\,1\,1\,1\,1\,0\,0\,0\,1\,1\,1\,4\,4\,4\,4 \end{bmatrix}$$

with the following corresponding sums in each column:

$$\left[\begin{array}{cccccccccccccccccccccccc} 13 & 18 & 4 & 4 & 5 & 8 & 5 & 2 & 2 & 2 & 5 & 5 & 5 & 10 & 17 & 1 & 0 & 0 & 5 & 10 & 10 & 4 & 5 & 13 & 13 \end{array}\right]$$

Now we are ready to apply the kernel function. For simplicity, we assume a uniform profile defined by some radius $r > 0$; see Fig. 5.14 for the simple step function defining a uniform profile.

The calculated sums need to be compared with r^2. For generating Fig. 5.12, $r = 1.6$ has been used; thus, $r^2 = 2.56$. Six squared Euclidean distance values are less than 2.56. These are the six feature points contained in the circle on the left in Fig. 5.12, defining the active feature point set

$$S = \{(2,4), (2,4), (4,4), (2,5), (3,5), (3,5)\}$$

for this step of the mean-shift iteration.

We calculate the mean of the set S (because of the uniform profile) as $\mathbf{u}_S = (2.67, 4.5)$. We compare $(2.67, 4.5)$ with the previous mean $(3, 5)$ and detect that the distance is still above the threshold $\tau = 0.1$.

We continue in the next iteration step with generating a new mean matrix $\mathbf{M}$, which has $(2.67, 4.5)$ in all of its columns, calculate again a vector of squared Euclidean distances to this mean (via a matrix $\mathbf{E}$), select again the set S of currently active feature points, which are in a distance less than r to $(2.67, 4.5)$, and calculate the new mean for this set S. We compare the new mean with $(2.67, 4.5)$ by using the threshold $\tau = 0.1$.

The process stops when the distance between two subsequent means is less than τ. This defines a final mean. The initial feature $\mathbf{u} = (3, 5)$ is assigned to this final mean.

After having processed all feature points in the feature space, we cluster the feature points if their final means are identical or just "close" to each other. This defines the equivalence classes of feature points.

The example used a uniform profile; we can also use the other profiles as illustrated in Fig. 5.14. This changes the way of approximating the local means (now by weighted sums of contributing feature values).

The algorithm in the example can be optimized. The use of the matrix $\mathbf{M}$ in the example for comparing with *all* the available features $\mathbf{u}$ is time-inefficient. Locating repeatedly points close to the current mean can be done more efficiently, for example by using hashing techniques. We next discuss the issue of time complexity.

Partitioning the Feature Space into Windows Consider an algorithm that starts with a partition of the feature space into "small" windows, as uniform as possible. See Fig. 5.15 for a segmentation result and Fig. 5.16, left, for a simple 2D feature space example.

We perform mean-shift operations for all of those windows in successive rounds until none of the windows moves anymore into a new position. We round the means to nearest integers; thus, we centre windows always at feature vectors. We assign

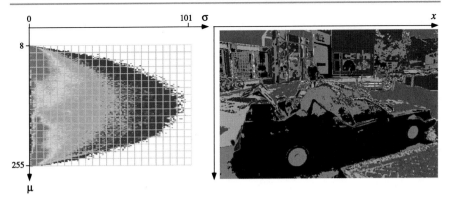

Fig. 5.15 *Left*: A sketch of a partitioned feature space for the image Odense shown in Fig. 5.11. *Right*: Segmentation result for this image using a feature space partition into windows of size 39×39, resulting in 33 labels

Fig. 5.16 The centres of the nine initial windows, shown on the *left*, are the considered as initial means. They move by subsequent mean-shifts into new locations and stop moving at blue or red cells, which are final means. The red cell indicates the only case where two initial windows moved into the same final mean, defining a merger of those two windows into one 2×6 equivalence class shown on the *right*

the feature vectors of all those original windows to the same equivalence class (i.e. a segment in the feature space) whose centres moved into the same final mean.

Example 5.5 (Pairwise-Disjoint Square Windows in Feature Space) Consider the 2D feature space represented as an 8×8 array on the left of Fig. 5.16, showing multiplicities of feature vectors. We apply a uniform profile in square windows (and not in a disc).

After the first round of mean-shifts of those nine initial windows, we notice that four of them do not move at all, identified by four blue cells. Five windows continue into the second round of mean-shifts. Now we notice that four of those five do not move any further, defining four more blue cells. Only one window needs to be considered in the third round of mean-shifts; its mean moves into the position of a previously already labelled blue cell, thus establishing a merger with the window defined by this cell. This merger is illustrated on the right.

In Fig. 5.17 we partition the same 8×8 feature space as before but now into smaller 2×2 windows. In the upper right we have a case where all values add up to 0; there is no occurrence of any feature in this window, thus, the end of the story

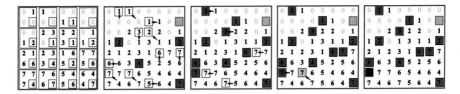

Fig. 5.17 The reference points of 16 initial windows, shown on the *left*, move by mean-shift into new locations. *Grey*: Irrelevant window. *Blue*: No further move. *Red*: Merger with a blue cell. *Black*: Merger with a red cell. *Yellow*: The most interesting case, where we arrive at a previously already considered location

Fig. 5.18 *Left to right*: The original 2×2 partition as in Fig. 5.17, final locations of means with indicated 4- or 8-adjacencies, the resulting equivalence classes defined by merged windows, the resulting equivalence classes if also merging due to 4-connectedness of final means, and resulting equivalence classes if also merging due to 8-connectedness

here. Blue cells show again a stop of movement, and red cells a merger with a blue cell. This time we also have a third window merging with two previously already merged windows, shown by the black cell. At the yellow cell we also notice that this location has been considered previously; thus, we can stop here and simply merge into the already-initialized calculation path for this location. This appears to be the case with the best potentials for reducing time when segmenting large-scale images.

We could also cluster final means (i.e. blue, red, or black cells in this case), for example defined by 4- or 8-connectedness. Clusters define then the equivalence classes. See Fig. 5.18.

Mean-Shift Algorithm when Partitioning the Feature Space into Windows
We use an n-channel representation of the given image I, defining thus an n-dimensional feature space for $n \geq 1$. We insert all the $|\Omega|$ features of a given image into a uniformly digitized feature space at grid-point locations (similar to the counters in the accumulator space for a Hough transform), using rounding of values where necessary. This defines an n-dimensional histogram.

We declare all initial n-dimensional windows in the feature space, defining a partition of this space, to be *active* (if containing at least one feature vector). The equivalence class of such a window contains at the moment of initialization only this window itself. We start the iterative mean-shift procedure.

In each run of the iteration, we move any active window into a new mean (i.e. rounded to a grid position in the feature space). We have two cases:

Fig. 5.19 *Left*: The colour image HowMany. *Right*: The segmentation result for this image using a 3D RGB feature space and a partitioning into $91 \times 91 \times 91$ windows for the described mean-shift algorithm when partitioning the feature space into windows without any clustering of final means

1. If the newly calculated mean is still the previous mean, we have a *stop*: the mean is a *final mean*; we delete this window from the list of active windows.
2. If in the current iteration step the means of two windows are identical, we have a *merger*: we merge the equivalence classes of both windows and delete the second window from the list of active windows.
3. If a move of a mean into a feature space location already occupied in a previous iteration step by another mean of another window, we have a *follower*: we merge the equivalence classes of both windows and delete the currently moved window from the list of active windows.

We stop the iteration if the list of active windows is empty. See Fig. 5.19 for an example of a result; 3D windows of size $91 \times 91 \times 91$ led here to 10 different means (labels).

The final result can be post-processed, for example by clustering 4- or 8-connected final means by merging the equivalence classes of windows assigned to those means. The algorithm can be further simplified by merging Cases (2) and (3); in both cases we move a newly calculated mean onto a previously already occupied position, with identical consequences.

The time-efficiency of this algorithm is paid by a "blocky structure" of equivalence classes of features **u** in the feature space and by the approximate character of considered moves by using regular grid points as the only possible locations for calculated means.

Mean-Shift Algorithm when Considering Individual Feature Vectors in Feature Space We consider now shifts of individual feature vectors in the feature space but continue to use regular grid points as the only possible locations for feature vectors or calculated means.

For doing so, we select a kernel function of some radius $r > 0$; due to the used discrete approximation of the feature space, we need r to be greater than 1, and larger values of r will define more significant moves of means, but will also increase the time complexity.

Fig. 5.20 *Left*: The segmentation result (26 labels) for the image HowMany shown in Fig. 5.19 using a 3D RGB feature space, the mean-shift algorithm for individual feature vectors, and the Gauss kernel function with $r = 25$. *Right*: All the same as before, but with merging final means, which are at a distance of ≤ 50 to each other, reducing 26 to 18 labels this way

We declare all non-zero vectors in the feature space to be *active means*; their initial equivalence class contains just their own initial location. We start the iterative mean-shift procedure.

In each run of the iteration, we move any active mean **u** into a new mean by using feature-space multiplicity values in the neighbourhood of **u**, weighted by the selected kernel function. This operation corresponds to the mean-shift in (5.19). We round the obtained mean to the nearest grid position in the feature space. We have two cases:

1. A newly calculated mean is still the previous mean. We have a *stop*. The mean is a *final mean*; we delete this mean from the list of active means.
2. A newly calculated mean is identical to a previously calculated mean. We have a *merger*. (See Exercise 5.7.) We merge the equivalence classes of both means and delete the newly calculated mean from the list of active means.

We stop the iteration if the list of active windows is empty. The final result can again be post-processed by clustering final means. See Fig. 5.20 for illustrations of results.

5.3   Image Segmentation as an Optimization Problem

This section describes segmentation as a particular labelling problem and belief-propagation as a method for solving such a problem. A labelling problem is specified by error terms (penalties for data issues and non-smoothness), and we outline how to go towards an optimized solution for such a problem.

5.3.1   Labels, Labelling, and Energy Minimization

When preparing for the Horn–Schunck algorithm in Sect. 4.2.1 (see (4.9) and the following text), we used labelling functions for assigning optic flow tuples (u, v) (i.e. the *labels*) to pixel locations (x, y). The definition of pairwise-disjoint segments, defining a *segmentation* of all pixels in Ω, is also a labelling problem. Figure 5.2 shows two examples.

Four Labels Are Sufficient When mapping a given image into a binary image, we assign to each pixel either label "white" or "black". We can decide to use 4-, 8-, or K-connectedness for defining image regions (see Sect. 3.1); the regions in the created binary image are the established *segments*.

When mapping a given image into a coloured map, we assign to each pixel a colour as its label. Again, 4-, 8-, or K-connected regions of the created colour map define the created *segments*. According to the *Four-Colour Theorem*, it is sufficient to use only four different colours for visualizing any image segmentation.

Insert 5.6 (Four-Colour Theorem) *About the middle of the* 19*th century, the hypothesis emerged that any partition of the plane into connected segments, called a* map, *could be coloured by using four different colours only such that border-adjacent (i.e. not just corner-adjacent) segments could be differently coloured. In* 1976 *it was proven by the US-American mathematician K. Appel* (1932–2013) *and W. Haken (born in* 1928 *in Germany) that this is a valid mathematical theorem, known as the* Four-Colour *theorem.*

The General Labelling Approach Labelling is a common way for modelling various computer vision problems (e.g. optic flow in Chap. 4, image segmentation in this chapter, integration of vector fields in Sect. 7.4.3, or stereo matching in Chap. 8). The set of labels can be discrete,

$$L = \{l_1, l_2, \ldots, l_m\} \quad \text{with } |L| = m \tag{5.22}$$

or continuous,

$$L \subset \mathbb{R}^n \quad \text{for } n \geq 1 \tag{5.23}$$

Image segmentation or stereo matching are examples for discrete sets of labels; optic flow uses labels in a set $L \subset \mathbb{R}^2$ and vector field integration in a set $L \subset \mathbb{R}$.

In this section we assume a discrete set of labels having cardinality $m = |L|$ and also the notation

$$h = f_p = f(p) \quad \text{or} \quad l = f_q = f(q) \tag{5.24}$$

Labels are assigned to *sites*, and sites in this textbook are limited to be pixel locations. For a given image, we have $|\Omega| = N_{cols} \cdot N_{rows}$ sites, which is a large number; thus, time-efficiency *is* of importance for identifying a labelling function

$$f : \Omega \to L \tag{5.25}$$

or, just in other notation,

$$f = \{(p, h) : p \in \Omega \wedge f(p) = h\} \tag{5.26}$$

We aim at calculating a labelling f that minimizes a given (total) *error* or *energy*

$$E(f) = \sum_{p \in \Omega} \left[E_{data}(p, f_p) + \sum_{q \in A(p)} E_{smooth}(f_p, f_q) \right] \quad (5.27)$$

where A is an adjacency relation between pixel locations as introduced in Sect. 3.1, with

$$q \in A(p) \quad \text{iff} \quad \text{pixel locations } q \text{ and } p \text{ are adjacent} \quad (5.28)$$

If not otherwise specified, we use 4-adjacency; see (3.1) for its definition. The error function E_{data} assigns non-negative penalties to a pixel location p when assigning a label $f_p \in L$ to this location. The error function E_{smooth} assigns non-negative penalties by comparing the assigned labels f_p and f_q at adjacent pixel positions p and q.

Equation (5.27) defines a model for an optimization problem characterized by local interactions along edges between adjacent pixels. This is an example of a *Markov random field* (MRF) model. In this section we apply belief propagation for solving this optimization problem approximately.

Insert 5.7 (Markov, Bayes, Gibbs, and Random Fields) *The Russian mathematician A.A. Markov (1856–1922) studied stochastic processes where the interaction of multiple random variables can be modelled by an undirected graph. These models are today known as* Markov random fields. *If the underlying graph is directed and acyclic, then we have a* Bayesian network, *named after the English mathematician T. Bayes (1701–1761). If we only consider strictly positive random variables, then an MRF is called a* Gibbs random field, *named after the US-American scientist J.W. Gibbs (1839–1903).*

The function E_{data} is the *data term*, and the function E_{smooth} is the *smoothness, continuity*, or *neighbourhood term* of the total energy E.

Informally speaking, $E_{data}(p, f_p) = 0$ means that the label f_p is "perfect" for pixel location p. The function E_{smooth} defines a prior that favours identical labels at adjacent pixels. This is a critical design problem: there are borders between segments (i.e. places where labels need to change); we cannot penalize such necessary changes too much for still making them possible.

A labelling problem is solved by assigning uniquely a label from a set L to each site in Ω. In case of a discrete label set L with $|L| = m$, we have $m^{|\Omega|}$ possible labelling functions. Taking the four-colour theorem as a guide, we can limit ourself to $4^{|\Omega|}$. This is still a large number.

Selecting a labelling that minimizes (accurately) the error defined in (5.27) is a challenge. As a compromise, we aim at obtaining an *approximately minimal solution*. Extreme choices of data or smoothness term can cause trivial optimum solutions for (5.27). For example, if the smoothness penalty is extremely large, then a constant labelling is optimal. On the other hand, if we choose the smoothness term to be close to 0, then only the pixel-wise data term defines the outcome, and this case is also not difficult to optimize. A dominating data or smoothness error term contribute to a simplification of the optimization task.

Observation 5.3 *The computational complexity of an optimum solution for the MRF defined by (5.27) depends on the chosen error terms.*

5.3.2   Examples of Data and Smoothness Terms

Regarding optic flow calculations, we have examples of data terms in (4.9) and (4.58) and examples of smoothness terms in (4.10) and (4.59).

Data Term Examples   We first decide about the number $m \geq 2$ of labels to be used for the different segments. We may have more than just m segments because the same label l_i can be used repeatedly for disconnected segments. Segments with the same label can be defined by some data similarity, such as the mean-shift feature vector convergence to the same peak in the feature space.

Example 5.6 (Data Term Based on Random Initial Seeds) We select m random pixels in the given scalar image I and calculate in their (say) 5×5 neighbourhood the mean and standard deviation, defining 3D feature vectors $\mathbf{u}_i = [I(x_i, y_i), \mu_i, \sigma_i]^\top$ for $1 \leq i \leq m$. We consider those m pixels as seeds for m feature classes to be labelled by m labels l_1 to l_m.

Consider $f_p = l_i$ at pixel location p. We define that

$$E_{data}(p, l_i) = \|\mathbf{u}_i - \mathbf{u}_p\|_2^2 = \sum_{k=1}^{n}(u_{i,k} - u_{p,k})^2 \tag{5.29}$$

if using the L_2-norm,

$$E_{data}(p, l_i) = \|\mathbf{u}_i - \mathbf{u}_p\|_1 = \sum_{k=1}^{n}|u_{i,k} - u_{p,k}| \tag{5.30}$$

if using the L_1-norm (less sensitive with respect to outliers compared to L_2), or

$$E_{data}(p, l_i) = \chi^2(\mathbf{u}_i, \mathbf{u}_p) = \sum_{k=1}^{n}\frac{(u_{i,k} - u_{p,k})^2}{u_{i,k} + u_{p,k}} \tag{5.31}$$

if using χ^2 (in general even less-sensitive with respect to outliers; χ^2 is not a metric because it does not satisfy the triangle inequality), where $\mathbf{u}_p$ is the feature vector defined by the mean and standard deviation in the 5×5 neighbourhood of pixel location p.

Initial seeds can be tested first on variance, selected several times in the image, and then the set that maximizes the variance is chosen. The size of the neighbourhood or used features can also vary.

Example 5.7 (Data Term Based on Peaks in Feature Space) The image feature space is an n-dimensional histogram, defined by nD feature values $\mathbf{u}$ at all Ω pixel locations. Grey levels only define the common 1D histogram, as discussed in Sect. 1.1.2. 2D features (e.g. the local mean and local standard deviation) define 2D histograms as sketched in Fig. 5.12.

We select m local peaks in the image feature space. For detecting those, we can start in the image feature space with m feature vectors and apply mean-shift to them, thus detecting $\leq m$ peaks $\mathbf{u}_i$ in the feature space, to be identified with label l_i. Then we define the data term E_{data} as in Example 5.6.

Priors provided by the approach in Example 5.7 appear to be more adequate for a meaningful segmentation than those proposed in Example 5.6 but require more computation time. We could even run mean-shift segmentation at first *completely* and then use those detected m peaks that have more pixels assigned than any remaining peaks. See Exercise 5.8.

Smoothness Term Examples   We consider a unary symmetric smoothness error term defined by the identity

$$E_{smooth}(l - h) = E_{smooth}(h - l) = E_{smooth}\big(|l - h|\big) \tag{5.32}$$

for labels $l, h \in L$. Binary smoothness terms $E_{smooth}(l, h)$ are the more general case, and including dependencies from locations in terms $E_{smooth}(p, q; l, h)$ is even more general.

Insert 5.8 (Origin of the Potts Model) *The model was introduced by the Australian mathematician R.B. Potts (1925–2005) in his 1951 PhD thesis on Ising models.*

Example 5.8 (Potts Model) In this model, any discontinuity between labels is penalized uniformly, by only considering equality or non-equality between labels:

$$E_{smooth}(l - h) = E_{smooth}(a) = \begin{cases} 0 & \text{if } a = 0 \\ c & \text{otherwise} \end{cases} \tag{5.33}$$

where $c > 0$ is a constant. This simple model is especially appropriate if feature vectors do have a minor variance within image regions and only significant discontinuities at region borders.

Example 5.9 (Linear Smoothness Cost) The linear cost function is as follows:

$$E_{smooth}(l - h) = E_{smooth}(a) = b \cdot |l - h| = b \cdot |a| \tag{5.34}$$

Fig. 5.21 *Left*: Linear
smoothness cost. *Right*:
Linear truncated smoothness
cost

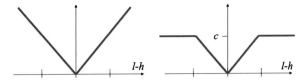

where $b > 0$ defines the *increase rate* in costs.

For the linear truncated case, we use a *truncation constant* $c > 0$ and have that

$$E_{smooth}(l - h) = E_{smooth}(a) = \min\{b \cdot |l - h|, c\} = \min\{b \cdot |a|, c\} \qquad (5.35)$$

(i.e. there is no cost increase if the difference reaches a level c). See Fig. 5.21 for linear and truncated linear case.

In general, *truncation* represents a balance between an appropriate change to a different label (by truncation of the penalty function) and occurrence of noise or minor variations, not yet requesting a change of a label (in the linear part). Occurring label differences below the truncation constant c are treated as noise and penalized (according to the given difference in labels).

Example 5.10 (Quadratic Smoothness Cost) We have the (unconstrained) quadratic case (we skip the formula) or the truncated quadratic cost function

$$E_{smooth}(l - h) = E_{smooth}(a) = \min\{b \cdot (l - h)^2, c\} = \min\{b \cdot a^2, c\} \qquad (5.36)$$

The positive reals b and c define the slope and truncation, respectively.

Observation 5.4 *Data terms are problem-specific, especially designed for matching tasks such as optic flow calculation or image segmentation, while smoothness terms are (typically) of general use.*

5.3.3 Message Passing

A *belief-propagation* (BP) algorithm passes messages (the *belief*) around in a local neighbourhood, defined by the underlying undirected graph of the MRF. We assume 4-adjacency in the image grid. Message updates are in iterations (you possibly already know such a message-passing strategy from the field of 2D cellular automata); messages are passed on in parallel, from a labelled pixel to its four 4-adjacent neighbours. See Fig. 5.22.

Informal Outlook   The thin black arrows in Fig. 5.22 indicate directions of message passing. For example (*left*), pixel p is left of pixel q, and pixel p sends a message to pixel q in the first iteration. The message from pixel p contains already messages received from its neighbours (*right*) in all the subsequent iterations. This occurs at pixel q in parallel for all four 4-adjacent pixels. In one iteration step, each

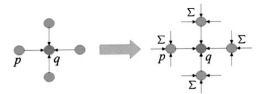

Fig. 5.22 The central pixel q receives messages from adjacent pixels such as p, and this occurs for all pixels in the image array in the same way. In the next iteration step, the central pixel q receives messages from adjacent pixels, representing all the messages those pixels (such as p) have received in the iteration step before

labelled pixel of the adjacency graph computes its message based on the information it had at the end of the previous iteration step and sends its (new) message to all the adjacent pixels in parallel.

Informally speaking, the larger the penalty $E_{data}(p, l)$ is, the "more difficult" it is to reduce the cost at p for label l by messages sent from adjacent pixels. The "influence" of adjacent pixels decreases when the data cost at this pixel for a particular label increases.

Formal Specification   Each *message* is a function that maps the ordered discrete set L of labels into a corresponding 1D array of length $m = |L|$ having a non-negative real as the *message value* in any of its m positions.

Let $m^t_{p \to q}$ be such a message, with message values for $l \in L$ in its m components, sent from node p to the adjacent node q at iteration t. For $l \in L$, let

$$m^t_{p \to q}(l) = \min_{h \in L} \left(E_{data}(p, h) + E_{smooth}(h - l) + \sum_{s \in A(p) \setminus q} m^{t-1}_{s \to p}(h) \right) \quad (5.37)$$

be the *message-update equation*, where l denotes a possible label at q, and h runs through L and is again just a possible label at p.

We accumulate at q all messages from adjacent pixel locations p and combine with the data cost values for labels l at q. This defines at pixel location q an 1D array of *costs*

$$E_{data}(q, l) + \sum_{p \in A(q)} m^t_{p \to q}(l) \quad (5.38)$$

for assigning a label l to q at time t. This cost combines the time-independent data term $E_{data}(q, l)$ with the sum of all $|A|$ received message values for $l \in L$ at time t.

Informal Interpretation   Understanding (5.37) and (5.38) is the key for understanding belief propagation. We provide an informal interpretation of both equations.

We are at node q. Node q inquires with its adjacent nodes, such as p, about their opinion about selecting label l at q. Node p, being asked about its opinion, scans through all the labels h and tells q the lowest possible cost when q decides for l.

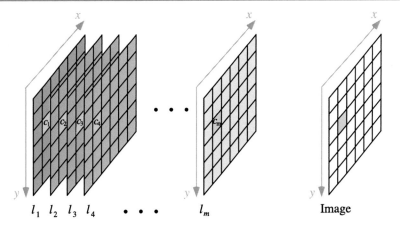

Fig. 5.23 A sketch of m message boards, each board for one label, and of a pixel in the input image. The cost value c_i is in message board No. i for label l_i; that label l_j will finally define the calculated value at the given pixel, which is identified by a minimum value of c_j compared to all c_i for $1 \le i \le m$

The smoothness term defines the penalty when q takes l and p takes h. Label h also creates the cost $E_{data}(p, h)$ at p. Finally, p also has the information available provided by all of its adjacent nodes at time $t - 1$, excluding q, because q cannot influence this way the opinion of p about label l.

Node q inquires at time t about all the possible labels l this way. For every label l, it asks each of its adjacent nodes.

In (5.38) we combine now the opinions of all adjacent nodes for label l at q. At this moment we also have to take the data cost of l at q into account. Smoothness costs have been taken care off already in the messages generated from p to q.

Message Boards Instead of passing on 1D arrays of length $m = |L|$, it appears to be more convenient to use m *message boards* of size $N_{cols} \times N_{rows}$, one board for each label. See Fig. 5.23. Message updates in these message boards follow the previously defined pattern, illustrated in Fig. 5.22. The 1D vectors of length m at all the pixel locations are just considered to be a stack of m scalar arrays, each for one label $l \in L$.

5.3.4 Belief-Propagation Algorithm

We present a general belief-propagation algorithm where the set Ω of pixel locations is the set of sites (or nodes) to be labelled. We have the following components in an iterative process: initialization, an update process (from iteration step $t - 1$ to iteration step t), and a termination criterion.

Initialization   We initialize all m message boards at all $|\Omega|$ positions by starting with initial messages

$$m_{p\to q}^0(l) = \min_{h\in L}\big(E_{data}(p,h) + E_{smooth}(h-l)\big) \tag{5.39}$$

resulting in initial costs

$$E_{data}(q,l) + \sum_{p\in A(q)} m_{p\to q}^0(l) \tag{5.40}$$

at pixel location $q \in \Omega$ in message board l.

Iteration Steps of the BP Algorithm   In iteration step $t \geq 1$ we calculate messages $m_{p\to q}^t(l)$, as defined in (5.37), and combine them to cost updates at all pixel locations $q \in \Omega$ and for any of the m message boards l, as defined in (5.38).

For discussing these iterations, we first rewrite the message-update equation (5.37) as follows:

$$m_{p\to q}^t(l) = \min_{h\in L}\big\{E_{smooth}(h-l) + H_{p,q}(h)\big\} \tag{5.41}$$

where

$$H_{p,q}(h) = E_{data}(p,h) + \sum_{s\in A(p)\setminus\{q\}} m_{s\to p}^{t-1}(h) \tag{5.42}$$

A straightforward computation of $H_{p,q}$ (for all $h \in L$) requires $O(m^2)$ time, assuming that $E_{data}(p,h)$ only requires constant time for calculation.

If using the Potts model for the smoothness term, then the message-update equation (5.41) simplifies to

$$m_{p\to q}^t(l) = \min\Big\{H_{p,q}(l), \min_{h\in L\setminus\{l\}} H_{p,q}(h) + c\Big\} \tag{5.43}$$

We compute the minimum over all h and compare with $H_{p,q}(l)$.

If using the linear model for the smoothness term, the non-truncated message-update equation (5.41) turns into

$$m_{p\to q}^t(l) = \min_{h\in L}\big(b \cdot |h-l| + H_{p,q}(h)\big) \tag{5.44}$$

where b is the parameter defining the linear cost. We consider an example.

Example 5.11 (Non-Truncated Linear Smoothness Model) Let $L = \{0,1,2,3\}$ and $b = 1$, with

$$H_{p,q}(0) = 2.5 \qquad H_{p,q}(1) = 1$$
$$H_{p,q}(2) = 1.5 \qquad H_{p,q}(3) = 0$$

Fig. 5.24 Example of four piecewise-linear functions. Minima are taken at *red points*. There is no minimum on the *green lines*. The *blue lines* define the lower envelope of all the given lines

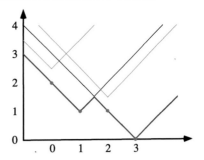

for a given combination of adjacent pixel locations p and q. These data are illustrated in Fig. 5.24 for the linear non-truncated case. The value $H_{p,q}(l)$ defines a vertical shift of the linear cost function (the *cone*) at label l.

The calculations corresponding to (5.44) are now as follows:

$$m^t_{p \to q}(0) = \min\{0 + 2.5, 1 + 1, 2 + 1.5, 3 + 0\}$$
$$= \min\{2.5, 2, 3.5, 3\} = 2$$
$$m^t_{p \to q}(1) = \min\{1 + 2.5, 0 + 1, 1 + 1.5, 2 + 0\}$$
$$= \min\{3.5, 1, 2.5, 2\} = 1$$
$$m^t_{p \to q}(2) = \min\{2 + 2.5, 1 + 1, 0 + 1.5, 1 + 0\}$$
$$= \min\{4.5, 2, 1.5, 1\} = 1$$
$$m^t_{p \to q}(3) = \min\{3 + 2.5, 2 + 1, 1 + 1.5, 0 + 0\}$$
$$= \min\{5.5, 3, 2.5, 0\} = 0$$

These calculated minima are labelled in Fig. 5.24 by red points. We note that the green lines are not incident with any of the minima. The minima are all on the *lower envelope* shown in blue.

The minimization of (5.44) (i.e. in the non-truncated linear case) can be formulated as follows: Calculate the lower envelope of m upward facing cones, each with identical slope defined by parameter b. Each cone is rooted at $(h, H_{p,q}(h))$. See Fig. 5.25. The minimum for label h is then simply on the lower envelope, shown as red dots.

The truncated linear model follows the same scheme. Message updates can be computed in $\mathcal{O}(m)$ time; we discussed the calculation of the lower envelope for families of parabolas before in Sect. 3.2.4, in the context of the general Euclidean distance transform (EDT).

If using the quadratic model for the smoothness term, the non-truncated message-update equation (5.41) turns into

$$m^t_{p \to q}(l) = \min_{h \in L}\left(b(h - l)^2 + H_{p,q}(h)\right) \tag{5.45}$$

Fig. 5.25 The general case: m labels, some contributing to minima (*black lines*), and some not (*green lines*)

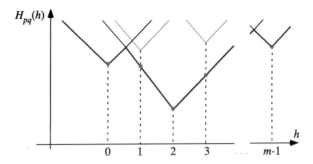

Fig. 5.26 The lower envelope of m parabolas

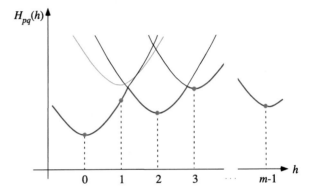

Again, minima are on the lower envelope of the parabolas defined by the quadratic penalty functions; see Fig. 5.26.

The parabolas are rooted at $(h, H_{p,q}(h))$, and this corresponds exactly to the input for the EDT; the calculation of lower envelopes is part of an EDT algorithm. The lower envelope can be calculated in time $\mathcal{O}(m)$; see Sect. 3.2.4.

Termination of the Iteration and Results of the Algorithm   A *termination criterion* tells the BP algorithm to stop when the program has done a pre-defined number of iterations. Other options, such as waiting that the mean of all changes in all message boards, between iterations $t-1$ and t, becomes less than a given positive threshold τ, are rather impractical (due to no guarantee of convergence).

At the moment t_0 of termination, each pixel location p has m cost values $(c_1^{t_0}, \ldots, c_m^{t_0})$ at location p in the m message boards, with cost value $c_i^{t_0}$ for label l_i for $1 \leq i \leq m$. The value of the algorithm at p equals $f_p^{t_0} = l_j$ for

$$j = \arg\min_{1 \leq i \leq m} c_i^{t_0} \qquad (5.46)$$

assuming a unique minimum; if several labels have the same minimum cost, then we decide for a label also present at a 4-adjacent pixel location of p.

Fig. 5.27 Checkerboard partition of Ω into red and black pixel locations

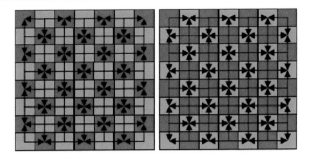

How to Improve Time Complexity? A first option is the so-called *red–black method*. Pixel locations in Ω are divided in being either *black* or *red*. At iteration t, messages are sent from black pixels to adjacent red pixels only; based on received messages, red pixels sent at iteration $t + 1$ messages to black pixels; see Fig. 5.27 for a possible partition of Ω.

Insert 5.9 (Jacobi and Gauss–Seidel Relaxations) *Consider a system of N linear equations* $\mathbf{Ax} = \mathbf{b}$, *with all diagonal elements of* $\mathbf{A}$ *being nonzero. Without loss of generality, we can consider each equation to be scaled so that its diagonal element is* 1. *Write* $\mathbf{A} = \mathbf{I} - \mathbf{L} - \mathbf{U}$, *where the square matrices* $\mathbf{L}$ *and* $\mathbf{U}$ *have their nonzero elements as minus the elements of* $\mathbf{A}$, *below and above the diagonal respectively. Then the N equations can be written as* $\mathbf{x} = (\mathbf{L} + \mathbf{U})\mathbf{x} + \mathbf{b}$.

   C.G.J. Jacobi (1804–1851) devised an iterative method for solving those linear equations for $\mathbf{x}$, *starting from an arbitrary initial estimate* $\mathbf{x}_0$ *and computing a sequence of vectors*

$$\mathbf{x}_{k+1} = (\mathbf{L} + \mathbf{U})\mathbf{x}_k + \mathbf{b}$$

Under suitable conditions, the sequence of vectors $\mathbf{x}_k$ *converges to the required solution* $\mathbf{x}$ *from any initial estimate* $\mathbf{x}_0$. *For example, if* $\sum_{j \neq i} |a_{ij}| < 1$ *for all* $i = 1, \ldots, N$, *then Jacobi's method converges. Jacobi's method requires storage space for two consecutive vectors in that sequence of estimates.*

   A modification of Jacobi's method was described by Gauss (see Insert 2.4) in 1823, in a private letter to his student C. L. Gerling (1788–1864), and a proof was published in 1874 by P.L. von Seidel (1821–1896). That Gauss–Seidel method requires storage for only one vector $\mathbf{x}$—*when each element gets updated, it replaces the previous value. It can be represented as*

$$\mathbf{x}_{k+1} = \mathbf{L}\mathbf{x}_{k+1} + \mathbf{U}\mathbf{x}_k + \mathbf{b}$$

*The first row of **L** has only zeros, and so the first element of $\mathbf{x}_{k+1}$ can be computed, followed successively by element 2, element 3, ..., element N.*

*Now consider matrices **A** with nonzero elements such that x can be partitioned into a red subvector and a black subvector, with each red element connected (by **A**) only to black elements and each black element connected only to red elements (as in Fig. 5.27). The following result has been proved (see* [D.W. Young. Iterative methods for solving partial difference equations of elliptic type. Trans. American Math. Society, vol. 76, pp. 92–111, 1954.] *for such matrices **A**: The Gauss–Seidel method converges iff Jacobi's method converges, and it converges (asymptotically) at twice the rate of Jacobi's method.*

A second way to achieve a speed-up is using *coarse-to-fine BP*, also called *pyramidal BP*. Coarse-to-fine BP not only helps to reduce computation time, it also contributes to achieving more reliable results.

We refer to the regular pyramid image data structure introduced in Sect. 2.2.2. Pixel locations in one 2×2 window in one layer of the pyramid are also adjacent to one node in the next layer (i.e. the pixel generated from this 2×2 window). This extends the used adjacency relation A in the BP algorithm. We only use a limited number of layers in the pyramid, such as (say) five.

Using such a pyramidal adjacency relation, the distances between pixels at the bottom layer are shortened, which makes message propagation more efficient.

What Needs to Be Specified for a BP Algorithm? We need to select the smoothness term, say, one of the three options (Potts, truncated linear, or truncated quadratic), with specification of a few parameters involved.

We need to specify the used adjacency relation, with 4-adjacency or a pyramidal extension of 4-adjacency as common standards.

Finally, the actual application (optic flow, image segmentation, and so forth) dictates possible choices for the data term.

Then we are ready to start the iterations and will decide about a way how or when to terminate the algorithm.

5.3.5 Belief Propagation for Image Segmentation

We provided two options for data terms for image segmentation in Examples 5.6 and 5.7. Both were examples for selecting initial feature vectors $\mathbf{u}_i$ for m segment labels, which will then lead to the calculation of m connected regions (segments) at least; each label can define multiple segments. There are many more possible ways for initializing feature vectors $\mathbf{u}_i$.

Figure 5.28 illustrates the application of pyramidal BP (using five pyramidal layers, including the original 1296×866 image itself at the ground layer) and not updating the initial seeds during the BP algorithm.

Fig. 5.28 *Upper left*: The original colour image Spring, showing a Spring scene at the University of Minnesota, Minneapolis. *Upper right*: The segmentation result after five iterations using pyramidal BP segmentation with a Potts smoothness term with $c = 5$ and a data term as proposed in Example 5.6 using the L_2-norm. *Lower left*: After 10 iterations, also for $c = 5$. *Lower right*: Also after 10 iterations but for $c = 10$

If the initial seeds $\mathbf{u}_i$, as proposed, e.g., in Examples 5.6 and 5.7, remain constant in the iterative process, then this is limiting the flexibility of the technique.

Observation 5.5 *It appears to be beneficial to update initial seeds $\mathbf{u}_i$ in each step of the BP iteration.*

For updating, we consider the results at the end of iteration step t of our BP algorithm. The value of the algorithm at p equals $f_p^t = l_j$ for

$$j = \underset{1 \le i \le m}{\arg \min} c_i^t \qquad (5.47)$$

at this moment. Identical labels define connected regions in the image, the segments at time t. Without specifying all the technical details, the basic idea can be to select the m largest segments (by area, i.e. number of pixels), reassign the m labels to those m segments, and use the centroids of those m largest segments as updated values $\mathbf{u}_i^t$ for the next iteration of the BP algorithm. See Fig. 5.29.

Because segment labels are just for identification, not for characterizing segment properties, only the Potts smoothness term appears to be meaningful for this particular application of BP. As an alternative, the smoothness term could also penal-

Fig. 5.29 The results for the image Spring shown in Fig. 5.28. *Left*: Segmentation result after five iterations using pyramidal BP segmentation with a Potts smoothness term with $c = 5$ and a data term as proposed in Example 5.6 but now using the χ^2-norm and updated centroids $\mathbf{u}_i^t$. *Right*: The result using the same algorithm but after 10 iterations and for $c = 10$

ize similarities of data represented by adjacent labels, meaning that different labels should truly reflect dissimilarities in image data.

Observation 5.6 *For replacing the Potts smoothness term by an alternative smoothness term in BP segmentation, it appears to be meaningful to include data characteristics into the smoothness term.*

This observation is stated here as a research suggestion; see also Exercise 5.10.

5.4   Video Segmentation and Segment Tracking

Video segmentation can benefit from the similarity of subsequent frames. Similarity can be defined by
1. *image-feature consistency*, meaning that corresponding segments have similar image feature statistics,
2. *shape consistency*, meaning that corresponding segments have about the same shape (to be refined by requests on scale invariance, rotation invariance, and so forth),
3. *spatial consistency*, meaning that corresponding segments have about the same location (due to the slow motion, also typically about the same size or even about the same shape), or
4. *temporal consistency*, meaning that corresponding segments can be tracked due to modelled camera and/or object movements in the scene (possibly supported by size or shape similarity).

This section discusses image-feature and temporal consistency. We discuss a mean-shift algorithm utilizing image-feature consistency in video data. For shape similarity, the shape features as discussed in Sect. 3.2 might be useful. Regarding spatial consistency, the moments and, in particular, the centroids of Sect. 3.3.2 are of relevance.

Fig. 5.30 *Left*: A frame of the sequence `tennisball`. *Middle and right*: Segment labelling by assigning colours as labels, showing inconsistency in labelling between Frame t and $t + 1$. Both frames have been mean-shift segmented individually

5.4.1   Utilizing Image Feature Consistency

Segments should remain stable over time, and there should be no appearance and disappearance of spurious segments over time. Mean-shift segmentation can be extended from still-image segmentation, as discussed before, to video segmentation.

When using colours for segment labelling, the colours should remain consistent over time and not change as illustrated in Fig. 5.30.

Local Peak Matching   We consider nD image feature vectors $\mathbf{u}$ at $|\Omega|$ pixel locations in each frame. For example, we can have $n = 3$ and $\mathbf{u} = (R, G, B)$ for colour images.

We assume consistency between local peaks of feature vectors $\mathbf{u}$ between segments in subsequent frames, meaning that the same peak is approached in two subsequent frames about at the same image coordinates. Thus, we extend the nD feature space to an $(n + 2)$D feature space, also taking the local coordinates x and y as feature components, but consider the spatial and value components as separated components $\mathbf{u}_s = (x, y)$ and $\mathbf{u}_v = \mathbf{u}$, respectively. The combined vectors $\mathbf{u}_c(t) = [\mathbf{u}_s(t), \mathbf{u}_v(t)]$ are now the elements in the $(n + 2)$D feature space for Frame t. For abbreviation, we again use

$$\mathscr{X}_{i,s} = \frac{1}{r_s^2} \left\| \mathbf{u}_s(t + 1) - \mathbf{u}_{i,s}(t) \right\|_2^2 \quad \text{and} \quad \mathscr{X}_{i,v} = \frac{1}{r_v^2} \left\| \mathbf{u}_v(t + 1) - \mathbf{u}_{i,v}(t) \right\|_2^2 \quad (5.48)$$

while assuming a kernel profile k_s with radius $r_s > 0$ for the spatial component and a kernel profile k_v with radius $r_v > 0$ for the value component.

At the beginning, Frame 1 is just segmented by mean-shift as a still image. Frame $t + 1$ needs to be segmented now, based on results for Frame t. Frame t has been processed; we have the values $\mathbf{u}_i(t)$, for $i = 1, \ldots, m$ being the combined feature vectors of Frame t.

In extension of the mean-shift for still images, as defined by (5.19), we have for the subsequent-frame case now the following:

$$m_g\big(\mathbf{u}_c(t + 1)\big) = \frac{\sum_{i=1}^m \mathbf{u}_i(t) \cdot g_s(\mathscr{X}_{i,s}) \cdot g_v(\mathscr{X}_{i,v})}{\sum_{i=1}^m g_s(\mathscr{X}_{i,s}) \cdot g_v(\mathscr{X}_{i,v})} - \mathbf{u}_c(t + 1) \quad (5.49)$$

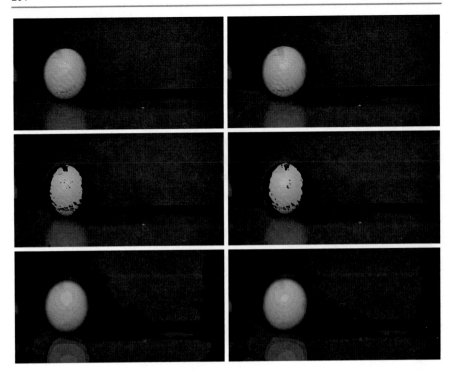

Fig. 5.31 *Top row*: Two subsequent frames of the sequence tennisball. *Middle row*: Black pixels (within the ball) are those which do not have matching peaks in the previous frame. *Bottom row*: Resultant segments

The mean-shift algorithm continues until $\mathbf{u}_c(t+1)$ converges to a local peak that matches value features in the previous frame, and all feature subsets are processed. A local peak for Frame $(t+1)$ is matched to the closest local peak for Frame t, assuming that the distance is reasonably small. Otherwise, the local peak for Frame $(t+1)$ creates a new class of segments.

Now we implement (5.49) analogously to the way how we did for still images for (5.19). We detect a new local peak when the mean-shift procedure converges, which means that the magnitude of the shift vector $m_g(\mathbf{u}_c(t+1))$ is below a threshold (e.g., below 100 in case of RGB colour images). Features of a pixel are replaced by the features of the assigned local peak. Figure 5.31 illustrates this for frames of the tennisball sequence, where features are 3D colour values. Corresponding local peaks can be mapped into false colours for better visibility of colour-labelled segments; see Fig. 5.32.

5.4.2 Utilizing Temporal Consistency

This subsection describes a simpler procedure, which only uses the spatial information and not the value distributions in segments. Figure 5.33 illustrates temporal

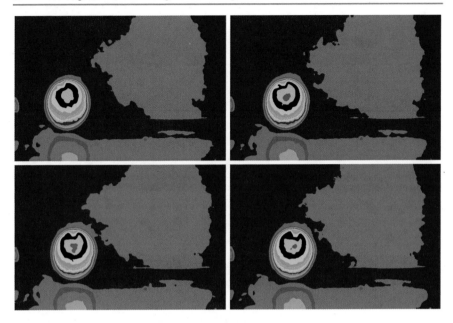

Fig. 5.32 False-coloured segments, mapping corresponding local peaks onto the same colour in four subsequent images of the recorded video sequence

Fig. 5.33 Bounding boxes of tracked segments for video sequences bicyclist and motorway

consistency (in vision-based driver assistance) where segment tracking can benefit from the fact that corresponding segments in subsequent frames have a substantial overlap of their pixel locations. Segments have been detected by stereo-image analysis (to be discussed later in this book), also allowing to label detected segments by distances (in meters) to the recording camera.

We select segments in subsequent frames of a video sequence that are of relevance for the given application (e.g. we ignore segments that are likely to be part of the background). For all the selected segments in Frame t, we like to know whether

Fig. 5.34 The symmetric
difference of sets A and B

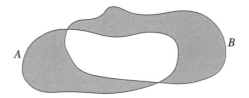

they "continue" in Frame $t + 1$. We assume that there are significant overlaps between corresponding segments in subsequent frames.

Outline of the Tracking Program   Let $\{A_0^t, A_1^t, \ldots, A_{n_t}^t\}$ be the family of segments selected for Frame t. We aim at pairing of segments A_i^t and A_j^{t+1} in Frames t
and $t + 1$, which defines *tracking* when performed along the whole video sequence.

An initially selected family $\{A_0^t, A_1^t, \ldots, A_{n_t}^t\}$ of segments defines our *active list
of segments*. We search for corresponding segments such that each A_i^t corresponds
to one A_j^{t+1} at most, and each A_j^{t+1} to at most one A_i^t. Some A_i^ts or A_j^{t+1}s may not
have corresponding segments. Without modelling camera or object movements, we
simply assume that we select corresponding segments based on overlaps between
segments A_i^ts or A_j^{t+1}s, also taking the motion of segment A_i^t into account as estimated by dense motion analysis (see Chap. 4).

If we cannot find a corresponding segment (also not by using the digital footprint
method defined below), then we remove a segment from the list of active segments.
There should also be a process for adding potentially new active segments to the list
from time to time.

Dissimilarity Measure   For measuring the dissimilarity of two segments A and
B, both given as sets of pixel locations in the same xy image domain Ω, we apply
a metric defined by the ratio of the cardinality of the *symmetric difference* of A and
B, see Fig. 5.34, to the cardinality of their union:

$$\mathscr{D}(A, B) = \frac{|(A \cup B) \setminus (A \cap B)|}{|A \cup B|} \tag{5.50}$$

This metric equals 0 if and only if both sets are equal and equals 1 if both sets have
no pixel location (x, y) in common.

Two-Frame Correspondences   Because the position of a segment A can change
from Frame t to Frame $t + 1$, we use the relative motion as obtained by a dense
optical flow algorithm (such as Horn–Schunck, Lucas–Kanade, BBPW, or others)
to compensate for a translational component. Let (u_p, v_p) be the optic flow at pixel
location p. We calculate the *mean flow* in the region occupied by A in Frame t as
follows:

$$\mathbf{u}_{A,t} = (u, v) = \frac{1}{|A|} \sum_{p \in A} (u_p, v_p) \tag{5.51}$$

We translate the pixel locations in a set A by $\mathbf{u}_{A,t}$ into a new set $\overline{A} = \mathbf{u}_{A,t}[A]$.

For segment A_i^t, $1 \le i \le n_t$, we identify now that index j_0 such that $\mathscr{D}(\overline{A_i^t}, A_j^{t+1})$ is minimal, for all $j = 1, \ldots, n_{t+1}$:

$$j_0 = \underset{j=1,\ldots,n_{t+1}}{\arg\min} \; \mathscr{D}(\overline{A_i^t}, A_j^{t+1}) \tag{5.52}$$

For excluding insignificant correspondences, we select a threshold T, $0 < T < 1$, such that we only accept correspondences if

$$\mathscr{D}(\overline{A_i^t}, A_{j_0}^{t+1}) < T \tag{5.53}$$

Altogether, we identified $A_{j_0}^{t+1}$ to be the segment in Frame $t + 1$ that corresponds to segment A_i^t in Frame t, formally denoted by

$$A \Rightarrow_{\mathbf{u}} B \tag{5.54}$$

for $A = A_i^t$, $B = A_{j_0}^{t+1}$, and $\mathbf{u} = \mathbf{u}_{A,t}$. Because, theoretically, there may be multiple segments A in Frame t that identify the same segment B in Frame $t + 1$ as being corresponding, we transform (5.54) into a one-to-one mapping by assigning B to the set A of selected candidates that minimizes the metric $\mathscr{D}(A, B)$.

History of Length τ   In order to track corresponding segments over multiple frames, we apply the two-frame correspondence procedure repeatedly and also try to deal with cases where segments change or even disappear for a short time. We apply a simple statistical filter.

The filter stores for each tracked segment its history of τ corresponding segments at previous time slots. For example, if recording at 25 Hz, we may use a value such as $\tau = 6$, thus less than a quarter of a second.

The *history of length* τ of a segment B in Frame t is defined by the sequence

$$A_1 \Rightarrow_{\mathbf{u}_1} A_2 \Rightarrow_{\mathbf{u}_2} \cdots \Rightarrow_{\mathbf{u}_{\tau-1}} A_\tau \Rightarrow_{\mathbf{u}_\tau} B \tag{5.55}$$

if there is always a corresponding segment defined when going backward from Frame $(t - i)$ to Frame $(t - [i + 1])$ for $i = 0, \ldots, \tau - 1$.

Mapping of History Segments into Frame t   The segment A_τ in Frame $t - 1$ was moved by $\mathbf{u}_\tau$ into $\mathbf{u}_\tau[A_\tau]$ when identifying the best match with B in Frame t. Segment $A_{\tau-1}$ in Frame $t - 2$ was moved by $\mathbf{u}_{\tau-1}$ into $\mathbf{u}_{\tau-1}[A_{\tau-1}]$ when identifying the best match with A_τ in Frame $t - 1$, thus defining set $\mathbf{u}_\tau[\mathbf{u}_{\tau-1}[A_{\tau-1}]]$ in Frame t when applying the next move $\mathbf{u}_\tau$ of the given history. In continuation, the segment A_1 moves into $\mathbf{u}_\tau[\mathbf{u}_{\tau-1}[\ldots\mathbf{u}_1[\ldots[A_1]\ldots]]]$ in Frame t.

In this way we map all the previous τ segments, detected to be in correspondence with segment B in Frame t, into their normalized locations in Frame t; the segment A_1 is translated τ times, the segment A_2 is translated $\tau - 1$ times, and so forth.

Temporal Relevance and Temporal Footprint   We assign a weight ω_i uniformly to each pixel location in the segment A_i for $1 \leq i \leq \tau$, with $\omega_1 \leq \omega_2 \leq \cdots \leq \omega_\tau \leq 1$. In this way we weight the *temporal relevance* of the segment A_i for its appearance in Frame t.

For example, for $\tau = 6$, we may use the weights $0.1, 0.1, 0.15, 0.15, 0.2, 0.3$, in this order, for $1 \leq i \leq 6$.

We accumulate now all those weights (by addition) at pixel locations resulting from the performed translations of the segments A_i into Frame t, defining the *temporal footprint* of the set A_τ over its history of length τ being the set of all pixel locations having an accumulated weight above the threshold 0.5.

Two-Frame Correspondence Revised   Two-frame correspondence search from Frame $(t - 1)$ to Frame t can now use this generated temporal footprint in Frame t. If there is no corresponding segment B in Frame t, then we use the temporal footprint of the set A_τ as segment B, defining now the new set A_τ by shifting all the history parameters forward for defining now a digital footprint in Frame $(t + 1)$ using the mean optical flow $\mathbf{u}_{B,t}$. We can use this kind of propagation (without having actually a corresponding segment in Frame t) for a limited time, for example for τ frames, assuming that a temporarily disappearing segment will show up again in a later frame, being only temporarily partitioned into other segments, merged with other segments, or not present due to similar operations. If a segment is not confirmed again, then it is discarded from the list of active segments used for frame tracking.

5.5   Exercises

5.5.1   Programming Exercises

Exercise 5.1 (Decrease in Number of Segments After Smoothing) As input, use grey-level images I of your choice, or generate grey-level images I with random grey levels in the range 0 to $G_{\max}$ (Hint: call the system function RANDOM for each visited pixel). Input images should be of decent size such as 500×500 at least. Process input images as follows:

1. Perform a 5×5 box filter on I for value smoothing.
2. Implement the fill-algorithm shown in Fig. 5.8 and count the number of resulting segments.
3. Repeat these two steps a few times (on the same generated image). Generate a diagram how the number of segments changes with the number of applications of the box filter.

    Compare results of your implementation with those of the function `flood-Fill` in OpenCV.

Fig. 5.35 *Left*: NPR of the image MissionBay; see Fig. 5.6 for original and stylization. *Right*: NPR of the image AnnieYukiTim; see Fig. 5.2 for original and stylization

Exercise 5.2 (Winnemöller Stylization, Mean-Shift Segmentation, and Simplification) This is a little project towards artistic rendering of taken photographs. Combine the following three processes into one solution for *non-photorealistic rendering* (NPR):

1. Derive binary edges for a given colour image based on Winnemöller stylization.
2. Perform mean-shift segmentation such that regions of constant colour value are created.
3. Do alpha-blending for the results obtained in the previous two processes and simplify the obtained colour image even further such that in regions circumscribed by edges as a general trend only one colour value is shown (i.e. enhance the posterization effect within regions defined by the obtained edges).

Figure 5.35 illustrates two results for such a combination of the briefly mentioned subprocesses.

Exercise 5.3 (Mean-Shift Segmentation in OpenCV) The function meanShift in OpenCV uses parameters for spatial radius (sp), colour radius (cr), and used levels in the image pyramid (L).

Parameter $k =$ sp defines the window size $(2k + 1) \times (2k + 1)$ in the spatial domain (i.e. carrier Ω). The parameter cr defines the window size in the feature space with "feature = colour" (i.e. consider all values (R, G, B) with

$$\left\| (R, G, B) - (R_0, G_0, B_0) \right\|_1 \leq \text{cr}$$

where (R_0, G_0, B_0) is the image value at the current pixel. The parameter L = maxLevel is greater than or equal to 0; this means that a pyramid of L $+1$ levels is used.

Figure 5.36 illustrates results for L = 1 (i.e. two levels); the top row illustrates the application of subsequent segment colouring using the function floodFill.

Discuss the meaning and impacts of the parameters cr, sp, and L with reference to provided explanations in this chapter and by using images of your choice, also including the image Spring as an example for a difficult segmentation.

Fig. 5.36 *Top*: Segmentation results for the image Aussies, where segments are pseudo–coloured rather than shown with the image value identified at the peak. Use of sp = 12 and sr = 19 (*left*), or use of sp = 5 and sr = 24 (*right*). *Bottom*: The image Xochicalco (*left*) and segmented image (*right*) using sp = 25 and sr = 25

Exercise 5.4 (Belief-Propagation Segmentation) Implement belief-propagation segmentation for the parameterization as specified in the captions for Figs. 5.28 and 5.29 (e.g. just use of the simple Potts model). Include the image Spring in your set of test images. Compare your segmentation results with those given in these two figures. Perform further variations in parameters of the algorithm, for example with the goal to reduce the number of segments, or with the goal to improve segments showing "just one person" or just a few "merged" persons.

Exercise 5.5 (Background Modelling) Images (e.g. in video surveillance) are often segmented into *objects* and *background*, i.e. a partition of Ω into only two types of pixels. Modelling the background by a *mixture of Gaussians* (e.g. three to five Gaussians) has been a standard approach in this area for some years. Figure 5.37 illustrates the application of this technique, which has been *not* described in this textbook. The original reference for the method is [C. Stauffer and W.E.L. Grimson. Adaptive background mixture models for real-time tracking. In Proc. Computer Vision Pattern Recognition, 1998], and there are many related materials available on the net, including sources.

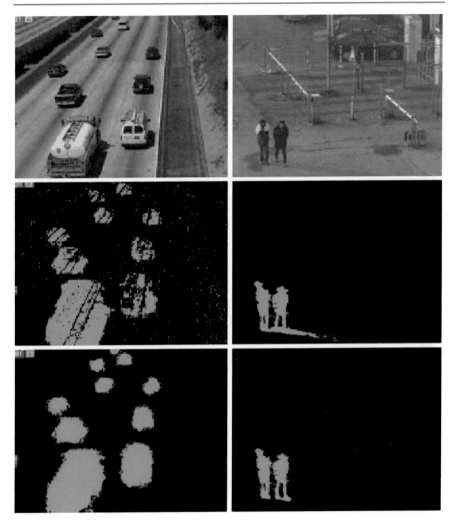

Fig. 5.37 *Top*: Original scenes. *Middle*: Background versus objects. *Bottom*: Post-processing with elimination of shadows in object areas

Record your own indoor or outdoor video data, study and understand the method, and model the background by a mixture of Gaussians, as proposed by Stauffer and Grimson.

Exercise 5.6 (Calculation of Recovery Rate) Select "simple" images that show only a small number of segments, such as less than 10. Provide the ground truth for those images, for example by manually identifying borders of segments.

Select a segmentation algorithm of your choice for these images and compare the obtained segments with the given ground truth by using the recovery rate measure as defined in Exercise 5.9.

5.5.2 Non-programming Exercises

Exercise 5.7 Suppose that the mean-shift algorithm for features clustering (as described on p. 188) uses a window of K grid points in a feature space, the histogram table includes C nonempty cells, and exactly $M \geq C$ different grid points are visited as the result of all mean calculations.

1. Show that the total time of the mean-shift algorithm is of *asymptotic time complexity*[3] $\mathcal{O}(MK + M^2)$, where power two comes from multiple visits over the same path from a given grid point to the stable mean point.
2. In order to avoid multiple visits, apply the ideas of the UNION-FIND algorithm (R. Tarjan 1975), i.e. when you visit the grid point $v = u + m_g(u)$ as the result of mean shifting to grid point u, then assign to q the following segment:

$$\mathrm{SEG}(v) = \mathrm{UNION}\big(\mathrm{SEG}(u), \mathrm{FIND}(q)\big)$$

   where v is rounded to the nearest grid point, and $\mathrm{FIND}(q)$ returns the segment q belongs to.

   Show that the use of UNION-FIND data structures reduces the time complexity for mean-shift clustering from $\mathcal{O}(MK + M^2)$ to $\mathcal{O}(MK)$.

Exercise 5.8 If we like to use the mean-shift idea to identify local maxima in a histogram in the feature space, then we find all grid points in the feature space for which the shift $m_g(u)$ is sufficiently small:

$$\overline{M} = \big\{u : \|m_g(u)\|_2 < \Delta u\big\}$$

where Δu is a grid step in the feature space.

Show that using a window with K grid points for the feature histogram with C nonempty cells requires $\mathcal{O}(CK)$ time to identify the set of grid points $\overline{M}$ approximating local maxima.

Exercise 5.9 We define the *recovery rate*, which is useful when comparing different segmentation or clustering techniques.

We consider clustering of vectors $\mathbf{x} \in \mathbb{R}^d$ for $d > 0$. For example, consider vectors $\mathbf{x} = [x, y, R, G, B]^\top$, with $d = 5$, for segmenting a colour image.

Our general definition is: A *clustering algorithm $\mathscr{A}$* maps a finite set S of points in $\mathbb{R}^d$ into a family of pairwise-disjoint clusters. A segmentation algorithm is an example for this more general definition.

Assume that we have an algorithm A which maps S into $m > 0$ pairwise disjoint clusters C_i (e.g. segments) for $i = 1, 2, \ldots, m$, containing $m_i = |C_i|$ vectors $\mathbf{x}_{ij} \in \mathbb{R}^d$. When segmenting an image, the sum of all m_is is equal to the cardinality $|\Omega|$. We call the C_is the *old clusters*.

---

[3]Consider increasing functions f and g from the set $\mathbb{N}$ of natural numbers into the set $\mathbb{R}^+$ of positive reals. We have $f(n) \in \mathcal{O}(g(n))$ *iff* there exist a constant $c > 0$ and an $n_0 > 0$ such that $f(n) \leq c \cdot g(n)$ for all $n \geq n_0$.

Now consider another clustering algorithm B, which maps the same set S into $n > 0$ pairwise disjoint clusters G_k for $k = 1, 2, \ldots, n$. We call the G_ks the *new clusters*. A new cluster G_k contains vectors $\mathbf{x}$ that were assigned by A to old clusters. Let

$$G_k = \bigcup_{j=1}^{s_k} G_{k_j}$$

where each G_{k_j} is a non-empty subset of exactly one old cluster C_i for $j = 1, 2, \ldots, s_k$. Indices or *names* i and k of old and new clusters are not related to each other, and in general we can expect that $n \neq m$. Let us assume that $n \leq m$ (i.e. the number of new clusters is upper bounded by the number of old ones).

An ideal *recovery* would be if each old cluster is equal to one of the new clusters, i.e. the two sets of clusters are just permutations by names, and $n = m$. Both algorithms A and B, would, for example, lead to the same image segmentation result; the segments might be just labelled by different colours.

Now we select contributing sets $G_{1_{j_1}}, G_{2_{j_2}}, \ldots, G_{n_{j_n}}$, one for each new cluster, which optimize the following two properties:

1. For each pair a_{j_a} and b_{j_b} of two different indices in the set $\{1_{j_1}, 2_{j_2}, \ldots, n_{j_n}\}$, there exist two different old clusters C_a and C_b such that $G_{a_{j_a}} \subseteq C_a$ and $G_{b_{j_b}} \subseteq C_b$.
2. Let C_k be the old cluster assigned to subset $G_{k_{j_k}}$ of the new cluster G_k in the sense of the previous item such that the sum

$$\sum_{k=1}^{m} \frac{|G_{k_{j_k}}|}{|C_k|}$$

is maximized; and this maximization is achieved for all possible index sets $\{1_{j_1}, 2_{j_2}, \ldots, n_{j_n}\}$.

The selected contributing sets $G_{1_{j_1}}, G_{2_{j_2}}, \ldots, G_{n_{j_n}}$ are thus assigning each new cluster G_k to exactly one old cluster C_k by maximizing the given sum. In particular, a chosen subset $G_{k_{j_k}}$ might be not the one of maximum cardinality in the partition of G_k; the selected contributing sets have been selected by maximizing the total sum. Then, the value

$$\mathcal{R}_A(B) = \sum_{k=1}^{n} \frac{|G_{k_{j_k}}|}{|C_k|} \times \frac{100\,\%}{n}$$

is called the *recovery rate* for a clustering algorithm B with respect to an algorithm A for input set S.

Note that we also do not need an algorithm A for comparison; just a given set of old clusters (say, the ground truth) is fine for calculating the recovery rate.

Discuss the asymptotic time complexity of the proposed measure for a recovery rate for clustering (and segmentation in particularly).

Exercise 5.10 Observation 5.6 suggest to replace the simple Potts smoothness term by an alternative smoothness term in BP segmentation. For example, if μ_1 and μ_2 are the intensity means in adjacent segments, then the constant c in (5.33) can be replaced by a term where c is scaled in dependency of the difference $|\mu_1 - \mu_2|$.

Specify modified smoothness functions based on (5.33) that include data characteristics into the smoothness term.

Exercise 5.11 Show that the dissimilarity measure $\mathscr{D}$ defined in (5.50) is a metric satisfying the three properties of a metric as specified in Sect. 1.1.3 on the family of sets of pixels. Each set of pixels has a defined cardinality (i.e. the number of pixels in this set).

Cameras, Coordinates, and Calibration

6

This chapter describes three basic components of a computer vision system. The geometry and photometry of the used cameras needs to be understood (to some degree). For modelling the projective mapping of the 3D world into images and for the steps involved in camera calibration, we have to deal with several coordinate systems. By calibration we map recorded images into normalized (e.g. geometrically rectified) representations, thus simplifying subsequent vision procedures.

Insert 6.1 (Niépce and the First Photograph) *The world's first photograph (image is in the public domain) was taken in 1826 in France by N. Niépce (1765–1833). It shows a view from a workroom on his farm at Le Gras:*

During eight hours of exposure time (note: buildings are illuminated by the sun from the right and from the left), the photograph was captured on a 20 × 25 cm oil-treated bitumen.

R. Klette, *Concise Computer Vision*, Undergraduate Topics in Computer Science, DOI 10.1007/978-1-4471-6320-6_6, © Springer-Verlag London 2014

Fig. 6.1 A drawing (in the public domain) of a camera obscura in the 17th century "Sketchbook on military art, including geometry, fortifications, artillery, mechanics, and pyrotechnics". Outside objects are projected top-down through a small hole onto a wall in the dark room

6.1 Cameras

The principle of a *camera obscura* is illustrated in Fig. 6.1. A small hole in the wall of a dark room projects the outside world top-down. This was known for thousands of years (e.g. about 2500 years ago in China), but it took till the beginning of the 19th century that projected images also were recorded on a medium, thus "frozen in time". By inserting a lens into the hole, the brightness and clarity of camera obscuras improved in the 16th century.

This section discusses features of cameras that may help you in the decision process which camera(s) should be used in your research or application. It also provides basic models for a single camera or a stereo-camera system, to be used in the following chapters.

6.1.1 Properties of a Digital Camera

A digital camera uses one or several *matrix sensors* for recording a projected image. See Fig. 6.2, left. A sensor matrix is an $N_{cols} \times N_{rows}$ array of *sensor elements* (phototransistors), produced either in *charge-coupled device* (CCD) or *complementary metal-oxide semiconductor* (CMOS) technology. The first digital camera was Sony's *Mavica* in 1981, after which other digital cameras were manufactured.

Fig. 6.2 *Left*: A sensor matrix. The individual cells are so tiny that they cannot be seen here, even after zooming in. *Right*: A sketch of the Bayer pattern

Fig. 6.3 The analysis of a car crash test (here at Daimler A.G., Sindelfingen, Germany) was based (in 2006) on high-resolution images captured at 1,000 pps

Computer Vision Cameras Computer vision benefits from the use of high-quality cameras. Important properties are, for example, the colour accuracy, reduced lens distortion, ideal aspect ratio, high spatial (also called high-definition) image resolution, large bit depth, a high dynamic range (i.e. value accuracy in dark regions of an image as well as in bright regions of the same image), and high speed of frame transfer. See Fig. 6.3 for an example of an application requiring high-quality cameras (e.g. for answering the question: "Did the mannequin's head hit the steering wheel?").

Computer vision cameras are typically permanently connected to a computer (via a video port or a frame grabber) and require software for frame capture or camera control (e.g., for time synchronization, panning, tilting, or zooming).

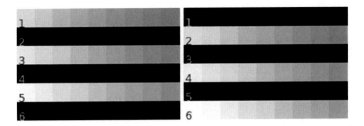

Fig. 6.4 Half-frames defined by either odd (*left*) or even (*right*) row indices

Digital Video Digital cameras provide normally both options of recording still images or video data. For a given camera, spatial times temporal resolution is typically a constant. For example, a camera which captures $7,680 \times 4,320$ (i.e. 33 Mpx) at 60 fps, records 1.99 Gpx (Gigapixels) per second. The same camera may also support to record $2,560 \times 1,440$ (i.e. 3.7 Mpx) at 540 fps, which also means 1.99 Gpx per second.

Interlaced digital video scans subsequent frames either at odd or even lines of the image sensor; see Fig. 6.4. Analog video introduced this technique for reducing transmission bandwidth. Reasons for interlaced video scans disappear with today's imaging technology.

Interlaced video is in particular disturbing for automated video analysis. Ways of combining both half-frames into one full frame can be (e.g.) by linear interpolation or simply by doubling rows in one half-frame.

Each frame contains the entire image in *progressive video*. This not only leads to better visual video quality, it also provides an appropriate input for video analysis.

Image Resolution and Bit Depth Each phototransistor is an $a \times b$ rectangular cell (e.g. a and b are about 2 μm each). Ideally, the *aspect ratio* a/b should be equal to 1 (i.e. square cells).

The image resolution $N_{cols} \times N_{rows}$ (= number of sensor elements) is commonly specified in *Megapixels* (Mpx). For example, a 4-Mpx camera has $\approx 4,000,000$ pixels in an image format such as $3:4$ or $9:16$. Without further mentioning, the number of pixels means "colour pixels". For example, Kodak offered in 1991 its DCS-100, which had a 1.3-Mpx sensor array.

A large number of pixels alone does not yet ensure image quality. As a simple example, more pixels means in general a smaller sensor area per pixel, thus less light per sensor area and a worse signal-to-noise ratio (SNR). The point-spread function of the optics used has to ensure that a larger number of pixels does not simply lead to additional noise in images. For computer vision applications, it is also often important to have more than just 8 bits per pixel value in one channel (e.g. it is of benefit to have 16 bits per pixel in a grey-level image when doing motion or stereo analysis).

Bayer Pattern or Beam Splitting The *Bayer pattern* (named after B. Bayer at Eastman Kodak) is commonly used on consumer digital cameras. One colour pixel is actually captured by four sensor elements, two for Green and one for Red and

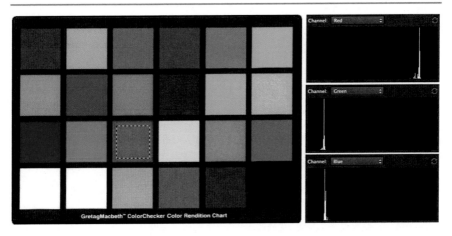

Fig. 6.5 A selected window in the red patch and histograms for the R, G, and B channels

Blue each. See Fig. 6.2, right. A sensor array of size $N_{cols} \times N_{rows}$ then actually records only colour images of resolution $\frac{N_{cols}}{2} \times \frac{N_{rows}}{2}$. Values R, G, and B at one recorded pixel are recorded at locations being one sensor element apart.

Alternatively, a *beam splitter* (e.g. using two dichroic prisms) is used in high-quality digital colour cameras to split light into three beams of differing wavelengths, one for the Red, one for the Green, and one for the Blue component. In this case, three $N_{cols} \times N_{rows}$ sensor arrays are used, and values R, G, and B at one pixel then actually correspond to the same pixel location.

Colour Accuracy A *colour checker* is a chart of squares showing different grey-levels or colour values. For example, see the colour checker from Macbeth™ in Figs. 1.32 and 6.5.

Example 6.1 (Colour Accuracy by Histogram Analysis) For evaluating colour accuracy, take an image of such a chart, preferably under diffuse illumination (for reducing the impact of lighting on colour appearance). Position a window within one patch of the acquired image. The histogram of such a window (if a colour patch, then three histograms for R, G, and B channels) should describe a "thin peak" for a camera with high colour accuracy. See Fig. 6.5.

Means of windows within different patches should relate (relatively, due to illumination effects) to each other as specified by the norm RGB values of those patches, provided by the producer of the colour checker.

Lens Distortion Optic lenses contribute the *radial lens distortion* to the projection process when capturing images, also known as the *barrel transform* or *pincushion transform*; see Fig. 6.6.

If a rectangular planar region is captured such that the projection centre is orthogonally in front of the centre of the region, then the region should ideally appear as a rectangle.

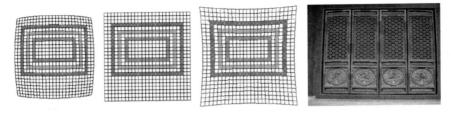

Fig. 6.6 *Left to right*: An image grid distorted by a barrel transform, an ideal rectangular image, an image grid distorted by a pincushion transform, and a projective and lens distortion combined in one image

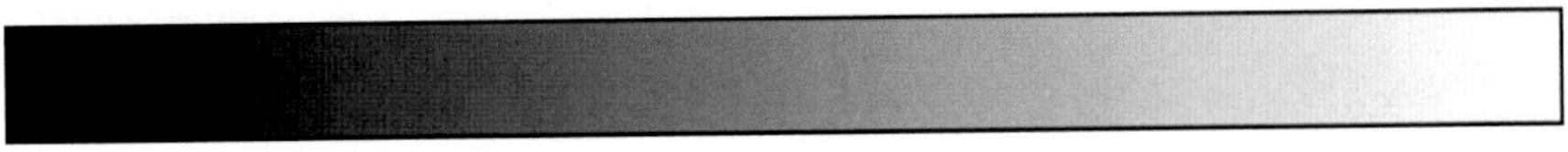

Fig. 6.7 Grey-level bar going linearly up from *Black* (value 0) to *White* (value G_{max})

Example 6.2 (Quantifying Lens Distortion) By capturing a regular grid (e.g., a checker board), the deviation of captured lines from the ideal of straight lines can be used to characterize the lens distortion of a camera. Effects of lens distortion depend on the distance to the test pattern and appear often together with projective distortions. See Fig. 6.6, right.

Linearity of a Camera Cameras are often designed in a way that they correspond to the perceived brightness in the human eye, which in nonlinear. For image analysis purposes, we either turn off the nonlinearity of created values, or, if not possible, it might be desirable to know a correction function for mapping captured intensities into linearly distributed intensities.

Patches of grey values, such as the bottom row of patches (representing grey levels) on the Macbeth™ colour checker or the linear bar in Fig. 6.7, can be used for testing the *linearity* of the measured intensity values $M = (R + G + B)/3$.

Assume that a black patch results in the mean intensity value u_{min} ($= 0$ in the ideal case) and a white patch results in the mean intensity value u_{max} ($= G_{max}$ in the ideal case). Now consider a patch which is a % white (i.e. $(100 - a)$ % black). Then this patch should get the corresponding linear value

$$u_{min} + \frac{a}{100}(u_{max} - u_{min}) \tag{6.1}$$

between u_{min} and u_{max}. Deviations from this expectation define correction values.

6.1.2 Central Projection

Ignoring radial distortions caused by the used optical lens, a projection through a small hole can be described by the theoretical *model of a pinhole camera*.

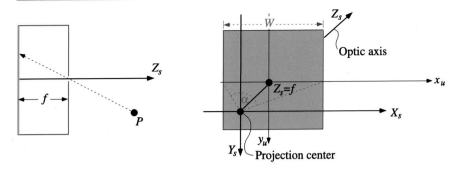

Fig. 6.8 *Left*: A sketch of an existing pinhole camera; a point P is projected through the hole (the projection centre) onto the image plane at distance f behind the hole; the projected image appears top-down. *Right*: A model of a pinhole camera, with an image of width W and viewing angle α; in the model we assume that the image plane is between world and projection centre

Model of a Pinhole Camera In this model, the diameter of the hole is assumed to be "very close" to zero. Existing pinhole cameras, also known as "shoebox cameras" (using either film or sensor matrices for image recording; see the web for photo examples) use indeed very small pinholes and long exposure times.

See Fig. 6.8, right, for the model of a pinhole camera. The pinhole is here called the *projection centre*. For avoiding top-down reversed images, the model has the projection centre behind the image plane.

We assume a right-hand $X_s Y_s Z_s$ camera coordinate system.[1] The Z_s-axis points into the world, called the *optic axis*. Because we exclude the consideration of radial distortion, we have *undistorted projected points* in the image plane with coordinates x_u and y_u. The distance f between the $x_u y_u$ image plane and the projection centre is the *focal length*.

In cases where the value of f is not (even in some abstract sense) defined by a focal length of a camera, it can also be called the *projection parameter*.

An ideal pinhole camera has a *viewing angle* (see Fig. 6.8, right) of

$$\alpha = 2 \arctan \frac{W}{2f}$$

The focal length f typically starts at 14 mm and can go up to multiples of 100 mm. For example, for $W = 36$ mm and $f = 14$ mm, the horizontal viewing angle equals about $\alpha = 104.25°$.[2] This model of a pinhole camera uses notions of optics in an abstract sense; it disregards the wave nature of light by assuming ideal geometric rays. It also assumes that objects are in focus, whatever their distance is to the camera. If projecting a visible surface point at close range, under practical circumstances we

---

[1]The subscript "s" comes from "sensor"; the camera is a particular sensor for measuring data in the 3D world. A laser range-finder or radar are other examples of sensors.

[2]For readers who prefer to define a *wide angle* accurately: let it be any angle greater than this particular $\alpha = 104.25°$, with $360°$ as an upper bound.

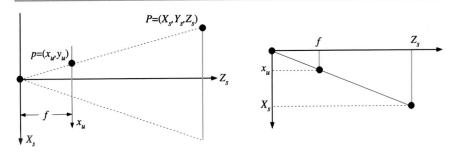

Fig. 6.9 *Left*: The central projection in the $X_s Z_s$ plane for focal length f. *Right*: An illustration of the ray theorem for x_u to X_s and f to Z_s

would have to focus an applied camera to this range (the parameter f of the camera increases to some $f + z$ this way).

Central Projection Equations   The $X_s Y_s Z_s$ Cartesian camera coordinate system can be used for representing any point in the 3D world. A visible point $P = (X_s, Y_s, Z_s)$ in the world is mapped by the *central projection* into a pixel location $p = (x_u, y_u)$ in the undistorted image plane; see Fig. 6.9, left. The ray theorem of elementary geometry tells us that f to Z_s (of point P) is the same as x_u (of pixel location p) to X_s (of point P), with analogous ratios in the $Y_s Z_s$ plane. Thus, we have that

$$x_u = \frac{f X_s}{Z_s} \quad \text{and} \quad y_u = \frac{f Y_s}{Z_s} \tag{6.2}$$

In the following we make use repeatedly of those two equations in (6.2).

The Principal Point   Figure 6.8, right, illustrates that the optical axis intersects the image somewhere close to its centre. In our assumed xy image coordinate system (see Fig. 1.1) we have the coordinate origin in the upper left corner of the image, and not somewhere close to its centre, as it occurs for the $x_u y_u$ image coordinates.

Let (c_x, c_y) be the intersection point of the optical axis with the image plane in xy coordinates. This point (c_x, c_y) is called the *principal point* in the xy image plane, and it needs to be determined by camera calibration. It follows that

$$(x, y) = (x_u + c_x, y_u + c_y) = \left(\frac{f X_s}{Z_s} + c_x, \frac{f Y_s}{Z_s} + c_y \right) \tag{6.3}$$

The pixel location (x, y) in our 2D xy image coordinate system also has the 3D coordinates $(x - c_x, y - c_y, f)$ in the $X_s Y_s Z_s$ camera coordinate system.

6.1.3   A Two-Camera System

For understanding the 3D geometry of a scene, it is convenient to use more than just one camera. Stereo vision requires two or more cameras.

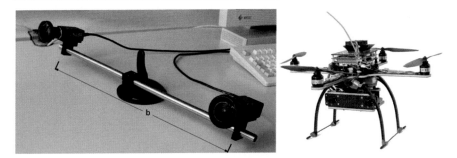

Fig. 6.10 *Left*: A stereo camera rig on a suction pad with indicated base distance b. *Right*: A forward-looking stereo camera system integrated into a quadcopter

Fig. 6.11 The canonical (or standard) stereo geometry

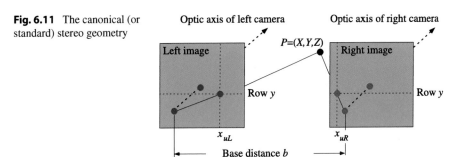

Stereo Camera System If we use two or more cameras in a computer vision application, then they should be as identical as possible for avoiding unnecessary difficulties. Calibration will then allow us to have virtually two identical copies of the same camera. The *base distance* b is the translational distance between the projection centres of two cameras. See Fig. 6.10, left. Figure 6.10, right, shows a quadcopter where the forward-looking integrated stereo camera system has a base distance of 110 mm (a second down-looking stereo camera system in this quadcopter has a base distance of 60 mm).

After calibrating two "nearly parallel" cameras, the base distance b is the only remaining parameter defining the relative pose of one camera with respect to the other.

Canonical Stereo Geometry As a result of calibration (to be described later), assume that we have two virtually identical cameras perfectly aligned as illustrated in Fig. 6.11. We describe each camera by using the model of a pinhole camera. The *canonical stereo geometry* of two cameras (also known as the *standard stereo geometry*) is characterized by having an identical copy of the camera on the left translated by the distance b along the X_s-axis of the $X_s Y_s Z_s$ camera coordinate system of the left camera. The projection centre of the left camera is at $(0, 0, 0)$ and the projection centre of the cloned right camera is at $(b, 0, 0)$. In other words, we have

1. two coplanar images of identical size $N_{cols} \times N_{rows}$,

Fig. 6.12 Omnidirectional cameras. *Left*: A fish-eye camera. *Right*: A digital camera with a hyperboloidal-shaped mirror

2. parallel optic axes,
3. an identical effective focal length f, and
4. collinear image rows (i.e., row y in one image is collinear with row y in the second image).

By applying the central projection equations of (6.2) for both cameras, a 3D point $P = (X_s, Y_s, Z_s)$ in the $X_s Y_s Z_s$ coordinate system of the left camera is mapped into undistorted image points

$$p_{uL} = (x_{uL}, y_{uL}) = \left(\frac{f \cdot X_s}{Z_s}, \frac{f \cdot Y_s}{Z_s} \right) \tag{6.4}$$

$$p_{uR} = (x_{uR}, y_{uR}) = \left(\frac{f \cdot (X_s - b)}{Z_s}, \frac{f \cdot Y_s}{Z_s} \right) \tag{6.5}$$

in the left and right image planes, respectively. Calibration has to provide accurate values for b and f for being able to use those equations when doing stereo vision.

6.1.4   Panoramic Camera Systems

Panoramic imaging sensor technology contributes to computer vision, computer graphics, robot vision, or arts. Panoramic camera systems can either record a wide-angle image in one shot or are designed for recording multiple images, to be stitched or combined into one wide-angle image.

Omnidirectional Camera System   Omnidirectional camera systems observe a 360-degree field of view; see Fig. 6.12 for two examples of such cameras. Omnidirectional imaging can be classified into catadioptric or dioptric systems.[3] A catadioptric system is a combination of a quadric mirror and a conventional camera; a

---

[3]*Catadioptric*: pertaining to, or involving both the reflection and the refraction of light; *dioptric*: relating to the refraction of light.

Fig. 6.13 *Upper row*: Original fish-eye images (180-degree fields of view, showing Prague castle and a group of people). *Lower row*: Resulting panoramic images

Fig. 6.14 An experimental rotating sensor-line camera configuration using a sensor-line camera mounted on a small turntable (for selecting a fixed viewing angle ω with respect to the normal of the rotation circle defined by the big turntable), which is on an extension slide, thus allowing us to chose a fixed distance R from the rotation centre of the big turntable

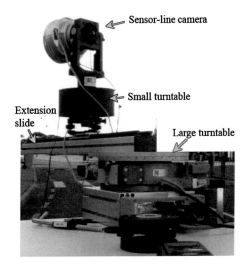

dioptric system has a specially designed refractor, which controls the angles of rays passing through the optical lens of the camera.

Figure 6.13 shows examples of recorded images. A mapping of a captured wide-angle field of view into a *cylindric panorama* is a solution to support common subsequent image analysis. Single-centre cylindric images possess perspective-like appearance and suppress circular distortion as given in catadioptric or dioptric images.

Fig. 6.15 A panoramic image of Auckland CBD recorded in 2001 from the top of Auckland Harbour Bridge using the sensor-line camera shown in Fig. 6.14

Rotating Sensor-Line Camera System   A rotating sensor-line camera produces cylindric panoramas when used in a configuration as illustrated in Fig. 6.14. The configuration is basically characterized by radius R and viewing angle ω.

The sensor-line camera records in one shot $1 \times N_{rows}$ pixels. It records subsequently (say, N_{cols} times) images during one rotation, thus allowing us to merge those N_{cols} line-images into one $N_{cols} \times N_{rows}$ array-image.

A benefit is that the length N_{rows} of the sensor line can be several thousands of pixels. The rotating sensor-line camera may record 360° panoramic images within a time frame needed for taking N_{cols} individual shots during one full rotation. Figure 6.15 shows an example of a $56{,}580 \times 10{,}200$ panorama captured in 2002 by a rotating sensor-line camera. The technology records dynamic processes in subsequent single-line images, which might be disturbing or desirable, depending on interests.

Stereo Vision with a Rotating Sensor-Line Camera System   A rotating sensor-line camera system can record a *stereo panorama* by rotating it once with a viewing angle ω and then again with a viewing angle $-\omega$, thus recording two cylindric array-images during both rotations, which define a stereo pair of images. See Fig. 6.16. If using a matrix-camera (i.e. of standard pinhole type), then it is sufficient to rotate this camera once and to compose panoramic images for a symmetric pair of angles ω and $-\omega$ just from a pair of image columns symmetric to the principle point of the camera used.

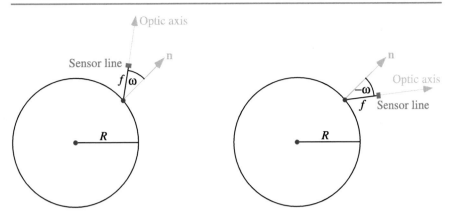

Fig. 6.16 *Left*: A top-view on a sensor-line camera with focal length f rotating at distance R to rotation centre and with viewing angle ω to normal of the rotation circle. *Right*: All the same but with viewing angle $-\omega$

Insert 6.2 (Panoramic Vision) *This is a very active field of research and applications, and we only provide two references here for further reading, the books* [K. Daniilidis and R. Klette, eds. Imaging Beyond the Pinhole Camera. Springer, Dordrecht, 2007] *and* [F. Huang, R. Klette, and K. Scheibe. Panoramic Imaging. Wiley, West Sussex, England, 2008].

6.2   Coordinates

This section discusses world coordinates, which are used as reference coordinates for cameras or objects in the scene. We also detail homogeneous coordinates, which provide a way to perform coordinate transforms uniformly by matrix multiplication (after extending the 3D world coordinate system by one more coordinate axis).

6.2.1   World Coordinates

We have cameras and 3D objects in the scenes to be analysed by computer vision. It is convenient to assume an $X_w Y_w Z_w$ *world coordinate system* that is not defined by a particular camera or other sensor. A camera coordinate system $X_s Y_s Z_s$ needs then to be described with respect to the chosen world coordinates; see Fig. 6.17. Figure 6.18 shows the world coordinate system at a particular moment during a camera calibration procedure.

Affine Transform   An *affine transform* of the 3D space maps straight lines into straight lines and does not change ratios of distances between three collinear points. The mathematical representation of an affine transform is by a *linear transform*

Fig. 6.17 Camera and world
coordinate systems

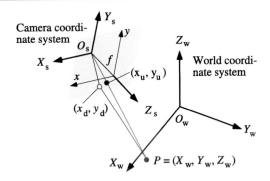

defined by a matrix multiplication and a translation. For example, we may first apply
a translation $\mathbf{T} = [t_1, t_2, t_3]^T$ followed by a rotation

$$\mathbf{R} = \begin{bmatrix} r_{11} & r_{12} & r_{13} \\ r_{21} & r_{22} & r_{23} \\ r_{31} & r_{32} & r_{33} \end{bmatrix} = \mathbf{R}_1(\alpha) \cdot \mathbf{R}_2(\beta) \cdot \mathbf{R}_3(\gamma) \tag{6.6}$$

where

$$\mathbf{R}_1(\alpha) = \begin{bmatrix} 1 & 0 & 0 \\ 0 & \cos\alpha & \sin\alpha \\ 0 & -\sin\alpha & \cos\alpha \end{bmatrix} \tag{6.7}$$

$$\mathbf{R}_2(\beta) = \begin{bmatrix} \cos\beta & 0 & -\sin\beta \\ 0 & 1 & 0 \\ \sin\beta & 0 & \cos\beta \end{bmatrix} \tag{6.8}$$

$$\mathbf{R}_3(\gamma) = \begin{bmatrix} \cos\gamma & \sin\gamma & 0 \\ -\sin\gamma & \cos\gamma & 0 \\ 0 & 0 & 1 \end{bmatrix} \tag{6.9}$$

are the individual rotations about the three coordinate axes, with *Eulerian rotation
angles* α, β, and γ, one for each axis. A translation preceded by rotation would lead
to a different rotation matrix and a different translation vector in general.

Observation 6.1 *Rotation and translation in the 3D space are uniquely determined
by six parameters* α, β, γ, t_1, t_2, *and* t_3.

World and Camera Coordinates   World and camera coordinates are transformed
into each other by a linear (or affine) transform. Consider the affine transform
of a point in the 3D space, given as $P_w = (X_w, Y_w, Z_w)$ in world coordinates,
into a representation $P_s = (X_s, Y_s, Z_s)$ in camera coordinates. Besides this *coordinate notation* for points used so far, we also use the *vector notation*, such as

$P_w = [X_w, Y_w, Z_w]^T$ for a point P_w. We have that

$$(X_s, Y_s, Z_s)^T = \mathbf{R} \cdot \left[(X_w, Y_w, Z_w)^T + \mathbf{T} \right] = \begin{bmatrix} r_{11} & r_{12} & r_{13} \\ r_{21} & r_{22} & r_{23} \\ r_{31} & r_{32} & r_{33} \end{bmatrix} \cdot \begin{bmatrix} X_w + t_1 \\ Y_w + t_2 \\ Z_w + t_3 \end{bmatrix}$$
(6.10)

for a rotation matrix $\mathbf{R}$ and a translation vector $\mathbf{T}$, which need to be specified by calibration. Note that $P_w = (X_w, Y_w, Z_w)$ and $P_s = (X_s, Y_s, Z_s)$ denote the *same* point in the 3D Euclidean space, just with respect to different 3D coordinate systems.

By multiplying the matrix and the vector in (6.10) we obtain that

$$X_s = r_{11}(X_w + t_1) + r_{12}(Y_w + t_2) + r_{13}(Z_w + t_3) \tag{6.11}$$

$$Y_s = r_{21}(X_w + t_1) + r_{22}(Y_w + t_2) + r_{23}(Z_w + t_3) \tag{6.12}$$

$$Z_s = r_{31}(X_w + t_1) + r_{32}(Y_w + t_2) + r_{33}(Z_w + t_3) \tag{6.13}$$

Projection from World Coordinates into an Image   Assume that a point $P_w = (X_w, Y_w, Z_w)$ in the 3D scene is projected into a camera and visible at an image point (x, y) in the xy coordinate system. The affine transform between world and camera coordinates is as defined in (6.11) to (6.13). Using (6.3), we have in camera coordinates that

$$\begin{bmatrix} x - c_x \\ y - c_y \\ f \end{bmatrix} = \begin{bmatrix} x_u \\ y_u \\ f \end{bmatrix} = f \begin{bmatrix} X_s/Z_s \\ Y_s/Z_s \\ 1 \end{bmatrix} = f \begin{bmatrix} \frac{r_{11}(X_w+t_1)+r_{12}(Y_w+t_2)+r_{13}(Z_w+t_3)}{r_{31}(X_w+t_1)+r_{32}(Y_w+t_2)+r_{33}(Z_w+t_3)} \\ \frac{r_{21}(X_w+t_1)+r_{22}(Y_w+t_2)+r_{23}(Z_w+t_3)}{r_{31}(X_w+t_1)+r_{32}(Y_w+t_2)+r_{33}(Z_w+t_3)} \\ 1 \end{bmatrix}$$
(6.14)

where we also model the shift in the image plane by $(c_x, c_y, 0)$ into the principal point in undistorted image coordinates.

6.2.2 Homogeneous Coordinates

In general, it is of benefit to use *homogeneous coordinates* rather than just inhomogeneous coordinates (as so far in this text). Just to mention one benefit: in homogeneous coordinates, the subsequent steps of matrix multiplication and vector addition in an affine transform, as, for example, in (6.10), reduce to just one matrix multiplication.

Homogeneous Coordinates in the Plane   We first introduce homogeneous coordinates in the plane before moving on to the 3D space. Instead of using only coordinates x and y, we add a third coordinate w. Assuming that $w \neq 0$, (x', y', w) represents now the point $(x'/w, y'/w)$ in the usual 2D inhomogeneous coordinates; the scale of w is unimportant, and thus we call (x', y', w) *homogeneous coordinates* for a 2D point $(x'/w, y'/w)$. Obviously, we can decide to use only $w = 1$ for representing points in the 2D plane, with $x = x'$ and $y = y'$.

Of course, you noticed that there is also the option to have $w = 0$. Homogeneous coordinates $(x, y, 1)$ define existing points, and coordinates $(x, y, 0)$ define *points at infinity*.

Lines in the Plane   A straight line in the plane is now represented by the equation

$$a \cdot x + b \cdot y + 1 \cdot c = [a, b, c]^T \cdot [x, y, 1] = 0 \qquad (6.15)$$

Consider two straight lines $\gamma_1 = (a_1, b_1, c_1)$ and $\gamma_2 = (a_2, b_2, c_2)$ in the plane, represented in the introduced homogeneous representation. They intersect at the point

$$\gamma_1 \times \gamma_2 = (b_1 c_2 - b_2 c_1, a_2 c_1 - a_1 c_2, a_1 b_2 - a_2 b_1) \qquad (6.16)$$

given in homogeneous coordinates. Formula (6.16) is also known as the *cross product* of two vectors. For parallel lines, we have that $a_1 b_2 = a_2 b_1$; the parallel lines intersect at a point at infinity. The calculus using homogeneous coordinates applies uniformly for existing points as well as for points at infinity.

Consider two different points $p_1 = (x_1, y_1, w_1)$ and $p_2 = (x_2, y_2, w_2)$; they define (i.e. are incident with) the line $p_1 \times p_2$. For example, assume that one of the two points is at infinity, say $p_1 = (x_1, y_1, 0)$. Then we have with $p_1 \times p_2 = (y_1 w_2, x_1 w_2, x_1 y_2 - x_2 y_1)$ an existing straight line. The point $p_1 = (x_1, y_1, 0)$ is at infinity in direction $[x_1, y_1]^T$.

If both points are at infinity, i.e. $w_1 = w_2 = 0$, then we have a straight line $p_1 \times p_2 = (0, 0, x_1 y_2 - x_2 y_1)$ at infinity; note that $x_1 y_2 \neq x_2 y_1$ for $p_1 \neq p_2$ in this case.

Example 6.3   Consider a point $p = (x, y)$ and a translation $\mathbf{t} = [t_1, t_2]^T$ in inhomogeneous 2D coordinates. The multiplication

$$\begin{bmatrix} 1 & 0 & t_1 \\ 0 & 1 & t_2 \\ 0 & 0 & 1 \end{bmatrix} \cdot [x, y, 1]^T = [x + t_1, y + t_2, 1]^T \qquad (6.17)$$

results in the point $(x + t_1, y + t_2)$ in inhomogeneous coordinates.

Observation 6.2 *Homogeneous coordinates allow us to perform uniquely defined calculations in the plane also covering the cases that we were not able to express before in our calculus when using only inhomogeneous xy coordinates.*

Homogeneous Coordinates in 3D Space   A point $(X, Y, Z) \in \mathbb{R}^3$ is represented by (X', Y', Z', w) in homogeneous coordinates, with $(X, Y, Z) = (X'/w, Y'/w, Z'/w)$. Affine transforms can now be represented by 4×4 matrix multiplications.

Example 6.4 Consider a point $P = (X, Y, Z)$ and a translation $\mathbf{t} = [t_1, t_2, t_3]^T$ in inhomogeneous 3D coordinates. The multiplication

$$
\begin{bmatrix}
1 & 0 & 0 & t_1 \\
0 & 1 & 0 & t_2 \\
0 & 0 & 1 & t_3 \\
0 & 0 & 0 & 1
\end{bmatrix} \cdot [X, Y, Z, 1]^T = [X + t_1, Y + t_2, Z + t_3, 1]^T \tag{6.18}
$$

results in the point $(X + t_1, Y + t_2, Z + t_3)$ in inhomogeneous coordinates.

Now consider an affine transform defined by rotation and translation, as given in (6.10). The 4×4 matrix multiplication

$$
\begin{bmatrix}
r_{11} & r_{12} & r_{13} & t_1 \\
r_{21} & r_{22} & r_{23} & t_2 \\
r_{31} & r_{32} & r_{33} & t_3 \\
0 & 0 & 0 & 1
\end{bmatrix} \cdot [X, Y, Z, 1]^T = \begin{bmatrix} \mathbf{R} & \mathbf{t} \\ \mathbf{0}^T & 1 \end{bmatrix} \cdot [X, Y, Z, 1]^T = [X_s, Y_s, Z_s, 1]^T
$$

$$\tag{6.19}$$

results in the point (X_s, Y_s, Z_s) in inhomogeneous coordinates.

By means of (6.19) we also introduced a notation of 4×4 matrices by means of a 3×3 submatrix $\mathbf{R}$, a column 3-vector $\mathbf{t}$, and a row 3-vector $\mathbf{0}^T$. We will use such a notation sometimes in the following.

6.3 Camera Calibration

Camera calibration specifies *intrinsic* (i.e. camera-specific) and *extrinsic* parameters of a given one- or multi-camera configuration.

Intrinsic or internal parameters are the (effective) focal length, dimensions of the sensor matrix, sensor cell size or aspect ratio of sensor height to width, radial distortion parameters, coordinates of the principal point, or the scaling factor. Extrinsic parameters are those of the applied affine transforms for identifying poses (i.e. location and direction) of cameras in a world coordinate system.

This section provides an overview on calibration such that you can perform camera calibration with calibration software as available on the net, with sufficient background knowledge for understanding what is happening *in principle*. The section is not detailing any particular calibration method, which is outside the scope of this textbook.

6.3.1 A User's Perspective on Camera Calibration

A camera-producer specifies normally some internal parameters (e.g. the physical size of sensor cells). The given data are often not accurate enough for being used in a computer vision application.

A Quick Guide   For camera calibration, we use geometric patterns on 2D or 3D surfaces that we are able to measure very accurately. For example, we can use a calibration rig that is either attached to walls (i.e. permanently positioned) or dynamically moving in front of the camera system while taking multiple images; see Fig. 6.18, right. The used geometric patterns are recorded, localized in the resulting images, and their appearance in the image grid is compared with the available measurements about their geometry in the real world.

Calibration may be done by dealing with only one camera (e.g. of a multi-camera system) at a time assuming that cameras are static or that we only calibrate internal parameters.

Typically, we have a movable multi-camera system in computer vision, and we follow a multi-camera approach for calibration, aiming at calibrating internal and external parameters. Recording may commence after having the parameters needed for calibration specified and the appropriate calibration rig and software at hand. Calibration needs to be redone from time to time.

When calibrating a multi-camera system, all cameras need to be exactly time-synchronized, especially if the calibration rig moves during the procedure.

Insert 6.3 (Calibration Software) *There is calibration software available online, such as the C sources provided by J.-Y. Bouget: a calibration rig is recorded under various poses*

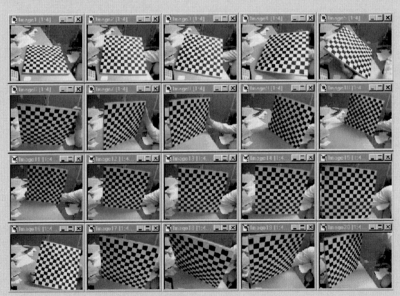

and processed as described on www.vision.caltech.edu/bouguetj/calib_doc/ or in the OpenCV *library.*

Fig. 6.18 *Left*: A 2D checkerboard pattern as commonly used for camera calibration. *Right*: A portable calibration rig; visible light reflections on the pattern would be a drawback when analysing recorded images of a calibration rig. Where is the world coordinate system?

> *Every new placement of the calibration rig in the 3D scene defines a different world coordinate system. Calibration provides internal and relative (i.e., one camera to other cameras) parameters. It is convenient for calibration accuracy if the calibration rig "fills" a captured image.*

Involved Transforms Each camera comes with its own camera coordinate system, having the origin at its projection centre as shown in Fig. 6.8, right. The calibration rig is commonly used for defining the world coordinates at the moment when taking an image (see Fig. 6.18, right). We need to consider the following transforms:

1. a coordinate transform from world coordinates (X_w, Y_w, Z_w) into camera coordinates (X_s, Y_s, Z_s),
2. a central projection of (X_s, Y_s, Z_s) into undistorted image coordinates (x_u, y_u),
3. the lens distortion involved, mapping (x_u, y_u) into the actually valid (i.e. distorted) coordinates (x_d, y_d); see Fig. 6.17,
4. a shift of $x_d y_d$ coordinates defined by the principal point (x_c, y_c), defining the sensor coordinates (x_s, y_s), and finally,
5. the mapping of sensor coordinates (x_s, y_s) into image memory coordinates (x, y) (i.e. the actual address of a pixel), as specified in Fig. 1.1.

Lens Distortion The mapping from a 3D scene into 2D image points combines a perspective projection and a deviation from the model of a pinhole camera, caused by radial lens distortion (see Sect. 6.1.1).

A (simplified) rule: Given a lens-distorted image point $p_d = (x_d, y_d)$, we can obtain the corresponding undistorted image point $p_u = (x_u, y_u)$ as follows:

$$x_u = c_x + (x_d - c_x)\left(1 + \kappa_1 r_d^2 + \kappa_2 r_d^4 + e_x\right) \tag{6.20}$$

$$y_u = c_y + (y_d - c_y)\left(1 + \kappa_1 r_d^2 + \kappa_2 r_d^4 + e_y\right) \tag{6.21}$$

for principal point (c_x, c_y) and $r_d = \sqrt{(x_d - c_x)^2 + (y_d - c_y)^2}$.

The errors e_x and e_y are insignificant and can be assumed to be zero. There is experimental evidence that approximating these series with only two lower-order components κ_1 and κ_2 corrects more than 90 % of the radial distortion. Using only the first-order radial symmetric distortion parameter κ_1 allows a precision of about 0.1 pixels in the image sensor array.

Lens distortion needs to be calibrated for each of the cameras, and this process may be separated from the remaining calibration processes. After having lens distortion corrected, the camera may be viewed as being an implementation of the pinhole-camera model.

Designing a Calibration Method   First, we need to define the set of parameters to be calibrated and a corresponding camera model having those parameters involved. For example, if the radial distortion parameters κ_1 and κ_2 need to be calibrated, then the camera model needs to include (6.20) and (6.21).

If we already know the radial distortion parameters and have used those for mapping recorded distorted images into undistorted images, then we can use equations such as (6.14). Points (X_w, Y_w, Z_w) on the calibration rig (e.g. corners of the squares) or *calibration marks* (i.e. special marks in the 3D scene where calibration takes place) are known by their physically measured world coordinates. For each point (X_w, Y_w, Z_w), we need to identify the corresponding point (x, y) (if possible, with subpixel accuracy) that is the projection of (X_w, Y_w, Z_w) in the image plane. Having, for example, 100 different points (X_w, Y_w, Z_w), this defines 100 equations in the form of (6.14), where only c_x, c_y, f, r_{11} to r_{33}, t_1, t_2, and t_3 appear as unknowns. We have an overdetermined equational system and need to find a "clever" optimization procedure for solving it for those few unknowns.

We can decide to refine our camera model. For example, we like to make a difference between a focal length f_x in the x-direction and a focal length f_y in the y-direction; we also like to include the edge length e_x and e_y of the sensor cells in the used sensor matrix in the camera, the transition from camera coordinates in world units to homogeneous camera coordinates in pixel units, or also a shearing factor s for evaluating the orthogonality of the recorded image array.

All such parameters can be used to add further details into the basic equation (6.14). Accordingly, the resulting equational systems will become more complex have more unknowns.

Thus, we briefly summarize the *general procedure*: known positions (X_w, Y_w, Z_w) in the world are related to identifiable locations (x, y) in recorded images. The equations defining our camera model then contain X_w, Y_w, Z_w, x, and y as known values and intrinsic or extrinsic camera parameters as unknowns. The resulting equation system (necessarily nonlinear due to central projection or radial distortion) needs to be solved for the specified unknowns, where over-determined situations provide for stability of a used numeric solution scheme.

We do not discuss any further such equation systems or solution schemes in this textbook.

Manufacturing a Calibration Board   A rigid board wearing a black and white checkerboard pattern is common. It should have 7×7 squares at least. The squares need to be large enough such that their minimum size, when recorded on the image plane during calibration, is 10×10 pixels at least (i.e. having a camera with an effective focal length f, this allows us to estimate the size of $a \times a$ cm for each square assuming a distance of b m between the camera and board).

A rigid and planar board can be achieved by having the calibration grid, e.g. printed onto paper or by using equally sized black squares, those glued onto a rigid board. This method is relatively cheap and reliable.

This grid can be created with any image-creating tool as long as the squares are all exactly of the same size.

Localizing Corners in the Checkerboard   For the checkerboard, *calibration marks* are the corners of the squares, and those can be identified by approximating intersection points of grid lines, thus defining the corners of the squares potentially with subpixel accuracy.

For example, assume 10 vertical and 10 horizontal grid lines on a checkerboard, as it is the case in Fig. 6.18, right. Then this should result in $10 + 10$ peaks in the $d\alpha$ Hough space for detecting line segments. Each peak defines a detected grid line, and the intersection points of those define the corners of the checkerboard in the recorded image.

Applying this method requires that lens distortion has been removed from the recorded images prior to applying the Hough-space method. Images with lens distortion will show bended lines rather than perfectly straight grid lines.

Localizing Calibration Marks   A calibration pattern can also be defined by marks such as circular or square dots. For example, this is a popular choice if cameras are calibrated in the same location, thus calibration marks can be permanently painted on walls or other static surfaces.

Assume that we identify an image region S of pixels as the area that shows a calibration mark, say, in grey levels. The position of the calibration mark can then be identified at subpixel accuracy by calculating the centroid of this region, as already discussed in Example 3.7.

6.3.2 Rectification of Stereo Image Pairs

Consider a two-camera recording system as discussed in Sect. 6.1.3. This is the common input for stereo vision, a basic procedure in computer vision for obtaining distance data by just using visual information.

The complexity of stereo vision is mainly defined by the task to identify the corresponding points in pairs of input images, recorded by two cameras. This task is the subject of Chap. 8. For reducing this complexity, it is convenient to warp the recorded image pairs such that it appears that they are actually recorded in canonical

Fig. 6.19 *Top*: Images recorded by two cameras with significant differences in extrinsic parameters and also (insignificant) differences in intrinsic parameters. *Bottom*: Two geometrically rectified images taken at different viewing locations by two cameras installed in a crash-test hall

stereo geometry (by a pair of identical cameras). We call this process short *geometric rectification*, without further mentioning the context of stereo vision (geometric rectification is also of relevance in other contexts).

A Multi-camera System   Often it is actually insufficient to use just two cameras for applying computer vision to complex environments or processes. For example, in a crash-test hall in the automotive industry there are many high-definition very fast cameras installed for recording the few seconds of a crash test from different viewing angles. Figure 6.19 illustrates two geometrically rectified images. How to achieve this?

We will answer this question in this subsection. We do not restrict the discussion to just a left camera and a right camera. We consider a general case of a Camera i or Camera j, where the numbers i and j identify different cameras in a multi-camera system.

The Camera Matrix   As (examples of) intrinsic camera parameters of Camera i, we consider here

1. the edge lengths e_i^x and e_i^y of camera sensor cells (defining the aspect ratio),
2. a skew parameter s_i,
3. the coordinates of the principal point $\mathbf{c}_i = (c_i^x, c_i^y)$ where the optical axis of Camera i and image plane intersect, and

4. the focal length f_i.

We assume that the lens distortion has been calibrated before and does not need to be included anymore in the set of intrinsic parameters.

Instead of the simple equation (6.14), defining a camera model just based on the intrinsic parameters f, c_x and c_y, we have now a refined projection equation in 4D homogeneous coordinates, mapping a 3D point $P = (X_w, Y_w, Z_w)$ into the image coordinates $p_i = (x_i, y_i)$ of the ith camera (as defined by Fig. 1.1) as follows:

$$
k \begin{bmatrix} x_i \\ y_i \\ 1 \end{bmatrix} = \begin{bmatrix} f_i/e_i^x & s_i & c_i^x & 0 \\ 0 & f_i/e_i^y & c_i^y & 0 \\ 0 & 0 & 1 & 0 \end{bmatrix} \begin{bmatrix} \mathbf{R}_i & -\mathbf{R}_i^T \mathbf{t}_i \\ \mathbf{0}^T & 1 \end{bmatrix} \begin{bmatrix} X_w \\ Y_w \\ Z_w \\ 1 \end{bmatrix}
$$

$$
= [\mathbf{K}_i | \mathbf{0}] \cdot \mathbf{A}_i \cdot [X_w, Y_w, Z_w, 1]^T \tag{6.22}
$$

where $\mathbf{R}_i$ and $\mathbf{t}_i$ denote the rotation matrix and translation vector in 3D inhomogeneous world coordinates, and $k \neq 0$ is a scaling factor.

By means of (6.22) we defined a 3×3 matrix $\mathbf{K}_i$ of intrinsic camera parameters, and a 4×4 matrix $\mathbf{A}_i$ of extrinsic parameters (of the affine transform) of Camera i. The 3×4 *camera matrix*

$$
\mathbf{C}_i = [\mathbf{K}_i | \mathbf{0}] \cdot \mathbf{A}_i \tag{6.23}
$$

is defined by 11 parameters if we allow for an arbitrary scaling of parameters; otherwise, it is 12.

Common Viewing Direction for Rectifying Cameras i and j   We identify a common viewing direction for Cameras i and j, replacing the given viewing directions along the optical axes of those two cameras. Let Π be a plane perpendicular to the baseline vector $\mathbf{b}_{ij}$ from the projection centre of Camera i to the projection centre of Camera j. See Fig. 6.20.

We project the unit vectors $\mathbf{z}_i^\circ$ and $\mathbf{z}_j^\circ$ of both optical axes into Π, which results in vectors $\mathbf{n}_i$ and $\mathbf{n}_j$, respectively. The algebraic relations are as follows:

$$
\mathbf{n}_i = \left(\mathbf{b}_{ij} \times \mathbf{z}_i^\circ\right) \times \mathbf{b}_{ij} \quad \text{and} \quad \mathbf{n}_j = \left(\mathbf{b}_{ij} \times \mathbf{z}_j^\circ\right) \times \mathbf{b}_{ij} \tag{6.24}
$$

We could also have used $\mathbf{b}_{ji}$ in both equations, but then uniformly four times.

Aiming at a "balanced treatment" of both cameras, we use the bisector of $\mathbf{n}_i$ and $\mathbf{n}_j$ for defining the unit vector

$$
\mathbf{z}_{ij}^\circ = \frac{\mathbf{n}_i + \mathbf{n}_j}{\|\mathbf{n}_i + \mathbf{n}_j\|_2} \tag{6.25}
$$

of the common direction.

Fig. 6.20 An illustration for calculating the common viewing direction for Cameras i and j

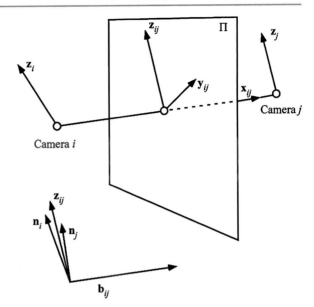

Consider the unit vector $\mathbf{x}_{ij}^{\circ}$ in the same direction as $\mathbf{b}_{ij}$, and the unit vector $\mathbf{y}_{ij}^{\circ}$ is finally defined by the constraint of ensuring (say) a left-hand 3D Cartesian coordinate system. Formally, we have that

$$\mathbf{x}_{ij}^{\circ} = \frac{\mathbf{b}_{ij}}{\|\mathbf{b}_{ij}\|_2} \quad \text{and} \quad \mathbf{y}_{ij}^{\circ} = \mathbf{z}_{ij} \times \mathbf{x}_{ij}^{\circ} = -\mathbf{x}_{ij}^{\circ} \times \mathbf{z}_{ij} \tag{6.26}$$

In general, for any vectors $\mathbf{a}$ and $\mathbf{b}$, $(\mathbf{a}, \mathbf{b}, \mathbf{a} \times \mathbf{b})$ defines a left-hand tripod. We have the left-hand tripod $(\mathbf{x}_{ij}^{\circ}, \mathbf{z}_{ij}^{\circ} \times \mathbf{x}_{ij}^{\circ}, \mathbf{z}_{ij}^{\circ})$ because

$$\mathbf{x}_{ij}^{\circ} \times \left(\mathbf{z}_{ij}^{\circ} \times \mathbf{x}_{ij}^{\circ}\right) = \mathbf{z}_{ij}^{\circ}\left(\mathbf{x}_{ij}^{\circ} \cdot \mathbf{x}_{ij}^{\circ}\right) - \mathbf{x}_{ij}^{\circ}\left(\mathbf{x}_{ij}^{\circ} \cdot \mathbf{z}_{ij}^{\circ}\right) = \mathbf{z}_{ij}^{\circ} \tag{6.27}$$

and $(\mathbf{x}_{ij}^{\circ}, \mathbf{x}_{ij}^{\circ} \times \mathbf{z}_{ij}^{\circ}, \mathbf{z}_{ij}^{\circ})$ would be a right-hand tripod.

The two images of Camera i and Camera j need to be modified as though both would have been taken in the direction $\mathbf{R}_{ij} = (\mathbf{x}_{ij}\mathbf{y}_{ij}\mathbf{z}_{ij})^T$, instead of the actually used directions $\mathbf{R}_i$ and $\mathbf{R}_j$.

Producing the Rectified Image Pair   The rotation matrices that rotate both cameras into their new (virtual) viewing direction are as follows:

$$\mathbf{R}_i^* = \mathbf{R}_{ij}\mathbf{R}_i^T \quad \text{and} \quad \mathbf{R}_j^* = \mathbf{R}_{ij}\mathbf{R}_j^T \tag{6.28}$$

In general, when rotating any camera around its projection centre about the matrix $\mathbf{R}$, the image is transformed by a rotation *homography* (i.e. a recalculated projective transformation)

$$\mathbf{H} = \mathbf{K} \cdot \mathbf{R} \cdot \mathbf{K}^{-1} \tag{6.29}$$

where $\mathbf{K}$ is the 3×3 matrix of intrinsic parameters of this camera. The matrix $\mathbf{K}^{-1}$ transfers pixel coordinates into camera coordinates in world units, the matrix $\mathbf{R}$ rotates them into the common plane, and the matrix $\mathbf{K}$ transfers them back into pixel coordinates.

A rectified image is calculated, pixel by pixel, using

$$p = \mathbf{H}^{-1} \hat{p} \qquad (6.30)$$

such that the new value at pixel location $\hat{p}$ is calculated based on the original image values in a neighbourhood of a point p (which is in general not exactly a pixel location), using (e.g.) bilinear interpolation.

Creating an Identical Twin   Assume that we want to have the image of Camera j after rotation homography with respect to the parameters of Camera i, i.e. we create an identical copy of Camera i at the pose of Camera j. For ensuring this effect, we simply apply the rotation homography

$$\mathbf{H}_{ij} = \mathbf{K}_i \cdot \mathbf{R}_j^* \cdot \mathbf{K}_j^{-1} \qquad (6.31)$$

which first transforms by $\mathbf{K}_j^{-1}$ the points in the jth image plane into a "normalized" coordinate system, then we apply $\mathbf{R}_j^*$ to perform the desired rotation, and, finally, $\mathbf{K}_i$ for transforming the rotation result according to the parameters of Camera i.

Insert 6.4 (Fundamental and Essential Matrix of Stereo Vision) *Following a publication by H.C. Longuet-Higgins in 1981, Q.T. Luong identified in 1992 in his PhD thesis two matrices, called the fundamental matrix and essential matrix, which describe binocular stereo geometry, either with including the characteristics of the used cameras or without, respectively.*

Fundamental and Essential Matrix   We go back to having just a left and a right camera. Let p_L and p_R be *corresponding stereo points*, i.e. the projections of a 3D point P in the left and right image planes. Assume that p_L and p_R are given in homogeneous coordinates. Then we have that

$$p_R^T \cdot \mathbf{F} \cdot p_L = 0 \qquad (6.32)$$

for some 3×3 matrix $\mathbf{F}$, defined by the configuration (i.e. intrinsic and extrinsic parameters) of the two cameras for *any* pair p_L and p_R of corresponding stereo points.

This matrix $\mathbf{F}$ is known as the *fundamental matrix*, sometimes also called the *epipolar matrix* or the *bifocal tensor*. For example, $\mathbf{F} \cdot p_L$ defines a line in the image plane of the right camera, and any stereo point corresponding to p_L needs to be on that line. (This is an *epipolar line*, and we discuss such a line later in the book.)

The matrix $\mathbf{F}$ is of rank 2 and uniquely defined (by the left and right cameras) up to a scaling factor. In general, seven pairs of corresponding points (in general position) are sufficient to identify the matrix $\mathbf{F}$. Interestingly, there is the relation

$$\mathbf{F} = \mathbf{K}_R^{-T} \cdot \mathbf{R}[\mathbf{t}]_\times \cdot \mathbf{K}_L^{-1} \tag{6.33}$$

for camera matrices $\mathbf{K}_R$ and $\mathbf{K}_L$. We go from pixel coordinates to camera coordinates in world units. Here, $[\mathbf{t}]_\times$ is the *cross product matrix* of a vector $\mathbf{t}$, defined by $[\mathbf{t}]_\times \cdot \mathbf{a} = \mathbf{t} \times \mathbf{a}$, or

$$[\mathbf{t}]_\times = \begin{bmatrix} 0 & -t_3 & t_2 \\ t_3 & 0 & -t_1 \\ -t_2 & t_1 & 0 \end{bmatrix} \tag{6.34}$$

The matrix

$$\mathbf{E} = \mathbf{R}[\mathbf{t}]_\times \tag{6.35}$$

is also known as the *essential matrix*; it has five degrees of freedom, and it is uniquely defined (by the left and right cameras) up to scaling.

Insert 6.5 (Geometry of Multi-Camera Systems) *This chapter provided a basic introduction into geometric issues related to single- or multiple-camera systems. Standard references for geometric subjects in computer vision are, for example, the books* [R. Hartley and A. Zisserman. Multiple View Geometry in Computer Vision, Second Edition. Cambridge University Press, Cambridge, 2004] *and* [K. Kanatani. Geometric Computation for Machine Vision. Oxford University Press, Oxford, 1993].

6.4   Exercises

6.4.1   Programming Exercises

Exercise 6.1 (Evaluation of Cameras) Evaluate (at least) two different digital cameras with respect to the properties of
1. colour accuracy,
2. linearity, and
3. lens distortion.
Even two cameras of the same brand might be of interest; it is expected that they result in (slightly) different properties.

Design, calculate and print at least one test image (test pattern) for each of those three properties. Try to provide a motivation why you decided for your test images. Obviously, printer quality will influence your tests.

Take measurements repeatedly (say, under varying conditions, such as having your test images, or further test objects, at different distances to the camera, or under varying light conditions). This needs to be followed by a statistical analysis (calculate the means and standard deviations for your measurement series).

Fig. 6.21 *Top*: Registered images. *Bottom*: Stitched images. Results of a project in 1998 at the University of Auckland

Note that property comparisons will typically not lead to a simple result such as "this camera is better than the other one", rather to a more sophisticated comparison such as "for this criterion, this camera performs better under given circumstances."

Exercise 6.2 (Image Stitching) Use a common (i.e. array- or pinhole-type) digital camera on a tripod and record a series of images by rotating the camera: capture each image such that the recorded scene overlaps to some degree with the scene recorded in the previous image.

Write your own simple and straightforward program of *stitching* those images onto the surface of one cylinder or into a rectangular panorama. The first step is *image registration*, i.e. spatially aligning the recorded images and defining cuts between those. See Fig. 6.21 for an illustration of registration and stitching steps.

(*Image stitching* is an area where many solutions have been published already; check the net for some inspirations.)

For comparison, use a commercial or freely available stitching software (note that often this already comes with the camera or is available via the camera web support) for mapping the images into a 360° panorama.

Compare the results with the results of your own image stitching program.

Exercise 6.3 (Stereo Panorama) Rotate a video camera on a tripod for generating stereo panoramas as described at the end of Sect. 6.1.4. The two columns generating your views for ω and $-\omega$ need to be chosen carefully; they need to be symmetric with respect to the principal point of your video camera. If not, the generated two-view panoramas do not have proper geometry for being stereo-viewable.

Regarding the chosen radius R and viewing angle ω, there are two recommended values that maximize the number of disparity levels between the closest object of interest at distance D_1 and the furthest object of interest at distance D_2. These two (uniquely defined) values can be looked up in the second book listed in Insert 6.2. You may also experiment with taking different values R and ω.

The generated stereo panoramas become stereo-viewable by using anaglyphs. Anaglyphic images are generated by combining the channel for Red from one image with the channels for Blue and Green from the other image. The order of filters in available anaglyphic eyeglasses decides which image contributes which the channel. Demonstrate your recorded stereo panoramas using anaglyphic eyeglasses.

Exercise 6.4 (Detection of Calibration Marks) Record images for camera calibration using a checkerboard pattern as illustrated in Insert 6.3. Implement or use an available program for line detection (see Sect. 3.4.1) and detect the corners in the recorded images at subpixel accuracy. Discuss the impact of radial lens distortion on your detected corners.

Exercise 6.5 (Building a Pinhole Camera) This is not a programming exercise, but a practical challenge. It is a suggestion for those who like to experience the simplest possible camera, which you can build yourself, basically just using a shoebox and photo-sensitive paper: check out on the net for "pinhole cameras", where there are some practical hints, and there is also an interesting collection of photos online recorded with those cameras.

6.4.2 Non-programming Exercises

Exercise 6.6 Check this chapter for equations given in inhomogeneous coordinates. Express all those in homogeneous coordinates.

Exercise 6.7 Specify the point at infinity on the line $31x + 5y - 12 = 0$. Determine the homogeneous equation of this line. What is the intersection point of this line with the line $31x + 5y - 14 = 0$ at infinity?

Generalize by studying the lines $ax + by + c_1 = 0$ and $ax + by + c_2 = 0$ for $c_1 \neq c_2$.

Exercise 6.8 Consider a camera defined by the following 3×4 camera matrix:

$$\mathbf{C} = \begin{bmatrix} 1 & 0 & 0 & 0 \\ 0 & 1 & 0 & 0 \\ 0 & 0 & 1 & 1 \end{bmatrix}$$

Compute the projections of the following 3D points (in world coordinates) with this camera:

$$\mathbf{P}_1 = \begin{bmatrix} 1 \\ 1 \\ 1 \\ 1 \end{bmatrix}, \quad \mathbf{P}_2 = \begin{bmatrix} 1 \\ 1 \\ -1 \\ 1 \end{bmatrix}, \quad \mathbf{P}_3 = \begin{bmatrix} 3 \\ 2 \\ 1 \\ 1 \end{bmatrix}, \quad \text{and} \quad \mathbf{P}_4 = \begin{bmatrix} 0 \\ 0 \\ 0 \\ 1 \end{bmatrix}$$

Exercise 6.9 Let $p_R = [x, y, 1]^\top$ and $p_L = [x', y', 1]^\top$. The equation

$$p_R^T \cdot \mathbf{F} \cdot p_L = 0$$

is equivalently expressed by

$$\begin{bmatrix} xx' & xy' & x & yx' & yy' & y & x' & y' & 1 \end{bmatrix} \begin{bmatrix} F_{11} \\ F_{21} \\ F_{31} \\ F_{12} \\ F_{22} \\ F_{32} \\ F_{13} \\ F_{23} \\ F_{33} \end{bmatrix} = 0$$

where F_{ij} are the elements of the fundamental matrix $\mathbf{F}$. Now assume that we have at least eight pairs of corresponding pixels, defining the matrix equation

$$\begin{bmatrix} x_1x_1' & x_1y_1' & x_1 & y_1x_1' & y_1y_1' & y_1 & x_1' & y_1' & 1 \\ x_2x_2' & x_2y_2' & x_2 & y_2x_2' & y_2y_2' & y_2 & x_2' & y_2' & 1 \\ \vdots & \vdots & \vdots & \vdots & \vdots & \vdots & \vdots & \vdots & \vdots \\ x_nx_n' & x_ny_n' & x_n & y_nx_n' & y_ny_n' & y_n & x_n' & y_n' & 1 \end{bmatrix} \begin{bmatrix} F_{11} \\ F_{21} \\ \vdots \\ F_{33} \end{bmatrix} = \begin{bmatrix} 0 \\ 0 \\ \vdots \\ 0 \end{bmatrix}$$

for $n \geq 8$, expressed in short as $\mathbf{A} \cdot \mathbf{f} = \mathbf{0}$. Solve this equation for the unknowns F_{ij}, considering noise or inaccuracies in pairs of corresponding pixels.

Exercise 6.10 Show that the following is true for any nonzero vector $\mathbf{t} \in \mathbb{R}^3$:
1. $[\mathbf{t}]_x \cdot \mathbf{t} = 0$,
2. the rank of matrix $[\mathbf{t}]_x$ is 2,
3. the rank of the essential matrix $\mathbf{E} = \mathbf{R}[\mathbf{t}]_x$ is 2,
4. the fundamental matrix $\mathbf{F}$ is derived from the essential matrix $\mathbf{E}$ by the formula
   $\mathbf{F} = \mathbf{K}_R^{-T}\mathbf{E}\mathbf{K}_L^{-1}$,
5. the rank of the fundamental matrix $\mathbf{F}$ is 2.

3D Shape Reconstruction

7

This chapter describes three different techniques for vision-based reconstruction of 3D shapes. The use of structured lighting is a relatively simple but accurate method. Stereo vision might be called *the* 3D shape-reconstruction method in computer vision; its actual stereo-matching challenges are a subject in the following chapter; here we only discuss how results of stereo matching are used to derive a 3D shape. Finally, as an alternative technique, we briefly describe shading-based 3D-shape understanding.

7.1 Surfaces

Computer vision reconstructs and analyses the visible world, typically defined by textured surfaces (e.g. not considering fully or partially transparent objects).

This section provides an introduction into the topology of surfaces, a parameterized description of surface patches, and the gradient space, a model for analysing relations between surface normals. We also define the surface curvature.

Insert 7.1 (3D City or Landscape Visualizations) *Camera or laser range-finder data have been used since about* 2000 *for large-scale and very detailed 3D city or landscape visualizations; see Fig. 7.1 for an example. Such 3D visualizations go beyond 2D representations of the Earth surface (by aerial images) or merged street-view images that do not yet represent 3D shapes of buildings or street geometry. Related computer-vision technology is described in the book [F. Huang, R. Klette, and K. Scheibe. Panoramic Imaging. Wiley, West Sussex, 2008].*

7.1.1 Surface Topology

The *surface S* (also known as the *border* or *frontier*) of an existing 3D object in the real world can be described as

R. Klette, *Concise Computer Vision*, Undergraduate Topics in Computer Science, DOI 10.1007/978-1-4471-6320-6_7, © Springer-Verlag London 2014

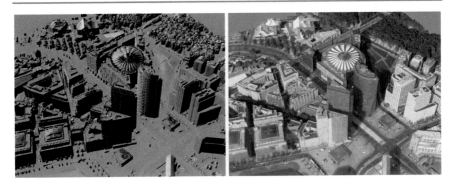

Fig. 7.1 *Left*: Surfaces reconstructed from image data recorded in an airplane. *Right*: Surfaces after texture mapping using recorded images. The scene shows the Sony Centre at Berlin, Germany

Fig. 7.2 *Left*: A polyhedral gap-free surface. *Middle and right*: Two smooth surfaces with gaps; the surface of a sphere without a few circular areas and the surface of a torus without one circular area

1. a *smooth surface* for which at every point $P \in S$, (a) continuous derivatives exist in any direction within S, and (b) there exists a neighbourhood in S that is topologically equivalent[1] to a disk, or as
2. a *polyhedral surface* composed of polygons (e.g. of triangles), thus with discontinuities at edges of the polyhedron, but also satisfying for any $P \in S$ the existence of a neighbourhood in S that is topologically equivalent to a disk.

The existence for any $P \in S$ of a neighbourhood in S that is topologically equivalent to a disk ensures that the surface S does not have any *gap*, which would allow us "to look into the interior of the given object". See Fig. 7.2, middle and right.

In the first case we speak about a *gap-free smooth surface*. For example, the surface of a sphere is a gap-free smooth surface, and so is the surface of a torus. In the second case we speak about a *gap-free polyhedral surface*; see Fig. 7.2, left. The surface shown in Fig. 7.1, left, is defined by a triangulation; by also including

---

[1]Two sets in Euclidean space are *topologically equivalent* if one of them can be mapped by a homeomorphism onto the other; a *homeomorphism* is a one-to-one continuous mapping such that its inverse is also continuous.

the covered region of the *ground plane* as one face and the faces of all *vertical sides* (see also Fig. 7.4), we can consider it to be a gap-free surface, provided that the calculated triangulation does not have any gap.

With respect to surface topology, it does not matter wether we have polygonal or smooth surface patches. A *gap-free surface* means either the first or the second case depending on a given context. Both cases are equivalent regarding surface topology.

Insert 7.2 (Euler Characteristics, Betti, and Jordan Surfaces) *The Euclidean topology was briefly recalled in Insert 3.6. Consider a connected compact set S in $\mathbb{R}^3$. Its frontier is known as* a surface. *The set may have* cavities, *which are not connected to the unbounded complement of the set, and it may have* handles.

The genus $g(S)$ *of the surface of S is the maximum number of cuts such that the surface does not yet become disconnected. For example, the genus of the surface of a sphere equals 0, and that of the surface of a torus equals 1.*

For a connected compact set S in $\mathbb{R}^3$ (e.g. a sphere with n handles), the most simple and combinatorial topological invariant is the Euler characteristic χ. *If the surface is connected (i.e. S has no cavities), then*

$$\chi(S) = 2 - 2 \cdot g(S)$$

The surface of the sphere (or any topological deformation of it, such as a cube for example) has Euler characteristic $\chi = 2$. The surface of the torus has Euler characteristic $\chi = 0$. If the surface of S is disconnected, and has $b \geq 2$ frontier components (i.e. $b - 1$ cavities), then

$$\chi(S) = 2 - 2 \cdot g(S) - (b - 1)$$

Now consider the surface S of a general bounded polyhedron in $\mathbb{R}^3$ (i.e. a bounded set with a frontier defined by a finite number of polygonal faces). Then we have that

$$\chi(S) = \alpha_2(S) - \alpha_1(S) + \alpha_0(S) - (b - 1)$$

where b is the number of components of S; for α_0 to α_2, see Insert 3.1. Alternatively, in the case $b = 1$ we also have that

$$\chi(S) = \beta_2(S) - \beta_1(S) + \beta_0(S)$$

where β_0, β_1, and β_2 are the Betti numbers *of a set S, named after the Italian mathematician E. Betti (1823–1892); β_0 is the number of components, β_1 is the number of "tunnels" (a "tunnel" is an intuitive concept; for a precise*

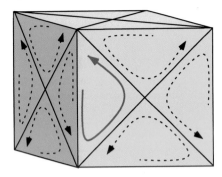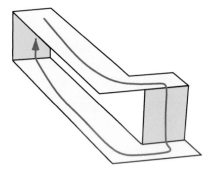

Fig. 7.3 *Left*: By selecting the orientation for the blue triangle we already specify the orientation of any other triangle in the triangulation of a gap-free surface. Complete the missing orientations on the *top* of the cube. *Right*: A *Moebius band* is a non-orientable surface. The shown *blue arc* can be continued so that it forms a loop that runs through all the faces of the band

definition of β_1, see, for example, Chap. 6 in the book [R. Klette and A. Rosenfeld: Digital Geometry. Morgan Kaufmann, San Francisco, 2004]), *and β_2 is the number of cavities. For example, the surface of a torus has $\beta_0 = 1$ (it is connected), $\beta_1 = 2$ (one tunnel inside of the surface, one through the "hole"), and $\beta_2 = 1$ (the interior of the surface).*

A Jordan surface (*C. Jordan*, 1887) *is defined by a parameterization that establishes a topological mapping onto the surface of a unit sphere. In computer vision we are usually not interested in global parameterizations of surfaces (just in local neighbourhoods), It is usually fine to stay globally with a topological definition of a surface. A theorem by I. Gawehn, 1927, says that any gap-free smooth surface is topologically equivalent to a gap-free polyhedral surface.*

Orientable Surfaces   An *oriented triangle* is a triangle with a direction on its frontier, say "clockwise" or "counter-clockwise", which is called the *orientation* of the triangle. The orientation of a triangle induces orientations of its edges. Two triangles in a triangulation that have a common edge are *coherently oriented* if they induce opposite orientations on their common edge.

A triangulation of a surface is *orientable* iff it is possible to orient all the triangles in such a way that every two triangles that have a common edge are coherently oriented; otherwise, it is called *non-orientable*.

A triangulation of an orientable surface can only have one of two possible orientations; by selecting an orientation for one triangle we already specify the orientation for the whole surface. See Fig. 7.3. If Z_1 and Z_2 are triangulations of the same surface, Z_1 is orientable iff Z_2 is orientable.

Observation 7.1 *The fact that orientability does not depend on the triangulation allows us to define a surface as* orientable *iff it has an orientable triangulation. Also note that the "orientation" (of a surface) and "direction" (of a vector) specify different mathematical concepts.*

The Euler Characteristic of a Surface   Let $\alpha_0, \alpha_1, \alpha_2$ be the numbers of vertices, edges, and triangles in a triangulation Z of a surface. The *Euler characteristic* of Z is

$$\chi(Z) = \alpha_0 - \alpha_1 + \alpha_2 \tag{7.1}$$

See Inserts 3.1 and 7.2. Two triangulations of the same surface have the same Euler characteristic. This fact allows us to speak about *the* Euler characteristic of a surface. The Euler characteristic is a topological invariant: topologically equivalent surfaces have the same Euler characteristic.

The Euler characteristic decreases with the topological complexity of a surface, with 2 being the maximum for a single (i.e. connected) surface. What is the Euler characteristic of the surface shown on the left in Fig. 7.3?

Example 7.1 (Euler Characteristics for Cube and Sphere Surfaces) The surfaces of a cube and of a sphere are topologically equivalent. Each face of a cube can be triangulated into two triangles. This results in 8 vertices, 18 edges, and 12 triangles, so that the Euler characteristic of the triangulation is 2. The surface of a sphere can be subdivided into four curvilinear triangles (e.g. consider a tetrahedron inscribed into the sphere; the vertices of the tetrahedron can be used as vertices of those four curvilinear triangles); this results in 4 vertices and 6 simple arcs, so that the Euler characteristic is again 2.

Separations by Jordan Surfaces in 3D Space   Section 3.1.1 discussed separations in the 2D Euclidean space $\mathbb{R}^2$ and in the digital image. A Jordan curve is topologically equivalent to a circle, and a *Jordan surface* is topologically equivalent to the surface of a sphere. L.E.J. Brouwer showed in 1911 that any Jordan surface separates $\mathbb{R}^3$ in the Euclidean topology into two connected subsets; the given Jordan surface is the frontier (also called border) of each of those two subsets.

7.1.2   Local Surface Parameterizations

Computer vision is usually not interested in providing globally parameterized representations of surfaces visible in the real world. Local parameterizations are useful when discussing shape reconstruction methods.

Representation of Surface Patches   A smooth or polyhedral surface can be partitioned into (connected) *surface patches*. Linear surface patches (also called *facets*, such as the triangles of a triangulated surface) are incident with a plane $Z = aX + bY + c$.

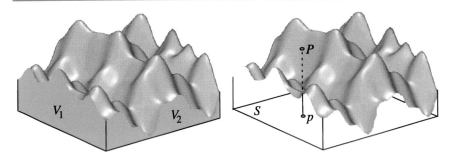

Fig. 7.4 The shown recovered surface can be seen as being one surface patch or as a surface composed into many smooth or linear patches (e.g. in case of triangulation). *Left*: Two visible faces V_1 and V_2 of vertical sides. *Right*: Illustration of a point p in a region S in the ground plane, corresponding one-to-one to a point P in the recovered surface

An *elevation map* is a recovered surface on top of a rectangular region S within a ground plane such that every point $P = (X, Y, Z)$ in the recovered surface corresponds one-to-one to a point $p = (X, Y) \in S$; see Fig. 7.4. A local patch of an elevation map can be given by an *explicit representation* $Z = F_e(X, Y)$, where the XY plane defines the ground plane, or by an *implicit representation* in the form $F_i(X, Y, Z) = 0$. For a smooth surface patch, we assume continuously differentiable (up to some appropriate order) explicit or implicit surface functions.

Example 7.2 (Surface of a Sphere) The visible surface of a sphere in $X_s Y_s Z_s$ camera coordinates is given as follows:

$$Z_s = F_e(X_s, Y_s) = a - \sqrt{r^2 - X_s^2 - Y_s^2} \tag{7.2}$$

assuming that the sphere is in front of the image plane $Z_s = f$, and the implicit form

$$F_i(X_s, Y_s, Z_s) = X_s^2 + Y_s^2 + (Z_s - a)^2 - r^2 = 0 \quad \text{with } a - r > f \tag{7.3}$$

represents the surface of the same sphere.

For a surface point $P = (X_s, Y_s, Z_s)$, we have the Euclidean distance $d_2(P, O) = \|P\|_2$ of P to the projection centre $O = (0, 0, 0)$ of the camera. The *depth* of P equals Z_s, the location of P with respect to the optical axis. We can also assume to have a *background plane* $Z = c$ behind (or below) the visible surfaces; the *height* of P is then defined by the difference $c - Z_s$. Accordingly, recovered surfaces can be visualized by *distance maps*, *depth maps*, or *height maps*, using a selected colour key for illustrating visualized values. See Fig. 7.5, right, for an example of a depth map, also illustrating the geometric complexity of real-world surfaces.

Surface Normals   The *gradient* of a surface $Z = F_e(X, Y)$ is the vector given by

$$\nabla Z = \mathbf{grad}\, Z = \left[\frac{\partial Z}{\partial X}, \frac{\partial Z}{\partial Y} \right]^\top \tag{7.4}$$

Fig. 7.5 *Left*: Input image `Bridge` for a surface recovery application (using stereo vision). *Right*: Visualized depth map using the colour key as shown on the *right*. Being not confident with a recovered depth value is shown at a pixel location by using a grey value rather than a value from the colour key. The small numbers in the colour key go from 5.01 to 155 (in a non-linear scale, with 10.4 about at the middle) and denote distances in meters

Fig. 7.6 The Gaussian
sphere is defined by radius 1

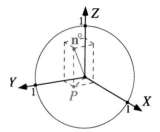

In case of a plane $aX + bY + Z = c$, we have the gradient $[a, b]^\top$. The *normal* is given by

$$\mathbf{n} = \left[\frac{\partial Z}{\partial X}, \frac{\partial Z}{\partial Y}, 1 \right]^\top = [a, b, 1]^\top \qquad (7.5)$$

We decided again, as already for (1.16) when defining the normal for an image, for a normal away from the image plane, and thus the value $+1$ in the third component. The *unit normal* (of length 1) is given as follows:

$$\mathbf{n}^\circ = [n_1, n_2, n_3]^\top = \frac{\mathbf{n}}{\|\mathbf{n}\|_2} = \frac{[a, b, 1]^\top}{\sqrt{a^2 + b^2 + 1}} \qquad (7.6)$$

By means of (7.5) and (7.6) we introduced also the general use of a and b for denoting the components of a normal.

Consider a sphere of radius 1 centred at the origin O (also called *Gaussian sphere*), as shown in Fig. 7.6. The angle between the vector $\mathbf{n}^\circ$ and the Z-axis is called the *slant* and denoted by σ. The angle between the vector from O to $P = (X, Y, 0)$ and the X-axis is called the *tilt* and denoted by θ. The point P is in the distance $\sin \sigma$ to O. The unit normal $\mathbf{n}^\circ$ defines a point on the surface of

Fig. 7.7 *Left*: Two orthogonal surface normals in the XYZ scene space. *Right*: The ab gradient space, illustrating the p and q values of the two normals $\mathbf{n}_1$ and $\mathbf{n}_2$

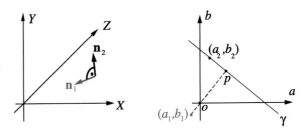

the Gaussian sphere that is uniquely represented by (σ, θ), also called the point's *spherical coordinates*.

Gradient Space   We define an ab coordinate space (see Fig. 7.7, right) where each point (a, b) represents a gradient $(a, b)^\top$ in the XYZ space (e.g. world coordinates) of the scene objects. This is the *gradient space*.

For example, consider the plane $Z = aX + bY + c$. Then, (a, b) represents in the gradient space all planes that are parallel to the given plane (i.e. for any $c \in \mathbb{R}$).

We consider a normal $\mathbf{n}_1 = [a_1, b_1, 1]^\top$ in the XYZ space that maps into point (a_1, b_1) in the gradient space, and a normal $\mathbf{n}_2 = [a_2, b_2, 1]^\top$ that is orthogonal to $\mathbf{n}_1$. See Fig. 7.7, left. For the dot product of both vectors, it follows that

$$\mathbf{n}_1 \cdot \mathbf{n}_2 = a_1 a_2 + b_1 b_2 + 1 = \|\mathbf{n}_1\|_2 \cdot \|\mathbf{n}_2\|_2 \cdot \cos \frac{\pi}{2} = 0 \qquad (7.7)$$

Assume that $\mathbf{n}_1$ is a given vector and we like to characterize the orthogonal direction $\mathbf{n}_2$. For given a_1 and b_1, we have a straight line g in the gradient space, defined by $a_1 a_2 + b_1 b_2 + 1 = 0$ and the unknowns a_2 and b_2. It can be geometrically described as follows:
1. the line incident with origin $o = (0, 0)$ and point p is orthogonal to line γ,
2. $\sqrt{a_1^2 + b_1^2} = d_2((a_1, b_1), o) = 1/d_2(p, o)$, and
3. p and (a_1, b_1) are in opposite quadrants.
The line γ is uniquely defined by these three properties. The line γ is called the *dual straight line* to the normal $\mathbf{n}_1$ or to (a_1, b_1). Any direction $\mathbf{n}_2$ orthogonal to $\mathbf{n}_1$ is located on γ.

7.1.3 Surface Curvature

This subsection is for a reader with interests in mathematics. It provides a guideline for analysing the curvature of surfaces reconstructed in computer vision. The given curvature definitions are not used further in the book except in Exercises 7.2 and 7.6. There are different ways for defining the curvature for a smooth surface.

Gaussian Curvature   C.F. Gauss defined the surface curvature at a surface point P by considering "small" surface patches S_ε of radius $\varepsilon > 0$ centred at P. For S_ε, let R_ε be the set of all endpoints of unit normals at points $Q \in S_\varepsilon$; the set R_ε is a

Fig. 7.8 A surface cut by a plane Π_η

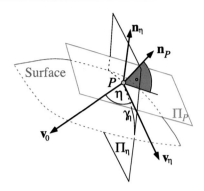

region on the surface of the unit sphere. Now let

$$\kappa_G(P) = \lim_{\varepsilon \to 0} \frac{\mathscr{A}(R_\varepsilon)}{\mathscr{A}(S_\varepsilon)} \tag{7.8}$$

where $\mathscr{A}$ denotes the area measure. This defines the *Gaussian curvature* at a surface point P.

Normal Curvature   We also define the two (often used) *principal curvature values* λ_1 and λ_2 for a point P in a smooth surface. On the way to there, we first define the *normal curvature*.

Let γ_1 and γ_2 be two different arcs in the given surface that intersect at P, and let $\mathbf{t_1}$ and $\mathbf{t_2}$ be the two tangent vectors to γ_1 and γ_2 at P. These vectors span the tangent plane Π_P at P. We assume angular orientations $0 \leq \eta < \pi$ in Π_P (a half-circle centred at P).

The surface normal $\mathbf{n}_P$ at P is orthogonal to Π_P and collinear with the cross product $\mathbf{t_1} \times \mathbf{t_2}$. Let Π_η be a plane that contains $\mathbf{n}_P$ and has orientation η; see Fig. 7.8.

Π_η makes a dihedral angle η with Π_0 and cuts the surface in an arc γ_η. (Π_η may cut the surface in several arcs or curves, but we consider only the one that contains P.) Let $\mathbf{t}_\eta$, $\mathbf{n}_\eta$, and κ_η be the tangent, normal, and curvature of γ_η at P.

κ_η is the *normal curvature* of any arc $\gamma \subset \Gamma \cap \Pi_\eta$ at P that is incident with P.

Example 7.3 (Two Examples of Normal Curvatures) Let the surface be a horizontal plane incident with $P = (0, 0, 0)$ in $\mathbb{R}^3$. Any γ_η is a straight line segment in the plane that is incident with $(0, 0, 0)$; we have $\kappa_\eta = 0$ and $\mathbf{t}_\eta = \gamma_\eta$.

Let the surface be a "cap" of a sphere centred at its north pole P, γ_η is a segment of a great circle on the sphere, $\mathbf{n}_\eta$ is incident with the straight line passing through P and the centre of the sphere, and $\kappa_\eta = 1/r$, where r is the radius of the sphere.

Principal Curvatures   Recall that the characteristic polynomial p of an $n \times n$ matrix $\mathbf{A}$ is defined as $p(\lambda) = \det(\mathbf{A} - \lambda \mathbf{I}) = (-\lambda)^n + \cdots + \det(\mathbf{A})$, where $\mathbf{I}$ is the $n \times n$ identity matrix. The eigenvalues λ_i of an $n \times n$ matrix $\mathbf{A}$ are the n roots of its characteristic polynomial $\det(\mathbf{A} - \lambda \mathbf{I}) = 0$.

Let $\mathbf{v}$ be a unit vector in Π_P. The negative derivative $-D_{\mathbf{v}}\mathbf{n}$ of the unit normal vector field $\mathbf{n}$ of a surface, regarded as a linear map from Π_P to itself, is called the *shape operator* (or *Weingarten map* or *second fundamental tensor*) of the surface.

Let $\mathbf{M}_P$ be the Weingarten map in the matrix representation at P (with respect to any orthonormal basis in Π_P), and let λ_1 and λ_2 be the eigenvalues of the 2×2 matrix $\mathbf{M}_P$. Note that these eigenvalues do not depend on the choice of an orthonormal basis in Π_P.

Then, λ_1 and λ_2 are called the *principal curvatures* or *main curvatures* of the given surface at P.

Euler Formula   Let $\mathbf{w}_1$ and $\mathbf{w}_2$ be any two orthogonal vectors that span the tangent plane Π_P at P, i.e. they are tangent vectors that define normal curvatures in directions η and $\eta + \pi/2$. Then the *Euler formula*

$$\kappa_\eta(p) = \lambda_1 \cdot \cos(\eta)^2 + \lambda_2 \cdot \sin(\eta)^2 \qquad (7.9)$$

allows us to calculate the normal curvature $\kappa_\eta(p)$ in any direction η at p from the principal curvatures λ_1 and λ_2 and the angle η.

Mean Curvature   The mean $(\lambda_1 + \lambda_2)/2$ is called the *mean curvature* of the given surface at a point P. The mean curvature is equal to $(\kappa_\eta(P) + \kappa_{\eta+\pi/2}(P))/2$ for any $\eta \in [0, \pi)$.

It can also be shown that the absolute value of the product $\lambda_1\lambda_2$ equals the Gaussian curvature $\kappa_G(P)$ as defined in (7.8).

Insert 7.3 (Meusnier) J.B.M. Meusnier (1754–1793) *was a French aeronautical theorist and military general.*

Theorem by Meusnier   We can also cut the given surface at P by a plane Π_c in some direction. The intersection of Π_c with the surface defines an arc γ_c in the neighbourhood of P, and we can estimate the 1D curvature κ_c of γ_c at P. However, we cannot assume that Π_c is incident with the surface normal $\mathbf{n}_P$ at P.

Let $\mathbf{n}_c$ be the principal normal of γ_c at p. A theorem of Meusnier tells us that the normal curvature κ_η in any direction η is related to the curvature κ_c and the normals $\mathbf{n}_P$ and $\mathbf{n}_c$ by

$$\kappa_\eta = \kappa_c \cdot \cos(\mathbf{n}_P, \mathbf{n}_c) \qquad (7.10)$$

Thus, by estimating two normal curvatures κ_η and $\kappa_{\eta+\pi/2}$ we can estimate the mean curvature.

Similarity Curvature   Let κ_1 and κ_2 be the two principal curvatures of a given surface at a point P in this surface (called λ_1 and λ_2 above). We define the curvature ratio κ_3 as follows:

$$\kappa_3 = \frac{\min(|\kappa_1|, |\kappa_2|)}{\max(|\kappa_1|, |\kappa_2|)} \qquad (7.11)$$

In the case where κ_1 and κ_2 are both equal to zero, κ_3 is defined as being equal to zero. It follows that $0 \leq \kappa_3 \leq 1$.

The *similarity curvature* $\mathscr{S}(P)$ is defined as follows:

$$\mathscr{S}(P) = \begin{cases} (\kappa_3, 0) & \text{if the signs of } \kappa_1 \text{ and } \kappa_2 \text{ are both positive} \\ (-\kappa_3, 0) & \text{if the signs of } \kappa_1 \text{ and } \kappa_2 \text{ are both negative} \\ (0, \kappa_3) & \text{if the signs of } \kappa_1 \text{ and } \kappa_2 \text{ differ and } |\kappa_2| \geq |\kappa_1| \\ (0, -\kappa_3) & \text{if the signs of } \kappa_1 \text{ and } \kappa_2 \text{ differ and } |\kappa_1| > |\kappa_2| \end{cases} \qquad (7.12)$$

Note that $\mathscr{S}(P) \in \mathbb{R}^2$.

Insert 7.4 (3D Scanners) *There are many products on the market for recovering 3D surfaces, typically called "3D scanner" or "3D digitizer". Structured light scanners (e.g. the Kinect 1), stereo vision, and surface reflectance-based systems are discussed in this chapter. For example, structured light scanners are popular for modelling human bodies (e.g. whole body scanners in the movie industry), and stereo vision is widely used for aerial imaging, 3D reconstructions of buildings, or even for real-time processing requiring a 3D understanding of the environment.*

Not discussed in this book, because (so far) not yet closely integrated into computer vision technologies, are, for example, the following:

Laser scanners are based on the "time-of-flight" principle, enhanced by modulated wave lengths for measuring very accurate distance values (the new Kinect 2 replaces structured light by time-of-flight, thus bringing time-of-flight closer into computer vision).

Holography is still not yet very common for 3D measurements but popular for 3D visualizations.

Touch probes, laser trackers, optic position trackers, or magnetic position trackers are all basically not using imaging technologies.

7.2   Structured Lighting

Structured lighting is the projection of a light pattern (e.g. a ray, a plane of light, a grid pattern, or encoded light in the form of subsequent binary illumination patterns) under calibrated geometric conditions onto an object whose shape needs to be recovered. Typically, we use one camera and one light source, and by calibration

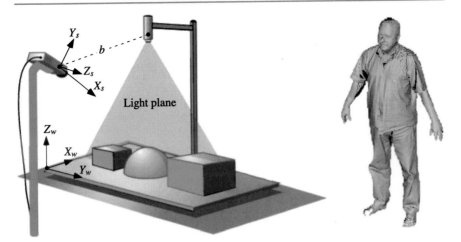

Fig. 7.9 *Left*: The (laser) light source projects a sweeping light plane (by fanning out a light beam into a "sheet of light"), which projects at each time a bright line across the objects of interest. *Right*: The recovered surface of a person using structured lighting

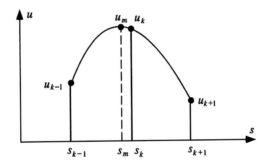

Fig. 7.10 The identified intensity profile in the row or column direction (aiming at being orthogonal to the tangential direction of a recorded light plane in an image). We consider pixels and their grey levels at location s_{k-1} on the left and s_{k+1} on the right of s_k for identifying an ideal location s_m (with a maximum u_m, which is actually not visible in the image) with subpixel accuracy

we need to determine the pose of the light source with respect to the camera. See Fig. 7.9, left, for an illustration of a possible set-up.

This section provides the necessary mathematics for reconstructing surfaces using structured light.

7.2.1   Light Plane Projection

Locating a Projected Light Plane   An illuminated line in the 3D world is visible in an image across multiple pixels. We analyse a projected line in 1D cuts, indexed by $k = 1, \ldots, k_{end}$, orthogonal to its tangential direction identified at pixel s_k where the image has a local maximum u_k. See Fig. 7.10.

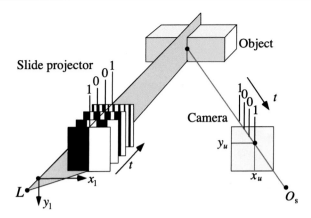

Fig. 7.11 A slide projector projects one binary pattern at a time, thus either illuminating surface points at this moment through the white columns or not (i.e. light is blocked by the *black columns*). A sequence of slides generates thus at a surface point a binary code (1 = illuminated by this slide, 0 = not illuminated). The figure illustrates one light plane defined by subsequent columns in the used binary patterns

We measure grey levels u_{k-1} and u_{k+1} at pixel locations s_{k-1} and s_{k+1}, which are at a selected distance to s_k. We assume a second-order polynomial $u = a \cdot s^2 + b \cdot s + c$ for intensities in the cut through the projected line. We calculate the parameters a, b, and c of the polynomial by using

$$
\begin{bmatrix} a \\ b \\ c \end{bmatrix} = \begin{bmatrix} s_{k-1}^2 & s_{k-1} & 1 \\ s_k^2 & s_k & 1 \\ s_{k+1}^2 & s_{k+1} & 1 \end{bmatrix}^{-1} \begin{bmatrix} u_{k-1} \\ u_k \\ u_{k+1} \end{bmatrix}
\tag{7.13}
$$

(Actually, c is not needed for s_m.) Then we obtain s_m for the location of the projected line in subpixel accuracy; the polynomial has its maximum at $s_m = -\frac{b}{2a}$. Why?

Generation of Light Planes by Encoded Light Instead of generating one light plane at a time, we can also use n projected binary patterns for generating 2^n light planes, encoded in the recorded n images.

Consider a slide projector for projecting n slides, each showing a binary pattern of resolution $2^n \times 2^n$. See Fig. 7.11. In each slide, a column is either black (i.e. blocking the light) or white. One column in those slides thus generates over time a particular light plane, identified by a binary sequence of "illuminated" or "not illuminated". By identifying such a sequence for one particular surface point we can understand which light plane was actually mapped onto this surface point.

By using n slides at times $t = 1, \ldots, n$, we record n images and have generated 2^n light planes. (For example, we can reduce to $n - 1$ slides based on the assumption that light planes on the left cannot be confused with light planes on the right of the recorded scene.)

For reasons of error reduction, it is recommended that the projected slides follow the *Gray code* rather than the usual binary code.

Insert 7.5 (Gray and the Gray Code) *This binary code was proposed by F. Gray (1887–1969), a US-American physicist. Consecutive integers are represented by binary numbers that differ in one digit only. The table below illustrates by examples, encoding integers 0 to 7:*

Integers	0	1	2	3	4	5	6	7
Usual code	000	001	010	011	100	101	110	111
Gray code	000	001	011	010	110	100	101	111

7.2.2 Light Plane Analysis

We recall the coordinate systems used for camera and world; see Figs. 6.17 and 7.9. Additionally, we now also have a light source.

Camera, Light Source, and World Coordinate Systems   The camera is positioned in a 3D space, with a, say, left-hand $X_s Y_s Z_s$ camera coordinate system. The projection centre is at the origin O_s. The optical axis of the camera coincides with the Z_s-axis. The image plane is parallel to the $X_s Y_s$ plane, at (effective) focal distance $Z_s = f$. The image has either (looking towards O_s) a left-hand xy coordinate system or (viewpoint at O_s) a right-hand xy coordinate system.

Due to lens distortions, a 3D point P is projected into a point $p_d = (x_d, y_d)$ in the image plane, where subscript d stands for "distorted". Assuming the model of a pinhole camera (i.e. central projection), the position of p_d is corrected into $p_u = (x_u, y_u)$, where the subscript u stands for "undistorted". By applying the ray theorem we obtained the central projection equations

$$x_u = \frac{f \cdot X_s}{Z_s} \quad \text{and} \quad y_u = \frac{f \cdot Y_s}{Z_s} \qquad (7.14)$$

3D points are given in an $X_w Y_w Z_w$ world coordinate system. The camera coordinates can be transformed into the world coordinates by a rotation and a subsequent translation, which is conveniently described in a 4D homogeneous world coordinate space.

Structured lighting requires (in general) also calibration of the used light source(s). It is necessary to have the pose (i.e. location and direction) of the light source in the world coordinates. For example, we need to determine the length b of the baseline defined by projection centre of the camera and the origin of the light rays, which are emerging from the light source. See Fig. 7.9.

2D Sketch   We first discuss the hypothetic case of a camera in a plane before going to the actual case of a camera in the 3D space. Assume that the angles α and β and the base distance b are given by calibration. We have to calculate P. See Fig. 7.12.

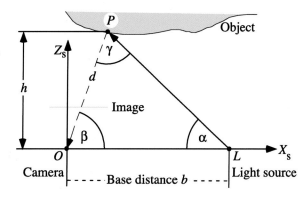

Fig. 7.12 A hypothetical simple case: The camera, light source, and unknown surface point P are all in one plane; L is assumed to be on the X_s-axis

The projection centres O and L and the unknown point P define a triangle. We determine the location of P by *triangulation*, using basic formulas about triangles such as the law of sines:

$$\frac{d}{\sin \alpha} = \frac{b}{\sin \gamma} \tag{7.15}$$

It follows that

$$d = \frac{b \cdot \sin \alpha}{\sin \gamma} = \frac{b \cdot \sin \alpha}{\sin(\pi - \alpha - \beta)} = \frac{b \cdot \sin \alpha}{\sin(\alpha + \beta)} \tag{7.16}$$

and, finally,

$$P = (d \cdot \cos \beta, d \cdot \sin \beta) \tag{7.17}$$

in the $X_s Z_s$ coordinates. The angle β is determined by the position of the projected (illuminated) point P in the hypothetical 1D image.

The 3D Case   Now we consider the actual 3D case. Assume that b is given by light source calibration and α by controlled light plane sweeping. See Fig. 7.13.

The ray theorem (of central projection) tells us that $X_s/x_u = Z_s/f = Y_s/y_u$, and from the trigonometry of right triangles we know that $\tan \alpha = Z_s/(b - X_s)$. It follows that

$$Z = \frac{X}{x} \cdot f = \tan \alpha \cdot (b - X) \quad \text{and} \quad X \cdot \left(\frac{f}{x} + \tan \alpha \right) = \tan \alpha \cdot b \tag{7.18}$$

The solution is

$$X = \frac{\tan \alpha \cdot b \cdot x}{f + x \cdot \tan \alpha}, \qquad Y = \frac{\tan \alpha \cdot b \cdot y}{f + x \cdot \tan \alpha}, \quad \text{and} \quad Z = \frac{\tan \alpha \cdot b \cdot f}{f + x \cdot \tan \alpha} \tag{7.19}$$

Why does γ not appear in these equations?

In general we need to consider the case that the light source L is not on the X_s axis, and the derivation of formulas for this case is left as an exercise. See also Exercise 7.7.

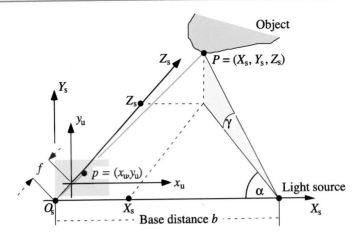

Fig. 7.13 For simplification, we consider the light source L on the X_s-axis

Fig. 7.14 A stereo vision input pair aiming at ensuring canonical stereo geometry by using accurately mounted cameras on an optical bench (1994, TU Berlin, Computer Vision lab). Today it is more efficient to use camera calibration and subsequent image rectification for preparing input data, as described in Sect. 6.3.2

7.3   Stereo Vision

Binocular vision works. The human visual system is a proof. The difficult part is to determine corresponding points in the left and right views of a scene (see Fig. 7.14 for an example) being projections of the same surface point. (We devote an extra chapter, Chap. 8, to this task.) Assuming that we already have those corresponding points and a pair of calibrated cameras (i.e. intrinsic and extrinsic parameters), then it is straightforward to calculate the depth or distance to the visible surface point.

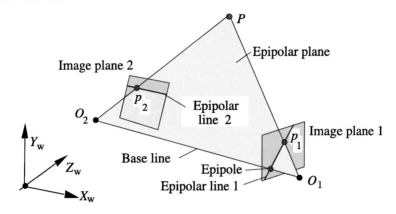

Fig. 7.15   A sketch of epipolar geometry for two cameras in general poses

This section explains the geometric model of stereo vision, having *epipolar geometry* and *disparity* as its central notions, and how to use disparities for calculating the depth or distance.

7.3.1   Epipolar Geometry

We have two cameras in general poses, not just "left" and "right". The cameras are considered in the pinhole-camera model having projection centres O_1 and O_2. See Fig. 7.15. We consider the Euclidean geometry in $\mathbb{R}^3$, ignoring digital limitations in the images for the time being.

A 3D point P in $X_w Y_w Z_w$ world coordinates is projected into a point p_1 in Image 1 (i.e. accurately, not just on a pixel location) and onto a *corresponding point* p_2 in Image 2. The task in *stereo correspondence analysis* (the subject in the following chapter) is to locate p_2 starting at a point p_1 in the first image.

Three non-collinear points in the 3D space define a plane. The points O_1, O_2 and the unknown point P define the *epipolar plane*. The points O_1, O_2 and the projection point p_1 define the same plane.

The intersection of an image plane with the epipolar plane forms an *epipolar line*. The search for a corresponding point p_2 can proceed along the epipolar line in Image 2.

Observation 7.2 *Knowing the projection centres O_1 and O_2 by camera calibration in world coordinates, a point p_1 in Image 1 already tells us the line we have to search in the second image for finding the corresponding point p_2; we do not have to search "everywhere" in Image 2.*

This restriction of the search space for stereo analysis is very useful to know.

Canonical Epipolar Geometry   Section 6.1.3 introduced canonical stereo geometry, which now defines *canonical epipolar geometry*. See Fig. 6.11. Here we have left and right cameras.

A 3D point P defines in this case an epipolar plane that intersects both image planes in the same row. When starting at a point $p_1 = (x_u, y_u)$ in the left camera, then the corresponding point (if P is visible in the right camera) is in the image row y_u in the right camera.

Where are the epipoles in canonical epipolar geometry? They can be described accurately in 4D homogeneous coordinates. They are points at infinity.

7.3.2   Binocular Vision in Canonical Stereo Geometry

After geometric rectification into canonical stereo geometry, two corresponding points in the left and right images are in the same image row. Starting, for example, with a pixel $p_L = (x_L, y)$ in the left image, the corresponding pixel $p_R = (x_R, y)$ in the right image satisfies $x_R \leq x_L$, which means that the pixel p_R is left of pixel p_L in the $N_{cols} \times N_{rows}$ array of all pixels. See Fig. 6.11 for an illustration of this order. Actually, to be precise, the c_{xL} and c_{xR} coordinates of the principal points in the left and right cameras might influence this order at places where x_L and x_R are nearly identical; see (6.3). But we assume, for formal simplicity, that $x_R \leq x_L$ holds as well as $x_{uR} \leq x_{uL}$ for the undistorted coordinates.

Disparity in the General Case   Assume two rectangular images I_i and I_j of identical size $N_{cols} \times N_{rows}$ as input for stereo vision; as in Sect. 6.3.2, we use indices i and j for the general case rather than just "left" and "right". We consider the overlay of both images, one on top of the other, in the xy image coordinate system, as illustrated in Fig. 7.16.

A 3D point $P = (X, Y, Z)$ is projected into a point p_i in the ith,\and into p_j in the jth image, defining the *disparity vectors* (i.e. virtual shifts)

$$\mathbf{d}_{ij} = p_i - p_j \quad \text{or} \quad \mathbf{d}_{ji} = p_j - p_i \qquad (7.20)$$

The scalar *disparity* value $d_{ij} = d_{ji}$ is defined as the magnitude $\|\mathbf{d}_{ij}\|_2 = d_2(p_i, p_j)$ of $\mathbf{d}_{ij}$. We have that $\|\mathbf{d}_{ij}\|_2 = \|\mathbf{d}_{ji}\|_2$.

Disparity for Canonical Stereo Geometry   We have left and right images in this case. The pixel $p_L = (x_L, y)$ in the left image corresponds to the pixel $p_R = (x_R, y)$ in the right image. Because of $x_R \leq x_L$, we have a disparity value equal to $x_L - x_R$.

Triangulation for Canonical Stereo Geometry   Now we have all together for going from stereo-image input data to results, that means recovered 3D points $P = (X, Y, Z)$ in camera or world coordinates.

We apply (6.4) and (6.5) and recover the unknown visible points P in the camera coordinate system of the left camera, $P = (X_s, Y_s, Z_s)$, using the undistorted image coordinates (x_{uL}, y_{uL}) and (x_{uR}, y_{uR}) as input, which satisfy $y_{uL} = y_{uR}$ and $x_{uR} \leq x_{uL}$.

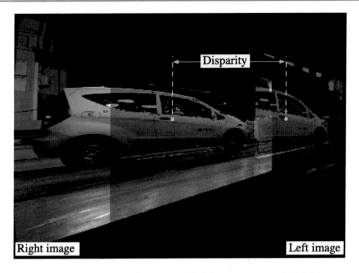

Fig. 7.16 In continuation of Fig. 6.19, two rectified images are overlaid in the same array of $N_{cols} \times N_{rows}$ pixels. Two corresponding points define a disparity

The base distance is denoted by $b > 0$, and, as always, f is the unified focal length. First, we are able to eliminate Z_s from (6.4) and (6.5) using

$$Z_s = \frac{f \cdot X_s}{x_{uL}} = \frac{f \cdot (X_s - b)}{x_{uR}} \tag{7.21}$$

We solve (7.21) for X_s and have that

$$X_s = \frac{b \cdot x_{uL}}{x_{uL} - x_{uR}} \tag{7.22}$$

By using this value of X_s, we also obtain from (7.21) that

$$Z_s = \frac{b \cdot f}{x_{uL} - x_{uR}} \tag{7.23}$$

Finally, using this value of Z_s in (6.4) or (6.5), we derive that

$$Y_s = \frac{b \cdot y_u}{x_{uL} - x_{uR}} \tag{7.24}$$

with $y_u = y_{uL} = y_{uR}$.

Observation 7.3 *Two corresponding pixels* $(x_L, y) = (x_{uL} + c_{xL}, y_{uL} + c_{yL})$ *and* $(x_R, y) = (x_{uR} + c_{xR}, y_{uR} + c_{yR})$ *identify its joint pre-image* $P = (X, Y, Z)$ *in the 3D space using the triangulation formulas in* (7.22), (7.23), *and* (7.24).

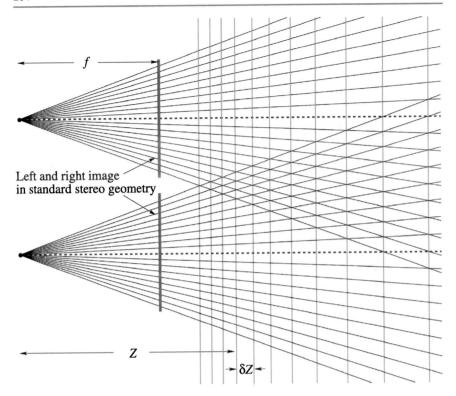

Fig. 7.17 The figure shows crossing lines passing through pixel locations in both stereo images. The intersections mark potential positions of points P in the 3D space located by the disparities defined by the pixel coordinate differences. The distances δZ between subsequent depth layers increase nonlinearly

Discussion of the Given Triangulation Formulas The disparity $x_{uL} - x_{uR} = 0$ means that the pre-image $P = (X, Y, Z)$ is at infinity. The larger the disparity $x_{uL} - x_{uR}$, the closer is the pre-image $P = (X, Y, Z)$ to the cameras.

Because we deal with integer coordinates in images, the disparity values $x_{uL} - x_{uR}$ are basically limited to integers as well (ignoring the constant but possibly non-integral shift by the principal point). Due to the nonlinearity of the triangulation equations, a difference of 1 between $x_{uL} - x_{uR} = 0$ and $x_{uL} - x_{uR} = 1$ means to go from infinity to a defined value, between $x_{uL} - x_{uR} = 1$ to $x_{uL} - x_{uR} = 2$ that pre-image points move much closer to the cameras, but between $x_{uL} - x_{uR} = 99$ and $x_{uL} - x_{uR} = 100$ only a very minor change in distance to the cameras. See Fig. 7.17.

Observation 7.4 *Without further attempts of refined measurements, the number of available disparity values between $d_{\max}$ and 0 defines the number of available depth levels; those depth levels are nonlinearly distributed, from dense close to the cameras to very sparse further away from the cameras.*

Fig. 7.18 *Left*: Sparse matches of a stereo correspondence method are shown as coloured points using a colour key for illustrating depth; a continuation of Fig. 7.16. *Right*: The input stereo pair Andreas (*top*), dense depth map using grey values as a key for illustrating depth, and a triangulated and texture-mapped surface representation of the obtained stereo results (Computer Vision lab, TU Berlin 1994)

A larger base distance b and a larger focal length f support an increase in depth levels but reduce the number of pixels that have corresponding pixels in the second image. An increase in the image resolution is a general way to improve the accuracy of depth levels, paid by an increase in computation costs.

Recovering Sparse or Dense Depth Data Pairs of corresponding points provide recovered 3D points. Correspondence search techniques can lead to many estimated matches between points in the stereo image data or only to a very few matches. In Fig. 7.18, left, the few sparse matches were generated close to edges in the image, using a local (non-hierarchical) correlation-based stereo matcher, demonstrating a stereo matching strategy as common in the early days of computer vision. Figure 7.18, right, shows dense matches, illustrating that hierarchical correlation-based stereo matching already supported reasonable results.

Correspondence analysis also comes with errors. Thus, even if only a few matches are detected, the quality of those still needs to be carefully analysed.

Recovering Sparse Depth Data for Embedded Vision Sparse stereo analysis is today still of interest for "small" embedded vision systems where time efficiency and accuracy of sparse results are crucial. Figure 7.19 illustrates the results of a stereo matcher using a modified FAST feature detector. The stereo images are recorded from a quadcopter.

Fig. 7.19 *Left*: Sparse matches using feature-based stereo analysis on a quadcopter (Tübingen University, 2013). *Right*: Stereo cameras are mounted on this quadcopter

Fig. 7.20 *Left* and *right cameras* are symmetric to the Z-axis; their optical axes intersect at a point C on the Z-axis, which is the point of convergence

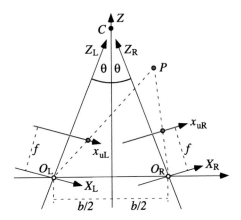

7.3.3   Binocular Vision in Convergent Stereo Geometry

For maximizing the space of objects being visible in both cameras, it can be useful to depart from canonical stereo geometry and to use a convergent set-up as illustrated in Fig. 7.20.

Tilted Cameras with Corresponding Image Rows   We assume a Cartesian XYZ coordinate system; Fig. 7.20 shows the X and Z axes; the Y-axis points towards the viewer. We have left and right cameras with optical axes intersecting at a point C on the Z-axis. For the left camera, we have the coordinates $X_L Y_L Z_L$, and for the right camera, we have the coordinates $X_R Y_R Z_R$. The projection centres are at O_L and O_R. The axis X is incident with both projection centres. The line segment $O_L O_R$

is the *base line* of the defined *convergent binocular vision system*, and b is the *base distance*.

The base distance between O_L and O_R equals b, and the optical axes Z_L and Z_R describe each the same angle θ with the Z-axis. A point P in the world is projected into both images with coordinates x_{uL} and x_{uR}, having the identical y-coordinates $y_u = y_{uL} = y_{uR}$ (i.e. this is the kind of rectification we ensure after camera calibration). There is the same focal length f for left and right cameras.

Coordinate Transforms The system XYZ can be transformed into the $X_L Y_L Z_L$ system by the rotation

$$\begin{bmatrix} \cos(-\theta) & 0 & -\sin(-\theta) \\ 0 & 1 & 0 \\ \sin(-\theta) & 0 & \cos(-\theta) \end{bmatrix} = \begin{bmatrix} \cos(\theta) & 0 & \sin(\theta) \\ 0 & 1 & 0 \\ -\sin(\theta) & 0 & \cos(\theta) \end{bmatrix} \tag{7.25}$$

by angle $-\theta$ about the Y-axis followed by the translation

$$\left[X - \tfrac{b}{2}, Y, Z \right]^\top \tag{7.26}$$

by $b/2$ to the left. This defines the affine transform

$$\begin{bmatrix} X_L \\ Y_L \\ Z_L \end{bmatrix} = \begin{bmatrix} \cos(\theta) & 0 & \sin(\theta) \\ 0 & 1 & 0 \\ -\sin(\theta) & 0 & \cos(\theta) \end{bmatrix} \begin{bmatrix} X - \tfrac{b}{2} \\ Y \\ Z \end{bmatrix} \tag{7.27}$$

Analogously,

$$\begin{bmatrix} X_R \\ Y_R \\ Z_R \end{bmatrix} = \begin{bmatrix} \cos(\theta) & 0 & -\sin(\theta) \\ 0 & 1 & 0 \\ \sin(\theta) & 0 & \cos(\theta) \end{bmatrix} \begin{bmatrix} X + \tfrac{b}{2} \\ Y \\ Z \end{bmatrix} \tag{7.28}$$

Consider a point $P = (X, Y, Z)$ in the XYZ-coordinate system projected into the left $x_{uL} y_u$ and the right $x_{uR} y_u$ coordinate systems. According to the general central projection equations, we know that

$$x_{uL} = \frac{f \cdot X_L}{Z_L}, \qquad y_u = \frac{f \cdot Y_L}{Z_L} = \frac{f \cdot Y_R}{Z_R}, \qquad \text{and} \qquad x_{uR} = \frac{f \cdot X_R}{Z_R} \tag{7.29}$$

In the centred XYZ-coordinate system we obtain that

$$x_{uL} = f \frac{\cos(\theta)(X - \tfrac{b}{2}) + \sin(\theta) \cdot Z}{-\sin(\theta)(X - \tfrac{b}{2}) + \cos(\theta) \cdot Z} \tag{7.30}$$

$$y_u = f \frac{Y}{-\sin(\theta)(X - \tfrac{b}{2}) + \cos(\theta) \cdot Z} \tag{7.31}$$

$$x_{uR} = f \frac{\cos(\theta)(X + \tfrac{b}{2}) - \sin(\theta) \cdot Z}{\sin(\theta)(X + \tfrac{b}{2}) + \cos(\theta) \cdot Z} \tag{7.32}$$

This leads to the following equational system:

$$\big[-x_{uL} \cdot \sin(\theta) - f \cdot \cos(\theta)\big]X + \big[x_{uL} \cdot \cos(\theta) - f \cdot \sin(\theta)\big]Z$$
$$= -\left[\frac{b}{2}x_{uL} \cdot \sin(\theta) + \frac{b}{2}f\right] \tag{7.33}$$

$$\big[-y_u \cdot \sin(\theta)\big]X + [-f]Y + \big[y_u \cdot \cos(\theta)\big]Z$$
$$= \left[\frac{b}{2}y_u \cdot \sin(\theta)\right] \tag{7.34}$$

$$\big[x_{uR} \cdot \sin(\theta) - f \cdot \cos(\theta)\big]X + \big[x_{uR} \cdot \cos(\theta) + f \cdot \sin(\theta)\big]Z$$
$$= -\left[\frac{b}{2}x_{uR} \sin(\theta) - \frac{b}{2}f\right] \tag{7.35}$$

Solving for the Unknown Point in 3D Space   This might look difficult now for calculating one projected point $P = (X, Y, Z)$. (Do humans "that" for all the corresponding image points in the left and right eyes when converging views for understanding the distances to objects?)

This equation system actually allows us to calculate the XYZ-coordinates of the projected point P accurately. (In human vision, we are not accurately measuring, just deriving distance estimates.)

Let $a_1 = [-x_{uL} \cdot \sin(\theta) - f \cdot \cos(\theta)], \dots, c_0 = -[\frac{b}{2}x_{uR} \cdot \sin(\theta) - \frac{b}{2}f]$ be the coefficients of the equation system above, which can all be determined assuming a fixed *tilt angle* θ, known focal length f, and a detected pair (x_{uL}, y_u) and (x_{uR}, y_u) of corresponding image points, being the projection of the same 3D point $P = (X, Y, Z)$:

$$a_1 X + a_3 Z = a_0 \tag{7.36}$$

$$b_1 X + b_2 Y + b_3 Z = b_0 \tag{7.37}$$

$$c_1 X + c_3 Z = c_0 \tag{7.38}$$

This can easily be solved for X, Y, and Z.

Observation 7.5 *Convergent stereo geometry does not lead to a large overhead in calculations, compared to the use of canonical stereo geometry.*

Vergence   If a point P is of particular interest for a human, then the human visual system focuses on P (called *vergence*). Geometrically, the tilt of both eyes changes so that the Z_L and Z_R axes (ideally) intersect at P. In such a case we do not have anymore two identical tilt angles θ. Future camera technology might be able to implement vergence. General linear algebra tools for coordinate changes would be then more efficient (in terms of briefness, clarity, and generality) for describing vergence.

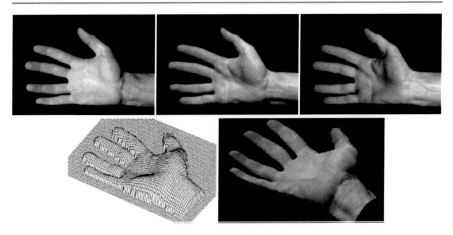

Fig. 7.21 *Top*: Three input images for PSM; the hand is not allowed to move when taking these images. *Bottom*: The reconstructed surface by using the 3-light-source PSM (in 1996 at TU Berlin)

7.4   Photometric Stereo Method

In the previous section we required a light source (usually the Sun) and two (or more) static or mobile cameras for reconstructing the 3D shape. Now we use one static camera and multiple static light sources, which can be switched on and off while taking images. The technology used is known as the *photometric stereo method* (PSM). See Fig. 7.21 for an example where three light sources have been used; the hand is illuminated by only one of those three at a time when taking one of the three images.

This section first discusses *Lambertian reflectance* as an example how surfaces reflect light. Then we consider the three-light-source PSM for deriving surface gradients. Finally, we discuss how surface gradients can be mapped into a 3D shape.

7.4.1   Lambertian Reflectance

Point Light Source Assumption   For simpler mathematical description, we assume that each of the used light sources can be identified by a single point in $\mathbb{R}^3$; this light source emits light uniformly in all directions. Of course, when talking about an existing light source, it illuminates only a limited range, it has a particular energy distribution curve $L(\lambda)$ (see Fig. 1.25, left, for an example), and it has a geometric shape. But we assume that the used light sources are "not very close" to the objects of interest, thus making possible the *point light source assumption*.

Relatively to the illuminated surfaces (of our object of interest), we assume that a light source L is in direction $\mathbf{s}_L = [a_L, b_L, 1]^\top$ and emits light with intensity E_L. This constant E_L can be seen as integral over the energy distribution curve of light source L in the visible spectrum of light.

Fig. 7.22 A light source in the direction **s**, a planar Lambertian reflector with surface normal **n**, and a camera in the viewing direction $\mathbf{v}_1$. The Lambertian reflector emits light into any direction $\mathbf{v}_1, \ldots, \mathbf{v}_4$ uniformly, as long as such a direction is in the hemisphere of possible viewing directions on the illuminated side of the planar Lambertian reflector

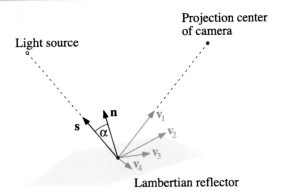

Light source

Projection center of camera

Lambertian reflector

Insert 7.6 (Lambert and his Cosine Law) *The Swiss mathematician and physicist J.H. Lambert (1728–1777) contributed to many areas, including geometric optics, colour models, and surface reflectance. He was also the first to prove that π is an irrational number. Lambertian reflectance is characterized by the cosine law, which he published in 1760.*

Lambert's Cosine Law   The radiant intensity observed from an *ideal diffusely reflecting surface* (also known as the *Lambertian reflector*) is directly proportional to the cosine of the angle α between the surface normal **n** and direction **s** to the light source. See Fig. 7.22. No matter which vector $\mathbf{v}_i$ defines the viewing direction to the camera, it will receive the same amount of emitted light.

Let $\mathbf{n}_P = [a, b, 1]^\top$ be the surface normal of a visible and illuminated surface point P. For the formal representation of Lambert's cosine law, first note that

$$\mathbf{s}^\top \cdot \mathbf{n}_P = \|\mathbf{s}\|_2 \cdot \|\mathbf{n}_P\|_2 \cdot \cos\alpha \tag{7.39}$$

resulting in

$$\cos\alpha = \frac{\mathbf{s}^\top \cdot \mathbf{n}_P}{\|\mathbf{s}\|_2 \cdot \|\mathbf{n}_P\|_2} \tag{7.40}$$

Second, the emitted light at the point P is scaled by

$$\eta(P) = \rho(P) \cdot \frac{E_L}{\pi} \tag{7.41}$$

where E_L was defined as a light source energy, which is reflected at P uniformly into all directions of a hemisphere (thus, we divide by π, which is the spatial angle of a hemisphere), and we also have a surface reflectance constant $\rho(P)$ with $0 \le \rho(P) \le 1$, called the *albedo*.[2]

---

[2]"Albedo" means "whiteness" in Latin.

Insert 7.7 (Albedo) *We defined the albedo simply by one scalar denoting the ratio of reflected radiation to incident radiation; the difference between both is absorbed at the surface point. This corresponds to the simplified use of E_L for the incident radiation.*

The general definition of albedo, introduced by J.H. Lambert for any type of surface reflectance, is as a function depending on the wavelength λ in the visible spectrum of light. Because we only discuss Lambertian reflectance here, it is actually sufficient to use a scalar albedo: the reflected light here does not depend on the incident energy distribution function.

Altogether, we observe the following emitted light at surface point P, called the *reflectance* at P:

$$R(P) = \eta(P) \cdot \frac{\mathbf{s}_L^\top \cdot \mathbf{n}_P}{\|\mathbf{s}_L\|_2 \cdot \|\mathbf{n}_P\|_2}$$

$$= \eta(P) \cdot \frac{a_L a + b_L b + 1}{\sqrt{a_L^2 + b_L^2 + 1} \cdot \sqrt{a^2 + b^2 + 1^2}} \tag{7.42}$$

The reflectance $R(P) \geq 0$ is a second-order function in unknowns a and b if we assume that the combined surface reflectance $\eta(P)$ is a constant (i.e. we continue to illuminate and to observe the same point but consider different slopes). The direction to a light source is considered to be constant (i.e. objects are small compared to the distance to the light source).

Reflectance Maps A *reflectance map* is defined in the ab gradient space of the normals $(a, b, 1)$; see Fig. 7.7; it assigns a reflectance value to each gradient (a, b) assuming that the given surface reflectance is uniquely defined by the gradient value (as it is the case for Lambertian reflectance).

Example 7.4 (Lambertian Reflectance Map) Consider a point P with albedo $\rho(P)$ and gradient (a, b).

If $\mathbf{n}_P = \mathbf{s}_L$, then $\alpha = 0$ and $\cos\alpha = 1$; the curve in (7.42) degenerates into $R(P) = \eta(P)$, and this is the maximal possible value. We have the value $\eta(P)$ at (a_L, b_L) in the gradient space.

If $\mathbf{n}_P$ is orthogonal to $\mathbf{s}_L$, then the surface point P is "just" not illuminated anymore; $\mathbf{n}_P$ is on the dual straight line to $\mathbf{s}_L$ (illustrated in Fig. 7.7, right). Because of $\alpha = \pi/2$ and $\cos\alpha = 0$; the curve in (7.42) degenerates into $R(P) = 0$, and this is the minimal possible value. Thus, we have the value 0 along the dual straight line to (a_L, b_L) in the gradient space, and we continue with value 0 in the halfplane defined by this straight line and not containing the point (a_L, b_L) (i.e. the gradients of surface points that cannot be illuminated by the light source L).

For all values of $R(P)$ between 0 and $\eta(P)$, the curve in (7.42) is either parabolic or hyperbolic. All these curves together define a *Lambertian reflectance map* in the gradient space, as illustrated in Fig. 7.23.

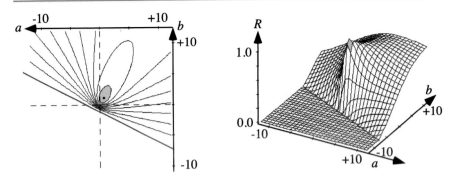

Fig. 7.23 Lambertian reflectance map. *Left*: Isolines. *Right*: A 3D view of values in this map

7.4.2 Recovering Surface Gradients

Assume that we have one static camera (on a tripod), but three different point light sources at directions $\mathbf{s}_i$ for $i = 1, 2, 3$. We assume that the reflectance value $R(P)$ is uniformly reduced by a constant factor $c > 0$ (due to the distance between object surface and camera) and mapped into a monochromatic value u in the image of the camera.

We capture three images. We turn only one light source on at a time, and a surface point P maps now (at the same pixel position) into three different intensity values given by

$$u_i = R_i(P) = \frac{\eta(P)}{c} \cdot \frac{\mathbf{s}_i^\top \cdot \mathbf{n}_P}{\|\mathbf{s_i}\|_2 \cdot \|\mathbf{n}_P\|_2} \tag{7.43}$$

defining three second-order curves in the gradient space, which (ideally) intersect at (a, b), where $\mathbf{n}_P = [a, b, 1]^\top$ is the normal at the point P.

An *n-source photometric stereo method* (*n*PSM) attempts to recover surface normals by some kind of practical implementation for determining this ideal intersection at (a, b) for $n \geq 3$. Three light sources are needed at least for a unique normal reconstruction; $n = 3$ defines the default 3-source *photometric stereo method* (PSM).

Albedo-Independent PSM We consider surfaces with Lambertian reflectance. For example, human skin satisfies Lambert's cosine law approximately, with critical issues at places of occurring specularity. There is also specularity in the (open) eyes.

We cannot assume that the albedo $\rho(P)$ is constant across a Lambertian surface. The colouring of surface points changes, and thus also the albedo. We need to consider *albedo-independent PSM*. We repeat (7.43) but replace $\eta(P)$ by its detailed definition:

$$u_i = E_i \cdot \frac{\rho(P)}{c\pi} \cdot \frac{\mathbf{s}_i^\top \cdot \mathbf{n}_P}{\|\mathbf{s_i}\|_2 \cdot \|\mathbf{n}_P\|_2} \tag{7.44}$$

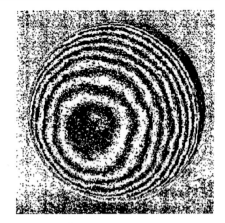

Fig. 7.24 *Left*: An image of a calibration sphere, ideally with uniform albedo and Lambertian reflectance. *Right*: An illustration of detected isointensity "lines", showing the noisiness involved

for light source energies E_i and $i = 1, 2, 3$. By multiplying the first equation (i.e. $i = 1$) by $u_2 \cdot \|s_2\|_2$ and the second equation (i.e. $i = 2$) by $-u_1 \cdot \|s_1\|_2$ and then adding both results, we obtain the following:

$$\rho(P) \cdot \mathbf{n}_P \cdot \left(E_1 u_2 \|s_2\|_2 \cdot s_1 - E_2 u_1 \|s_1\|_2 \cdot s_2\right) = 0 \qquad (7.45)$$

This means that the vector $\mathbf{n}_P$ is orthogonal to the specified difference of vectors s_1 and s_2, assuming that $\rho(P) > 0$. We divide both sides by $\rho(P)$ using this assumption; using the first and third images, we have that

$$\mathbf{n}_P \cdot \left(E_1 u_3 \|s_3\|_2 \cdot s_1 - E_3 u_1 \|s_1\|_2 \cdot s_3\right) = 0 \qquad (7.46)$$

Altogether, $\mathbf{n}_P$ is collinear with the cross product

$$\left(E_1 u_2 \|s_2\|_2 \cdot s_1 - E_2 u_1 \|s_1\|_2 \cdot s_2\right) \times \left(E_1 u_3 \|s_3\|_2 \cdot s_1 - E_3 u_1 \|s_1\|_2 \cdot s_3\right) \quad (7.47)$$

Knowing that we are looking for a surface normal away from the camera, we uniquely derive the desired unit normal $\mathbf{n}_P^\circ$.

Note that we only need relative intensities of light sources for this technique and no absolute measurements.

Direction to Light Sources by Inverse PSM For the calibration of directions s_i to the three light sources, we apply *inverse photometric stereo*. We use a *calibration sphere* that has (about) Lambertian reflectance and uniform albedo. See Fig. 7.24. The sphere is positioned about at the same location where object normals will be recovered later on. It is of benefit for the accuracy of the calibration process if the sphere is as large as possible, that means, it is "filling" the image taken by the fixed camera.

We identify the circular border of the imaged sphere. This allows us to calculate the surface normals (of the sphere) at all points P projected into pixel positions within the circle. Due to the expected inaccuracy with respect to Lambertian reflectance (see approximate isointensity "lines" on the right of Fig. 7.24), more than just three points P (say, about 100 uniformly distributed points with their normals in the circular region of the sphere, in the image recorded for light source i) should be used to identify the direction $\mathbf{s}_i$ by least-square optimization, using (7.44): We have the values u_i and normals $\mathbf{n}_P$; we solve for the unknown direction $\mathbf{s}_i$. We also measure this way the energy ratios between the intensities E_i of the three light sources.

Regarding the set-up of the light sources relatively to the location of the objects (or of the calibration sphere), it has been estimated that the angle between two light source directions (centred around the viewing direction of the camera) should be about $56°$ for optimized PSM results.

Albedo Recovery   Consider (7.44) for $i = 1, 2, 3$. We know the three values u_i at a pixel location p being the projection of surface point P. We also have (approximate) values for the unit vectors $\mathbf{s}_i^{\circ}$ and $\mathbf{n}_P^{\circ}$. We have measured the relative intensities of the three light sources.

The only remaining unknown is $\rho(P)$. In the described albedo-independent PSM, we combined the first and second images and the first and third images. We still can combine the second and third images. This all supports a robust estimation of $\rho(P)$.

Why Albedo Recovery?   The knowledge of the albedo is of importance for light-source-independent modelling of the surface of an object, defined by geometry and texture (albedo). In general (if not limited to Lambertian reflectance), the albedo depends upon the wavelength of the illuminating light. As a first approximation, we may use light sources of different colours, such as red, green, or blue light, to recover the related albedo values. Note that after knowing $\mathbf{s}^{\circ}$ and $\mathbf{n}^{\circ}$, we only have to change the wave length of illuminations (e.g. using transparent filters), assuming that the object is not moving in between.

It has been shown that such a technique is of reasonable accuracy for recovering the albedo values of a human face. See Fig. 7.25 for an example.

7.4.3   Integration of Gradient Fields

A discrete field of normals (or gradients) can be transformed into a surface by *integration*. As known from mathematical analysis, integration is not unique (when dealing with smooth surfaces). The result is only determined up to an additive constant.

Ill-Posedness of the Surface Recovering Problems   The results of PSM are expected to be discrete and erroneous surface gradient data. Considered surfaces are often also "non-smooth", for example polyhedral surfaces with discontinuous changes in surface normals at edges of polygonal faces.

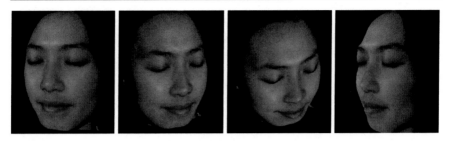

Fig. 7.25 A face recovered by 3PSM (at The University of Auckland in 2000). Closed eyes avoid the recording of specularity

Fig. 7.26 Assuming that a surface patch is defined on a simply connected set and its explicit surface function satisfies the integrability condition, the local integration along different paths will lead (in the continuous case) to identical elevation results at a point (x_1, y_1), after starting at (x_0, y_0) with the same initial elevation value

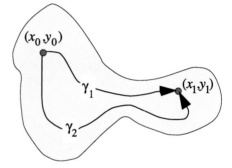

For illustrating the reconstruction difficulty by an example, assume that we look onto a staircase, orthogonal to the front faces. All recovered normals will point straight towards us, and there is no chance to recover the staircase from these normals, which also match the normals of a plane.

In general, the densities of recovered surface normals do not correspond uniformly to the local surface slopes.

Local Integration Methods In the continuous case we have that values of a depth function $Z = Z(x, y)$, defined on a simply connected set, can be recovered by starting at one point (x_0, y_0) with an initial value $Z(x_0, y_0)$ and then by integrating the gradients along a path γ that is completely in the set. It then holds that different integration paths lead to an identical value at (x_1, y_1). To be precise, the depth Z also needs to satisfy the *integrability condition*

$$\frac{\partial Z^2}{\partial x \partial y} = \frac{\partial Z^2}{\partial y \partial x} \tag{7.48}$$

at all points (x, y) in the considered simply connected set; but this is more of theoretical interest only. For a sketch of two different paths, see Fig. 7.26.

Local integration methods implement integration along selected paths (e.g. one or multiple scans through the image as illustrated in Fig. 2.10) by using initial Z-values and local neighbourhoods at a pixel location when updating Z-values incrementally.

Two-Scan Method   We present a local method for depth recovery from gradients. We want to recover a depth function Z such that

$$\frac{\partial Z}{\partial x}(x, y) = a_{x,y} \tag{7.49}$$

$$\frac{\partial Z}{\partial y}(x, y) = b_{x,y} \tag{7.50}$$

for all the given gradient values $a_{x,y}$ and $b_{x,y}$ at pixel locations $(x, y) \in \Omega$.

Consider grid points $(x, y + 1)$ and $(x + 1, y + 1)$; since the line connecting points $(x, y + 1, Z(x, y + 1))$ and $(x + 1, y + 1, Z(x + 1, y + 1))$ are approximately perpendicular to the average normal between these two points, the dot product of the slope of this line and the average normal is equal to zero. This gives

$$Z(x + 1, y + 1) = Z(x, y + 1) + \frac{1}{2}(a_{x,y+1} + a_{x+1,y+1}) \tag{7.51}$$

Similarly, we obtain the following recursive relation for pixel locations $(x + 1, y)$ and $(x + 1, y + 1)$:

$$Z(x + 1, y + 1) = Z(x + 1, y) + \frac{1}{2}(b_{x+1,y} + b_{x+1,y+1}) \tag{7.52}$$

Adding above two recursions together and dividing the result by 2 give

$$Z(x + 1, y + 1) = \frac{1}{2}\big(Z(x, y + 1) + Z(x + 1, y)\big)$$

$$+ \frac{1}{4}(a_{x,y+1} + a_{x+1,y+1} + b_{x+1,y} + b_{x+1,y+1}) \tag{7.53}$$

Suppose further that the total number of points on the object surface be $N_{cols} \times N_{rows}$. If two arbitrary initial height values are preset at pixel locations $(1, 1)$ and (N_{cols}, N_{rows}), then the *two-scan algorithm* consists of two stages; the first stage starts at the left-most, top-most corner $(1, 1)$ of the given gradient field and determines the height values along the x-axis and y-axis by discretizing (7.49) in terms of the forward differences:

$$Z(x, 1) = Z(x - 1, 1) + a_{x-1,1} \tag{7.54}$$

$$Z(1, y) = Z(1, y - 1) + b_{1,y-1} \tag{7.55}$$

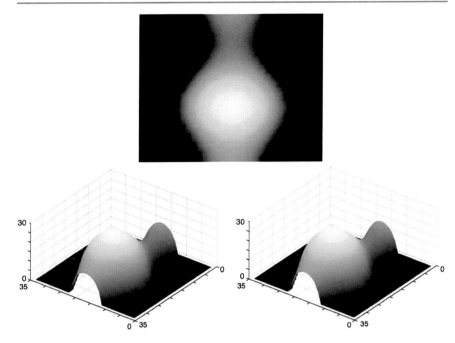

Fig. 7.27 The results of the two-scan method for a synthetic vase object. *Left*: The original image. *Middle*: A 3D plot of the vase object. *Right*: The reconstruction result using the two-scan method

where $x = 2, \ldots, N_{cols}$ and $j = 2, \ldots, N_{rows}$. Then scan the image vertically using (7.53). The second stage starts at the right-most, bottom-most corner (N_{cols}, N_{rows}) of the given gradient field and sets the height values by

$$Z(x - 1, N_{rows}) = Z(x, N_{rows}) - a_{x, N_{rows}} \tag{7.56}$$

$$Z(N_{cols}, y - 1) = Z(N_{cols}, y) - b_{N_{cols}, y} \tag{7.57}$$

Then scan the image horizontally using the following recursive equation:

$$Z(x - 1, y - 1) = \frac{1}{2}\big(Z(x - 1, y) + Z(x, y - 1)\big)$$
$$- \frac{1}{4}(a_{x-1,y} + a_{x,y} + b_{x,y-1} + b_{x,y}) \tag{7.58}$$

Since the estimated height values may be affected by the choice of the initial height value, we take the average of the two scan values for the final depth values.

For an illustration of the results for the two-scan method, see Fig. 7.27. The shown synthetic vase is generated by using the following explicit surface equation:

$$Z(x, y) = \sqrt{f^2(y) - x^2},$$

where $f(y) = 0.15 - 0.1 \cdot y(6y + 1)^2(y - 1)^2(3y - 2)^2$

for $-0.5 \le x \le 0.5$ and $0.0 \le y \le 1.0$ \hfill (7.59)

The image of this synthetic vase object is shown on the left of Fig. 7.27. The 3D plot of the reconstructed surface, using the provided two-scan algorithm, is shown on the right of Fig. 7.27.

Global Integration   Assume that we have a gradient vector estimated at any pixel location $p \in \Omega$. We aim at mapping this uniform and dense gradient vector field into a surface in a 3D space, which is likely to be the actual surface that caused the estimated gradient vector field. The depth values $Z(x, y)$ define labels at pixel locations (x, y), and we are back to a labelling problem with error (or energy) minimization.

Similar to the total variations considered in Chap. 4, we combine again the data term

$$E_{data}(Z) = \sum_{\Omega} \left[(Z_x - a)^2 + (Z_y - b)^2 \right] + \lambda_0 \sum_{\Omega} \left[(Z_{xx} - a_x)^2 + (Z_{yy} - b_y)^2 \right]$$

$$(7.60)$$

with the smoothness term

$$E_{smooth}(Z) = \lambda_1 \sum_{\Omega} \left[Z_x^2 + Z_y^2 \right] + \lambda_2 \sum_{\Omega} \left[Z_{xx}^2 + 2Z_{xy}^2 + Z_{yy}^2 \right] \qquad (7.61)$$

where Z_x and Z_y are the first-order partial derivatives of Z, a_x and b_y are the first-order partial derivatives of a and b, and Z_{xx}, $Z_{xy} = Z_{yx}$, and Z_{yy} are the second-order partial derivatives. With $\lambda_0 \ge 0$ we control the consistency between the surface curvature and changes in available gradient data. With $\lambda_1 \ge 0$ we control the smoothness of the surface, with $\lambda_2 \ge 0$ we go one step further and control also the smoothness of surface curvature. Altogether, we like to determine a surface Z (i.e. the labelling function) such that the total error (or total energy)

$$E_{total}(Z) = E_{data}(Z) + E_{smooth}(Z) \qquad (7.62)$$

is minimized, having gradients (a, b) as inputs at pixel locations (x, y).

Insert 7.8 (Fourier-Transform-Based Methods) *The optimization problem, defined by (7.62), can be solved by using the theory of projections onto convex sets. The given gradient field $(a_{x,y}, b_{x,y})$ is projected onto the nearest integrable gradient field in the least-square sense, using the Fourier transform for optimizing in the frequency domain. See [R.T. Frankot and R. Chellappa.*

> *A method for enforcing integrability in shape from shading algorithms. IEEE Trans. Pattern Analysis Machine Intelligence, vol. 10, pp. 439–451, 1988] for the case that the second part of the data constraint is not used as well as no smoothness constraint at all.*
>
> *In order to improve accuracy and robustness and to strengthen the relation between the surface function Z and the given gradient field, (7.62) also contains additional constraints as introduced in [T. Wei and R. Klette. Depth recovery from noisy gradient vector fields using regularization. In Proc. Computer Analysis Images Patterns, pp. 116–123, LNCS 2756, Springer, 2003].*

Fourier-Transform-Based Methods   To solve the minimization problem (7.62), Fourier-transform techniques can be applied. The 2D Fourier transform (see Sect. 1.2) of the surface function $Z(x, y)$ is defined by

$$\mathbf{Z}(u, v) = \frac{1}{|\Omega|} \sum_{\Omega} Z(x, y) \cdot \exp\left[-i 2\pi \left(\frac{xu}{N_{cols}} + \frac{yv}{N_{rows}}\right)\right] \qquad (7.63)$$

and the inverse Fourier transform is defined by

$$Z(x, y) = \sum_{\Omega} \mathbf{Z}(u, v) \cdot \exp\left[i 2\pi \left(\frac{xu}{N_{cols}} + \frac{yv}{N_{rows}}\right)\right] \qquad (7.64)$$

where $i = \sqrt{-1}$ is the imaginary unit, and u and v represent the frequencies in the 2D Fourier domain.

In addition to the Fourier pairs provided in Sect. 1.2, we also have the following:

$$Z_x(x, y) \Leftrightarrow i u \mathbf{Z}(u, v)$$

$$Z_y(x, y) \Leftrightarrow i v \mathbf{Z}(u, v)$$

$$Z_{xx}(x, y) \Leftrightarrow -u^2 \mathbf{Z}(u, v)$$

$$Z_{yy}(x, y) \Leftrightarrow -v^2 \mathbf{Z}(u, v)$$

$$Z_{xy}(x, y) \Leftrightarrow -u v \mathbf{Z}(u, v)$$

Those Fourier pairs define the appearance of the considered derivatives of the function Z in the frequency domain.

Let $\mathbf{A}(u, v)$ and $\mathbf{B}(u, v)$ be the Fourier transforms of the given gradients $A(x, y) = a_{x,y}$ and $B(x, y) = b_{x,y}$, respectively. We also use Parseval's theorem; see (1.31).

Frankot–Chellappa Algorithm and Wei–Klette Algorithm   We obtain an equivalence of the optimization problem (7.62) in the spatial domain to the optimization problem in the frequency domain that we are looking for a minimization of

$$\sum_{\Omega}\left[(iu\mathbf{Z} - \mathbf{A})^2 + (iv\mathbf{Z} - \mathbf{B})^2\right]$$

$$+ \lambda_0 \sum_{\Omega}\left[\left(-u^2\mathbf{Z} - iu\mathbf{A}\right)^2 + \left(-v^2\mathbf{Z} - iv\mathbf{B}\right)^2\right]$$

$$+ \lambda_1 \sum_{\Omega}\left[(iu\mathbf{Z})^2 + (iv\mathbf{Z})^2\right]$$

$$+ \lambda_2 \sum_{\Omega}\left[\left(-u^2\mathbf{Z}\right)^2 + 2(-uv\mathbf{Z})^2 + \left(-v^2 Z_F\right)^2\right] \tag{7.65}$$

The above expression can be expanded into

$$\sum_{\Omega}\left[u^2\mathbf{ZZ}^\star - iu\mathbf{ZA}^\star + iu\mathbf{Z}^\star\mathbf{A} + \mathbf{AA}^\star + v^2\mathbf{ZZ}^\star - iv\mathbf{ZB}^\star + iv\mathbf{Z}^\star\mathbf{B} + \mathbf{BB}^\star\right]$$

$$+ \lambda_0 \sum_{\Omega}\left[u^4\mathbf{ZZ}^\star - iu^3\mathbf{ZA}^\star + iu^3\mathbf{Z}^\star\mathbf{A} + u^2\mathbf{AA}^\star + v^4\mathbf{ZZ}^\star\right.$$

$$\left. - iv^3\mathbf{ZB}^\star + iv^3\mathbf{Z}^\star\mathbf{B} + v^2\mathbf{BB}^\star\right]$$

$$+ \lambda_1 \sum_{\Omega}\left(u^2 + v^2\right)\mathbf{ZZ}^\star + \lambda_2 \sum_{\Omega}\left(u^4 + 2u^2v^2 + v^4\right)\mathbf{ZZ}^\star \tag{7.66}$$

using $\star$ for denoting the complex conjugate.

Differentiating the above expression with respect to $\mathbf{Z}^\star$ and setting the result to zero, we can deduce the necessary condition for a minimum of the cost function (7.62) as follows:

$$\left(u^2\mathbf{Z} + iu\mathbf{A} + v^2\mathbf{Z} + iv\mathbf{B}\right) + \lambda_0\left(u^4\mathbf{Z} + iu^3\mathbf{A} + v^4\mathbf{Z} + iv^3\mathbf{B}\right)$$

$$+ \lambda_1\left(u^2 + v^2\right)\mathbf{Z} + \lambda_2\left(u^4 + 2u^2v^2 + v^4\right)\mathbf{Z} = 0 \tag{7.67}$$

A rearrangement of this equation then yields

$$\left[\lambda_0\left(u^4 + v^4\right) + (1 + \lambda_1)\left(u^2 + v^2\right) + \lambda_2\left(u^2 + v^2\right)^2\right]\mathbf{Z}(u, v)$$

$$+ i\left(u + \lambda_0 u^3\right)\mathbf{A}(u, v) + i\left(v + \lambda_0 v^3\right)\mathbf{B}(u, v) = 0 \tag{7.68}$$

Solving the above equation with $(u, v) \neq (0, 0)$, we obtain that

$$\mathbf{Z}(u, v) = \frac{-i(u + \lambda_0 u^3)\mathbf{A}(u, v) - i(v + \lambda_0 v^3)\mathbf{B}(u, v)}{\lambda_0(u^4 + v^4) + (1 + \lambda_1)(u^2 + v^2) + \lambda_2(u^2 + v^2)^2} \tag{7.69}$$

1: **input** gradients $a(x, y), b(x, y)$; parameters $\lambda_0, \lambda_1,$ and λ_2
2: **for** $(x, y) \in \Omega$ **do**
3:     **if** $(|a(x, y)| < c_{max}$ & $|b(x, y)| < c_{max})$ **then**
4:         $A1(x, y) = a(x, y)$; $A2(x, y) = 0$;
5:         $B1(x, y) = b(x, y)$; $B2(x, y) = 0$;
6:     **else**
7:         $A1(x, y) = 0$; $A2(x, y) = 0$;
8:         $B1(x, y) = 0$; $B2(x, y) = 0$;
9:     **end if**
10: **end for**
11: Calculate Fourier transform in place: $A1(u, v), A2(u, v)$;
12: Calculate Fourier transform in place: $B1(u, v), B2(u, v)$;
13: **for** $(u, v) \in \Omega$ **do**
14:     **if** $(u \neq 0$ & $v \neq 0)$ **then**
15:         $\Delta = \lambda_0(u^4 + v^4) + (1 + \lambda_1)(u^2 + v^2) + \lambda_2(u^2 + v^2)^2$;
16:         $H1(u, v) = [(u + \lambda_0 u^3)A2(u, v) + (v + \lambda_0 v^3)B2(u, v)]/\Delta$;
17:         $H2(u, v) = [-(u + \lambda_0 u^3)A1(u, v) - (v + \lambda_0 v^3)B1(u, v)]/\Delta$;
18:     **else**
19:         $H1(0, 0)$ = average depth; $H2(0, 0) = 0$;
20:     **end if**
21: **end for**
22: Calculate inverse Fourier transform of $H1(u, v)$ and $H2(u, v)$ in place: $H1(x, y), H2(x, y)$;
23: **for** $(x, y) \in \Omega$ **do**
24:     $Z(x, y) = H1(x, y)$;
25: **end for**

Fig. 7.28 The Fourier-transform-based Wei–Klette algorithm (generalizing the Frankot–Chellappa algorithm, which has $\lambda_0 = \lambda_1 = \lambda_2 = 0$, thus not using the second part of the data constraint and no smoothness constraint at all) for calculating an optimum surface for a given dense gradient field

This is the Fourier transform of the unknown surface function $Z(x, y)$ expressed as a function of the Fourier transforms of the given gradients $A(x, y) = a_{x,y}$ and $B(x, y) = b_{x,y}$. The resulting algorithm is shown in Fig. 7.28.

The constant c_{max} eliminates gradient estimates that define angles with the image plane close to $\pi/2$, and the value $c_{max} = 12$ is an option. The real parts are stored in arrays A1, B1, and H1, and imaginary parts in arrays A2, B2, and H2. The initialization in Line 19 can be by an estimated value for the average depth of the visible scene. The parameters λ_0, λ_1, and λ_2 should be chosen based on experimental evidence for the given scene.

Figure 7.29 shows three captured images of a Beethoven plaster statue using a static camera and three light sources. The gradients were generated using albedo-independent 3PSM. The figure illustrates the recovered surfaces for the same dense gradient field as input but using either $\lambda_0 = 0$ (i.e. the Frankot–Chellappa algorithm) or $\lambda_0 = 0.5$ (i.e. the Wei–Klette algorithm); positive values of λ_1 and λ_2 can be used for further fine-tuning of the recovered surface.

Test on Noisy Gradients   Generally speaking, local methods provide unreliable reconstructions for noisy gradient inputs since errors propagate along the scan paths. We illustrate global integration for the synthetic vase already used in Fig. 7.27. We

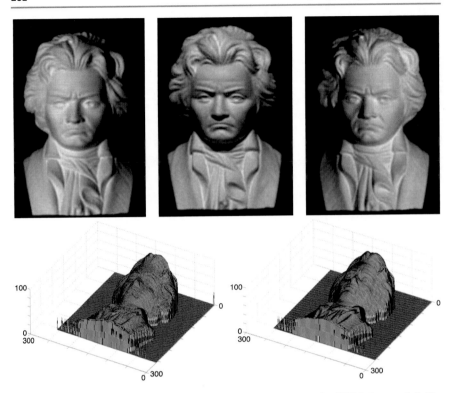

Fig. 7.29 *Top*: An Image triplet of a Beethoven statue used as input for 3PSM. *Bottom, left:* The recovered surface using the Frankot–Chellappa algorithm. *Bottom, right:* The recovered surface using the Wei–Klette algorithm with $\lambda_0 = 0.5$ and $\lambda_1 = \lambda_2 = 0$

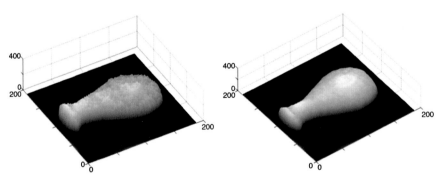

Fig. 7.30 The results for a noisy gradient field for the synthetic vase shown in Fig. 7.27. *Left*: The reconstructed surface using the Frankot–Chellappa algorithm. *Right*: The reconstructed surface using the Wei–Klette algorithm with $\lambda_0 = 0$, $\lambda_1 = 0.1$, and $\lambda_2 = 1$

generate a discrete gradient vector field for this synthetic vase and add Gaussian noise (with mean set to zero and standard deviation set to 0.01) to this gradient field. See Fig. 7.30 for results.

Fig. 7.31 *Left*: An example of an input image of a cylindrical shape with glued-on label. *Middle*: An approximate location of occluding contours of cylinder, generated by manual interaction. *Right*: An extracted flat label from multiple input images

7.5 Exercises

7.5.1 Programming Exercises

Exercise 7.1 (Map Surface of Cylindrical Shape into a Plane) Provide a solution for the following task: Given is a set of images showing one cylindrical object such as a can or a bottle (see Fig. 7.31). The occluding contour of the cylindrical object may be generated interactively rather than by an automated process.

Use multiple images of the cylindrical object showing an "interesting" part of the surface (such as the label in Fig. 7.31). Your program needs to ensure the following:
1. For each image, map it onto one generic cylinder of some fixed radius.
2. Use *image stitching* for merging segments of mapped images on the surface of this generic cylinder.
3. Finally, map the stitched image into the plane.
Thus, you provide a planar view on some surface parts of the given cylindrical object, as illustrated in Fig. 7.31 for an example.

Exercise 7.2 (Visualization of Similarity Curvature) Visualize similarity curvature for 3D surfaces. The values of similarity curvature are in $\mathbb{R}^2$. Figure 7.32 illustrates two possible colour keys for the first (horizontal axis) and the second (vertical axis) value in tuples specifying the similarity curvature and shows also the application of this colour scheme for a few simple shapes.

Select a few 3D shapes of your choice, each at different scales, and visualize their similarity curvature by mapping the colour key values onto the surfaces of the selected shapes.

Summarize your experience when visualizing the similarity curvature for the same shape but given at different scales (sizes).

Exercise 7.3 (Building a Simple 3D Scanner) This project is about a "very basic" way to build a 3D scanner. We assume that you have a digital camera and a planar light source (such as an overhead slide projector or a light display similar to those for reading X-rays; both are actually outdated technologies) at hand.

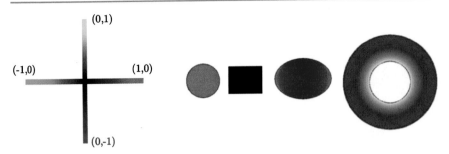

Fig. 7.32 *Left*: A possible colour key for the similarity curvature. *Right*: Application of this colour key for sphere, cylinder, ellipsoid, and torus

Use cardboard to build a disk such that 20 to 50 cm large objects (such as a wooden statue) fit onto it, mark its border by degrees (say, in steps of 5 degrees), position it onto a desk, draw a circle around it, and make a mark on the circle indicating where the 0 degree mark of the disk is at the start, before doing subsequent rotations of the disk within the circle by the marked angular increases.

Now project a fixed light plane towards the rotation axis of the disk by covering your planar light source by two sheets of paper, leaving just a very narrow gap between both. (An even better solution is actually to have a laser light and an optical wedge for generating a light plane.)

Position the camera so that it "sees" the rotating disk and calibrate distances as follows: move an object such as a book in the area of the disk in measured distance increments and identify the image column(s) that show the projected light plane on the object at a given distance; this way you create a look-up table for illuminated columns in the camera and the corresponding distances.

Now you are ready to identify 3D points on the surface of an object, positioned on your rotating disk. Report about the experiment and submit input images as well as a reconstructed set of 3D surface points.

Exercise 7.4 (Uncertainty in Stereo Reconstruction) Figure 7.17 illustrates the uncertainties of calculated disparity values. Intersections of lines mark potential positions in 3D space, which are specified by calculated disparities, but the actual position of the surface point creating this disparity can be in a trapezoid around the intersection point. The area of the trapezoids (i.e. the uncertainty) increases with distance to the cameras.

Actually, the figure only shows one plane defined by one row in the left and right images. The regions of uncertainties are (3D) polyhedra; the trapezoids are only 2D cuts trough those polyhedra.

This exercise requires a geometric analysis of the volume of those polyhedra (the area of trapezoids could be used as a simplification) and a graphical representation of uncertainties as a function of distance to the cameras.

Assume two cameras of fixed resolution $N_{rows} \times N_{cols}$ in canonical stereo geometry, defined by the focal length f and base distance b. Provide a graphical representation of uncertainties as a function of distance to the cameras; change only

f and represent the changes in uncertainties; now change only b and represent the changes in uncertainties again. A program interface allowing interactive changes of f and b would be ideal.

Exercise 7.5 (Removal of Minor Highlights) The described PSM method only works if surface reflectance is close to Lambertian. However, minor specularities can be "removed" if the surface texture is "not very detailed", by using the *dichromatic reflectance model* for coloured surfaces.

Use an object where the surface only has patches of (roughly) constant colour, which show minor specularities. Take images of this object and map the pixel values being within one patch of constant colour into the RGB colour cube. These values should form a T or an L in the RGB cube, defined by a base line (the diffuse component) and higher-intensity values away from the base line (the specularity).

Approximate the base line and map the RGB values orthogonally onto the base line. Replace in the image the mapped values by the obtained values on the baseline.

This is a way to remove minor highlights. Demonstrate this for a few images taken from your test object under different viewing angles and lighting conditions.

7.5.2 Non-programming Exercises

Exercise 7.6 A *smooth compact* 3D set is compact (i.e., connected, bounded, and topologically closed), and the curvature is defined at any point of its frontier (i.e., its surface is differentiable at any point).

Prove (mathematically) that the similarity curvature measure $\mathscr{S}$, as defined in (7.12), is (positive) scaling invariant for any smooth 3D set.

Exercise 7.7 Instead of applying a trigonometric approach as on p. 259, specify the required details for implementing a linear-algebra approach for structured lighting along the following steps:
1. From calibration we know the implicit equation for each light plane expressed in world coordinates.
2. From calibration we also know in world coordinates the parametric equation for each ray from the camera's projection centre to the centre of a square pixel for each pixel.
3. Image analysis gives us the ID of the light plane visible at a given pixel location.
4. An intersection of the ray with the light plane gives us the surface-point coordinates.

Exercise 7.8 Specify the fundamental matrix $\mathbf{F}$ for canonical stereo geometry. Consider also a pair of tilted cameras as shown in Fig. 7.20 and specify also the fundamental matrix $\mathbf{F}$ for such a pair of two cameras.

Exercise 7.9 Describe the Lambertian reflectance map in spherical coordinates on the Gaussian sphere (hint: isointensity curves are circles in this case). Use this model to answer the question why two light sources are not yet sufficient for identifying a surface normal uniquely.

Exercise 7.10 Why the statement "We also use Parseval's theorem..." on p. 279?

Stereo Matching

This chapter discusses the search for corresponding pixels in a pair of stereo images. We consider at first correspondence search as a labelling problem, defined by data and smoothness error functions and by the applied control structure. We describe belief-propagation stereo and semi-global matching. Finally, we also discuss how to evaluate the accuracy of stereo-matching results on real-world input data, particularly on stereo video data.

Figure 8.1 shows a pair of geometrically rectified input images, defining a *stereo pair*. We considered two-camera systems in Sect. 6.1.3, their calibration and geometric rectification in Sect. 6.3, stereo-vision geometry in Sect. 7.3.1, and the use of detected corresponding pixels for 3D surface reconstruction in Sect. 7.3.2, assuming a stereo pair in canonical stereo geometry. It remains to answer the question: *How to detect pairs of corresponding pixels in a stereo pair?*

This chapter always assumes stereo pairs that are already geometrically rectified and possibly also preprocessed for reducing brightness issues (e.g. see Sect. 2.3.5). Corresponding pixels are thus expected to be in the left and right images in the same image row, as illustrated in Fig. 6.11 for standard stereo geometry. Figure 8.2 illustrates a calculated disparity map.

8.1 Matching, Data Cost, and Confidence

Stereo matching is an example of the labelling approach as outlined in Sect. 5.3.1. A labelling function f assigns a label $f_p \in L$, a disparity, to each pixel location $p \in \Omega$, applying error functions E_{data} and E_{smooth} as specified in (5.30) for a general case, which we recall here for better reference:

$$E(f) = \sum_{p \in \Omega} \left[E_{data}(p, f_p) + \sum_{q \in A(p)} E_{smooth}(f_p, f_q) \right] \qquad (8.1)$$

R. Klette, *Concise Computer Vision*, Undergraduate Topics in Computer Science, DOI 10.1007/978-1-4471-6320-6_8, © Springer-Verlag London 2014

Fig. 8.1 A stereo pair Crossing. Starting at pixel location p in the left image, we search along the epipolar line for a corresponding pixel location q. How to detect q (e.g. in a homogeneously textured region as shown here)? A correct q would be to the right of the shown q

Fig. 8.2 Visualization of a calculated disparity map for the stereo pair Crossing shown in Fig. 8.1, using a colour key for visualizing different disparities. Black illustrates a pixel where confidence was low in the calculated disparity

The *accumulated costs* of label f_p at p are the combined data and adjacent smoothness error values:

$$A_{data}(p, f_p) = E_{data}(p, f_p) + \sum_{q \in A(p)} E_{smooth}(f_p, f_q) \qquad (8.2)$$

Examples for a (general) smoothness error or energy term E_{smooth} (also called continuity or neighbourhood term) are provided in Sect. 5.3.2, starting with the simple Potts model and continuing with the linear (truncated) and quadratic (truncated) cost functions.

This section describes the stereo-matching problem at an abstract level, specifies data-cost functions E_{data} as applicable for solving stereo-matching problems, and also a way for selecting an appropriate data-cost function for stereo data of interest. The section ends with providing measures for confidence in calculated disparity values.

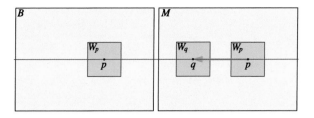

Fig. 8.3 Assume that the left image is the base image (i.e. $B = L$) and the right image is the match image (i.e. $M = R$). We start at a pixel p in the base image, consider its neighbourhood defined by a square window, and compare with neighbourhoods around pixels q on the epipolar line (i.e. on the same row due to canonical stereo geometry) in the match image

8.1.1   Generic Model for Matching

We have a left and a right image, denoted by L and R, respectively. One of both is now the *base image*, and the other the *match image*, denoted by B and M, respectively. For a pixel $(x, y, B(x, y))$ in the base image, we search for a *corresponding pixel* $(x + d, y, M(x + d, y))$ in the match image, being on the same epipolar line identified by row y. The two pixels are corresponding if they are projections of the same point $P = (X, Y, Z)$ in the shown scene, as illustrated in Fig. 6.11. (In this figure it is $B = L$ and $M = R$, $x = x_{uL}$, and $x + d = x_{uR}$.)

Base and Match Images and Search Intervals   Figure 8.3 illustrates the case $B = L$ (and thus $M = R$). We initiate a search by selecting $p = (x, y)$ in B. This defines the *search interval* of points $q = (x + d, y)$ in M with $\max\{x - d_{\max}, 1\} \leq x + d \leq x$. In other words, we have that

$$0 \leq -d \leq \min\{d_{\max}, x - 1\} \tag{8.3}$$

(Section 7.3.2 explained that we only need to search to the left of x.) For example, if we start at $p = (1, y)$ in B, then we can only consider $d = 0$, and point P would need to be "at infinity" for having corresponding pixels. If we start at $p = (N_{cols}, y)$ and we have that $N_{cols} > d_{\max}$, then we have that $-d \leq d_{\max}$, and the search interval stops on the left already at $N_{cols} - d_{\max}$.

If we change to $B = R$ (and thus $M = L$), the sign of d will swap from negative to positive, and we have that

$$0 \leq d \leq \min\{d_{\max}, N_{cols} - x\} \tag{8.4}$$

See Fig. 8.4. We initiate a search again by selecting $p = (x, y)$ in $B = R$ and have the search interval of points $q = (x + d, y)$ in $M = L$ with $x \leq x + d \leq \min\{N_{cols}, x + d_{\max}\}$.

Fig. 8.4 Here we take the
right image as the base image
(i.e. $B = R$) and the *left
image* as the match image
(i.e. $M = L$)

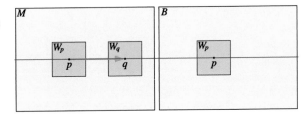

Label Set for Stereo Matching For not having to discriminate in the following
between positive and negative values, we assume right-to-left matching and refer to
the following label set:

$$L = \{-1, 0, 1, \ldots, d_{\max}\} \qquad (8.5)$$

where -1 denotes "no disparity assigned", and all the non-negative numbers are
possible disparity values, with $d_{\max} > 0$. In case of left-to-right matching, we have
the label set $L = \{+1, 0, -1, \ldots, -d_{\max}\}$.

Using intrinsic and extrinsic camera parameters, the value $d_{\max}$ can be estimated
by the closest objects in the scene that are "still of interest". For example, when
analysing a scene in front of a driving car, everything closer than, say, 2 m is out of
interest, and the threshold 2 m would identify $d_{\max}$. See Exercise 8.7.

Neighbourhoods for Correspondence Search For identifying corresponding
points, a straightforward idea is to compare neighbourhoods (rectangular windows
for simplicity) around a pixel p in the image I. We consider $(2l + 1) \times (2k + 1)$
windows $W_p^{l,k}(I)$. The window $W_p^{0,k}(I)$ is only along one image row.[1] We only
consider grey-level images with values between 0 and $G_{\max}$.

We always consider one image row y at a time. We just write B_x for $B(x, y)$, or
$W_x^{l,k}(B)$ for $W_p^{l,k}(B)$, and M_{x+d} for $M(x + d, y)$, or $W_{x+d}^{l,k}(M)$ for $W_q^{l,k}(M)$. We
speak about the pixel location x in B and pixel location $x + d$ in M, not mentioning
the current row index y.

Windows are centred at the considered pixel locations. The data in both windows
around the start pixel location $p = (x, y)$ and around the candidate pixel location
$q = (x + d, y)$ are identical *iff* the data cost measure

$$E_{SSD}(p, d) = \sum_{i=-l}^{l} \sum_{j=-k}^{k} \left[B(x + i, y + j) - M(x + d + i, y + j) \right]^2 \qquad (8.6)$$

---

[1]This notation is short for $W_p^{2l+1, 2k+1}(I)$, the notation used in Sect. 1.1.1.

results in value 0, where SSD stands for the *sum of squared differences*. The same would be true if we use the data cost defined by the *sum of absolute differences* (SAD) as follows:

$$E_{SAD}(p,d) = \sum_{i=-l}^{l} \sum_{j=-k}^{k} \left| B(x+i, y+j) - M(x+d+i, y+j) \right| \quad (8.7)$$

In both equations we compare every pixel in the window $W_x^{l,k}(B)$ with that pixel in the window $W_{x+d}^{l,k}(M)$ that is relatively at the same location (i, j). In the extreme case of $l = k = 0$ we just compare the pixel value with the pixel value. For example, the *absolute difference* (AD)

$$E_{AD}(p,d) = \left| B(x, y) - M(x+d, y) \right| \quad (8.8)$$

may be seen as the simplest possible data cost function.

Five Reasons Why Just SSD or SAD Will Not Work We list five difficulties that prevent a simple use of the SSD or SAD data cost measure from succeeding when looking for corresponding pixels:

1. *Invalidity of ICA*. Stereo pairs often do not satisfy the ICA; the intensity values at corresponding pixels, and in their neighbourhoods, are typically impacted by lighting variations or just by image noise.
2. *Local reflectance differences*. Due to different viewing angles, P and its neighbourhood will also reflect light differently to cameras recording B and M (except in the case where having Lambertian reflectance at P).
3. *Differences in cameras*. Different gains or offsets in the two cameras used result in high SAD or SSD errors.
4. *Perspective distortion*. The 3D point $P = (X, Y, Z)$, projected into a pair of corresponding points, is on a sloped surface. The local neighbourhood around P on this surface is differently projected into images B and M because both images see this neighbourhood around P under (slightly) different viewing angles (i.e. the shape of windows W_p and W_q should ideally follow to projected shape of the local neighbourhood).
5. *No unique minimum*. There might be several pixel locations q defining the same minimum, such as in the case of a larger region being uniformly shaded, or in the case of a periodic pattern.

We will provide better data measures in the next subsection.

3D Data Cost Matrix Consider a base image B and a match image M. A data cost measure $E_{data}(p, l)$ with $p \in \Omega$ (i.e. the carrier of image B) and $l \in L \setminus \{-1\}$ defines the 3D *data cost matrix* $\mathbf{C}_{data}$ of size $N_{cols} \times N_{rows} \times (d_{max} + 1)$ with elements (assuming that $B = R$)

$$C_{data}(x, y, d) = \begin{cases} E_{data}(x, y, d) & \text{if } 0 \le d \le \min\{d_{max}, N_{cols} - x\} \\ -1 & \text{otherwise} \end{cases} \quad (8.9)$$

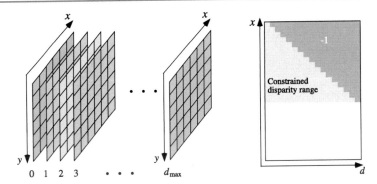

Fig. 8.5 *Left*: The 3D data cost matrix for a data cost function E_{data}. A position contains either the value $E_{data}(x, y, d)$ or -1. *Right*: The top view on this matrix, assuming $N_{cols} > d_{max}$ and $B = R$, showing all those columns (in the y-direction) in *dark grey*, which have the value -1; the rows in *light grey* indicate a constrained disparity range because there is at least one column (in the y-direction) labelled by -1

For example, the data measures *SSD* and *SAD* define the cost matrices $\mathbf{C}_{SSD}$ and $\mathbf{C}_{SAD}$.

A 3D data-cost matrix is a comprehensive representation of all the involved data costs, and it can be used for further optimization (e.g. by using the smoothness-cost function) in the control structure of the *stereo matcher* (i.e. an algorithm for stereo matching). Figure 8.5 illustrates data matrices. Each disparity defines one *layer* of the 3D matrix. In the case of $B = R$, the columns indicated by dark grey do have the value -1 in all their positions. The rows in light grey indicate the cases of x-coordinates where the available range of disparities is constrained, not allowing to go to a maximum of d_{max}.

If we consider one image row y at a time, and a fixed data-cost function, the notation can simplify to $C(x, d)$ by not including the current image row y or cost function.

8.1.2   Data-Cost Functions

A stereo matcher is often defined by the used data and smoothness-cost terms and by a control structure how those terms are applied for minimizing the total error of the calculated labelling function f. The smoothness terms are very much generically defined, and we present possible control structures later in this chapter. Data-cost calculation is the "core component" of a stereo matcher. We define a few data-cost functions with a particular focus on ensuring some invariance with respect to lighting artifacts in recorded images or brightness differences between left and right images.

Zero-Mean Version   Instead of calculating a data-cost function such as $E_{SSD}(x, l)$ or $E_{SAD}(x, l)$ on the original image data, we first calculate the mean $\overline{B}_x$ of a used window $W_x^{l,k}(B)$ and the mean $\overline{M}_{x+d}$ of a used window $W_{x+d}^{l,k}(M)$, subtract $\overline{B}_x$

from all intensity values in $W_x^{l,k}(B)$ and $\overline{M}_{x+d}$ from all values in $W_{x+d}^{l,k}(M)$, and then calculate the data-cost function in its *zero-mean version*. This is one option for reducing the impact of lighting artefacts (i.e. for not depending on the ICA).

We indicate this way of processing by starting the subscript of the data-cost function with a Z. For example, E_{ZSSD} or E_{ZSAD} are the zero-mean SSD or zero-mean SAD data-cost function, respectively, formally defined by

$$E_{ZSSD}(x,d) = \sum_{i=-l}^{l} \sum_{j=-k}^{k} \left[(B_{x+i,y+j} - \overline{B}_x) - (M_{x+i+d,y+j} - \overline{M}_{x+d}) \right]^2 \quad (8.10)$$

$$E_{ZSAD}(x,d) = \sum_{i=-l}^{l} \sum_{j=-k}^{k} \left| [B_{x+i,y+j} - \overline{B}_x] - [M_{x+d+i,y+j} - \overline{M}_{i+d}] \right| \quad (8.11)$$

NCC Data Cost The normalized cross correlation (NCC) was defined in Insert 4.11 for comparing two images. The NCC is already defined by zero-mean normalization, but we add the Z to the index for uniformity in notation. The *NCC data cost* is defined by

$$E_{ZNCC}(x,d) = 1 - \frac{\sum_{i=-l}^{l} \sum_{j=-k}^{k} [B_{x+i,y+j} - \overline{B}_x][M_{x+d+i,y+j} - \overline{M}_{x+d}]}{\sqrt{\sigma_{B,x}^2 \cdot \sigma_{M,x+d}^2}}$$

$$(8.12)$$

where

$$\sigma_{B,x}^2 = \sum_{i=-l}^{l} \sum_{j=-k}^{k} [B_{x+i,y+j} - \overline{B}_x]^2 \quad (8.13)$$

$$\sigma_{M,x+d}^2 = \sum_{i=-l}^{l} \sum_{j=-k}^{k} [M_{x+d+i,y+j} - \overline{M}_{x+d}]^2 \quad (8.14)$$

ZNCC is also an option for going away from the ICA.

The Census Data-Cost Function The *zero-mean normalized census cost function* is defined as follows:

$$E_{ZCEN}(x,d) = \sum_{i=-l}^{l} \sum_{j=-k}^{k} \rho(x+i, y+j, d) \quad (8.15)$$

with

$$\rho(u,v,d) = \begin{cases} 0 & B_{uv} \perp \overline{B}_x \text{ and } M_{u+d,v} \perp \overline{M}_{x+d} \\ 1 & \text{otherwise} \end{cases} \quad (8.16)$$

with $\perp$ either $<$ or $>$ in both cases. By using B_x instead of $\overline{B}_x$ and M_{x+d} instead of $\overline{M}_{x+d}$, we have the census data-cost function E_{CEN} (without zero-mean normalization).

Example 8.1 (Example for Census Data Cost) Consider the following 3×3 windows $W_x(B)$ and $W_{x+d}(M)$:

2	1	6
1	2	4
2	1	3

5	5	9
7	6	7
5	4	6

We have that $\overline{B}_x \approx 2.44$ and $\overline{M}_{x+d} \approx 6.11$.

Consider $i = j = -1$, resulting in $u = x - 1$ and $v = y - 1$. We have that $B_{x-1,y-1} = 2 < 2.44$ and $M_{x-1+d,y-1} = 5 < 6.11$, and thus $\rho(x - 1, y - 1, d) = 0$.

As a second example, consider $i = j = +1$. We have that $B_{x+1,y+1} = 3 > 2.44$, but $M_{x+1+d,y+1} = 6 < 6.11$, and thus $\rho(x + 1, y + 1, d) = 1$.

In the case $i = j = -1$, the values are in the same relation with respect to the mean, but at $i = j = +1$ they are in opposite relationships. For the given example, it follows that $E_{ZCEN} = 2$. The spatial distribution of ρ-values is illustrated by the matrix

0	0	0
1	0	0
0	0	1

The following vector $\mathbf{c}_{x,d}$ lists these ρ-values in a left-to-right, top-to-bottom order: $[0, 0, 0, 1, 0, 0, 0, 0, 1]^\top$.

Let $\mathbf{b}_x$ be the vector listing results $\text{sgn}(B_{x+i,y+j} - \overline{B}_x)$ in a left-to-right, top-to-bottom order, where sgn is the signum function. Similarly, $\mathbf{m}_{x+d}$ lists the values $\text{sgn}(M_{x+i+d,y+j} - \overline{M}_{x+d})$. For the values in Example 8.1, we have that

$$\mathbf{b}_x = [-1, -1, +1, -1, -1, +1, -1, -1, +1]^\top \tag{8.17}$$

$$\mathbf{m}_{x+d} = [-1, -1, +1, +1, -1, +1, -1, -1, -1] \tag{8.18}$$

$$\mathbf{c}_{x,d} = [0, 0, 0, 1, 0, 0, 0, 0, 1]^\top \tag{8.19}$$

The vector $\mathbf{c}_{x,d}$ shows exactly the positions where the vectors $\mathbf{b}_x$ and $\mathbf{m}_{x+d}$ differ in values; the number of positions where two vectors differ is known as the *Hamming distance* of those two vectors.

Observation 8.1 *The zero-mean normalized census data cost $E_{ZCEN}(x, d)$ equals the Hamming distance between the vectors $\mathbf{b}_x$ and $\mathbf{m}_{x+d}$.*

By adapting the definition of both vectors $\mathbf{b}_x$ and $\mathbf{m}_{x+d}$ to the census data-cost function E_{CEN}, we can also obtain those costs as the Hamming distance.

Fig. 8.6 *Left*: Dependency from 4-adjacent pixels. *Right*: Dependency of 4-adjacent pixels from their 4-adjacent pixels

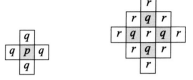

> **Insert 8.1** (Hamming) *The US-American mathematician R.W. Hamming (1915–1998) contributed to computer science and telecommunications. The Hamming code, Hamming window, Hamming numbers, and the Hamming distance are all named after him.*

By replacing the values -1 by 0 in the vectors $\mathbf{b}_x$ and $\mathbf{m}_{x+d}$, the Hamming distance for the resulting binary vectors can be calculated very time-efficiently.[2]

8.1.3 From Global to Local Matching

The data-cost and smoothness-cost functions together define the minimization problem for the total error defined in (8.1). The smoothness term uses an adjacency set $A(p)$, typically specified by 4-adjacency or an even larger adjacency set.

Growing 4-Adjacency into the Image Carrier Assume that A is just defined by 4-adjacency. A label f_p (i.e. the disparity in the stereo-matching case) at pixel p depends via the smoothness term on labels assigned to its four 4-adjacent pixels $q \in A_4(p)$; see Fig. 8.6, left.

The labels at pixels q also depend, according to the smoothness constraint, on the labels at all the 4-adjacent pixels r of those pixels q; see Fig. 8.6, right.

The labels at pixels r depend now again on labels at all 4-adjacent pixels of those pixels r. By continuing the process we have to conclude that the label at pixel p depends on the labels at all the pixels in carrier Ω. If A is a larger set than 4-adjacency, then data dependencies cover all Ω even faster.

The data term defines local value dependency from image values, but the smoothness term defines global dependency from all the assigned disparity values for making sure that the minimization problem of (8.1) is actually solved accurately.

Global Matching and Its Time Complexity *Global matching* (GM) is approximated by less time-expensive control structures of a stereo matcher. We briefly discuss time requirements of GM.

Consider extremely large smoothness penalties such as, say, $E_{smooth}(f_p, f_q) = G_{max} \cdot N_{cols} \cdot N_{rows}$ whenever $f_p \neq f_q$ (or even higher penalties). This leads to a situation where a (common) data term does not matter anymore; any constant

---

[2]See [H.S. Warren. Hacker's Delight, pp. 65–72, Addison-Wesley Longman, New York, 2002].

disparity map for all pixels in B would solve the optimization problem in this case, and a solution would be possible in a time needed to write the same constant in any pixel location in B. As another case, assume that the smoothness penalties are insignificant; decisions can be based on the data cost only. In this case ("The Winner Takes It All", see more about this below) we can also have a time-efficient and accurate solution to the minimization problem.

Observation 8.2 *The data term, adjacency set, and smoothness term in* (8.1) *influence the time needed to solve this minimization problem accurately.*

Consider images B and M of size $N_{cols} \times N_{rows}$. For implementing GM, each pixel in B needs to communicate with any other pixel in B, say via 4-adjacency; a longest path is then of length $N_{cols} + N_{rows}$ (if a pixel is in a corner of Ω), and those communication paths have length $(N_{cols} + N_{rows})/2$ as average. Each of the $N_{cols} \cdot N_{rows}$ pixels needs to communicate with the other $N_{cols} \cdot N_{rows} - 1$ pixels. This leads to an asymptotic run time in

$$t_{one} = \mathcal{O}\big((N_{cols} + N_{rows})N_{cols}^2 \cdot N_{rows}^2\big) \tag{8.20}$$

for evaluating globally *one* labelling f (i.e. a run time in $\mathcal{O}(N^5)$ if $N = N_{cols} = N_{rows}$). The set of all possible labellings has the cardinality

$$c_{all} = |L|^{|\Omega|} \in \mathcal{O}\big(d_{max}^{N_{cols} \cdot N_{rows}}\big) \tag{8.21}$$

Thus, an exhaustive testing of all possible labellings would require a time of $c_{all} \cdot t_{one}$. Of course, this is a worst-case scenario, which can be avoided; there are constraints for possible labellings, and communication between pixels can be reduced by not propagating the same information repeatedly through the image B or by using a pyramid image data structure (see Sect. 2.2.2) for reducing the lengths of communication paths between pixel locations. No serious attempt is known to achieve GM (e.g. on some parallel hardware).

Area of Influence   When deciding about a label f_p at pixel p, the control structure of the used stereo matcher consults pixels in a set $p + S$ via the smoothness constraint about possible feedback for the selection of f_p. We call the set S the *area of influence*.

Figure 8.7, left, illustrates such an area defined by the intersection of digital rays with Ω; in the shown case, 16 rays run towards the pixel location p. The area of influence is now not covering the whole Ω, as in case of GM, but also is not locally bounded; the rays run all the way to the image borders. This defines an area of influence for (ray-based) *semi-global matching* (SGM).

Figure 8.7, right, illustrates an area of influence created by repeatedly expanding into 4-adjacent pixels around the previous area of influence. The number of expansions defines the radius of the created 4-disc. This defines an area of influence as used in *belief-propagation matching* (BPM).

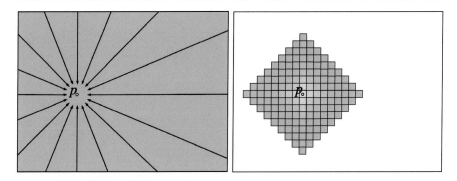

Fig. 8.7 *Left*: A search space defined by 16 rays running from the image border to pixel p. *Right*: A search space defined by including eight times repeated also 4-adjacent pixels into the decisions

GM is one extreme case for the area of influence, and $S = \{(0, 0)\}$ defines the other extreme case where the area of influence $p + S = p$ does not include any other pixel in B; in this case we do not consider smoothness with labels in adjacent pixels, and the data function also only takes the value at p into account (e.g. the data cost function E_{AD}).

Local Matching By defining an area of influence that is bounded by some fixed constant, a stereo algorithm applies local matching. Of course, the use of $S = \{(0, 0)\}$ defines local matching. If the number of repetitive applications of 4-adjacency (see Fig. 8.7, right) is fixed, then we also have a local matcher. If this number increases with the size $N_{cols} \times N_{rows}$ of the given images B and M, then we have a (disc-based) semi-global matcher.

See Fig. 8.8 for an example when using both a local and a semi-global stereo matcher on the same scene.

8.1.4 Testing Data Cost Functions

For testing the accuracy of different data cost functions with respect to identifying the correct corresponding pixel in M, we may apply a stereo matcher that is not impacted by a designed control structure and not by a chosen smoothness term, and we need to have stereo pairs with ground truth, telling us which is actually the correct corresponding pixel.

The Winner Takes It All We reduce the minimization of the total error for a labelling function f to the minimization of

$$E(f) = \sum_{p \in \Omega} E_{data}(p, f_p) \tag{8.22}$$

Fig. 8.8 *Top*: An input image of a recorded stereo sequence at the University of Auckland. *Middle*: A disparity map using a local matcher (block matching, as available in `OpenCV` beginning of 2013. *Bottom*: A disparity map using `iSGM`, a semi-global stereo matcher

Because a corresponding pixel in M needs to be on the same image row (i.e. the epipolar line), we can simply optimize by calculating, for any $p = (x, y)$ and any possible disparity f_p [see (8.3) and (8.4)], all the values $E_{data}(p, f_p)$ and achieve accurately the minimum for (8.22) by taking for each p the disparity f_p that minimizes $E_{data}(p, f_p)$. For doing so, we generate the 3D data cost matrix $\mathbf{C}_{data}$, select a pixel location $p = (x, y)$, go through all layers $d = 0$, $d = 1$, to $d = d_{max}$ (see Fig. 8.5), and compare all values $C_{data}(x, y, d) \geq 0$ for finding the disparity

$$f_p = \operatorname*{argmin}_{0 \leq d \leq d_{max}} \left\{ C_{data}(x, y, d) \geq 0 \right\} \tag{8.23}$$

that defines the minimum. In other words, for any $p = (x, y) \in \Omega$, we apply the control structure shown in Fig. 8.9.

Fig. 8.9 The winner takes it all at $p = (x, y) \in \Omega$ while applying left-to-right matching

```
1: Let d = d_min = 0 and E_min = E_data(p, 0);
2: while d < x do
3:     Let d = d + 1;
4:     Compute E = E_data(p, d);
5:     if E < E_min then
6:         E_min = E and d_min = d;
7:     end if
8: end while
```

This stereo matcher will create depth artifacts. We are not considering it as an applicable stereo matcher; we are just curious to understand how different data-cost functions behave in identifying correct matches. This test is not affected by a smoothness constraint or a sophisticated control structure.

Ground Truth Data for Measuring Accuracy of Stereo Matching Insert 4.12 introduced the term "ground truth". Assume that a measurement method provided (fairly) accurate disparity values at pixel locations for a set or sequence of stereo pairs B and M. The measurement method might be defined by synthetic stereo pairs generated for a 3D world model and the use of a 3D rendering program for calculating the stereo pairs, or by the use of a laser range-finder for measuring distances in a real-world 3D scene. See Insert 2.12 for examples of data provided online; the website vision.middlebury.edu/ at Middlebury College is another example for online test data.

A location $p \in \Omega$ defines a *bad pixel* in B iff the disparity calculated at p differs by (say) more than 1 from the value provided as the ground truth disparity. The percentage of non-bad pixels defines a common *accuracy measure* for stereo matching.

The experiment can then be as follows: Select the set of test data where ground truth disparities are available. Select the cost data functions you are interested in for comparison. Do a statistical analysis of the percentage of bad pixels when applying the control structure described in Fig. 8.9 for your data cost functions on the selected set of test data. Figure 8.10 shows an example for test data (long stereo sequences) where ground truth disparities are available.

8.1.5 Confidence Measures

At the beginning of Sect. 2.4.2 we defined confidence measures. A confidence measure can be used if ground truth is not available. In the given context, a confidence value $\Gamma(p)$ at $p \in \Omega$ (in base image B) needs to be accumulated based on stereo-matching models or plausible assumption about the matching process.

Left–Right Consistency The *left–right consistency check* is defined as follows: Let $B = R$ and perform right-to-left stereo matching, resulting in the disparity $f_p^{(R)}$ at p, then let $B = L$ and perform left-to-right stereo matching, resulting in the disparity $f_p^{(L)}$ at p. In both cases we consider the calculated disparities as positive

Fig. 8.10 *Left*: The original image `Set2Seq1Frame1` from EISATS. *Right*: A disparity map visualized with the disparity colour code used throughout the book

Fig. 8.11 Parabola fit at disparity d_0 defining the minimum of accumulated costs. The parabola also defines a subpixel accurate disparity at its minimum (see the *dashed line*)

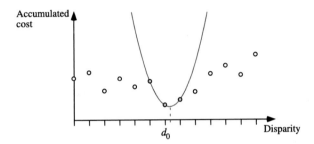

numbers. For comparing the disparity results $f_p^{(R)}$ and $f_p^{(L)}$, let

$$\Gamma_1(p) = \frac{1}{|f_p^{(R)} - f_p^{(L)}| + 1} \tag{8.24}$$

with $\Gamma_1(p) = 1$ for $f_p^{(R)} = f_p^{(L)}$ and $0 < \Gamma_1(p) < 1$ otherwise. For example, if $\Gamma_1(p) < 0.5$, then reject the calculated disparities as being inconsistent.

This confidence measure is based on an expectation that two consistent results support each other; but daily life often tells us different stories (just think about two newspapers telling different lies).

Fitted Parabola   It appears to be more appropriate to have confidence measures that are based on applied data cost functions, their values, or matching models.

For a pixel location p, consider a parabola fit $ax^2 + bx + c$ to accumulated costs [see (8.2)] in a neighbourhood of the disparity d_0 where the accumulated cost values $A_p(d) = A_{data}(p, d)$ take the global minimum. See Fig. 8.11. The minimum of such a parabola identifies the disparity at *subpixel accuracy*; the distance unit 1 between two subsequent disparities is defined by the distance unit 1 between two 4-adjacent pixel locations.

The parameter a defines the curvature of the parabola, and this value can be taken as a confidence measure. For deriving a, consider the following equation system:

$$a(d_0 - 1)^2 + b(d_0 - 1) + c = A_p(d_0 - 1) \tag{8.25}$$

$$a d_0^2 + b d_0 + c = A_p(d_0) \tag{8.26}$$

$$a(d_0 + 1)^2 + b(d_0 + 1) + c = A_p(d_0 + 1) \tag{8.27}$$

It follows that

$$\Gamma_2(p) = 2a = A_p(d_0 - 1) - 2 \cdot A_p(d_0) + A_p(d_0 + 1) \tag{8.28}$$

is a possible confidence measure, with minimum $\Gamma_2(p) = 0$ if $A_p(d_0 - 1) = A_p(d_0) = A_p(d_0 + 1)$ and $a > 0$ otherwise.

Perturbation Perturbation quantifies a deviation from an ideal cost function, which has a global minimum at d_0 and which is "very large" elsewhere. Nonlinear scaling is applied:

$$\Gamma_3(p) = d_{\max} - \sum_{d \neq d_0} \exp\left(-\frac{[A_p(d_0) - A_p(d)]^2}{\psi^2}\right) \tag{8.29}$$

The parameter ψ depends on the range of accumulated cost values. For $A_p(d_0) = A_p(d)$, for all $d \neq d_0$, and $\psi = 1$, it follows that $\Gamma_3(p) = 0$, the minimum value.

Peak Ratio Let d_1 be a disparity where the accumulated costs take a local minimum that is second after the local minimum at d_0, which is also the global minimum. The peak ratio confidence measure compares those two lowest local minima:

$$\Gamma_4(p) = 1 - \frac{A_p(d_0)}{A_p(d_1)} \tag{8.30}$$

The value d_1 is *not* defined by the second smallest accumulated cost value; this might occur just adjacent to d_0. Again, if all values $A_p(d)$ are equal, then $\Gamma_4(p)$ takes its minimum value 0.

Use of Confidence Measures When performing dense (i.e. at every pixel $p \in \Omega$) stereo matching, it might be appropriate to replace the resulting disparities with low confidence by the special label -1. Subsequent processes may then aim at "filling in reasonable" disparity values at those locations, for example by applying interpolation to the disparities at nearby locations having high confidence values. See Fig. 8.12 for an illustration of labeled low-confidence pixels.

8.2 Dynamic Programming Matching

Dynamic programming is a method for efficiently solving optimization problems by caching subproblem solutions rather than recomputing them again.

Fig. 8.12 *Left*: An image of stereo pair `Bridge`. *Right*: Disparity map where disparities with low confidence values are replaced by *grey*. The small numbers in the colour key, shown in a column on the *right*, go from 5.01 to 155 (in a non-linear scale, with 10.4 about at the middle) and denote distances in meter

---

Insert 8.2 (Dynamic Programming, Bellman, and Computer Vision) *Dynamic programming was introduced in* 1953 *into algorithm design by the US-American applied mathematician R. Bellman (1920–1984) for planning, decision making, and optimal control theory.*

Dynamic programming became popular in the 1960s *for various computing-related applications (e.g. recognition of context-free languages, optimizing matrix multiplication).*

For early examples of path optimization techniques applied for edge detection, see [V.A. Kovalevsky. Sequential optimization in pattern recognition and pattern description. In Proc. IFIP, pp. 1603–1607, 1968], [U. Montanari. On the optimal detection of curves in noisy pictures. Comm. ACM, vol. 14, pp. 335–345, 1971], *and* [A. Martelli. Edge detection using heuristic search methods. CGIP, vol. 1, pp. 169–182, 1972].

This section briefly recalls the dynamic programming methodology and applies it then to stereo analysis, thus defining *dynamic-programming matching* (DPM).

8.2.1 Dynamic Programming

To solve a problem by dynamic programming, it has to satisfy the following requirements:

1. The problem can be divided into multiple decision stages, and each stage is solvable on its own.
2. Those stages may be ordered along the time scale so that all previous stages whose results are needed at a later stage can be solved beforehand.
3. There exists a recursive relationship between the stages.
4. The solution of one stage must be independent of the decision history when solving the previous stages.

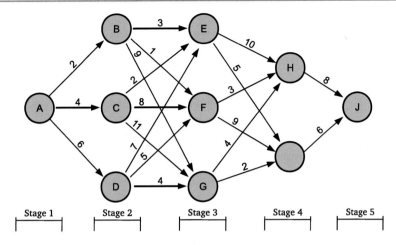

Fig. 8.13 An example of a weighted graph. The nodes are already graphically sorted into stages

5. The solution of the final stage must be self-contained.

Shortest Path Problems in Weighted Graphs We consider the calculation of a shortest path in a weighted graph. For graphs, see Insert 3.2. A *weighted graph* has positive weights assigned to its edges. See Fig. 8.13 for an example.

A weighted graph can be understood as being a road network, and the aim is to calculate a shortest path from one of its nodes to another node, where weights at edges are interpreted as the lengths of road segments between nodes.

Example 8.2 (Dynamic Programming for Solving a Shortest Path Problem) Consider the directed weighted graph in Fig. 8.13. The task is to find a shortest path from node A to node J. Arrows show possible directions for a move. The network can be divided into five stages, as illustrated in the figure, where Stage 1 contains node A, Stage 2 contains nodes B, C, and D, Stage 3 contains E, F, and G, Stage 4 contains nodes H and I, and Stage 5 contains node J.

Let X and Y denote the nodes in stages m and $m + 1$ with the distance $d(X, Y)$ between X and Y. For calculating the shortest path distance from a node X to J, use the recursive function

$$E_m(X) = \min_{Y \text{ in stage } m+1} \{d(X, Y) + E_{m+1}(Y)\} \qquad (8.31)$$

where $E_5(J) = 0$. $E_1(A)$ defines the minimum. See Table 8.1.

At stage m, the results are used as already obtained before for nodes at stage $m + 1$; there is no need to go (again) all the way to J. *Backtracking* provides the shortest path from node A to J. The solution does not have to be unique.

Table 8.1 The shortest distances $E_m(X)$ to node J

Stage	Shortest distance	Path
5	$E_5(J) = 0$	J
4	$E_4(H) = d(H, J) + E_5(J) = 8$	H, J
	$E_4(I) = d(I, J) + E_5(J) = 6$	I, J
3	$E_3(E) = d(E, I) + E_4(I) = 11$	E, I, J
	$E_3(F) = d(F, H) + E_4(H) = 11$	F, H, J
	$E_3(G) = d(G, I) + E_4(I) = 8$	G, I, J
2	$E_2(B) = d(B, F) + E_3(F) = 12$	B, F, H, J
	$E_2(C) = d(C, E) + E_3(E) = 13$	C, E, I, J
	$E_2(D) = d(D, G) + E_3(G) = 12$	D, G, I, J
1	$E_1(A) = d(A, B) + E_2(B) = 14$	A, B, F, H, J

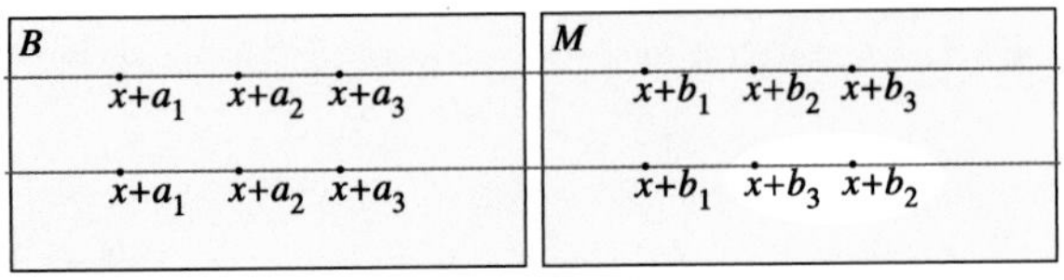

Fig. 8.14 The *upper row* satisfies the ordering constraint but not the *lower row*

8.2.2 Ordering Constraint

We prepare now for applying dynamic programming for calculating disparities along one image row y. We did this before by using the algorithm in Fig. 8.9 (the winner takes it all); in this case the decision at a pixel p was only guided by the data cost; there was no constraint defined for looking at neighbours of p for reconfirming a decision. Thus, there is also no possibility (or need) to apply dynamic programming. This need is given when we include dependencies between adjacent pixels into the optimization problem. One option is to apply the smoothness constraint, and we will do so in the next section. Another option is to use the *ordering constraint*, which also defines dependencies between disparities assigned to adjacent pixels.

Ordering Constraint for Scene Geometry When using stereo vision from an airplane with cameras far away compared to the height of visible objects on the surface of the Earth, we can assume that the correspondences are *ordered* along an epipolar line. Assume that $(x + a_i, y)$ in B corresponds to $(x + b_i, y)$ in M for $i = 1, 2, 3$. The given stereo geometry satisfies the *ordering constraint iff*

$$0 \le a_1 < a_2 < a_3 \quad \text{implies that} \quad x + b_1 \le x + b_2 \le x + b_3 \qquad (8.32)$$

for any configuration as assumed. If $B = L$, then it may be that $b_1 < 0$ but $0 < b_2 < b_3$. If $B = R$, then it may be that $0 < b_1$ but $b_3 < b_2 < 0$. See Fig. 8.14.

Figure 8.15 illustrates a case of a scene geometry where the ordering constraint is not satisfied. Basically, this is always possible if there are significant differences in depth compared to the distance between cameras and objects in the scene.

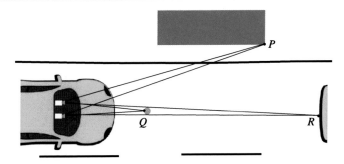

Fig. 8.15 The *left camera* sees the three 3D points in the order P, R, and Q, but the *right camera* in the order P, Q, and R

Epipolar Profiles An *epipolar profile* can be used for illustrating matching results for an image row y in B with image row y in M; we do not need to make reference to y. The profile is a digital arc going "basically" from the upper left to the lower right in a digital square of size $N_{cols} \times N_{cols}$; the x-coordinates in B correspond to columns, and the x-coordinates in M to rows. The disparity f_p at $p = (x, y)$ identifies the grid point $(x - f_p, x)$ in the square; the subsequent identified grid points are connected by straight segments forming a polygonal arc. This arc is the *epipolar profile*.

The profile is a cut through the 3D scene as seen by both cameras in (rectified) rows y from North–East (i.e. diagonally down from the upper right corner of the square).

Example 8.3 (Two Epipolar Profiles) Let $N_{cols} = 16$, $d_{max} = 3$, and $B = L$. We only consider pixels with $x = 4, 5, \ldots, 16$ in the left image for a correspondence search; for $x = 1, 2, 3$, we cannot consider the values up to d_{max}. For a row y, we calculate 13 labels (disparities) $f_4, f_5, \ldots, f_{16}$. We assume two vectors as results:

$$\mathbf{d}_1 = [f_4, f_5, \ldots, f_{16}]^\top = [0, 1, 2, 2, 3, 2, 3, 0, 1, 0, 0, 1, 1]^\top$$
$$\mathbf{d}_2 = [f_4, f_5, \ldots, f_{16}]^\top = [3, 3, 3, 1, 2, 0, 3, 1, 0, 0, 1, 2, 3]^\top$$

Figure 8.16 illustrates the epipolar profiles for both vectors.

Figure 8.16 shows on the left a profile that goes monotonically down to the lower right corner, illustrating that the recorded scene satisfies the ordering constraint for the given row y (at least according to the calculated disparities). The epipolar profile on the right illustrates that there is a kind of a "post" in the scene at the grid point $(7, 10)$ causing that the scene does not satisfy the ordering constraint in row y illustrated by this diagram.

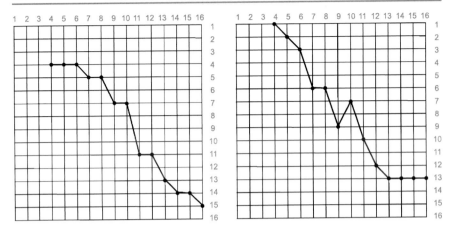

Fig. 8.16 *Left*: The epipolar profile for the vector $\mathbf{d}_1$. *Right*: The epipolar profile for the vector $\mathbf{d}_2$

Insert 8.3 (Origin of Epipolar Profiles) [*Y. Ohta and T. Kanade. Stereo by intra- and inter-scanline search using dynamic programming. IEEE Trans. Pattern Analysis Machine Intelligence, vol. 7, pp. 139–154, 1985] is the paper that introduced epipolar profiles and also pioneered dynamic programming matching (see Sect. 8.2) by giving for the first time a detailed description of this technique. A sketch of dynamic-programming matching was already contained in [H.H. Baker and T.O. Binford. Depth from edge and intensity based stereo. Stanford AI Lab Memo, 1981].*

Observation 8.3 *The epipolar profile for disparities calculated in one image row y provides a simple way to test whether the calculated disparities satisfy the ordering constraint: the epipolar profile needs to be monotonically decreasing.*

8.2.3   DPM Using the Ordering Constraint

DPM stereo analysis specifies a minimization algorithm, which is global within one *scanline* or row y.

Its accuracy is often (depending on application area) surpassed by many of today's top performing stereo matchers. When dealing with specific data (e.g. night vision or relatively low image resolution) or a particular application context (e.g. real-time, all-weather, and so forth), dynamic programming stereo might be still an option.

Optimization Problem   Given is a pair of rectified stereo images and a data cost function E_x; for abbreviation, let $E_x(f_x) = E_{data}(p, f_x)$ for $p = (x, y)$. We assume that $L = B$. We like to calculate an optimal labelling function f that

1. minimizes the error

$$E(f) = \sum_{x=1}^{N_{cols}} E_x(f_x) \tag{8.33}$$

2. satisfies the ordering constraint, and
3. for any pixel in L, we can assign a corresponding pixel in R (*uniqueness constraint*).

Despite the left-to-right process, we assume the values f_x in the set $\{0, 1, \ldots, d_{max}\}$. Thus, starting at (x, y) in the left image, a corresponding pixel is of the form $(x_r, y) = (x - f_x, y)$.

Derivation of Upper and Lower Bounds   A corresponding pixel $(x_r, y) = (x - f_x, y)$ needs to be visible in the right image (i.e. not occluded and $1 \leq x_r \leq N_{cols}$), which is expressed by the inequalities in (8.3). We rewrite this here as

$$0 \leq f_x \leq \min\{x - 1, d_{max}\} \tag{8.34}$$

If $x \leq d_{max}$, then f_x can only take a value in the set $\{0, 1, \ldots, x - 1\}$. If $f_x = x - 1$, then $x_r = x - (x - 1) = 1$, which satisfies that $1 \leq x_r \leq N_{cols}$. If $f_x = d_{max}$ and $d_{max} \leq x - 1$, we have that $x_r = x - d_{max} \geq x - (x - 1) = 1$. For example, if $d_{max} = 5$ and $x = 3$, then f_x is limited to take values only in $\{0, 1, 2\}$. Thus, it is very likely that we will assign incorrect points (x_r, y) to pixels (x, y), which are close to the left border of the left image.

Now we study impacts of the ordering constraint. If (x, y) in L is assigned to $(x_r, y) = (x - f_x, y)$ in R, then $(x_r - 1, y)$ can only be corresponding to some location $(x - a, y)$ in the left image for $a \geq 1$ (if there is a corresponding pixel at all). Thus, $x_r - 1 = (x - a) - f_{x-a}$.

Case 1   Assume that (x, y) in L was the first pixel in row y (from the left) assigned to the pixel (x_r, y) in R. The value a may specify the first pixel in L (in row y, from the left) assigned to $(x_r - 1, y)$ in R, and all the pixels $(x - a, y), (x - a + 1, y), \ldots, (x - 1, y)$ in L are assigned to $(x_r - 1, y)$ in R. It follows that

$$x_r = x - f_x > x_r - 1 = (x - 1) - f_{x-1} \tag{8.35}$$

Thus,

$$x - f_x > x - f_{x-1} - 1 \tag{8.36}$$

which is equivalent to

$$f_x - f_{x-1} < 1 \tag{8.37}$$

where (x, y) is the first pixel in L, counted from the left, which is assigned to the pixel (x_r, y) in R.

Case 2   Now assume that (x, y) in L is assigned to the same pixel (x_r, y) in R as $(x - 1, y)$ in L. Then we have that $x_r = x - f_x = (x - 1) - f_{x-1}$ and $f_x = f_{x-1} + 1$. This also satisfies the inequality in (8.37).

The inequalities in (8.34) and both cases above together lead to

$$\max\{0, f_x - 1\} \le f_{x-1} \le \min\{x - 2, d_{max}\} \tag{8.38}$$

This specifies a dependency between the disparities f_x and f_{x-1}, to be used in the dynamic programming algorithm.

Observation 8.4 *Having labels (disparities) that satisfy the inequality in (8.38) is a necessary and sufficient condition that the calculated solution satisfies ordering and uniqueness constraints.*

Stages   So, how to define the "stages" of the problem for applying dynamic programming? We use a *partial error function* $E_m(f)$, which is only the sum of $E_x(f_x)$ values for $1 \le x \le m$:

$$E_m(f) = \sum_{x=1}^{m} E_x(f_x) \tag{8.39}$$

At stage m we need to have assignments of labels f_x, for all x with $1 \le x \le m$; at stage m we have not yet assignments for $x > m$.

Results at Stages   Towards minimizing the total energy $E(f) = E_M(f)$, we calculate at stage m the errors as follows:

$$E_m(f) = \min_{0 \le d \le d_{max}} \{E_m(d) + E_{m-1}(f)\} \tag{8.40}$$

where f is always a labelling for all the pixel values up to the indexed stage (e.g. for $E_{m-1}(f)$, we need to have $m - 1$ values in f, from left to right), and $E_m(d)$ only addresses the error when selecting the disparity d for $x = m$.

We start at $m = 1$ in image B; we use $E_{m-1}(f) = E_0(f) = 0$ for initialization and start with $f_1 = 0$ and value $E_1(0)$.

For $m = 2$, we may already decide between $d = 0$ or $d = 1$, and so forth. We have to satisfy the inequalities in (8.38).

When arriving at stage $x = M$, we have the optimum value $E(f)$, and we identify the used labels that allowed us to arrive at this optimum by backtracking, step by step, first from $x = M$ to $x = M - 1$, then from $x = M - 1$ to $x = M - 2$, and so forth.

Example 8.4 (A Simple Example) Consider corresponding rows y in the left and right images as given in Fig. 8.17. We have $d_{max} = 3$ and $N_{cols} = 7$. We assume the absolute differences (AD) as a data cost function; see (8.8).

| 2 | 3 | 1 | 2 | 3 | 3 | 1 |

| 1 | 2 | 3 | 1 | 4 | 0 | 2 |

Fig. 8.17 An example of rows y in *left* and *right images*

We start with $E_1(f) = E_1(0) = |2 - 1| = 1$ for $f_1 = 0$. There is no other option. Next, we calculate $E_2(f)$. Considering $E_2(0) = |3 - 2| = 1$ and $E_2(1) = |3 - 1| = 2$, we may take $f_2 = 0$ as our preferred choice with $E_2(f) = E_2(0) + E_1(f) = 1 + 1 = 2$.

Note that $f_2 = f_1$, and this satisfies the inequalities in (8.38). These inequalities also allow us to take $f_2 = 1$ as an option, and this would define $E_2(f) = 1 + 2 = 3$. We indicate the used choices in the E-function as an initial f-sequence with $E(0, 0) = 2$ and $E(0, 1) = 3$.

For $E_3(f)$, we may consider the disparities 0, 1, or 2 (in case of $E_3(0, 0, \cdot)$, only 0 and 1, due to (3), with $D_3(0) = 2$ and $D_3(1) = 1$). Thus, we have that $E_3(0, 0, 0) = 2 + 2 = 4$ and $E_3(0, 0, 1) = 2 + 1 = 3$. In case of $E_3(0, 1, \cdot)$ we may consider 0, 1, and 2, with $E_3(0, 1, 0) = 3 + 2 = 5$, $E_3(0, 1, 1) = 3 + 1 = 4$, and $E_3(0, 1, 2) = 3 + 0 = 3$.

For $m = 4$, we have the following:

$$E_4(0, 0, 0, 0) = 4 + 1 = 5, \qquad E_4(0, 0, 0, 1) = 4 + 1 = 5,$$

$$E_4(0, 0, 1, 0) = 3 + 1 = 4, \qquad E_4(0, 0, 1, 1) = 3 + 1 = 4,$$

$$E_4(0, 0, 1, 2) = 3 + 0 = 3, \qquad E_4(0, 1, 0, 0) = 5 + 1 = 6,$$

$$E_4(0, 1, 0, 0) = 5 + 1 = 6, \qquad E_4(0, 1, 1, 0) = 4 + 1 = 5,$$

$$E_4(0, 1, 1, 1) = 4 + 1 = 5, \qquad E_4(0, 1, 1, 2) = 4 + 0 = 4,$$

$$E_4(0, 1, 2, 0) = 3 + 1 = 4, \qquad E_4(0, 1, 2, 1) = 3 + 1 = 4,$$

$$E_4(0, 1, 2, 2) = 3 + 0 = 3, \qquad E_4(0, 1, 2, 3) = 3 + 1 = 4.$$

At this point it may appear like that we have to memorize all the partial labellings at stage $m - 1$ (i.e., sequences of length $m - 1$) for continuing at stage m. Wrong!

The inequalities in (8.38) express that there is only a relation to be considered between f_{m-1} and f_m, and in (8.40) we select d based on the label f_{m-1} only (and the minimization of the sum).

Thus, from all those values $E_4(f_1, f_2, f_3, f_4)$ we only have to memorize the minimum values $E_4(\ldots, 0) = 4$, $E_4(\ldots, 1) = 4$, $E_4(\ldots, 2) = 3$, and $E_4(\ldots, 3) = 4$, and for each of these minima, we keep a note, the label of which was used at stage 3 to arrive at this minimum:

```
backtrack(4, 0) = 1   (see E₄(0, 0, 1, 0) = 3 + 1 = 4)

backtrack(4, 1) = 1   (see E₄(0, 0, 1, 1) = 3 + 1 = 4)

backtrack(4, 2) = 1   (see E₄(0, 0, 1, 2) = 3 + 0 = 3)

backtrack(4, 3) = 2   (see E₄(0, 1, 2, 3) = 3 + 1 = 4)
```

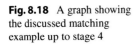

Fig. 8.18 A graph showing the discussed matching example up to stage 4

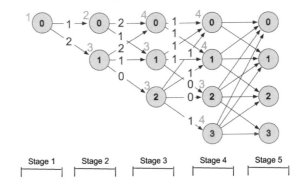

Compare with the shortest path example in Sect. 8.2.1: at stage m we have between one and $d_{max} + 1$ nodes, each node f_m is a possible label (disparity) at stage m, and the `backtrack`-function connects this node with a label f_{m-1} (note: this is not uniquely defined in general), which allowed us to generate a minimum $E_m(\dots, f_{m-1}, f_m)$.

The graph in Fig. 8.18 sketches the example up to stage 4. Each node is also labelled by the minimum cost, accumulated along paths from stage 1 to this node.

The only possible node at stage 1 comes with an initial cost of 1. Arrows between the node f_n at stage n and f_{n+1} at stage $n + 1$ are labelled by the additional cost due to using the disparity f_{n+1} at stage $n + 1$.

At stage M we have one node defining the minimum $E(f) = E_M(f)$, which means that we decide for only one possible disparity f_M. The disparities f_{M-1}, $f_{M-2}, \dots$ are then identified by backtracking.

The Algorithm At stage M we have a node with minimum cost and backtrack the arrows that lead to this minimum cost.

We return again to the more complete notation $E(x, y, d) = E_x(d)$ for row y, and `backtrack`(x, d) is an array of size $N_{cols} \times (d_{max} + 1)$. E_{min} is the partial energy minimum, called $E_m(f)$ above. We compute $f_M, f_{M-1}, \dots, f_1$ in this order. See the algorithm in Fig. 8.19.

The data cost function E can be any of the data cost functions discussed in Sect. 8.1.2.

Error Propagation Dynamic programming tends to propagate errors along the scanline (in the given algorithm with $B = L$ from left to right), resulting in horizontal streaks in the calculated disparity or depth map. See Fig. 8.20. The figure also shows that a "better" data cost function improves results significantly. See also Fig. 8.28.

```
for y = 1, 2, ..., N_rows do
    compute E(1, y, 0) {only d = 0 for x = 1}
    for x = 2 to N_cols do
        for d = 0 to min{x − 1, d_max} do
            E_min = +∞
            for d* = max{0, d − 1} to min{x − 2, d_max} do
                if E(x − 1, y, d*) < E_min then
                    E_min = E(x − 1, y, d*); d_min = d*
                end if
                E(x, y, d) = E_min + E(x, y, d); backtrack(x, d) = d_min
            end for
        end for
    end for
    E_min = +∞ {preparing for backtracking at x = M}
    for d = 0 to min{N_cols − 1, d_max} do
        if E(N_cols, y, d) < E_min then
            E_min = E(N_cols, y, d); d_min = d
        end if
    end for
    f_N_cols = d_min {E_min is the energy minimum for row y}
    for x = N_cols to 2 do
        f_{x−1} = backtrack(x, f_x)
    end for
end for
```

Fig. 8.19 A DPM algorithm when using the ordering constraint and $B = L$

8.2.4   DPM Using a Smoothness Constraint

The ordering constraint does not apply to all scenes, as illustrated by the sketch in Fig. 8.15. We replace the ordering constraint now by a smoothness constraint along the scanline. In the previous subsection, the scanline was limited to be an epipolar line (i.e. an image row) because the ordering constraint has been designed for the epipolar line.

By using a smoothness constraint along a scanline instead of the ordering constraint, we are not limited anymore to the epipolar line, and this is even a better contribution than being also applicable to scenes that do not satisfy the ordering constraint; we can use now more than one scanline. Possible scanlines are shown in Fig. 8.7, left.

Two-Step Potts Model for Smoothness Cost   We split the smoothness function, to be applied along one scanline, into two terms as follows:

$$E_{smooth}(f_p, f_q) = \chi_1(f_p, f_q) + \chi_2(f_p, f_q) \tag{8.41}$$

where p and q are adjacent pixel locations on the scanline, and

$$\chi_1(f_p, f_q) = \begin{cases} c_1 & \text{if } |f_p - f_q| = 1 \\ 0 & \text{otherwise} \end{cases} \tag{8.42}$$

Fig. 8.20 Disparity maps using DPM for stereo pair `Crossing` shown in Fig. 8.1. Low confidence values are replaced by black, using the left–right consistency check with threshold 1. *Upper left*: Use of AD as a data cost function. *Upper right*: Use of 5×5 census. *Lower left*: Use of 5×5 zero-mean census. *Lower right*: Use of 3×9 zero-mean census

$$\chi_2(f_p, f_q) = \begin{cases} c_2(p,q) & \text{if } |f_p - f_q| > 1 \\ 0 & \text{otherwise} \end{cases} \qquad (8.43)$$

for $c_1 > 0$ and $c_2(p,q) > c_1$. We have that $\chi_1(f_p, f_q) + \chi_2(f_p, f_q) = 0$ *iff* $f_p = f_q$.

The constant c_1 defines the penalty for a small difference in disparities for adjacent pixels. The function c_2 contributes a larger penalty than c_1 for cases of larger disparity differences.

Reduced Penalty at Step-Edges   By

$$c_2(p,q) = \frac{c}{|B(p) - B(q)|} \qquad (8.44)$$

for some constant $c > 0$ we define a scaling (by a very simple approximation of the image gradient in image B between pixel locations p and q). This way a disparity difference at a step-edge in the stereo pair causes a reduced penalty.

Error Minimization Along One Scanline   Figure 8.21 illustrates calculated disparity maps when performing DPM along one scanline only. For a given scanline, consider the segment $p_0, p_1, \ldots, p_m = p$, where p_0 is on the image bor-

Fig. 8.21 Resulting disparity maps for KITTI stereo data when using only *one* scanline for DPM with the discussed smoothness constraint and a 3×9 ZCEN data cost function. From *top* to *bottom*: Horizontal scanline (*left* to *right*), diagonal scanline (*lower left* to *upper right*), vertical scanline (*top* to *bottom*), and diagonal scanline (*upper left* to *lower right*). Pink pixels are for low-confidence locations

der in the base image B, and $p = (x, y)$ is the current pixel, i.e. the one for which we are searching for a corresponding pixel $p = (x + d, y)$ in the match image M.

Analogously to (8.40), we define the dynamic programming equations (i.e. the result at stage i in dependency of the results at stage $(i - 1)$) here as follows:

$$E(p_i, d) = E_{data}(p_i, d) + E_{smooth}(p_i, p_{i-1}) - \min_{0 \le \Delta \le d_{max}} E(p_{i-1}, \Delta) \qquad (8.45)$$

with

$$E_{smooth}(p, q) = \min \begin{cases} E(q, f_q) & \text{if } f_p = f_q \\ E(q, f_q) + c_1 & \text{if } |f_p - f_q| = 1 \\ \min_{0 \le \Delta \le d_{max}} E(q, \Delta) + c_2(p, q) & \text{if } |f_p - f_q| > 1 \end{cases}$$
$$(8.46)$$

where $E_{data}(p_i, d)$ is the data cost at pixel p_i for disparity d, and c_1 and c_2 are the penalties of the smoothness term as defined for (8.43). The smoothness term in (8.46) specifies equation (8.41) in this way that we only consider smoothness between a disparity at a pixel p_i on the scanline and the disparity at the previous pixel p_{i-1}. We subtract $\min_{0 \le \Delta \le d_{max}} E(p_{i-1}, \Delta)$ in (8.45) to restrict the range of resulting values, without affecting the minimization procedure.

Data Cost Matrix into Integration Matrix   We calculate the 3D data cost matrix as specified in (8.9) and calculate an *integration matrix* for the specified scanline. We start with $E(p_0, d) = E_{data}(p_0, d)$ on the image border. We perform dynamic programming along the scanline by applying (8.45). The obtained minimum, when arriving at the opposite border, specifies (via backtracking) optimum disparities along the scanline.

Example 8.5 (Efficiencies of Different Scanlines on Simple or Difficult Data) Consider recording of stereo video data in a car (e.g. for vision-based driver assistance). Recorded scenes can have very different levels of complexity, e.g. caused by lighting artifacts, night, snow, rain, density of traffic, shape of visible surfaces (e.g. when overtaking a truck), average distance to objects, and so forth, which can be classified into *situations* or *scenarios*. We have simple scenarios (e.g. a flat and well-marked road, bright and homogeneous light, sparse traffic) or difficult scenarios, such as illustrated by Fig. 8.22.

The figure shows a stereo pair taken in the rain. The wiper affects the image on the right, and there are specularities on the road. Figure 8.23 illustrates single-scanline (horizontal or vertical) reconstructions for this stereo pair and also for a simple situation.

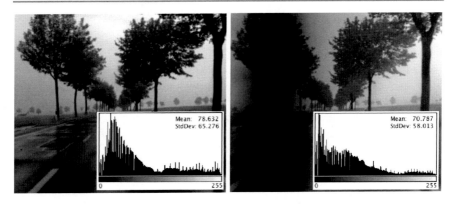

Fig. 8.22 A stereo pair of the sequence `rain` from the HCI data set with embedded histograms

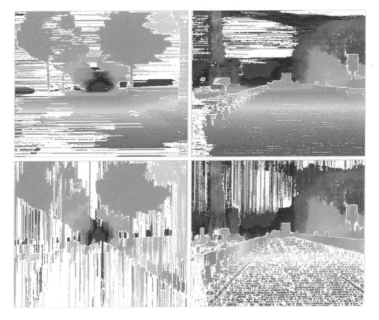

Fig. 8.23 *Left*: Challenging `rain` stereo data; see Fig. 8.22. *Right*: Simple highway data. *Top*: Disparity results for horizontal scanline. *Bottom*: Disparity results for vertical scanline

In case of the simple situation, the vertical scan also provides a "reasonable" estimate of disparities, while matching along the vertical scanline fails in case of the difficult situation.

Observation 8.5 *DPM with smoothness constraint supports the use of multiple scanlines. Results along scanlines contribute differently to an overall accuracy of disparity maps. Horizontal scanline results are particularly useful for scenes where a ground manifold (such as a road) can be expected.*

Insert 8.4 (Origin of Multi-Scanline DPM) *Multi-scanline DPM, called* semi-global matching (SGM), *has been introduced in the paper* [*H. Hirschmüller. Accurate and efficient stereo processing by semi-global matching and mutual information. In Proc. Conf. Computer Vision Pattern Recognition, vol. 2, pp. 807–814, 2005*]. *This stereo matcher has been designed for generating 3D city maps as illustrated in Fig. 7.1. Today it is used in many fields of applications, for example for cameras installed in cars used for vision-based driver assistance or autonomous driving.*

Basic and Iterative Semi-global Matching   After DPM with smoothness constraint along one scanline **a**, we do have cost values $E_\mathbf{a}(f_p)$ at every pixel in B. By adding the resulting cost values for multiple scanlines and selecting that disparity defining the overall minimum, we have a simple way for unifying results along multiple scanlines into one disparity at a pixel location. We call this the *basic semiglobal matching* (bSGM) algorithm.

Several variants of SGM have been proposed since the original paper was published in 2005. For example, this includes adding features such as pyramidal processing of costs, introducing iterations into the process and different weights when combining results from different scanlines, and the use of *priors* to ensure that (e.g.) "thin vertical" shapes in the scene are detected if prioritizing the results for horizontal scanlines; these listed features characterize *iterative SGM* (algorithm iSGM).[3]

Figure 8.24 shows combined results for the rain stereo pair shown in Fig. 8.22, using either bSGM or iSGM. The prioritization of results obtained from horizontal scanlines is adequate for those road scenes having a dominant ground-plane component.

8.3   Belief-Propagation Matching

Section 5.3 introduced belief propagation as a general optimization framework, which allows us to assign labels to all pixel locations based on given data and smoothness-cost terms, and using a message-passing process which defines a search space as illustrated in Fig. 8.7, right. This short section defines *belief-propagation matching* (BPM).

---

[3]Published in [S. Hermann and R. Klette. Iterative semi-global matching for robust driver assistance systems. In Proc. Asian Conf. Computer Vision 2012, LNCS 7726, pp. 465–478, 2012]; this stereo matcher was awarded the *Robust Vision Challenge* at the European Conference on Computer Vision in 2012.

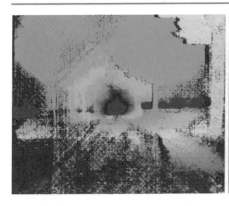

Fig. 8.24 Disparity maps for stereo pair `rain`; see Fig. 8.22. *Left*: Applying `bSGM`. *Right*: Applying `iSGM`

Insert 8.5 (Origin of BPM) *The paper [J Sun, N.-N. Zheng, and H.-Y. Shum. Stereo matching using belief propagation. IEEE Trans. Pattern Analysis Machine Intelligence, vol. 25, pp. 1–14, 2003] described how to use the general optimization strategy of belief propagation for stereo matching. The approach became very popular especially due to the paper [P.F. Felzenszwalb and D.P. Huttenlocher. Efficient belief propagation for early vision. Int. J. Computer Vision, vol. 70, pp. 41–54, 2006].*

BPM solves the stereo-matching problem by pixel labelling, having Ω (in the base image B) as the set of sites that will receive a label in the set $L = \{0, 1, \ldots, d_{max}\}$ by aiming at optimizing the error function

$$E(f) = \sum_{p \in \Omega} \left(E_{data}(p, f_p) + \sum_{(p,q) \in A} E_{smooth}(f_p - f_q) \right) \qquad (8.47)$$

where the smoothness-cost function can be assumed to be unary, just defined by the difference between labels at adjacent pixels. BPM applies the message-passing mechanism as described in Sect. 5.3.

Possible options for smoothness functions are described in Sect. 5.3.2. For data cost functions for stereo matching, see Sect. 8.1.2.

Example 8.6 (BPM Example) Figure 8.25 illustrates a simple example showing two 5×7 images forming a stereo pair. The image L is assumed to be the base image. We search for a corresponding pixel for pixel (x, y).

We assume that $d_{max} = 3$. Thus, we have four message boards, all of size 5×7, but we do not show the d_{max} columns left of x in Fig. 8.25 (for saving space in the figure).

Each pixel in the left image has potentially $d_{max} + 1$ matching pixels in the right image. For pixel (x, y) in the left image, potentially matching pixels are (x, y), $(x - 1, y)$, $(x - 2, y)$, and $(x - 3, y)$ in the right image.

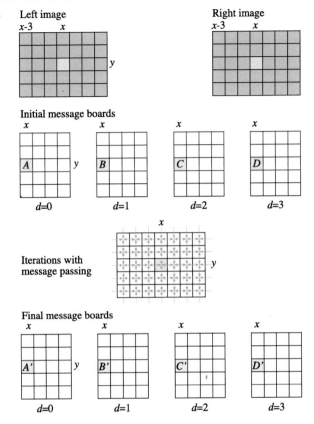

Fig. 8.25 A simple example for discussing BPM

We have $d_{max} + 1$ message boards. The disparity between pixels (x, y) and (x, y) equals 0; thus, the cost for assigning the disparity 0 to pixel (x, y) is at position (x, y) in Board 0; the disparity between pixels (x, y) and $(x - 1, y)$ equals 1; thus, the cost for assigning the disparity 1 to pixel (x, y) is at position (x, y) in Board 1, and so forth.

Initially, we insert data cost values into position (x, y) for all the $d_{max} + 1$ message boards. Thus, the data cost value differences $A = E_{data}((x, y), 0)$, analogously B, C, and D, go into the four message boards at position (x, y). This defines the *initialization of the boards*.

Now we start at $t = 1$ and send messages between adjacent pixels. Each pixel p sends a message vector of length $d_{max} + 1$ to an adjacent pixel with message values for $d \in L$ in its $d_{max} + 1$ components. Let $m^t_{p \to q}$ be such a message vector, sent from pixel at p to adjacent pixel at q in iteration t. For $d \in L$, we have that [see (5.40)]

$$m^t_{p \to q}(d) = \min_{h \in L} \left(E_{data}(p, h) + E_{smooth}(h - d) + \sum_{s \in A(p) \backslash q} m^{t-1}_{s \to p}(h) \right) \quad (8.48)$$

defines the message-update. We accumulate at q all messages from adjacent pixel locations p, combine with time-independent data cost values, and have the accumulated cost

$$E_{data}(q, d) + \sum_{p \in A(q)} m^t_{p \to q}(d) \qquad (8.49)$$

at pixel location q for assigning the disparity d to q at time t.

Back to our example, after a number of iterations, the iteration stops and defines new cost values A', B', C', and D' in the message boards at location (x, y).

The minimum of those cost values defines the disparity (i.e. the label) that will be assigned to the pixel at (x, y) as the result of the BPM process. For example, if $B' = \min\{A', B', C', D'\}$, then we have the disparity 1 for the pixel at (x, y) in the left image.

Pyramidal BPM   By using a regular pyramidal data structure for each image (left and right images), as defined in Sect. 2.2.2, we can shorten the distances between pixels for message passing. We decide to use $k > 1$ layers in the two pyramids, with the first (the bottom) layer being the original image.

The message boards are also transformed into the corresponding k-layer data structure. We initialize with data cost in the first layer and also for the $k - 1$ layer on top.

The adjacency set of a pixel location in one of the layers contains now also pixel locations in adjacent layers, with connections defined by the regular generation of the pyramids.

Now we follow exactly the message-passing process as defined in Sect. 5.3 for the general belief-propagation case and as illustrated in particular in Example 8.6.

Two Properties of Message Passing   The "strength" of message passing, from low-contrast areas in image B to contrast areas, is less than the "strength" of message passing from a high-contrast area to low-contrast area. We need to be aware of this *asymmetry*. Accordingly, BPM is "fine" with generating consistent labels (disparities) in textureless regions but may have difficulties when textures change.

In dependency of the chosen data and smoothness-cost functions, message passing can be "blocked" more or less by step-edges. This *influence of image-discontinuities* has often the positive effect of preserving depth discontinuities at intensity discontinuities.

Figure 8.26 shows an example when applying BPM for low-contrast, real-world image sequences. This stereo pair `Set1Seq1` from Sequence 1 of EISATS causes problems for BPM if the selection of the data cost function is based on ICA. This can be resolved by preprocessing input data (e.g. Sobel edge maps

Fig. 8.26 *Top*: The stereo pair `Set1Seq1`. *Middle*: The Sobel edge images of the stereo pair. *Bottom*: The BPM result for the original image data (*left*) and for the Sobel edge images (*right*); use of the AD cost function in both cases

or residuals w.r.t. smoothing) or by taking zero-mean variants of data cost functions.

8.4   Third-Eye Technique

When performing stereo-analysis for video data, it is desirable to have a control mechanism that decides about the quality of the produced disparity data by just one summarizing quality weight, say, in the range between 0 to 1. When discussing accuracy (by comparing against ground truth) or confidence of calculated disparities, we were interested in pixel-wise evaluations. Now we specify a method for time-efficient and summarizing (over the whole stereo pair) performance evaluation of stereo matchers.

This section answers two questions: How to map a reference image of a pair of stereo cameras into the pose of a third camera? How to measure the similarity between created virtual image and the actually recorded third image?

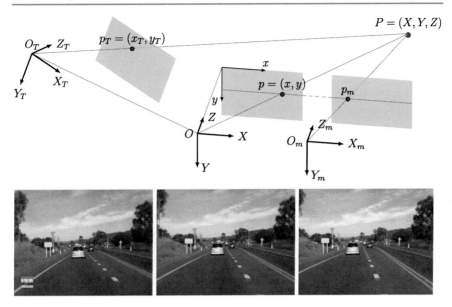

Fig. 8.27 *Top*: Three-camera coordinate systems. *Bottom*: An example of three recorded images, from *left* to *right*: third, left, and right image

8.4.1 Generation of Virtual Views for the Third Camera

Stereo matching is performed for sequences recorded by two cameras, and a third camera is used for evaluating the obtained results. (We could also, for example, use the second and third cameras for stereo matching and then unify the results with disparities obtained from the first and second cameras, and so forth.)

Three Cameras We calibrate three cameras for stereo sequence recording, as illustrated in Fig. 8.27.

For example, when recording traffic scenes in a car (as illustrated by the example in Fig. 8.27, bottom), the base distance between left and right cameras can be about 30 cm, and the third camera about 40 cm left of the left camera (for better identification of matching errors; a third camera centred between left and right cameras would make it more difficult to identify "issues"). For the shown example, all three cameras were mounted on one bar behind the windscreen for approximating already canonic stereo geometry. Images of the left and right cameras are geometrically rectified for stereo matching.

Third-Eye Technique The basic outline of the *third-eye technique* is as follows:[4]
1. Record stereo data with two cameras and calculate disparities.

---

[4]See [S. Morales and R. Klette. A third eye for performance evaluation in stereo sequence analysis. In Proc. Computer Analysis Images Patterns, LNCS 5702, pp. 1078–1086, 2009].

Fig. 8.28 *Left*: The third image. *Right*: The virtual image, to be compared with the third image. The virtual image was calculated using DPM with ordering constraint and the simple AD cost function for $L = B$; it shows a streaking-effect as is common for this one-scanline-only DPM technique. *Blue pixels* (on *top*) differ due to geometric rectification of the *left image*. *Green pixels* are not filled-in at all due to "missing" disparities of the stereo matcher. The parabolic *black arcs* are due to image warping and cannot be taken as problems related to the stereo matcher used

2. Have also a third calibrated camera looking into the same space as the other two cameras.
3. Use the calculated disparities for mapping the recorded image of the (say) left camera into the image plane of the third camera, thus creating a *virtual image*.
4. Compare the virtual image with the image recorded by the third camera.
If the virtual and third images "basically coincide", then the stereo matcher provides "useful" disparities.

How to Generate the Virtual View?   *Image warping* maps windows of an input image I into a resultant image J according to a coordinate transformation K, with the general intention to keep image values unaltered (which is, due to the discrete nature of the images, actually not possible without making some concessions). Examples for K are rotation, translation, or mirroring.

Because grid points will not map exactly on grid points in general, some kind of interpolation is common for rendering (according to a backward transform K^{-1}) as many pixels as possible in the image J. In our case here we are *not* interested in generating "nice images", we like to see the "issues". For example, the black parabolic arcs, visible in the virtual image in Fig. 8.28, right, would normally be filled with interpolated values if interested in rendering "nice images"; they are due to gaps defined by the geometric mapping K, not due to mismatches of the used stereo matcher.

The three cameras are calibrated, and the third image is available in the image plane of the reference camera (which was chosen to be the left camera above). We consider the pixels in the left camera for which the left and right cameras (using the given stereo matcher) provided the disparity values and thus also depth values because the cameras have been calibrated. Let d be the disparity between a pair (with $p = (x, y)$ in the left image) of corresponding pixels. According to (7.22), (7.24), and (7.23), the coordinates of the projected 3D point $P = (X, Y, Z)$ are as follows:

$$X = \frac{b \cdot x}{d}, \qquad Y = \frac{b \cdot y}{d}, \quad \text{and} \quad Z = f \frac{b}{d} \qquad (8.50)$$

Example 8.7 (Translation Only) In this example we assume that the camera coordinate system of the third camera is only a translation of the camera coordinate system of the left camera.

Step 1. We write the coordinates of a 3D point in terms of the camera coordinate system of the third camera, having an origin with coordinates (t_X, t_Y, t_Z) in the camera coordinate system of the left camera. This defines the translative relation

$$(X_T, Y_T, Z_T) = (X - t_X, Y - t_Y, Z - t_Z) \qquad (8.51)$$

between both coordinate systems.

Step 2. Central projection maps a point P into the third camera image plane at

$$(x_T, y_T) = f_T \left(\frac{X_T}{Z_T}, \frac{Y_T}{Z_T} \right) \qquad (8.52)$$

where f_T is the focal length calibrated for the third camera.

Step 3. According to Step 1 and (8.50), we can write the right term in (8.52) as follows:

$$(x_T, y_T) = f_T \left(\frac{X - t_X}{Z - t_Z}, \frac{Y - t_Y}{Z - t_Z} \right) = f_T \left(\frac{x \frac{b}{d} - t_X}{f \frac{b}{d} - t_Z}, \frac{y \frac{b}{d} - t_Y}{f \frac{b}{d} - t_Z} \right) \qquad (8.53)$$

This provides

$$x_T = f_T \frac{bx - dt_X}{fb - dt_Z} \quad \text{and} \quad y_T = f_T \frac{by - dt_Y}{fb - dt_Z} \qquad (8.54)$$

Thus, a point $P = (X, Y, Z)$, which was mapped into a pixel (x, y) in the left image, is also mapped into a point (x_T, y_T) in the third image, and (x_T, y_T) is now expressed in terms of (x, y), not in terms of (X, Y, Z), by using the calibrated translation (t_X, t_Y, t_Z), the base distance b, the focal length f_T, and the disparity d provided by the given stereo matcher.

Step 4. Now we map the intensity value at pixel (x, y) in the reference (i.e., left) image into the plane of the third image. We just map onto the nearest grid point. In case that multiple values (from different pixels in the reference image) are mapped onto the same pixel in the image plane of the third image, we can apply a confidence measure for selecting this value defined by that disparity having the maximum confidence for the given candidates.

Example 8.8 (Rotation About one Axis) As a modification of Example 8.7, let us assume that the camera coordinate system of the third camera is defined by (only) a rotation by angle θ about the horizontal X-axis of the camera coordinate system of the left camera. We have that

$$
\begin{pmatrix} X_T \\ Y_T \\ Z_T \end{pmatrix} = \begin{pmatrix} 1 & 0 & 0 \\ 0 & \cos\theta & -\sin\theta \\ 0 & \sin\theta & \cos\theta \end{pmatrix} \begin{pmatrix} X \\ Y \\ Z \end{pmatrix} = \begin{pmatrix} X \\ Y\cos\theta - Z\sin\theta \\ Y\sin\theta + Z\cos\theta \end{pmatrix} \tag{8.55}
$$

and obtain, as an intermediate result, that

$$
x_T = f_T \frac{X}{Y\sin\theta + Z\cos\theta} \quad \text{and} \quad y_T = f_T \frac{Y\cos\theta - Z\sin\theta}{Y\sin\theta + Z\cos\theta} \tag{8.56}
$$

and finally

$$
x_T = f_T \frac{x\frac{b}{d}}{y\frac{b}{d}\sin\theta + f\frac{b}{d}\cos\theta} = f_T \frac{x}{y\sin\theta + f\cos\theta} \tag{8.57}
$$

$$
y_T = f_T \frac{y\frac{b}{d}\cos\theta - f\frac{b}{d}\sin\theta}{y\frac{b}{d}\sin\theta + f\frac{b}{d}\cos\theta} = f_T \frac{y\cos\theta - f\sin\theta}{y\sin\theta + f\cos\theta} \tag{8.58}
$$

This is again the projection of P in the third image plane (not necessarily a grid point).

We leave the general case of an affine transform from the coordinate system of the left camera to the third camera as an exercise.

8.4.2   Similarity Between Virtual and Third Image

Due to lighting artifacts or brightness variations in recorded multi-camera video, a direct SAD or SSD comparison is out of the question.

How to Compare Virtual and Third Image   We compare the virtual image V (generated for time t) with the third image T (recorded at time t). The normalized cross-correlation (NCC, see Insert 4.11) appears to be an option.

Let Ω_t be the set of pixels that are used for the comparison for frames at time t. We will not include pixels where values in the virtual image remain black, thus differing from the third image due to (see Fig. 8.28)

1. geometric rectification of the left image,
2. "missing" disparities (i.e. being not in the image of mapped values), or
3. missed pixels for the applied coordinate transform K (i.e. being on the parabolic arcs).

Thus, according to those rules, Ω_t is simply the set of all pixel locations that are rendered by a mapped image value from the left image.

The mean and standard deviation are calculated within Ω_t, using symbols μ_V and σ_V, or μ_T and σ_T for the virtual V or third image T at time t, respectively. The NCC has then the form

$$M_{NCC}(V, T) = \frac{1}{|\Omega_t|} \sum_{p \in \Omega_t} \frac{[T(p) - \mu_T][V(p) - \mu_V]}{\sigma_T \sigma_V} \tag{8.59}$$

with $0 \leq M_{NCC}(I, J) \leq 1$ and a perfect identity in case of $M_{NCC}(I, J) = 1$.

The rules for defining the set Ω_t influence the performance evaluation. If a stereo matcher results into a relatively small set Ω_t, but with correctly rendered intensities on those sparsely distributed values, it would rank high. Thus, including the cardinality $|\Omega_t|$ into the measure used might be a good idea.

A more significant issue are homogeneously textured regions in an image. If the mapped intensity comes in the left image from such a region, is mapped incorrectly into another location in the virtual image, but still in the same region, then NCC for Ω_t as defined above will not notice such incorrect warpings. Therefore, it is recommended that the set Ω_t be further constrained: We only include pixels into Ω_t if they are "close" to an edge in the left image. This closeness defines a *mask*, and Ω_t becomes a subset of this mask.

Example 8.9 Fig. 8.29 illustrates an application of the third-eye technique for comparing BPM on a given video sequence of 120 frames. The scale for NCC is in percent. The pyramidal BPM algorithm used the simple AD data cost function, which is based on the ICA, and this is an incorrect assumption for real-world recording as for the illustrated sequence.

Two methods for data preprocessing are used, Sobel edge maps or residuals with respect to smoothing. See Fig. 8.30 for examples of pre-processed images, used as an input for stereo matching rather than the original stereo frames. Both methods improve the results according to the NCC measure used, defined for a masked set Ω_t, using as mask pixels being in a distance of at most 10 from the closest Canny edge pixel.

Analysis of NCC Diagrams Figure 8.29 indicates a significant drop in stereo-matching performance about at Frame 60. This is one of the important opportunities provided by the third-eye technique: identify the situations where recorded video sequences cannot be processed properly by a given stereo matcher and start your research into the question how to resolve the issue for the given situation. How to generalize the identified situation by a geometric or photometric model? How to adapt stereo matchers to identified situations?

The NCC values provided can also be used to compare the performance of stereo matchers on very long sequences, for example by comparing frame by frame and by measuring the total sum of signed differences in NCC values or just the total number of frames where one matcher was winning against the other.

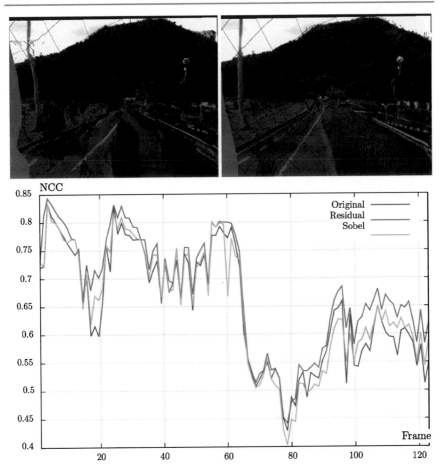

Fig. 8.29 A test of BPM on the stereo sequence `south` by using the same stereo matcher on three different input data: original data, residuals with respect to smoothing, and Sobel edge maps; see Fig. 8.30

8.5   Exercises

8.5.1   Programming Exercises

Exercise 8.1 (Segmentation of Disparity Maps and Generation of Mean Distances) Use as input stereo data recorded in a driving car (see, e.g., data provided on KITTI, HCI, or EISATS). Apply a segmentation algorithm on disparity maps, calculated by a selected stereo matcher (e.g. in `OpenCV`), with the goal to identify segments of objects "meaningful" for the traffic context. Consider the use of temporal consistency for segments as discussed in Sect. 5.4.2.

Calculate mean distances to your object segments and visualize those in a generated video, which summarizes your results. See Fig. 8.31 for an example.

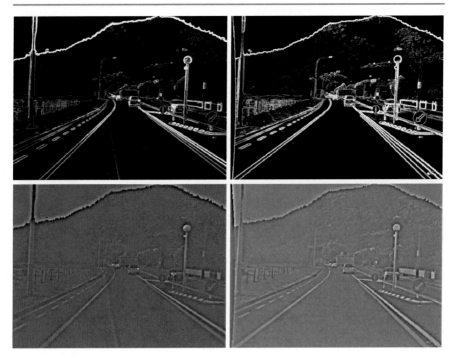

Fig. 8.30 Pre-processing of data for the stereo sequence south. *Top*: Sobel edge maps. *Bottom*: Residuals with respect to smoothing

Fig. 8.31 The mean distances to segmented objects. *Left*: The distances to objects within the lane area only. *Right*: The distances to all the detected objects

Exercise 8.2 (Confidence Measures on Challenging Stereo Data) Select or program two different stereo matchers and apply those on challenging HCI stereo sequences. See Fig. 8.32 for examples.

Select three different confidence measure for calculated disparities and visualize confidence-measure results as a graphical overlay on the input sequence for (say) the left camera.

Fig. 8.32 Challenging HCI stereo sequences and examples of calculated disparity maps (using iSGM)

Discuss the "visible correlation" between low-confidence values and shown situations in input sequences.

Exercise 8.3 (DPM with Ordering Constraint and Variations in Data Cost Functions) Implement DPM as specified in Fig. 8.19, using the ordering constraint and at least three different data cost functions, including AD and ZCEN (with a window of your choice).

Illustrate the obtained disparity maps similar to Fig. 8.20 based on a selected colour key and the exclusion of low-confidence disparity values.

As input, use

1. simple stereo data (e.g. indoor),
2. challenging outdoor stereo data that do not satisfy the ICA, and
3. *random-dot stereograms* as described in the book [D. Marr. Vision: A Computational Investigation into the Human Representation and Processing of Visual Information. The MIT Press, Cambridge, Massachusetts, 1982].

Discuss visible differences in obtained (coloured) disparity maps.

Exercise 8.4 (Multi-Scanline DPM with Smoothness Term) Implement multi-scanline DPM (also known as SGM) with the two-level Potts smoothness term as discussed in Sect. 8.2.4. Use either the ZCEN or the ZSAD data cost.

Compare visually (i.e. coloured disparity maps) results when using

1. only horizontal scanlines,
2. only horizontal and vertical scanlines,
3. also diagonal scanlines.

Use a confidence measure of your choice for calculating percentages of pixels where results are considered to be of "high confidence" for the different scanline choices.

Use input data as listed in Exercise 8.3.

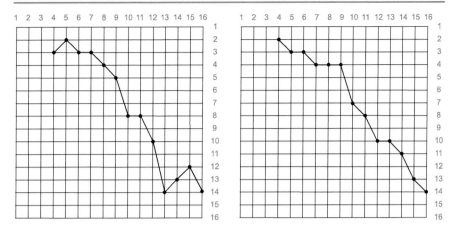

Fig. 8.33   Two epipolar profiles

Exercise 8.5 (BPM, Accuracy, and Time Complexity)   Implement pyramidal BPM. Note that there are BPM sources available on the net. Use the ZCEN data cost function and a smoothness term of your choice.

Analyse the influence of chosen layers in the pyramid on run-time and visible accuracy of generated depth maps (using a colour key for optimized visual presentation).

Use input data as listed in Exercise 8.3.

Exercise 8.6 (Evaluation of Stereo Matchers Using the Third-Eye Technique)   Implement the third-eye technique for evaluating stereo matchers. For example, use the trinocular sequences in Set 9 of EISATS as input data. Evaluate your favourite stereo matcher on those data.

Use either the original video sequences for stereo matching or preprocess those sequences using the Sobel operator and apply your stereo matcher on the obtained Sobel edge maps.

Apply the proposed NCC measure either with a mask (i.e. only pixels close to edges) or without a mask. Altogether, this defines two variants of your stereo matcher and two variants for analysing the results.

Discuss the obtained NCC value diagrams obtained for the four variants on the selected trinocular video sequences.

8.5.2   Non-programming Exercises

Exercise 8.7   Assume that our stereo system needs to analyse objects being in a distance of at least a metres from our binocular stereo camera system. We have intrinsic and extrinsic camera parameters calibrated. Determine the value $d_{\max}$ based on those parameters and known value a.

Fig. 8.34 A stereo pair

Exercise 8.8 Figure 8.33 shows two profiles. Do these epipolar profiles represent the disparity vector **d**? If so, which disparity vector? In reverse: Given are the disparity vectors

$$\mathbf{d}_1 = [f_4, f_5, \ldots, f_{16}]^\top = [1, 0, 1, 2, 3, 0, 1, 1, 0, 1, 2, 3, 2]^\top$$
$$\mathbf{d}_2 = [f_4, f_5, \ldots, f_{16}]^\top = [4, 3, 2, 1, 0, 1, 2, 4, 1, 2, 3, 2, 2]^\top$$

Draw the epipolar profiles defined by those two disparity vectors.
    Which profiles and which vectors satisfy the ordering constraint?

Exercise 8.9 At the beginning of Sect. 8.1.3, we discussed how 4-adjacency "grows" into the image carrier by repeated creations of dependencies between adjacent pixels. At time $t = 0$ it is just the pixel itself ($n_0 = 1$), at time $t = 1$ also the four four-adjacent pixels ($n_1 = n_0 + 4 = 5$), at time $t = 2$ also eight more pixels ($n_2 = n_1 + 8 = 13$). How many pixels are in this growing set at time $t \geq 0$ in general, assuming no limitation by image borders. At the time τ when terminating the iteration, n_τ defines the cardinality of the area of influence.
    Now replace 4-adjacency by 8-adjacency and do the same calculations. As a third option, consider 4-adjacency but also a regular image pyramid "on top" of the given image.

Exercise 8.10 Stereo matchers have to work on any input pair? Fine, here is one—see Fig. 8.34. Assume the simple AD data cost function and discuss (as a "Gedanken experiment") outcomes of "The winner takes all", of DPM with ordering constraint, of multi-scanline DPM with smoothness constraint, and of BPM for this stereo pair.

Feature Detection and Tracking 9

This chapter describes the detection of keypoints and the definition of descriptors for those; a keypoint and a descriptor define a feature. The given examples are SIFT, SURF, and ORB, where we introduce BRIEF and FAST for providing ORB. We discuss the invariance of features in general and of the provided examples in particular. The chapter also discusses three ways for tracking features: KLT, particle filter, and Kalman filter.

9.1 Invariance, Features, and Sets of Features

Figure 9.1 illustrates on the left detected keypoints and on the right circular neighbourhoods around detected keypoints, which can be used for deriving a descriptor.

This section defines invariance properties, which are of interest when characterizing (or designing) features. For the detection of keypoints in the scale space, it considers the related *disk of influence*, also for using its radius for introducing *3D flow vectors* as an extension of 2D optic flow vectors. The sets of features in subsequent frames of a video sequence need to be correlated to each other, and here we introduce the *random sample consensus* (RANSAC) as a possible tool for achieving this.

9.1.1 Invariance

Images are taken under varying illumination, different viewing angles, at different times, under different weather conditions, and so forth. When taking an aerial shot from an airplane, we do have a random rotation of shown objects, and *isotropy* (rotation invariance) has been mentioned before in the book (see Sect. 2.1.2).

In outdoor scene analysis, we often request types of invariance with respect to some operations, such as illumination changes or recording images at different distances to the object of interest.

R. Klette, *Concise Computer Vision*, Undergraduate Topics in Computer Science,
DOI 10.1007/978-1-4471-6320-6_9, © Springer-Verlag London 2014

Fig. 9.1 An illustration of DoG scale space keypoints. *Left:* The detected keypoints in a traffic scene. *Right:* The keypoints with their disks of influence; the radius of a disk is defined by the scale for which the keypoint has been detected

Fig. 9.2 A recorded scene itself may support invariance (e.g. isotropy by the scene on the *left*)

Procedure $\mathscr{X}$ Assume that we have input images I of scenes $S \in \mathscr{S}$ and a camera (i.e. an imaging process) C. For images $I = C(S)$, a defined analysis procedure $\mathscr{X}$ maps an image I into some (say) vectorial output $R(I) = \mathbf{r}$, the *result*. For example, this can be a list of detected features. Altogether, we have that

$$R(I) = R\big(C(S)\big) = \mathbf{r} \tag{9.1}$$

Invariance w.r.t. Changes in the Scene   Now assume that we have a change in the recorded scene S due to object moves, lighting changes, a move of the recording camera, and so forth. This defines a new scene $S_{new} = N(S)$, with $I_{new} = C(S_{new})$. A procedure $\mathscr{X}$ is invariant to the change N (in an ideal way) if we obtain with

$$R(I_{new}) = R\big(C\big(N(S)\big)\big) = \mathbf{r} \tag{9.2}$$

still the same result $\mathbf{r}$ for I_{new} as we had for I before.

For example, if the change N is defined by (only) a variation in lighting within a defined range of possible changes, then $\mathscr{X}$ is *invariant to illumination changes* in this particular range. If the change N is defined by a rotation of the scene, as recorded from an airplane flying along a different trajectory at the same altitude under identical weather conditions, then $\mathscr{X}$ is *isotropic*. See Fig. 9.2.

Fig. 9.3 Four keypoint detectors in OpenCV. *Upper left*: The keypoints detected with FAST. *Upper right*: The keypoints detected with ORB. *Lower left*: The keypoints detected with SIFT. *Lower right*: The keypoints detected with SURF

Invariance w.r.t. Used Camera   Now assume a modification M in the imaging procedure I (e.g. the use of a different camera or just of a different lens), $C_{mod} = M(C)$, with $I_{mod} = C_{mod}(S)$. A procedure $\mathscr{X}$ is invariant to the modification M if we obtain with

$$R(I_{mod}) = R\big(M\big(C(I)\big)\big) = \mathbf{r} \tag{9.3}$$

still the same result $\mathbf{r}$ for I_{mod} as we had for I before.

9.1.2   Keypoints and 3D Flow Vectors

A *keypoint* (or *interest point*) is defined by some particular image intensities "around" it, such as a corner; see Sect. 2.3.4. Figure 9.3 shows the keypoints detected by four different programs.

A keypoint can be used for deriving a *descriptor*. Not every keypoint detector has its particular way for defining a descriptor. A descriptor is a finite vector that summarizes properties for the keypoint. A descriptor can be used for classifying the keypoint. A keypoint and a descriptor together define a *feature* in this chapter.

Fig. 9.4 The pixel location $p = (x, y)$ in layer n of a scale space with its 26-adjacent locations in layers $n - 1, n,$ and $n + 1$

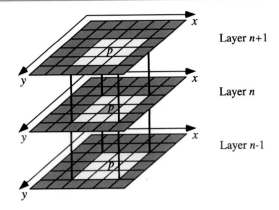

Keypoints Defined by Phase Congruency Phase-congruency is a possible way for detecting features; see Sect. 1.2.5. A local maximum of measure $\mathcal{P}_{ideal\_phase}(p)$, defined in (1.33), identifies a keypoint p. A descriptor $\mathbf{d}(p)$ can be derived from the properties extracted from the neighbourhood of p in the given image I; for example, the vector $D(p) = [\lambda_1, \lambda_2]^\top$ of eigenvalues of the matrix defined in (2.56).

> **Insert 9.1** (Origin of Keypoint Detection in Scale Space) *The paper* [T. Lindeberg. Feature detection with automatic scale selection. Int. J. Computer Vision, vol. 30, pp. 79–116, 1998] *was pioneering the use of a scale space for identifying keypoints.*

Keypoints Defined in LoG or DoG Scale Space See Sect. 2.4.1 for those two scale spaces. We explain the definition of keypoints in the DoG scale space notation; in the LoG scale space it is the same approach. We recall the difference of Gaussians (DoG) for scale σ and scaling factor $a > 1$ for combining two subsequent layers in the Gaussian scale space into one layer in the DoG scale space:

$$D_{\sigma,a}(x, y) = L(x, y, \sigma) - L(x, y, a\sigma) \tag{9.4}$$

We use an initial scale $\sigma > 0$ and apply the scaling factors a^n, $n = 0, 1, 2, \ldots,$ and so forth, for generating a finite number of layers in the DoG scale space.

The layers D_{σ,a^n}, $n = 0, \ldots, m$, define a 3D data array; each array position (x, y, n) in this 3D array has 17 or 26 adjacent array positions: eight in layer n (in the way of 8-adjacency), nine in layer $n - 1$ if $n > 1$, and nine in layer $n + 1$ if $n < m$. See Fig. 9.4. The array position (x, y, n) and those 17 or 26 adjacent positions define the *3D neighbourhood* of (x, y, n).

A *keypoint* is detected at $p = (x, y)$ if there is a layer n, $0 \leq n \leq m$, such that $D_{\sigma,a^n}(x, y)$ defines a local minimum or local maximum within the 3D neighbourhood of (x, y, n). (Keypoints detected in layers 0 and m for 17 adjacent positions only can be considered to be of "lower quality" and skipped.)

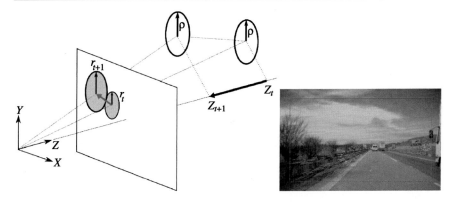

Fig. 9.5 *Left*: An illustration of a disk in a 3D space moving towards the image plane, generating there disks of influence of different radii. *Right*: The 2D projections of the detected 3D flow vectors; the colour key used represents different directions and magnitudes of motion in the 3D space

With a detected keypoint in the original image I at a pixel location $p = (x, y)$, we also have the scale $\sigma \cdot a^n$, where it has been detected; this scale defines the radius of the *disk of influence* for this keypoint p.

3D Flow Vectors   Assume a sequence of frames $I(\cdot, \cdot, t)$ and detected keypoints in the scale space for each frame, together with the radius of their disk of influence. Also assume that we have a way to solve the keypoint-correspondence problem between keypoints in frames $I(\cdot, \cdot, t)$ and $I(\cdot, \cdot, t + 1)$. (See Sect. 9.3 later in this chapter.) Some of the keypoints may not have a corresponding keypoint in the next frame.

Now consider a keypoint $p_t = (x_t, y_t)$ in a frame $I(\cdot, \cdot, t)$ with radius $r_t > 0$ of its disk of influence, assumed to be moving into a keypoint $p_{t+1} = (x_{t+1}, y_{t+1})$ in the frame $I(\cdot, \cdot, t + 1)$ with radius $r_{t+1} > 0$ of its disk of influence. Assume that those both disks of influence are projections of a local "circular situation" in the scene; see Fig. 9.5, left.

The increase in radius from r_t to r_{t+1} (in the example shown) is inversely proportional to the speed that the centre point of this local "circular situation" is moving towards the camera (see Example 9.1). If this centre point would move away, then the projected radius would increase. Thus, this changing radius of the disk of influence defines a 3D move of the centre point of the projected local "circular situation". See Fig. 9.5, right, for an illustration of derived 3D flow vectors.[1]

Example 9.1 (Disks in 3D Space Moving Towards a Camera) Figure 9.5 illustrates a disk of radius ρ moving towards a camera. Let f be the focal length of the camera, and let the disk move parallel to the XY-plane of the XYZ-camera coordinate

---

[1]The described generation of 3D flow vectors has been published in [J.A. Sanchez, R. Klette, and E. Destefanis. Estimating 3D flow for driver assistance applications. Pacific-Rim Symposium Image Video Technology, LNCS 5414, pp. 237–248, 2009].

system. For simplicity, assume that the radius is parallel to the Y-axis, going from Y_c to Y_e, from the centre point P_c to the end point P_e on the circle.

A 3D point $P = (X, Y, Z)$ in camera coordinates projects into a point $p = (x, y, f)$ in the image plane, with $x = f\frac{X}{Z}$ and $y = f\frac{Y}{Z}$. The point P_c projects into $p_c = (x_c, y_c, f)$, and P_e projects into $p_e = (x_e, y_e, f)$.

The moving disk is at time t at distance Z_t and projected into an image $I(\cdot, \cdot, t)$ as a disk of radius r_t having the area

$$\mathscr{A}_t = \pi r_t^2 = \pi (y_c - y_e)^2 = f\frac{\pi}{Z_t^2}(Y_c - Y_e)^2 = \pi f \frac{\rho^2}{Z_t^2} \tag{9.5}$$

The radius ρ of the disk is constant over time; the product $\mathscr{A}_t Z_t^2 = \pi f \rho^2$ does not change over time. It follows that

$$\frac{Z_{t+1}}{Z_t} = \sqrt{\frac{\mathscr{A}_t}{\mathscr{A}_{t+1}}} \tag{9.6}$$

which provides a robust estimator for this ratio of distance values.

Keypoints at Subpixel Accuracy The keypoints as detected above in the scale space, in the layer defined by the scale $\sigma \cdot a^n$, are at pixel locations (i.e. with integer coordinates). We interpolate a 2D second-order polynomial $g(x, y)$ to the detected keypoint and its four 4-adjacent neighbours, using for the function g the values in the layer defined by the scale $\sigma \cdot a^n$, take the derivatives of $g(x, y)$ in the x- and y-directions, and solve the resulting equation system for a subpixel-accurate minimum or maximum.

9.1.3 Sets of Keypoints in Subsequent Frames

We compare the detected sets of keypoints in two subsequent frames of an image sequence. The goal is to find corresponding keypoints. There will be *outliers* that have no corresponding keypoints in the other image. We discuss correspondence here as a (global) set problem, not as a point-by-point problem. (Fig. 9.24 illustrates the point-by-point matching problem.)

Considering matching as a set problem, we assume that there is a global pattern of keypoints, and we want to match this global pattern with another global pattern of keypoints. See Fig. 9.6 for an example. If two images only differ in size, then the global matching approach is appropriate.

Random Sample Consensus RANSAC, short for the *random sample consensus*, is an iterative estimation technique of parameters of an assumed mathematical model. Given is a set of data, called *inliers*, which follow this model, there is also additional data, called *outliers*, which do not follow the model, considered to be noise. For applying RANSAC, the probability of selecting inliers needs to be reasonably high.

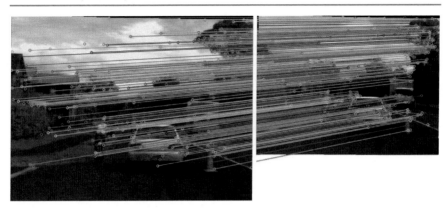

Fig. 9.6 *Left*: Set of SIFT keypoints. *Right*: The set of SIFT keypoints in the demagnified image. The *coloured lines* show a match between corresponding keypoints, represented by one uniform global affine transform, identified by RANSAC

For example, the data together, inliers and outliers, might be a noisy representation of a straight line $y = ax + b$, and the task is to estimate a and b. In our case here, the data are sets of keypoints in two different images, and the model is given by a geometric transform for defining keypoint correspondence. This is an example of a *matching problem*. For the given case, we consider an affine transform as being sufficiently general; it covers rotation, translation, and scaling. See Fig. 9.6 for an illustration of correspondences calculated by estimating one affine transform.

Insert 9.2 (Origin of RANSAC) *The method was first published in the paper* [M.A. Fischler and R.C. Bolles. Random sample consensus: A paradigm for model fitting with applications to image analysis and automated cartography. Comm. ACM, vol. 24, pp. 381–395, 1981.]

RANSAC Algorithm We need to have a test for evaluating whether some data *satisfy* or *fit* the parameterized model. In our case, a keypoint p in one image I is mapped by the parameterized affine transform onto a point q in the other image J. The test can be as follows: If there is a keypoint r in J at distance $d_2(q, r) \leq \varepsilon$, then we say that p satisfies the given parameterized affine transform. The tolerance threshold $\varepsilon > 0$ determines whether data fit the model.

For initialization of the process, select a random subset S of the given data (in our case, keypoints in the image I), consider all those as being inliers, and fit the model by estimating model parameters.

Test the parameterized model for all the other data; all the data satisfying the model go into the *consensus set* (i.e. the consensus set contains S).

Compare the cardinality of the consensus set against the cardinality of all data. If the percentage is reasonably high, then stop this iterative procedure. Otherwise, estimate updated model parameters based on the given consensus set, called a *refined*

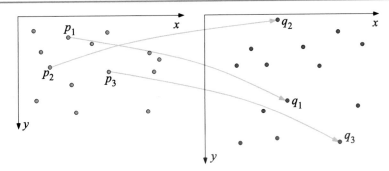

Fig. 9.7 The definition of an affine transform by three pairs of points in images I (on the *left*) and J

model. We continue with the refined model if its newly established consensus set is of larger cardinality than the cardinality of the previously established consensus set. If the cardinality did not increase, then we can go back to the initialization step by selecting another random subset S.

RANSAC for Feature Matching A feature is defined by a keypoint and a descriptor. For estimating the parameters of an affine transform, we utilize descriptors for estimating matching features in the other image. The initial set S can be three randomly selected keypoints in the image I. For those keypoints, we can search for three keypoints with reasonably matching descriptors in the image J. For the initial set S, we can also replace the random selection by a systematic evaluation of the "strength" of a feature, based on defining properties for descriptors, and a measure for those properties.

Example 9.2 (Estimating an Affine Transform) A point $p = (x, y, 1)$ in homogeneous coordinates in an image I is mapped into a point $q = (u, v, 1)$ in an image J by an affine transform

$$\begin{bmatrix} u \\ v \\ 1 \end{bmatrix} = \begin{bmatrix} r_{11} & r_{12} & t_1 \\ r_{21} & r_{22} & t_2 \\ 0 & 0 & 1 \end{bmatrix} \begin{bmatrix} x \\ y \\ 1 \end{bmatrix} \tag{9.7}$$

representing the linear equation system

$$u = r_{11}x + r_{12}y + t_1 \tag{9.8}$$

$$v = r_{21}x + r_{22}y + t_2 \tag{9.9}$$

We have six unknowns. When considering three non-collinear points p_1, p_2, and p_3 in I, we can determine those six unknowns. See the sketch in Fig. 9.7.

For the calculated affine transform $A(p) = q$, we now apply A to all the keypoints p in I, obtaining the points $A(p)$ in J. A point p goes into the consensus set if there is a keypoint q in J in the Euclidean distance to $A(p)$ less than $\varepsilon > 0$

```
 1: M_L = matchFeatures(I_L) {keypoints in left image};
 2: M_R = matchFeatures(I_R) {keypoints in right image};
 3: S = [] {empty list; will store the 3D points};
 4: for p in M_L do
 5:    d = findDisparity(p, M_R);
 6:    P = (p.x, p.y, d) · P {project detected point pair into 3D by multiplying with projection
       matrix};
 7:    append(S, P) {add the projected 3D point P to the set of 3D points};
 8: end for
 9: Π_1 = ransacFitPlane(S);
10: Π_2 = ransacRefinePlaneModel(S, Π_1);
```

Fig. 9.8 Fitting a plane into sparsely detected 3D points

with a "reasonable" match of descriptors, defining the expected image q_p of p in J. Obviously, the initially used points p_1, p_2, and p_3 pass this test.

We can expect to have a consensus set of more than just three points in I. We update the affine transform now by calculating the optimum transform for all the established pairs p in I and q_p in J, thus defining a refined affine transform. See the linear least-squares solution technique in Sect. 4.3.1.

Note that the value ε cannot be "very small"; this would not allow one to move away from the initial transform (for a better match between both sets of keypoints).

Example 9.3 (Estimating a plane in a 3D Cloud of Points) We assume a stereo camera system in a quadcopter; see Fig. 6.10, right, for an illustration. At a time t we record left and right images, I_L and I_R. In both images we apply a keypoint detector (e.g. a time-efficient detector such as FAST), providing sets M_L and M_R of keypoints.

For each keypoint p in M_L, we detect a matching keypoint in M_R (if it exists), defined by a disparity d. Feature descriptors can help to identify a match. Having a projection matrix $\mathbf{P}$ for the left camera, we can map p based on d and $\mathbf{P}$ into a point P in the 3D space. Such 3D points P are collected in a set S. After having all the keypoints processed at time t, we fit a plane into the set S using RANSAC (see Exercise 9.8). See Fig. 9.8 for pseudocode for this procedure.

The estimated plane can be used by the quadcopter for control while landing on a planar surface. Figure 9.9 illustrates a situation where the quadcopter is close to landing.

9.2 Examples of Features

This section defines three popular types of features, known under the acronyms SIFT, SURF, and ORB, and it also provides a comparative performance discussion for those three types of features with respect to invariance properties.

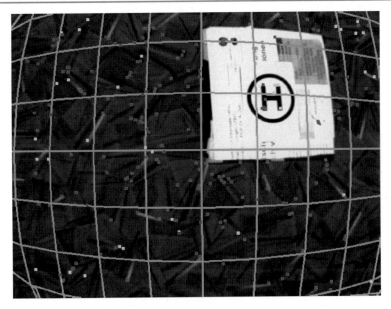

Fig. 9.9 An illustration of a fitted plane to a set of 3D points. The points have been calculated with a sparse stereo matcher using a modified FAST feature detector (implemented in a quadcopter). *Yellow points* are outliers. The fitted plane is back-projected into the non-rectified recorded image, thus resulting in a curved manifold due to lens distortion. The 3D points have been detected with a downward-looking stereo camera system integrated into the quadcopter shown in Fig. 6.10, right

9.2.1   Scale-Invariant Feature Transform

Assume that we have detected keypoints in the DoG or LoG scale space. For a keypoint $p \in \Omega$, we also have the scale $\sigma \cdot a^n$, which defines the radius $r_p = \sigma \cdot a^n$ of the disk of influence for this keypoint. Taking this disk, centred at p, in all layers of the scale space, we define a *cylinder of influence* for the keypoint. The intersection of this cylinder with the input image is also a disk of radius r_p centred at p.

Eliminating Low Contrast and Keypoints on Edges Typically, we are not interested in keypoints in low-contrast regions or on edges. The detected keypoints in low-contrast regions can easily be removed by following the model defined by (1.10). For example, if the bottom layer of the DoG scale space has a small value at p, then the given image has a low contrast at p.

For deciding whether one of the remaining keypoints p is on an edge, we can consider the gradient $\triangle I(p) = [I_x(p), I_y(p)]^\top$. If both components differ significantly in magnitude, then we can conclude that p is on an edge, which is (about) perpendicular to the coordinate axis along which the component had the dominant magnitude.

Another option is that we take only those keypoints that are at a corner in the image; see Sect. 2.3.4. A corner can be identified by the eigenvalues λ_1 and λ_2 of the Hessian matrix at a pixel location p. (See Insert 2.8). If the magnitude of both eigenvalues is "large", then we are at a corner; one large and one small eigenvalue identify a step-edge, and two small eigenvalues identify a low-contrast region.

Thus, after having already eliminated keypoints in low-contrast regions, for the remaining, we are only interested in the ratio

$$\frac{\lambda_1}{\lambda_2} = \frac{(I_{xx} + I_{yy})^2 + 4I_{xy}\sqrt{4I_{xy}^2 + (I_{xx} - I_{yy})^2}}{(I_{xx} + I_{yy})^2 - 4I_{xy}\sqrt{4I_{xy}^2 + (I_{xx} - I_{yy})^2}} \qquad (9.10)$$

for discriminating between keypoints being on a corner or on an edge.

We now assign the descriptors $\mathbf{d}(p)$ to the remaining keypoints p. The *scale-invariant feature transform* (SIFT) aims at implementing rotation invariance, scale invariance (actually addressing "size invariance", not really invariance w.r.t. scale σ), and invariance w.r.t. brightness variations.

Insert 9.3 (Origin of SIFT) *The paper* [D.G. Lowe. Object recognition from local scale-invariant features. In Proc. Int. Conf. Computer Vision, vol. 2, pp. 1150–1157, 1999] *defined the SIFT descriptor.*

Rotation-Invariant Descriptor The disk of influence with radius $r_p = \sigma \cdot a^n$ in the layer $D_{\sigma,a^n}(x, y)$ of the used DoG scale space can be analysed for a *main direction* along a main axis and rotated so that the main direction coincides with a (fixed) predefined direction. For example, (3.41) can be applied as is for identifying the main axis in the disk of influence in the layer $D_{\sigma,a^n}(x, y)$.

SIFT applies a heuristic approach. For pixel locations (x, y) in the disk of influence in layer $L(x, y) = D_{\sigma,a^n}(x, y)$, centred at a keypoint p, a local gradient is approximated by using

$$m(x, y) = \sqrt{\left[L(x, y + 1) - L(x, y - 1)\right]^2 + \left[L(x + 1, y) - L(x - 1, y)\right]^2} \quad (9.11)$$
$$\theta(x, y) = \text{atan} 2\left(\left[L(x, y + 1) - L(x, y - 1)\right], \left[L(x + 1, y) - L(x - 1, y)\right]\right) \quad (9.12)$$

as simple approximation formulas of magnitude and direction (for function atan 2, see footnote on p. 21). The directions are mapped onto 36 counters, each representing an interval of 10 degrees. The counters have the initial value 0. If a direction is within the 10 degrees represented by a counter, then the corresponding magnitude is added to the counter. Altogether, this defines a *gradient histogram*.

Local maxima in counter values, being at least at 80 % of the global maximum, define the *dominant directions*. If there are more than one dominant direction, then the keypoint is used in connection with each of those dominant directions.

Analogously to the processing of a main direction, the disk of influence is rotated so that a detected dominant direction coincides with a (fixed) predefined direction.

Fig. 9.10 *Upper left*:
A square containing a disk of
influence. *Upper right*:
A gradient map for deriving
the gradient histograms for
16 squares. *Lower left*:
A sketch of the detected
gradients. *Lower right*:
A sketch of the gradient
histograms

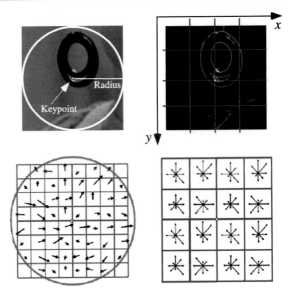

Brightness Invariance   For defining brightness-invariant features, we are interested in describing the disk of influence in the input image (and not for the layer defined where the keypoint has been detected). We can apply any of the transforms discussed in Sect. 2.3.5 for removal of lighting artifacts.

SIFT calculates features for gradients in the disk of influence by subdividing this disk into square windows; for a square window (for the size see below) in the input image, we generate a gradient histogram as defined above for identifying dominant directions, but this time for intervals of 45 degrees, thus only eight counters, each being the sum of gradient magnitudes.

Scale Invariance   We partition the rotated (see under "Rotation Invariance") disk of influence in the input image into 4×4 squares (geometrically "as close as possible"). For each of the 16 squares, we have a vector of length 8 representing the counter values for the gradient histogram for this square. By concatenating all 16 vectors of length 8 each we obtain a vector of length 128. This is the SIFT descriptor $\mathbf{d}_{SIFT}(p)$ for the considered keypoint p. See Fig. 9.10.

9.2.2   Speeded-Up Robust Features

The detector, known as *speeded-up robust features* (SURF), follows similar ideas as SIFT. It was designed for better run-time performance. It utilizes the integral images I_{int} introduced in Sect. 2.2.1 and simplifying filter kernels rather than convolutions with derivatives of the Gauss function.

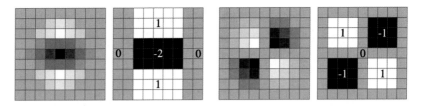

Fig. 9.11 An illustration for $\sigma = 1.2$, the lowest scale, and 9×9 discretized and cropped Gaussian second-order partial derivatives and corresponding filter kernels in SURF. *Pair on the left*: The derivative in the y-direction and SURF's simplifying approximation. *Pair on the right*: The derivative in the diagonal (*lower left* to *upper right*) direction and SURF's corresponding filter kernel

SURF Masks and the Use of Integral Images   Two of the four used masks (or filter kernels) are illustrated in Fig. 9.11; SURF's masks for the x-direction and the other diagonal direction are analogously defined. The size of the mask corresponds to the chosen scale. After 9×9, SURF then uses masks of sizes 15×15, 21×21, 27×27, and so on (subdivided into octaves; but here, as mentioned earlier, we do not discuss these implementation-specific issues) with corresponding increases of rectangular sub-windows.

Values in those filter kernels are either 0, -1, $+1$, or -2. The values -1, $+1$, and $+2$ are constant in rectangular subwindows W of the mask. This allows us to use formula (2.13) for calculating time-efficiently the sum S_W of all intensity values in W. It only remains to multiply the sum S_W with the corresponding coefficient (i.e., the value -1, $+1$, or -2). The sum of those three or four products is then the convolution result at the given reference pixel for one of the four masks.

Insert 9.4 (Origin of SURF)   *The paper* [H. Bay, A. Ess, T. Tuytelaars, and L. Van Gool. SURF: Speeded up robust features. Computer Vision Image Understanding, vol. 110, pp. 346–359, 2008] *defined SURF features.*

Scales and Keypoint Detection   The value $\sigma = 1.2$, as illustrated in Fig. 9.11, is chosen for the lowest scale (i.e. the highest spatial resolution) in SURF. Convolutions at a pixel location p in the input image I with four masks approximate the four coefficients of the Hessian matrix [see (2.28) and (2.29)]. The four convolution masks produce the values $D_{x,x}(p, \sigma)$ and $D_{x,y}(p, \sigma)$, assumed to be equal to $D_{y,x}(p, \sigma)$ and $D_{y,y}(p, \sigma)$. The value

$$S(p, \sigma) = D_{x,x}(p, \sigma) \cdot D_{y,y}(p, \sigma) - \left(c_\sigma \cdot D_{x,y}(p, \sigma)\right)^2 \qquad (9.13)$$

is then chosen as an approximate value for the determinant of the Hessian matrix at the scale σ, where c_σ with $0 < c_\sigma < 1$ is a weighting factor that could be optimized for each scale. However, SURF uses a constant $c_\sigma = 0.9$ as weight optimization appears to have no significant influence on results.

A keypoint p is then detected by a local maximum of a value $S(p, \sigma)$ within a $3 \times 3 \times 3$ array of S-values, analogously to keypoint detection in the LoG or DoG scale space.

SURF Descriptor The SURF descriptor (a 64-vector of floating-point values) combines local gradient information, similar to the SIFT descriptor, but uses again weighted sums in rectangular subwindows (known as *Haar-like features*; see Sect. 10.1.4 for a discussion of those in their original historic context) around the keypoint for a simplifying and more time-efficient approximation of gradient values.

9.2.3 Oriented Robust Binary Features

Before introducing *oriented robust binary features* (ORB), we first have to specify *binary robust independent elementary features* (BRIEF) because this feature descriptor and the keypoint detector FAST (see Sect. 2.3.4) together characterize ORB.

Binary Patterns BRIEF reduces a keypoint descriptor from a 128-vector (such as defined for SIFT) to just 128 bits. Given floating-point information is binarized into a much simpler representation. This idea has been followed when designing the census transform (see Sect. 8.1.2) by the use of *local binary patterns* (LBPs; see Fig. 9.12, left, for the definition) and by proposing a simple test for training a set of classification trees (see the next chapter for this subject).

Insert 9.5 (Origins of LBP) *The paper* [D.C. He and L. Wang. Texture unit, texture spectrum, and texture analysis. IEEE Trans. Geoscience Remote Sensing, vol. 28, pp. 509–512, 1990] *introduced the basic idea of local binary patterns (LBPs), which have been popularized by the work* [T. Ojala, M. Pietikäinen, and D. Harwood. Performance evaluation of texture measures with classification based on Kullback discrimination of distributions. In Proc. Int. Conf. Pattern Recognition, vol. 1, pp. 582–585, 1994] *and subsequent publications on using the* Kullback–Leibler distance *in pattern recognition, named after the US-American mathematicians S. Kullback (1907–1994) and R. Leibler (1914–2003).*

BRIEF For BRIEF, the LBP is defined for a selection of n pixel pairs (p, q), selected around the current pixel in some defined order in a $(2k + 1) \times (2k + 1)$ neighbourhood (e.g. $k = 4$ to $k = 7$) after performing some Gaussian smoothing defined by $\sigma > 0$ in the given image I. Thus, the order of those pairs and the parameters k and σ define a particular version of a BRIEF descriptor. In general, smoothing can be minor (i.e. a small σ), and the original paper suggested a random order for pairs of pixel locations. See Fig. 9.12, right. Thus, scale or rotation invariance was not intended by the designers of the original BRIEF.

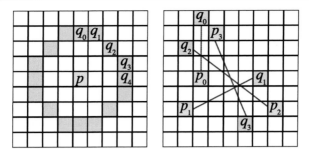

Fig. 9.12 *Left*: The figure shows one pixel location p in an image I and 16 pixel locations q on a discrete circle around p. Let $s(p, q) = 1$ if $I(p) - I(q) > 0$ and 0 otherwise. Then $s(p, q_0) \cdot 2^0 + s(p, q_1) \cdot 2^1 + \cdots + s(p, q_{15}) \cdot 2^{15}$ defines the LBP code at pixel location p, i.e. a binary code of 16 bits. *Right*: BRIEF suggests the use of an order defined by random pairs of pixels within the chosen square neighbourhood, illustrated here by four pairs (p_i, q_i), defining $s(p_0, q_0) \cdot 2^0 + s(p_1, q_1) \cdot 2^1 + s(p_2, q_2) \cdot 2^2 + s(p_3, q_3) \cdot 2^3$

Insert 9.6 (Origins of BRIEF and ORB) *The paper* [M. Calonder, V. Lepetit, C. Strecha, and P. Fua. BRIEF: Binary robust independent elementary features. In Proc. European Conf. Computer Vision, pp. 778–792, 2010] *defined BRIEF, and for the proposal of ORB, see* [E. Rublee, V. Rabaud, K. Konolige, and G. Bradski. ORB: An efficient alternative to SIFT or SURF. In Proc. Int. Conf. Computer Vision, pp. 2564–2571, 2011].

ORB ORB, which can also be read as an acronym for *oriented FAST and rotated BRIEF*, combines keypoints, defined by extending the corner detector FAST (see Sect. 2.3.4), with an extension of the feature descriptor BRIEF:

1. ORB performs a multi-scale detection following FAST (for scale invariance), it calculates a dominant direction, and
2. ORB applies the calculated direction for mapping the BRIEF descriptor into a steered BRIEF descriptor (for rotation invariance).

The authors of ORB also suggest ways for analysing the variance and correlation of the components of the steered BRIEF descriptor; a test data base can be used for defining a set of BRIEF pairs (p_i, q_i) that de-correlate the components of the steered BRIEF descriptor for improving the discriminative performance of the calculated features.

Multi-scale, Harris Filter, and Direction The authors of ORB suggested to use FAST for a defining discrete circle of radius $\rho = 9$; Fig. 2.22 illustrated FAST for a discrete circle of radius $\rho = 3$. (Of course, the chosen radius depends on the resolution and signal structure of the given images.) A scale pyramid of the input image is used for detecting FAST keypoints at different scales. The cornerness measure in 2.30 (of the Harris detector) is then used to select the T "most cornerness" keypoints at those different scales, where $T > 0$ is a pre-defined threshold for the numbers of keypoints. This is called a *Harris filter*.

The moments m_{10} and m_{01} [see (3.36)] of the disk S used, defined by the radius ρ, specify the direction

$$\theta = \text{atan} \, 2(m_{10}, m_{01}) \qquad (9.14)$$

By the definition of FAST it can be expected that $m_{10} \neq m_{01}$. Let $\mathbf{R}_\theta$ be the 2D rotation matrix about an angle θ.

Descriptor with a Direction   The pairs (p_i, q_i) for BRIEF with $0 \leq i \leq 255$ are selected by a Gaussian distribution within the disk used (of radius ρ). They form a matrix $\mathbf{S}$ that is rotated into

$$\mathbf{S}_\theta = \mathbf{R}_\theta \mathbf{S} = \mathbf{R}_\theta \begin{bmatrix} p_0 & \cdots & p_{255} \\ q_0 & \cdots & q_{255} \end{bmatrix} = \begin{bmatrix} p_{0,\theta} & \cdots & p_{255,\theta} \\ q_{0,\theta} & \cdots & q_{255,\theta} \end{bmatrix} \qquad (9.15)$$

A *steered* BRIEF descriptor is now calculated as the sum $s(p_{0,\theta}, q_{0,\theta}) \cdot 2^0 + \cdots + s(p_{255,\theta}, q_{255,\theta}) \cdot 2^{255}$, where s is as defined in the caption of Fig. 9.12. By going from the original BRIEF descriptor to the steered BRIEF descriptor, the values in the descriptor become more correlated.

For time-efficiency reasons, a used pattern of 256 BRIEF pairs (generated by a Gaussian distribution) is rotated in increments of $2\pi/30$, and all those patterns are stored in a look-up table. This eliminates the need for an actual rotation; the calculated θ is mapped on the nearest multiple of $2\pi/30$.

9.2.4   Evaluation of Features

We evaluate the presented feature detectors with respect to invariance properties. We change the frames in given sequences systematically, as illustrated in Fig. 9.13. For example, we reduce the size of an image. If a feature detector is scale-invariant, then it should detect (ideally) the same features in the demagnified image.

Feature Evaluation Test Procedure   We discuss four different types of systematic changes for frames, namely rotation, scaling (demagnification and magnification), brightness changes, and blurring.[2] For a given sequence of frames, we select one feature detector and do the following:

1. Read next frame I, which is a grey-level image.
2. Detect the keypoints p in I and their descriptors $\mathbf{d}(p)$ in I.
3. Let N_k be the number of keypoints p in I.
4. For the given frame, generate four image sequences:

---

[2]See [Z. Song and R. Klette. Robustness of point feature detection. In Proc. Computer Analysis Images Patterns, LNCS 8048, pp. 91–99, 2013].

Fig. 9.13 *Top, left*: A rotated image; the original frame from the sequence `bicyclist` from EISATS is 640 × 480 and recorded at 10 bit per pixel. *Top, right*: A demagnified image. *Bottom, left*: Uniform brightness change. *Bottom, left*: A blurred image

    (a) Rotate I around its centre in steps of 1 degree; this generates a sequence of 360 rotated images.

    (b) Resize I in steps of 0.01, from 0.25 to 2 times the original size; this generates a sequence of 175 scaled images.

    (c) Change the image brightness in I globally by adding a scalar to pixel values, in increments of 1 from -127 to 127; this generates a sequence of 255 brightness-transformed images.

    (d) Apply Gaussian blur to I with increments of 2 for σ from 3 to 41; this generates a sequence of 20 blurred versions of I.

5. Apply the feature detector again for each transformed image I_t; calculate the keypoints p_t and descriptors $\mathbf{d}(p_t)$.

6. Let N_t be the number of keypoints p_t for the transformed image.

7. Use the descriptors $\mathbf{d}(p)$ and $\mathbf{d}(p_t)$ to identify matches between features in I and I_t.

8. Use RANSAC to remove the inconsistent matches.

9. Let N_m be the number of detected matches.

Repeatability Measure We define the *repeatability* $\mathscr{R}(I, I_t)$ as the ratio of the number of detected matches to the number of keypoints in the original image:

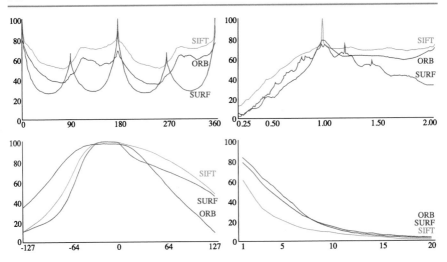

Fig. 9.14 Repeatability diagrams. *Top, left*: For rotation. *Top, right*: For scaling. *Bottom, left*: For brightness variation. *Bottom, right*: For blurring

Table 9.1 The mean values for 90 randomly selected input frames. The fourth column is the numbers of keypoints for the frame used for generating the transformed images shown in Fig. 9.13

Feature detector	Mean time per frame	Mean time per keypoint	Number N_k of keypoints
SIFT	254.1	0.55	726
SURF	401.3	0.40	1,313
ORB	9.6	0.02	500

$$\mathscr{R}(I, I_t) = \frac{N_m}{N_k} \qquad (9.16)$$

We report means for selected frames in test sequences, using OpenCV default parameters for the studied feature detectors and a set of 90 randomly selected test frames. See Fig. 9.14.

Discussion of the Experiments Invariance certainly has its limits. If scaling, brightness variation, or blurring passes these limits that image data get totally distorted, then we cannot expect repeatability anymore. Rotation is a different case; here we could expect invariance close to the ideal case (of course, accepting that digital images do not rotate as continuous 2D functions in $\mathbb{R}^2$.

Table 9.1 reports the run-time per input image, the mean run-time per keypoint, and the numbers of detected keypoints for the frame used for generating the transformed images shown in Fig. 9.13.

The experiments illustrate that SIFT is performing well (compared to SURF and ORB) for rotation, scaling, and brightness variation, but not for blurring. All results are far from the ideal case of invariance. If there is only a minor degree of brightness variation or blurring, then invariance can be assumed. But rotation or scaling leads already to significant drops in repeatability for small angles of rotation or minor scale changes. There was no significant run-time difference between SIFT and SURF, but a very significant drop in computation time for ORB, which appears (judging from this comparison) as a fast and reasonably competitive feature detector.

9.3   Tracking and Updating of Features

Here is an example of an application scenario: Consider a car that is called the *ego-vehicle* because it is the reference vehicle where the considered system is working in, in distinction to "other" vehicles in a scene. This ego-vehicle is equipped with a stereo vision system, and it drives through a street, providing reconstructed 3D clouds of points for each stereo frame at time t. After understanding the motion of the ego-vehicle, these 3D clouds of points can be mapped into a uniform 3D world coordinate system supporting 3D surface modelling of the road sides. Figure 9.15 illustrates such an application of stereo vision.[3]

For understanding the motion of the ego-vehicle, we track the detected features from frame t to frame $t+1$, being the input for a program calculating the *ego-motion* of the car. Such a program is an interesting subject on its own; in this section we only describe techniques how to track features from frame t to frame $t+1$.

9.3.1   Tracking Is a Sparse Correspondence Problem

In binocular stereo, the point or feature correspondence is calculated between images taken at the same time; the correspondence search is within an epipolar line. Thus, stereo matching is a *1D correspondence problem*.

For dense motion (i.e. optic flow) analysis, the point or feature correspondence is calculated between the images taken at subsequent time slots. Movements of pixels are not constrained to be along one straight line only; they may occur in any direction. Thus, dense motion analysis is a *2D correspondence problem*.

Tracking feature points in an image sequence is a sparse 2D correspondence problem. Theoretically, its solution could also be used for solving stereo or dense motion analysis, but there are different strategies for solving a dense or sparse correspondence problem. In sparse correspondence search we cannot utilize a smoothness term and first need to focus more on achieving accuracy based on the data term only, but can then use global consistency of tracked feature point patterns for stabilizing the result.

Tracking with Understanding 3D Changes   For a pair of 3D points $P_t = (X_t, Y_t, Z_t)$ and $P_{t+1} = (X_{t+1}, Y_{t+1}, Z_{t+1})$, projected at times t and $t+1$ into $p_t = (x_t, y_t, f)$ and $p_{t+1} = (x_{t+1}, y_{t+1}, f)$, respectively, when recording a video

---

[3] See [Y. Zeng and R. Klette. Multi-run 3D streetside reconstruction from a vehicle. In Proc. Computer Analysis Images Patterns, LNCS 8047, pp. 580–588, 2013].

Fig. 9.15 *Top*: Tracked feature points in a frame of a stereo video sequence recorded in a car. *Middle*: Tracked feature points are used for calculating the motion of the car; this allows one to map 3D points provided by stereo vision into a uniform 3D world coordinate system. *Bottom*: The stereo matcher iSGM has been used for the shown example (example of a disparity map for the recorded sequence)

sequence, we define the *Z-ratio* as follows:

$$\psi_Z = \frac{Z_{t+1}}{Z_t} \tag{9.17}$$

Based on this Z-ratio, we can also derive the X- and Y-ratios:

$$\psi_X = \frac{X_{t+1}}{X_t} = \frac{Z_{t+1}}{Z_t} \cdot \frac{x_{t+1}}{x_t} = \psi_Z \frac{x_{t+1}}{x_t} \tag{9.18}$$

$$\psi_Y = \frac{Y_{t+1}}{Y_t} = \frac{Z_{t+1}}{Z_t} \cdot \frac{y_{t+1}}{y_t} = \psi_Z \frac{y_{t+1}}{y_t} \tag{9.19}$$

This defines the following update equation:

$$
\begin{bmatrix} X_{t+1} \\ Y_{t+1} \\ Z_{t+1} \end{bmatrix} = \begin{bmatrix} \psi_X & 0 & 0 \\ 0 & \psi_Y & 0 \\ 0 & 0 & \psi_Z \end{bmatrix} \cdot \begin{bmatrix} X_t \\ Y_t \\ Z_t \end{bmatrix} \tag{9.20}
$$

In other words, knowing ψ_Z and the ratios $\frac{x_{t+1}}{x_t}$ and $\frac{y_{t+1}}{y_t}$ allows us to update the position of point P_t into P_{t+1}. Assuming that P_t and P_{t+1} are the positions of a 3D point P, from time t to time $t + 1$, we only have to solve two tasks:
1. decide on a technique to track points from t to $t + 1$, and
2. estimate ψ_Z.
If an initial position P_0 of a tracked point P is known, then we may identify its 3D position at subsequent time slots. Without having an initial position, we only have a 3D direction P_t to P_{t+1}, but not its 3D position.

Stereo vision is the general solution for estimating the Z-values or (just) ratios ψ_Z. Equation (9.17) specifies an alternative way for estimating ψ_Z in a monocular sequence from scale-space results. In the next subsections we discuss how to track points from t to $t + 1$ by providing three different techniques.

Insert 9.7 (Origin of the Lucas–Kanade Tracker) *The method was published in* [B.D. Lucas and T. Kanade: An iterative image registration technique with an application to stereo vision. In Proc. Int. Joint Conf. Artificial Intelligence, pp. 674–679, 1981]. *The selection of "good features" for matching (or tracking) was later discussed by C. Tomasi, first together with T. Kanade and then also with other co-authors; in recognition of this the Lucas–Kanade tracker is sometimes also called the KLT tracker.*

9.3.2   Lucas–Kanade Tracker

We match a *template* W_p, being a $(2k + 1) \times (2k + 1)$ window around keypoint $p = (x, y)$ in a base image I, with windows $W_{p,\mathbf{a}}$ in a match image J, where the method should be general enough to allow for translation, scaling, rotation, and so forth between a base window W_p and a match window $W_{p,\mathbf{a}}$ in J. Vector $\mathbf{a}$ parameterizes the transform from p into a new centre pixel, and also the transformation of a window W into a new shape. See Fig. 9.16.

Insert 9.8 (Newton, Raphson, and the Newton–Raphson Iteration) *I. Newton (1642–1727 in the Julian calendar, which was then used in England) and J. Raphson (about 1648–about 1715). The* Newton–Raphson iteration *calcu-*

Fig. 9.16 A template or base window W_p in a base image I is compared with a match window $W_{p,\mathbf{a}}$ in a match image J. In the shown case, the dissimilarity vector $\mathbf{a}$ is defined by a translation $\mathbf{t}$ and a scaling of height h into a smaller height. The figure also indicates that a disk of influence is contained in W_p. The pixel location p in J is the same as in I; it defines the start of the translation

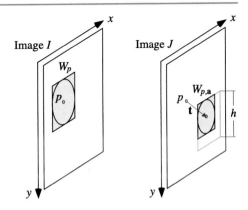

lates the zeros of a unary function f and generalizes an ancient method used by the Babylonians for approximating square roots.

We calculate a zero of a smooth unary function $\phi(x)$ for $x \in [a, b]$, provided that we have $\phi(a)\phi(b) < 0$. Inputs are the two reals a and b. We also have a way to calculate $\phi(x)$ and the derivative $\phi'(x)$ (e.g. approximated by difference quotients) for any $x \in [a, b]$. We calculate a value $c \in [a, b]$ as an approximate zero of ϕ:

1: *Let $c \in [a, b]$ be an initial guess for a zero.*
2: **while** *STOP CRITERION = false* **do**
3:     *Replace c by $c - \frac{\phi(c)}{\phi'(c)}$*
4: **end while**

The derivative $\phi'(c)$ is assumed to be non-zero. If ϕ has a derivative of constant sign in $[a, b]$, then there is just one zero in $[a, b]$.

An initial value of c can be specified by (say) a small number of binary-search steps for reducing the run-time of the actual Newton–Raphson iteration. A small $\varepsilon > 0$ is used for specifying the STOP CRITERION "$|\phi(c)| \le \varepsilon$".

The method converges in general only if c is "sufficiently close" to the zero z. However, if $\phi''(x)$ has a constant sign in $[a, b]$, then we have the following: if $\phi(b)$ has the same sign as $\phi''(x)$, then the initial value $c = b$ gives the convergence to z, otherwise chose the initial value $c = a$.

The figure below shows a smooth function $\phi(x)$ and an interval $[a, b]$ with $\phi(a)\phi(b) < 0$. Assume that we start with $c = x_1$. The tangent at $(x_1, \phi(x_1))$ intersects the x-axis at x_2, which is defined by

$$x_2 = x_1 - \frac{\phi(x_1)}{\phi'(x_1)}$$

We have that $\phi'(x_1) \neq 0$. Now we continue with $c = x_2$. This defines a new tangent and a new x-intercept x_3, and so forth.

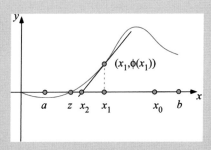

For initial value x_1, the sequence of values $x_2, x_3, \ldots$ converges to the zero z. If we would have started with $c = x_0$, then the algorithm would have failed. Note that $\phi''(x)$ does not have a constant sign in $[a, b]$. We need to start in the "same valley" where z is located. We search for the zero in the direction of the (steepest) decent. If we do not start in the "same valley", then we cannot cross the "hill" in between.

Following the Newton–Raphson Iteration   The *Lucas–Kanade tracker* uses approximate gradients (i.e. approximate derivatives in the x- and y-directions), which are robust against variations in intensities.[4] For window matching, an error function E is defined based on an LSE optimization criterion.

Translation   In the simplest case we only calculate a translation vector $\mathbf{t} = [t.x, t.y]^\top$ such that $J(x + t.x + i, y + t.y + j) \approx I(x + i, y + j)$ for all i, j, with $-k \leq i, j \leq k$, defining relative locations in template W_p.

For simplifying notation, we assume that $p = (x, y) = (0, 0)$ and use W or $W_\mathbf{a}$ instead of W_p or $W_{p,\mathbf{a}}$, respectively. Thus, in case of translation-only, the task is to approximate a zero (i.e. a minimum) of the error function

$$E(\mathbf{t}) = \sum_{i=-k}^{k} \sum_{j=-k}^{k} \left[J(t.x + i, t.y + j) - I\big(W(i, j)\big) \right]^2 \qquad (9.21)$$

where $\mathbf{t} = [t.x, t, y]^\top$ and $W(i, j) = (i, j)$.

Goal for General Warps   We present the tracker not just for translations but for general *warps* defined by an affine transform, with a vector $\mathbf{a}$ parameterizing the transform.

Let $J(W_\mathbf{a}(q))$ be the value at that point $W_\mathbf{a}(q)$ in J that results from a warping pixel location $q = (i, j)$ with $-k \leq i, j \leq k$, according to the parameter vector $\mathbf{a}$. Warping will not map a pixel location onto a pixel location; thus, we also apply some kind of interpolation for defining $J(W_\mathbf{a}(q))$.

---

[4]The presentation follows the Lucas–Kanade tracker introduction by *T. Svoboda* on cmp.felk.cvut. cz/cmp/courses/Y33ROV/Y33ROV_ZS20082009/Lectures/Motion/klt.pdf.

For example, for a translation with $\mathbf{a} = [t.x, t.y]^\top$, it follows that $W_{\mathbf{a}}(q) = (t.x, t.y) + q$ and $J(W_{\mathbf{a}}(q)) = J(t.x + i, t.y + j)$ for $q = (i, j)$.

Back to the general case, the goal is to calculate a *dissimilarity vector* $\mathbf{a}$ that minimizes the error function

$$E(\mathbf{a}) = \sum_q \left[J\left(W_{\mathbf{a}}(q)\right) - I\left(W(q)\right) \right]^2 \tag{9.22}$$

Iterative Steepest-Ascent Algorithm Assume that we are already at a parameter vector $\mathbf{a} = [a_1, \dots, a_n]^\top$. Similarly to the mean-shift algorithm for image segmentation, we calculate here a shift $m_{\mathbf{a}} = [m_1, \dots, m_n]^\top$ such that

$$E(\mathbf{a} + m_{\mathbf{a}}) = \sum_q \left[J\left(W_{\mathbf{a}+m_{\mathbf{a}}}(q)\right) - I\left(W(q)\right) \right]^2 \tag{9.23}$$

is minimized, as a partial step for going towards the minimum for (9.22). For solving this LSE optimization problem, we consider a Taylor expansion of $J(W_{\mathbf{a}}(q))$ with respect to dissimilarity vector $\mathbf{a}$ and a minor shift $m_{\mathbf{a}}$, given as follows:

$$J\left(W_{\mathbf{a}+m_{\mathbf{a}}}(q)\right) = J\left(W_{\mathbf{a}}(q)\right) + m_{\mathbf{a}}^\top \cdot \mathbf{grad}\, J \cdot \frac{\partial W_{\mathbf{a}}}{\partial \mathbf{a}} + e \tag{9.24}$$

Recall that we did the analog operation for deriving the Horn–Schunck constraint; here we also assume that $e = 0$ and thus the linearity of values of image J in a neighbourhood of the pixel location $W_{\mathbf{a}}(q)$.

In (9.24), the second term on the right-hand side is a product of the transpose of the shift vector $m_{\mathbf{a}}$, the derivative $\mathbf{grad}\, J$ of the outer function (i.e. the usual image gradient), and the derivative of the inner function, which also results in a scalar, as we have a scalar on the left-hand side. The window function W defines a point with x- and y-coordinates. For its derivative with respect to locations identified by parameter vector $\mathbf{a}$, we have that

$$\frac{\partial W_{\mathbf{a}}}{\partial \mathbf{a}}(q) = \begin{bmatrix} \frac{\partial W_{\mathbf{a}}(q).x}{\partial x} & \frac{\partial W_{\mathbf{a}}(q).x}{\partial y} \\ \frac{\partial W_{\mathbf{a}}(q).y}{\partial x} & \frac{\partial W_{\mathbf{a}}(q).y}{\partial y} \end{bmatrix} \tag{9.25}$$

known as the *Jacobian matrix* of the warp. For C.G.J. Jacobi, see Insert 5.9.

We insert the Taylor expansion of (9.24) into (9.23). The minimization problem is now defined by

$$\sum_q \left[J\left(W_{\mathbf{a}}(q)\right) + m_{\mathbf{a}}^\top \cdot \mathbf{grad}\, J \cdot \frac{\partial W_{\mathbf{a}}}{\partial \mathbf{a}} - I\left(W(q)\right) \right]^2 \tag{9.26}$$

We follow the standard LSE optimization procedure (see Insert 4.5) for calculating an optimum shift $m_{\mathbf{a}}$.

LSE Procedure   We calculate the derivative of the sum in (9.26) with respect to shift $m_{\mathbf{a}}$, set this equal to zero, and obtain the following equation:

$$2 \sum_q \left[\mathbf{grad}\, J \frac{\partial W_{\mathbf{a}}}{\partial \mathbf{a}} \right]^{\top} \left[J\big(W_{\mathbf{a}}(q)\big) + m_{\mathbf{a}}^{\top} \cdot \mathbf{grad}\, J \cdot \frac{\partial W_{\mathbf{a}}}{\partial \mathbf{a}} - I\big(W(q)\big) \right] = \mathbf{0} \quad (9.27)$$

with the 2×1 zero-vector $\mathbf{0}$ on the right-hand side. Here,

$$H = \sum_q \left[\mathbf{grad}\, J \frac{\partial W_{\mathbf{a}}}{\partial \mathbf{a}} \right]^{\top} \left[\mathbf{grad}\, J \frac{\partial W_{\mathbf{a}}}{\partial \mathbf{a}} \right] \quad (9.28)$$

is the 2×2 Hessian matrix, which combines the second-order derivatives. (For L.O. Hesse, see Insert 2.8.) The solution of (9.27),

$$m_{\mathbf{a}}^{\top} = H^{-1} \sum_q \left[\mathbf{grad}\, J \frac{\partial W_{\mathbf{a}}}{\partial \mathbf{a}} \right]^{\top} \left[I\big(W(q)\big) - J\big(W_{\mathbf{a}}(q)\big) \right] \quad (9.29)$$

defines the optimum shift vector $m_{\mathbf{a}}$ from a given parameter vector $\mathbf{a}$ to an updated parameter vector $\mathbf{a} + m_{\mathbf{a}}$.

Analogy to the Newton–Raphson Iteration   Starting with an initial dissimilarity vector $\mathbf{a}$, new vectors $\mathbf{a} + m_{\mathbf{a}}$ are calculated in iterations, following the steepest ascent. A possible stop criterion is that the error value in (9.22), or the length of shift vector $m_{\mathbf{a}}$ is below a given $\varepsilon > 0$, or a predefined maximum of iterations is reached.

Example 9.4 (Translation Case) Assume that we only look for a translation vector $\mathbf{a}$ with $W_{\mathbf{a}}(q) = [t.x + i, t_y + j]^{\top}$ for $q = (i, j)$. For the Jacobian matrix, we have that

$$\frac{\partial W_{\mathbf{a}}}{\partial \mathbf{a}}(q, \mathbf{a}) = \begin{bmatrix} \frac{\partial W_{\mathbf{a}}(q).x}{\partial x} & \frac{\partial W_{\mathbf{a}}(q).x}{\partial y} \\ \frac{\partial W_{\mathbf{a}}(q).y}{\partial x} & \frac{\partial W_{\mathbf{a}}(q).y}{\partial y} \end{bmatrix} = \begin{bmatrix} 1 & 0 \\ 0 & 1 \end{bmatrix} \quad (9.30)$$

The Hessian matrix equals[5]

$$H = \sum_q \left[\mathbf{grad}\, J \frac{\partial W_{\mathbf{a}}}{\partial \mathbf{a}} \right]^{\top} \left[\mathbf{grad}\, J \frac{\partial W_{\mathbf{a}}}{\partial \mathbf{a}} \right] = \sum_q \begin{bmatrix} \left(\frac{\partial J}{\partial x}\right)^2 & \frac{\partial J^2}{\partial x \partial y} \\ \frac{\partial J^2}{\partial x \partial y} & \left(\frac{\partial J}{\partial y}\right)^2 \end{bmatrix} \quad (9.31)$$

Furthermore, the steepest ascent is simply

$$\mathbf{grad}\, J \cdot \frac{\partial W_{\mathbf{a}}}{\partial \mathbf{a}} = \mathbf{grad}\, J \quad (9.32)$$

---

[5]We use a (practically acceptable) approximation of the Hessian. Instead of mixed derivatives, we apply the product of the first-order derivatives.

1: Let **a** be an initial guess for a dissimilarity vector.
2: **while** STOP CRITERION = false **do**
3:     For the given vector **a**, compute the optimum shift $m_\mathbf{a}$ as defined by (9.29).

4:     Let $\mathbf{a} = \mathbf{a} + m_\mathbf{a}$.
5: **end while**

Fig. 9.17 Lucas–Kanade algorithm

and

$$I\big(W(q)\big) - J\big(W_\mathbf{a}(q)\big) = I\big(W(q)\big) - J(q + \mathbf{a}) \qquad (9.33)$$

Altogether,

$$m_\mathbf{a}^\top = H^{-1} \sum_q \left[\mathbf{grad}\, J \frac{\partial W_\mathbf{a}}{\partial \mathbf{a}} \right]^\top \left[I\big(W(q)\big) - J\big(W_\mathbf{a}(q)\big) \right]$$

$$= \left[\sum_q \begin{bmatrix} (\frac{\partial J}{\partial x})^2 & \frac{\partial J^2}{\partial x \partial y} \\ \frac{\partial J^2}{\partial x \partial y} & (\frac{\partial J}{\partial y})^2 \end{bmatrix} \right]^{-1} \sum_q [\mathbf{grad}\, J]^\top \left[I\big(W(q)\big) - J(q + \mathbf{a}) \right]$$

After approximating the derivatives in image J around the current pixel locations in window W, defining the Hessian and the gradient vector, we only have to perform a sum of differences for identifying the shift vector $m_\mathbf{a}$.

Lucas–Kanade Algorithm Given is an image I, its gradient image $\mathbf{grad}\, I$, and a local template W (i.e. a window) containing (e.g.) the disk of influence of a keypoint. The algorithm is given in Fig. 9.17.

Line 3 in the algorithm requires calculations for all pixels q defined by the template W and basically in the main steps:
1. Warp W in I into $W_\mathbf{a}(q)$ in J.
2. Calculate the Jacobian matrix and its product with $\mathbf{grad}\, J$.
3. Compute the Hessian matrix.
The algorithm performs magnitudes faster than an exhaustive search algorithm for an optimized vector $\mathbf{a}$. A program for the Lucas–Kanade algorithm is also available in OpenCV.

Dents and Hills Assume that we only have a 2D vector $\mathbf{a}$ (e.g. for translation only). The error value of (9.22) is then defined on the plane, and for different values of $\mathbf{a}$, it describes a "hilly terrain" with local minima, possibly a uniquely defined global minimum, local maxima, and possibly a uniquely defined global maximum. See Fig. 9.18. For illustration purposes, let us reverse the meaning of minima and maxima (i.e. we are now interested to go by steepest descent to a global maximum).

The iteration scheme can only potentially lead to a uniquely defined global minimum (by steepest ascent) if the initial parameter vector is such that subsequent shifts (by steepest ascent) may lead to this global minimum.

Fig. 9.18 The *blue point* "cannot climb" by steepest descent to a global maximum; it is in a valley surrounded by local maxima only. The same is true for the *red point*, which is already at a local maximum. The *yellow dot* in the "central valley" (a global minimum) can iterate to the global peak (in the *middle* of the figure) by repeated shifts defined by steepest descent

Fig. 9.19 Two points are tracked from row *y* to row *y* − 1. Both points are integrated into one feature specifying coordinates *l* and *r* and further parameters, combined into one model-dependent descriptor **a**. The next feature on row *y* − 1 needs to be selected by an optimized match with the feature model

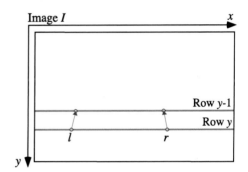

There is also the possibility of a *drift*. The individual local calculation can be accurate, but the composition of several local moves may result in significant errors after some time, mainly due to the discrete nature of the data.

9.3.3 Particle Filter

We consider now a different tracking scenario. Features (each defined by a keypoint and a descriptor) need to be tracked according to a general ("vague") model about the movement of those features. Tracking can be from frame to frame, or just within the same image. See Fig. 9.19.

Particles, Weighting, and Iterative Condensation Assume that features are defined by a specific, application-dependent model, not by a generic model of having (only) a disk of influence. This allows a more specific *weighting* of consistencies between feature locations and model correspondence.

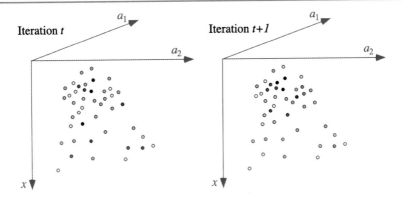

Fig. 9.20 A 3D particle space, combining one spatial component x and two descriptor components a_1 and a_2. Condensation maps weighted particles from iteration t to iteration $t + 1$. *Grey values* indicate weights; the weights change in the iteration step due to the particular condensation algorithm chosen from a set of many options

A *particle filter* is appropriate for such a scenario: a *particle* represents a feature in a multi-dimensional space; the dimensions of this space combine locations, such as (x, y) in the image, or just x on a specified row in the image, with descriptor values in a parameter vector $\mathbf{a} = (a_1, a_2, \ldots, a_m)$. See Fig. 9.20.

A particle filter can track parameter vectors over time or within a space, based on evaluating consistency with a defined model. By evaluating the consistency of a particle with the model, we assign a weight (a non-negative real) to the particle.

A *condensation algorithm* is then used to analyse a cluster of weighted particles for identifying a "winning particle". Many different strategies have been designed for condensation. Typically, the weights are recalculated in iterations for the given cluster of weighted particles. When iteration stops, some kind of mean or local maxima is taken as a winning particle. In the shown example in Fig. 9.20, the particles stay at their positions, only the weights are changing. In general, condensation can also merge particles, change positions, or create new particles.

Considered Example   We present a simple case. We have a feature that combines a left point and a right point in the same image row. It needs to be tracked in the same image. Movement is from one image row to the next, say, bottom-up. The translational movement of both contributing points to the feature can (slightly) differ. Figure 9.19 is for this situation.

This simple example allows us to present the core ideas of a particle filter while using a particular application (detection of lanes of a road in video data recorded in a driving ego-vehicle).[6] Here is a brief outline of the general workflow in this application; see Fig. 9.21 for an illustration of those steps:

---

[6]A particle filter for lane detection was suggested in [S. Sehestedt, S. Kodagoda, A. Alempijevic, and G. Dissanayake. Efficient lane detection and tracking in urban environments. In Proc. European Conf. Mobile Robots, pp. 126–131, 2007].

Fig. 9.21 *Top, left to right*: An input frame, bird's eye view, and the detected vertical edges. *Bottom, left to right*: The row components of EDT, shown as absolute values, detected centre of lane and lane borders, and lane borders projected back into the perspective view of the recorded frames

1. Map recorded video frames into a bird's-eye view being an orthogonal top-down projection.
2. Detect dominantly vertical edges in bird's-eye images; remove edge-artifacts.
3. Perform the Euclidean distance transform (EDT) for calculating the minimum distances between pixel locations $p = (x, y)$ to those edge pixels; use the *signed row components* $x - x_{edge}$ of the calculated distances $\sqrt{(x - x_{edge})^2 + (y - y_{edge})^2}$ for identifying centres of lanes at places where signs are changing and the distance values about half of the expected lane width.
4. Apply a particle filter for propagating detected lane border pixels bottom-up, row by row, such that we have the most likely pixels as lane border pixels again in the next row.

Step 2 can be done by assuming a step-edge and using approximations of partial derivative I_x only. For the removal of edge artifacts, see Exercise 3.2. For the EDT in Step 3, see Sect. 3.2.4.

Generating a Bird's-Eye View   Step 1 can be done by an *inverse perspective mapping* using the calibration data for the used camera or simply by marking four pixels in the image, supposed to be corners of a rectangle in the plane of the road (thus appearing as a trapezoid in the perspective image), and by applying a *homography*, which maps those marked four points into a rectangle, and at the same time the perspective view into a bird's-eye view.

Model-Based Particles   A lane-border model is illustrated in Fig. 9.21. For a detected centre of a lane, where positive and negative row components of the EDT meet (with absolute values which differ by 1 at most) in the bird's-eye view, we apply a fixed height h and have (applying the positive and negative row components) an angle α that identifies the x-coordinates l and r. Local approximations of the tan-

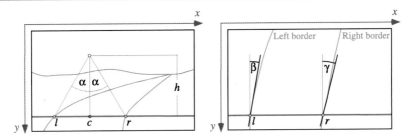

Fig. 9.22 *Left*: Model visualization for the perspective image. The *centre point c* defines, at fixed height h, the angle α that identifies *left* and *right lane border points* at l and r, respectively. *Right*: Bird's-view image. The model parameters are defined in this view. At detected points l and r, we have the tangent angles β and γ to the *left* and *right borders*, detected as dominantly vertical edges

gents at l and r to the detected lane borders define the angles β and γ. See Fig. 9.22 for an illustration of those parameters.

The height h and angle α are shown in the figure using the perspective view for illustration of the model. The coordinates l and r are actually defined in the bird's-eye view.

Altogether, a feature combining two points (l, y) and (r, y) in row y on the left and right lane borders (or one keypoint (c, y)) is defined by one vector $\mathbf{a} = [c, \alpha, \beta, \gamma]^\top$. Thus, we have a 4D particle space.

Initialization of the Tracking Process   Having a sequence of frames, the results from the previous frame can be used for initializing a feature in a row close to the bottom of the current frame. Let us assume that we are at the very first frame of the sequence or at a frame after lane borders had been lost in the previous frame.

The *start row* y_0 is close to the bottom of the first frame:

- Option (1): We search for a pixel (c, y) with a positive row-distance value, having an adjacent pixel in the same row with a negative row-distance value; possibly, we need to move up to the next row until we have a proper initial value c.
- Option (2): we run special detectors for points (l, y) and (r, y).

These initial values define the first feature vector

$$\mathbf{a}_0 = [c_0, \alpha_0, \beta_0, \gamma_0]^\top \tag{9.34}$$

for the start row. The angles β_0 and γ_0 can be chosen to be 0, to be specified better within the next particle propagation step.

Updating the Feature Vector of the Particle Filter   We track the feature vector $\mathbf{a} = [c, \alpha, \beta, \gamma]^\top$ from the start row upward to a row that defines the upper limit for expected lane borders.

The row parameter y is calculated incrementally by applying a fixed increment Δ, starting at y_0 in the birds-eye image. The row at step n is identified by $y_n = (y_0 + n \cdot \Delta)$. In the update process, a particle filter applies the following two models:

The Dynamic Model A dynamic model matrix $\mathbf{A}$ defines a default motion of particles in the image. Let p_n be the keypoint in step n, expressed as a vector. A prediction value $\hat{p}_n$ is generated from p_{n-1} by using $\hat{p}_n = \mathbf{A} \cdot p_{n-1}$. A general and simple choice is the identity matrix $\mathbf{A} = \mathbf{I}$ (i.e. in the given application it expresses a smoothness assumption for lane boundaries).

The Observation Model The observation model determines the weight of a particle during resampling. The points (c_n, y_n) are assumed to have large absolute row-distance values. Let L_n and R_n be short digital line segments, centred at (l_n, y_n) and (r_n, y_n), representing the tangential lines at those two points in the bird's-eye view. It is assumed that these two line segments are formed by pixels that have absolute row-distance values close to 0. We assume that L_n and R_n are formed by an 8-path of length $2k + 1$, with points (l_n, y_n) or (r_n, y_n) at the middle position.

Generation of Random Particles In each step, when going forward to the next row, we generate $N_{part} > 0$ particles randomly around the predicted parameter vector (following the dynamic model) in the mD particle space. For better results, use a larger number of generated particles (e.g. $N_{part} = 500$). Figure 9.20 illustrates 43 particles in a 3D particle space. Let

$$\hat{\mathbf{a}}_n^i = \left[\hat{c}_n^i, \hat{\alpha}_n^i, \hat{\beta}_n^i, \hat{\gamma}_n^i \right]^\top \tag{9.35}$$

be the ith particle generated in step n for $1 \leq i \leq N_{part}$.

Example 9.5 (Particle Generation Using a Uniform Distribution) We may apply a uniform distribution for generated particles in the mD particle space. For the discussed example, this can be implemented as follows:

For the first component we assume an interval $[c - 10, c + 10]$ and select uniformly random values for the c-component in this interval. This process is independent from the other components of a vector $\hat{\mathbf{a}}_n^i$. For the second component, we assume the interval (say) of $[\alpha - 0.1, \alpha + 0.1]$, for the third component, the interval $[\beta - 0.5, \beta + 0.5]$, and similar for γ.

Example 9.6 (Particle Generation Using a Gauss Distribution) We can also decide for a Gauss (or normal) distribution for the generated particles in the mD particle space. For the discussed example, this can be implemented as follows:

A zero-mean distribution produces values around the predicted value. For the individual components, we assume a standard deviation $\sigma > 0$ such that we generate values about in the same intervals as specified for the uniform distribution in Example 9.5. For example, we use $\sigma = 10$ for the c-component.

Particle Weights We define a weight for the ith particle $\hat{\mathbf{a}}_n^i$. The left position equals

$$l_n^i = \hat{c}_n^i - h \cdot \tan \hat{\alpha}_n^i \tag{9.36}$$

The sum of absolute row-distance values $d_r(x, y) = |x - x_{edge}|$, as provided by the EDT in the bird's-eye view, along the line segment L (assumed to be an 8-path of length $2k + 1$) equals

$$S_L^i = \sum_{j=-k}^{k} |d_r(l_n^i + j \cdot \sin \hat{\beta}_n^i, y_n + j \cdot \cos \hat{\beta}_n^i)| \qquad (9.37)$$

We calculate S_R^i for the second line segment in an analogous way and obtain the weight

$$w_{dist}^i = \frac{1}{2\sigma_l\sigma_r\pi} \exp\left(-\frac{(S_L^i - \mu_l)^2}{2\sigma_l} - \frac{(S_R^i - \mu_r)^2}{2\sigma_r}\right) \qquad (9.38)$$

with respect to the distance values on L and R, where μ_l, μ_r, σ_l, and σ_r are estimated constants (say, zero-mean $\mu_l = \mu_r = 0$ for the ideal case) based on experiments for the given application.

For the generated centre point (c_n^i, y_n), the weight equals

$$w_{centre}^i = \frac{1}{\sigma_c\sqrt{2\pi}} \exp\left(-\frac{(|\frac{1}{d_r(c_n^i, y_n)}| - \mu_c)^2}{2\sigma_c}\right) \qquad (9.39)$$

where μ_c and σ_c are again estimated constants.

Finally, the total weight for the ith particle $\hat{\mathbf{a}}_n^i$, at the beginning of the iterative condensation process, is given by

$$w_i = w_{dist}^i \cdot w_{centre}^i \qquad (9.40)$$

These weights decide about the "influence" of the particles during the condensation process. A normalization of all the N_{part} weights is normally required before applying one of the common condensation programs. See Fig. 9.23 for an illustration of results. By using more than just one row for defining a particle, the results can be improved in general. But using only three rows forward appears to be more reasonable than, say, eight rows forward. The number of used rows should be changed dynamically according to the state of lane borders, such as being straight or curved.

Condensation   The iterative condensation process decides now which of the randomly generated particles (generated "near" the predicted particles) is taken as a result for the next image row.

One iteration of condensation is also called *resampling*. Such a resampling step can possibly also merge particles, delete particles, or create new particles; the goal is to improve the "quality" of the particles.

A particle with a high weight is very likely to "survive" the resampling process. Resampling takes all the current weighted particles as input and outputs a set of weighted particles. Often, particles "shift" towards the particles that had a higher

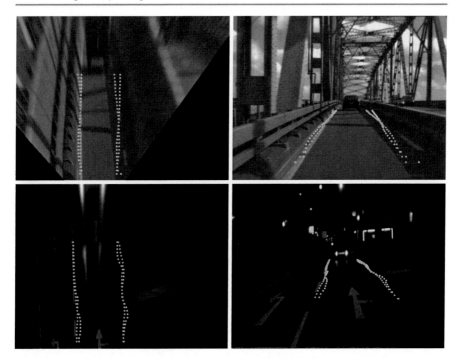

Fig. 9.23 *Top, left*: Generated points (l_n, y_n) and (r_n, y_n) using the described method (in *yellow*) and an extended method, where particles are defined by two rows backward and eight rows forward (in *cyan*). *Top, right*: Generated points backprojected into the corresponding source frame. *Bottom*: The *cyan points* are here for two rows backward and only three rows forward

weight in the input data. OpenCV provides a particle filter procedure; see CvCon-Densation.

A small number of iterations or resamplings is appropriate (e.g. 2 to 5). At the end of the iterations, the particle with the highest weight or the weighted mean of all particles is taken as the result.

9.3.4 Kalman Filter

The Kalman filter is a very powerful tool for controlling noisy systems. The basic idea is: "Noisy data in, and, hopefully, less noisy data out."

Applications of Kalman filters are numerous, such as tracking objects (e.g., balls, faces, heads, hands), fitting Bezier patches to point data, economics, navigation, and also many computer vision applications (e.g. stabilizing depth measurements, feature tracking, cluster tracking, fusing data from radar, laser scanner, and stereo-cameras for depth and velocity measurement). In the presentation here we provide the basics and aim at applications for feature tracking.

Continuous Equation of a Linear Dynamic System   We assume a continuous *linear dynamic system* defined by

$$\dot{\mathbf{x}} = \mathbf{A} \cdot \mathbf{x} \tag{9.41}$$

The nD vector $\mathbf{x} \in \mathbb{R}^n$ specifies the *state* of the process, and $\mathbf{A}$ is a constant $n \times n$ *system matrix*. The notation $\dot{\mathbf{x}}$ is short for the derivative of $\mathbf{x}$ with respect to time t.

The signs and magnitudes of the roots of the eigenvalues of $\mathbf{A}$ (i.e. the roots of the characteristic polynomial $\det(\mathbf{A} - \lambda\mathbf{I}) = 0$) determine the *stability* of the dynamic system. *Observability* and *controllability* are further properties of dynamic systems.

Example 9.7 (Moving Object with Constant Acceleration) A video camera captures an object moving along a straight line. Its centroid (i.e. the location) is described by the coordinate x on this line, and its motion by the speed v and *constant* acceleration a. We do not consider the start or end of this motion.

The process state is characterized by the vector $\mathbf{x} = [x, v, a]^\top$, and we have that $\dot{\mathbf{x}} = [v, a, 0]^\top$ because of

$$\dot{x} = v, \qquad \dot{v} = a, \qquad \dot{a} = 0 \tag{9.42}$$

It follows that

$$\dot{\mathbf{x}} = \begin{bmatrix} v \\ a \\ 0 \end{bmatrix} = \begin{bmatrix} 0 & 1 & 0 \\ 0 & 0 & 1 \\ 0 & 0 & 0 \end{bmatrix} \cdot \begin{bmatrix} x \\ v \\ a \end{bmatrix} \tag{9.43}$$

This defines the 3×3 system matrix $\mathbf{A}$. It follows that

$$\det(\mathbf{A} - \lambda\mathbf{I}) = -\lambda^3 \tag{9.44}$$

Thus, we have identical eigenvalues $\lambda_{1,2,3} = 0$, meaning that the system is "very stable".

Discrete Equations of a Linear Dynamic System   We map the continuous linear system, defined by the matrix $\mathbf{A}$ in (9.41), into a time-discrete system. Let Δt be the actual time difference between time slots t and $t + 1$. We recall the power series

$$e^x = 1 + \sum_{i=1}^{\infty} \frac{x^i}{i!} \tag{9.45}$$

for the Euler number for any argument x. Accordingly, let

$$\mathbf{F}_{\Delta t} = e^{\Delta t \mathbf{A}} = \mathbf{I} + \sum_{i=1}^{\infty} \frac{\Delta t^i \mathbf{A}^i}{i!} \tag{9.46}$$

be the *state transition matrix* for Δt. We assume that Δt is uniformly defined and will not use it anymore as a subscript in the sequel.

Note that there is typically an $i_0 > 0$ such that $\mathbf{A}^i$ equals the matrix having 0 in all its columns for all $i \geq i_0$. In such a case, (9.46) is a finite sum for the matrix $\mathbf{F}$ of a discrete system

$$\mathbf{x}_t = \mathbf{F}\mathbf{x}_{t-1} \qquad (9.47)$$

with $\mathbf{x}_0$ as initial state at time slot $t = 0$. Sometimes we use "time t" short for time $t_0 + t \cdot \Delta t$.

The state transition matrix $\mathbf{F}$ transforms the internal system states at time slot t (of the continuous linear system defined by a matrix $\mathbf{A}$) into the internal states at time slot $t + 1$.

Discrete Linear System with Control and Noise   In the real world we have noise and often also system control. Equation (9.47) is thus replaced by the following more detailed discrete system equations:

$$\mathbf{x}_t = \mathbf{F}\mathbf{x}_{t-1} + \mathbf{B}\mathbf{u}_t + \mathbf{w}_t$$

$$\mathbf{y}_t = \mathbf{H}\mathbf{x}_t + \mathbf{v}_t$$

Here we also have a *control matrix* $\mathbf{B}$, which is applied to a *control vector* $\mathbf{u}_t$ of the system, *system noise* vectors $\mathbf{w}_t$, an *observation matrix* $\mathbf{H}$, noisy *observations* $\mathbf{y}_t$, and *observation noise* vectors $\mathbf{v}_t$. The system noise and observation noise vectors, at different time slots, are all assumed to be mutually independent. *Control* defines some type of system influence at time t, which is not inherent to the process itself.

Example 9.8 (Continuation: Moving Object with Constant Acceleration) We continue Example 9.7. We have system vectors $\mathbf{x}_t = [x_t, v_t, a_t]^\top$ with $a_t = a$. We have a state transition matrix $\mathbf{F}$ (verify for the provided $\mathbf{A}$ by applying (9.46)) defined by

$$\mathbf{x}_{t+1} = \begin{bmatrix} 1 & \Delta t & \frac{1}{2}\Delta t^2 \\ 0 & 1 & \Delta t \\ 0 & 0 & 1 \end{bmatrix} \cdot \mathbf{x}_t = \begin{bmatrix} x_t + \Delta t \cdot v_t + \frac{1}{2}\Delta t^2 a \\ v_t + \Delta t \cdot a \\ a \end{bmatrix} \qquad (9.48)$$

Consider the observation $\mathbf{y}_t = [x_t, 0, 0]^\top$; we only observe the current location. This defines the observation matrix $\mathbf{H}$ as used in the following equation:

$$\mathbf{y}_t = \begin{bmatrix} 1 & 0 & 0 \\ 0 & 0 & 0 \\ 0 & 0 & 0 \end{bmatrix} \cdot \mathbf{x}_t \qquad (9.49)$$

The noise vectors $\mathbf{w}_t$ and $\mathbf{v}_t$ were not part of Example 9.7; they would be the zero vectors under ideal assumptions. The control vector and control matrix are also not used in the example.

Time-Discrete Prediction   Given is a sequence $\mathbf{y}_0, \mathbf{y}_1, \ldots, \mathbf{y}_{t-1}$ of noisy observations for a linear dynamic system. The goal is to estimate $\mathbf{x}_t = [x_{1,t}, x_{2,t}, \ldots, x_{n,t}]^\top$, which is the internal state of the system at time slot t. The estimation error should be minimized (i.e., we want to look "one step ahead").

Let $\hat{\mathbf{x}}_{t_1|t_2}$ be the *estimate* of the state $\mathbf{x}_{t_1}$ based on the knowledge as listed below, available at time t_2.

Let $\mathbf{P}_{t_1|t_2}$ be the variance matrix of the *prediction error* $\mathbf{x}_{t_1} - \hat{\mathbf{x}}_{t_1|t_2}$. The goal is to minimize $\mathbf{P}_{t|t}$ in some defined (i.e., mathematical) way.

Available Knowledge at Time of Prediction   When approaching this prediction problem at time slot t, we summarize the assumptions about the available knowledge at this time:

1. A state transition matrix $\mathbf{F}$, which is applied to the ("fairly known") previous state $\mathbf{x}_{t-1}$.
2. A control matrix $\mathbf{B}$, which is applied to the control vector $\mathbf{u}_t$ if at all there is a control mechanism built into the given system.
3. An understanding about the system noise $\mathbf{w}_t$ (e.g. modelled as a multivariate Gaussian distribution) by specifying a variance matrix $\mathbf{Q}_t$ and expected values $\mu_{i,t} = E[w_{i,t}] = 0$ for $i = 1, 2, \ldots, n$.
4. An observation vector $\mathbf{y}_t$ for state $\mathbf{x}_t$.
5. An observation matrix $\mathbf{H}$ ("how to observe $\mathbf{y}_t$"?).
6. An understanding about the observation noise $\mathbf{v}_t$ (e.g. modelled as a multivariate Gaussian distribution) by specifying a variance matrix $\mathbf{R}_t$ and expected values $\mu_{i,t} = E[v_{i,t}] = 0$ for $i = 1, 2, \ldots, n$.

Prediction and Filter   The key idea is now that we do not simply focus on having one after the other prediction by applying the available knowledge as outlined above. Instead, we define a *filter* that aims at updating our knowledge about the system noise, based on experienced prediction errors and observations so far, and we want to use the improved knowledge about the system noise for reducing the prediction error.

More basic problems in a followed approach, such as assuming an incorrect state transition matrix or an incorrect control matrix, are *not* solved by the filter. Here, a more general analysis is required to understand whether the assumed system matrices are actually a correct model for the underlying process.

Predict Phase of the Filter   In this first phase of the filter, we calculate the predicted state and the predicted variance matrix as follows, using the state transition matrix $\mathbf{F}$ and control matrix $\mathbf{B}$, as given in the model. We also apply the system noise variance matrix $\mathbf{Q}_t$:

$$\hat{\mathbf{x}}_{t|t-1} = \mathbf{F}\hat{\mathbf{x}}_{t-1|t-1} + \mathbf{B}\mathbf{u}_t \tag{9.50}$$

$$\mathbf{P}_{t|t-1} = \mathbf{F}\mathbf{P}_{t-1|t-1}\mathbf{F}^{\top} + \mathbf{Q}_t \tag{9.51}$$

Update Phase of the Filter   In the second phase of the filter, we calculate the *measurement residual vector* $\tilde{\mathbf{z}}_t$ and the *residual variance matrix* $\mathbf{S}_t$ as follows, using the observation matrix $\mathbf{H}$ of the assumed model. We also apply the observation noise variance matrix $\mathbf{R}_t$ and aim at improving these noise matrices:

$$\tilde{\mathbf{z}}_t = \mathbf{y}_t - \mathbf{H}\hat{\mathbf{x}}_{t|t-1} \tag{9.52}$$

$$\mathbf{S}_t = \mathbf{H}\mathbf{P}_{t|t-1}\mathbf{H}^\top + \mathbf{R}_t \qquad (9.53)$$

For an updated state-estimation vector (i.e. the prediction solution at time t), we now also consider an *innovation step* of the *filter* at time t:

$$\hat{\mathbf{x}}_{t|t} = \hat{\mathbf{x}}_{t|t-1} + \mathbf{K}_t\tilde{\mathbf{z}}_t \qquad (9.54)$$

Can we define a matrix $\mathbf{K}_t$ such that this innovation step makes sense? Is there even an optimal solution for this matrix $\mathbf{K}_t$? The answer is "yes", and it was given by R.E. Kalman.

Insert 9.9 (Kalman, Swerling, Thiele, the Linear Kalman Filter, and Apollo 8) *R.E. Kalman (born 1930 in Hungary) defined and published in* [R.E. Kalman. A new approach to linear filtering and prediction problems. J. Basic Engineering, vol. 82, pp. 35–45, 1960] *a recursive solution to the linear filtering problem for discrete signals, today known as the* linear Kalman filter. *Related ideas were also studied at that time by the US-American radar theoretician P. Swerling (1929–2000). The Danish astronomer T.N. Thiele (1838–1910) is also cited for historic origins of involved ideas. Apollo 8 (December 1968), the first human spaceflight from Earth to an orbit around the moon, would certainly not have been possible without the linear Kalman filter.*

Optimal Kalman Gain   The matrix

$$\mathbf{K}_t = \mathbf{P}_{t|t-1}\mathbf{H}^\top\mathbf{S}_t^{-1} \qquad (9.55)$$

minimizes the mean square error $E[(\mathbf{x}_t - \hat{\mathbf{x}}_{t|t})^2]$, which is equivalent to minimizing the trace (= sum of elements on the main diagonal) of $\mathbf{P}_{t|t}$. This mathematical theorem is due to R.E. Kalman.

The matrix $\mathbf{K}_t$ is known as the *optimal Kalman gain*, and it defines the *linear Kalman filter*. The filter also requires an updated estimate of the variance matrix

$$\mathbf{P}_{t|t} = (\mathbf{I} - \mathbf{K}_t\mathbf{H}_t)\mathbf{P}_{t|t-1} \qquad (9.56)$$

of the system noise for being prepared for the prediction phase at time $t + 1$. The variance matrix $\mathbf{P}_{0|0}$ needs to be initialized at the beginning of the filter process.

Example 9.9 (Moving Object with Random Acceleration) We continue Examples 9.7 and 9.8. The object (e.g. a car) is still assumed to move (e.g. in front of a camera) along a straight line, but now with *random* acceleration a_t between time $t - 1$ and time t. For modelling randomness, we assume the Gauss distribution with zero mean and variance σ_a^2. Measurements of positions of the object are also assumed to be noisy; again, we assume the Gaussian noise with zero mean and variance σ_y^2.

The state vector of this process is given by $\mathbf{x}_t = [x_t, \dot{x}_t]^\top$, where $\dot{x}_t$ equals the speed v_t. Again, we do not assume any process control (i.e. $\mathbf{u}_t$ is the zero vector).

We have that (note that a random acceleration cannot be part of the state anymore; what is the matrix $\mathbf{A}$ of the continuous model?)

$$\mathbf{x}_t = \begin{bmatrix} 1 & \Delta t \\ 0 & 1 \end{bmatrix} \begin{bmatrix} x_{t-1} \\ v_{t-1} \end{bmatrix} + a_t \begin{bmatrix} \frac{\Delta t^2}{2} \\ \Delta t \end{bmatrix} = \mathbf{F}\mathbf{x}_{t-1} + \mathbf{w}_t \tag{9.57}$$

with variance matrix $\mathbf{Q}_t = \mathrm{var}(\mathbf{w}_t)$. Let $\mathbf{G}_t = [\frac{\Delta t^2}{2}, \Delta t]^\top$. Then we have that

$$\mathbf{Q}_t = E[\mathbf{w}_t \mathbf{w}_t^\top] = \mathbf{G}_t E[a_t^2] \mathbf{G}_t^\top = \sigma_a^2 \mathbf{G}_t \mathbf{G}_t^\top = \sigma_a^2 \begin{bmatrix} \frac{\Delta t^4}{4} & \frac{\Delta t^3}{2} \\ \frac{\Delta t^3}{2} & \Delta t^2 \end{bmatrix} \tag{9.58}$$

That means that not only $\mathbf{F}$ but also $\mathbf{Q}_t$ and $\mathbf{G}_t$ are independent of t. Thus, we just denote them by $\mathbf{Q}$ and $\mathbf{G}$. (In general, the matrix $\mathbf{Q}_t$ is often only specified in the form of a diagonal matrix.)

In the assumed example, we measure the position of the object at time t (but not its speed); that means that we have the following:

$$\mathbf{y}_t = \begin{bmatrix} 1 & 0 \\ 0 & 0 \end{bmatrix} \mathbf{x}_t + \begin{bmatrix} v_t \\ 0 \end{bmatrix} = \mathbf{H}\mathbf{x}_t + \mathbf{v}_t \tag{9.59}$$

with observation noise $\mathbf{v}_t$ that has the variance matrix

$$\mathbf{R} = E[\mathbf{v}_t \mathbf{v}_t^\top] = \begin{bmatrix} \sigma_y^2 & 0 \\ 0 & 0 \end{bmatrix} \tag{9.60}$$

The initial position equals $\hat{\mathbf{x}}_{0|0} = [0, 0]^\top$. If this position is accurately known, then we have the zero variance matrix

$$\mathbf{P}_{0|0} = \begin{bmatrix} 0 & 0 \\ 0 & 0 \end{bmatrix} \tag{9.61}$$

Otherwise, we have that

$$\mathbf{P}_{0|0} = \begin{bmatrix} c & 0 \\ 0 & c \end{bmatrix} \tag{9.62}$$

with a suitably large real $c > 0$.

Now we are ready to deal with $t = 1$. First, we predict $\hat{\mathbf{x}}_{1|0}$ and calculate its variance matrix $\mathbf{P}_{1|0}$, following the prediction equations

$$\hat{\mathbf{x}}_{t|t-1} = \mathbf{F}\hat{\mathbf{x}}_{t-1|t-1} \tag{9.63}$$

$$\mathbf{P}_{t|t-1} = \mathbf{F}\mathbf{P}_{t-1|t-1}\mathbf{F}^\top + \mathbf{Q} \tag{9.64}$$

Then we calculate the auxiliary data $\tilde{\mathbf{z}}_1$ and $\mathbf{S}_1$, following the update equations

$$\tilde{\mathbf{z}}_t = \mathbf{y}_t - \mathbf{H}\hat{\mathbf{x}}_{t|t-1} \tag{9.65}$$

$$\mathbf{S}_t = \mathbf{HP}_{t|t-1}\mathbf{H}^\top + \mathbf{R} \tag{9.66}$$

This allows us to calculate the optimal Kalman gain $\mathbf{K}_1$ and to update $\hat{\mathbf{x}}_{1|1}$, following the equations

$$\mathbf{K}_t = \mathbf{P}_{t|t-1}\mathbf{H}^\top \mathbf{S}_t^{-1} \tag{9.67}$$

$$\hat{\mathbf{x}}_{t|t} = \hat{\mathbf{x}}_{t|t-1} + \mathbf{K}_t\tilde{\mathbf{z}}_t \tag{9.68}$$

Finally, we calculate $\mathbf{P}_{1|1}$ to prepare for $t = 2$, following the equation

$$\mathbf{P}_{t|t} = (\mathbf{I} - \mathbf{K}_t\mathbf{H})\mathbf{P}_{t|t-1} \tag{9.69}$$

Note that those calculations are basic matrix or vector algebra operations but formally already rather complex. On the other hand, implementation is quite straightforward.

Tuning the Kalman Filter   The specification of the variance matrices $\mathbf{Q}_t$ and $\mathbf{R}_t$, or of the constant $c \geq 0$ in $\mathbf{P}_{0|0}$, influences the number of time slots (say, the "convergence") of the Kalman filter such that the predicted states converge to the true states.

Basically, assuming a higher uncertainty (i.e. larger $c \geq 0$ or larger values in $\mathbf{Q}_t$ and $\mathbf{R}_t$) increases the values in $\mathbf{P}_{t|t-1}$ or $\mathbf{S}_t$; due to the use of the inverse $\mathbf{S}_t^{-1}$ in the definition of the optimal Kalman gain, this decreases the values in $\mathbf{K}_t$ and the contribution of the measurement residual vector in the (update) equation (9.54).

For example, in the extreme case that we are totally sure about the correctness of the initial state $\mathbf{z}_{0|0}$ (i.e. $c = 0$) and that we do not have to assume any noise in the system and in the measurement processes (as in Example 9.7), the matrices $\mathbf{P}_{t|t-1}$ and $\mathbf{S}_t$ degenerate to zero matrices; the inverse $\mathbf{S}_t^{-1}$ does not exist (note: a case to be considered in a program), and $\mathbf{K}_t$ remains undefined. The predicted state is equal to the updated state; this is the fastest possible convergence of the filter.

Alternative Model for Predict Phase   If we have the continuous model matrix $\mathbf{A}$ for the given linear dynamic process $\dot{\mathbf{x}} = \mathbf{A} \cdot \mathbf{x}$, then it is more straightforward to use the equations

$$\dot{\hat{\mathbf{x}}}_{t|t-1} = \mathbf{A}\hat{\mathbf{x}}_{t-1|t-1} + \mathbf{B}_t\mathbf{u}_t \tag{9.70}$$

$$\mathbf{P}_{t|t-1} = \mathbf{AP}_{t-1|t-1}\mathbf{A}^\top + \mathbf{Q}_t \tag{9.71}$$

rather than those using discrete matrices $\mathbf{F}$. (Of course, this also defines a modified matrix $\mathbf{B}$, now defined by the impact of control on the derivatives of state vectors.) This modification in the prediction phase does not have any formal consequence on the update phase.

9.4   Exercises

9.4.1   Programming Exercises

Exercise 9.1 (RANSAC versus Hough) Detect straight lines in images as illustrated in Fig. 3.40; write a generator for noisy line segments if not yet done before. Compare the performance of Hough-transform-based line detection versus RANSAC-based line detection using the ground truth available due to your noisy-line generator.

Design and implement the Hough transform or RANSAC for the two detection processes if not available from other sources. However, in any case, describe how the RANSAC-based method works in detail.

Exercise 9.2 (Box-Filter Scale Space) For $n \geq 0$, apply a 3×3 box filter, as defined in Eq. (2.7), n times repeatedly on a given image I, thus generating a blurred image $B^n(I)$. For $n = 0$, we have the original image $I = B^0(I)$.

Generate a *box-filter scale space* by selecting a finite set of layers defined by $n = 0 < n_1 < \cdots < n_m$. From this we derive a *residual scale space* of corresponding $m + 1$ layers

$$R_n(I) = I - B^n(I)$$

Let keypoints be defined by local maxima or minima as in the LoG or DoG scale space. The radius of the disk of influence is defined by the iteration number n where the keypoint has been detected.

Compare the performance of this keypoint detector with a DoG keypoint detector, following the ideas presented in Sect. 9.2.4.

Exercise 9.3 (Image Retrieval—Query by Example) Search for a "similar" image (similarity by visual content, not by textual description) in a given data base of images. The used data base should contain at least, say, 300 images. Your program allows one to submit any image (not necessarily already in the given database), and the output is a subset of the data base (say, 10 images) sorted by similarity.

Define "similarity" based on the distance between the descriptors of image features. The number of pairs of descriptors being "nearly identical", scaled by the total number of detected keypoints, defines a *measure of similarity*.

Figure 9.24 illustrates such individual best-point-by-point matches between keypoints having "nearly identical" SURF-descriptors. The figure illustrates that those matches do not define one consistent affine (or perspective) transform, such as illustrated in Fig. 9.6, where we assumed similarity between global patterns of keypoints.

Include also the "typical colour" at a keypoint into the descriptor of the used feature detector (e.g. the mean colour in a small neighbourhood). Generate these extended descriptors for the images in your data base.

The algorithmically interesting task now is the following: for a submitted image ("query by example"), calculate the extended descriptors for this image and aim at detecting the "most similar" images in the data base having the similarity definition

Fig. 9.24 Matches between SURF features in both images identified by similarity of descriptors

in mind as given above. In other words, you have to design a particular *classifier* for solving this task. The use of *KD-trees* (not described in this book; see other sources for their definition) can speed up the involved comparison of higher-dimensional vectors.

If the data base can be clustered into classes of "different" images, then a first step might be to calculate the *Mahanalobis distance* (not described in this book; see other sources for its definition) between the input image and the given clusters for identifying then the best matches in the cluster that minimizes the Mahanalobis distance.

Exercise 9.4 (Particle Filter for Lane Detection) Implement the particle filter as described in Sect. 9.3.3 for the single-row model. You may use the distance transform (for EDT) and condensation procedure (for the iteration step in the particle filter) as available in OpenCV. Regarding input sequences, Set 3 in EISATS provides, for example, simple day-time sequences showing clearly marked lane borders.

Exercise 9.5 (Linear Kalman Filter) Implement the Kalman filter described in Example 9.8.

Assume a random sequence of increments $\Delta x_t = x_{t+1} - x_t$ between subsequent positions, e.g. by using the system function RANDOM modelling the uniform distribution.

Modify (increase or decrease) the input parameters $c \geq 0$ and the noise parameters in the variance matrices $\mathbf{Q}$ and $\mathbf{R}$.

Discuss the observed impact on the filter's convergence (i.e. the relation between predicted and updated states of the process).

Note that you have to apply the assumed measurement noise model on the generation of the available data $\mathbf{y}_t$ at time t.

Exercise 9.6 (Integrating Disparity Measurements) Implement a Kalman-filter-based solution for improving the disparities calculated when operating a stereo-vision system in a driving vehicle in a static environment.

1. *Understanding the situation.* Assume an ego-vehicle driving in a static environment. Due to ego-motion, we experience some change in disparity. If we also assume that every pixel is independent, then we can set up *iconic Kalman filters* (i.e. one Kalman filter at each pixel of the image).

2. *Model the state process.* The disparity would be constant in a totally static world (i.e. also no ego-motion; $x_t = d_t = d_{t-1}$ and $\mathbf{F}_{\Delta t} = 1$).

However, we have a moving platform, so this disparity *will* change when the car is moving. The (x, y) pixel position will also change. As the car moves forward, all pixels move outward from the *focus of expansion*.[7] This is where we can use our control variables $\mathbf{B}$ and $\mathbf{u}$.

The state (the disparity) at time t is defined by a disparity at time $t - 1$ (in general at a different pixel) and the control variables.

We assume that the ego-motion is given by inertial sensors because most modern cars will give you velocity v and yaw ψ (amount of angle turned through) in a time frame. This can help us derive where pixels will be moving to in the next time frame.

Mathematically, the control variables are hard to derive and result in nonlinear equations. But we can take a more logical way of thinking. Since we know the vehicle movement in real-world coordinates, we could also use our control variables in the same way. This cannot be shown in a linear mathematical way (by using $\mathbf{B}$ and $\mathbf{u}$).

This process involves triangulating and backprojecting the pixel coordinates plus disparity, i.e. the disparity-map pixels $p = (x, y, d)$ and real-world coordinates $\mathbf{P} = [X, Y, Z]^{\top}$ (in vector format) w.r.t. the ego-vehicle.

For each measurement, we apply the following process:

1. Transform the coordinates (x_{t-1}, y_{t-1}) at time $t - 1$ into the real-world coordinates $\mathbf{P}_{t-1}$, as being a standard in stereo vision.
2. Predict the new position of $\mathbf{P}_{t-1}$ in real-world coordinates using the prediction from motion; for velocity v and yaw ψ, we have that

$$\mathbf{R}_t = \begin{bmatrix} \cos(\psi) & 0 & -\sin(\psi) \\ 0 & 1 & 0 \\ \sin(\psi) & 0 & \cos(\psi) \end{bmatrix} \quad \text{and} \quad \mathbf{T}_t = \frac{v \cdot \Delta t}{\psi} \begin{bmatrix} 1 - \cos(\psi) \\ 0 \\ -\sin(\psi) \end{bmatrix}$$

3. Transform the new real-world coordinates $\mathbf{P}_t = \mathbf{R}_t \mathbf{P}_{t-1} + \mathbf{T}_t$ back to pixel coordinates (x_t, y_t) using backprojection.

Here, $\mathbf{R}_t$ is the rotation matrix in the XZ-plane, due to the change in yaw, and $\mathbf{T}_t$ is the translation matrix between times t and $t - 1$; the angle ψ is the total yaw, and v is the velocity of the car during Δt.

Starting at a pixel (x, y) and disparity d at time $t - 1$, this provides an estimated disparity d' at a pixel (x', y') at time t, identified with being the value of $\mathbf{F}_{\Delta t} \hat{\mathbf{x}}_{t-1|t-1} + \mathbf{B}_t \mathbf{u}_t$ at (x', y'), where $\mathbf{u}_t$ is defined by the yaw rate $\dot{\psi}(t)$ and velocity v_t.

---

[7]This is the retinal point where lines parallel to translatory motion meet, also assuming a corresponding direction of gaze.

3. *Model the measurement process.* In our model, we are filtering our measurements directly (i.e. calculating the disparity). Therefore, for the individual pixel, $\mathbf{y} = y$ and $\mathbf{H} = 1$.

4. *Model the noise.* Disparity measurements have a Gaussian noise distribution in the depth direction (i.e. for sub-pixel measurements), and these can fluctuate to either side. The main state error is in the depth direction; thus, we will assume that $\mathbf{P} = P = \sigma_d^2$.

For our model, both the process and measurement noise (at a single pixel) are scalars. Therefore, $\mathbf{Q} = q_d$ and $\mathbf{R} = r_d$. We could assume that these values change between each iteration t, but we will assume that they remain to be constant.

5. *Test the filter.* The equations simplify at a single pixel as follows:

Predict:

$$\hat{x}_{t|t-1} = \text{as derived above using } \mathbf{u}_t$$

$$P_{t|t-1} = P_{t-1|t-1} + q_d$$

Update:

$$\hat{x}_{t|t} = \hat{x}_{t|t-1} + K_t(y_t - \hat{x}_{t|t-1})$$

$$K_t = P_{t|t-1}(P_{t|t-1} + r)^{-1}$$

$$P_{t|t} = (1 - K_t)P_{t|t-1}$$

The matrix $\mathbf{B}$ in this case is defined by projection at time $t-1$, affine transform, and backprojection at time t. This may be implemented pixel by pixel or for the whole image at once.

The idea here is to choose some logical noise parameters. A logical measurement noise is $r_d = 1$, considering to be up to 1 pixel out in our measurement.

If we want to filter out all moving objects, then a logical process parameter is $q_d = 0.0001$ (i.e., some small value portraying that we assume the model to be good).

This ends the description of the iconic Kalman filter approach. For testing, you need stereo video data recorded in a driving car, with known ego-motion parameters of the car. For example, check KITTI and EISATS for such data. Figure 9.25 illustrates the results when following the proposed method. Compare whether you achieve similar improvements above the original data when not using the iconic Kalman filters. Because we assumed a static world, we can expect that there will be errors on moving objects such as the cyclist in Fig. 9.25.

Insert 9.10 (Iconic Kalman Filters) *For the iconic Kalman filters in Exercise 9.6, see* [T. Vaudrey, H. Badino, and S. Gehrig. Integrating disparity images by incorporating disparity rate. In Proc. Robot Vision, pp. 29–42, 2008].

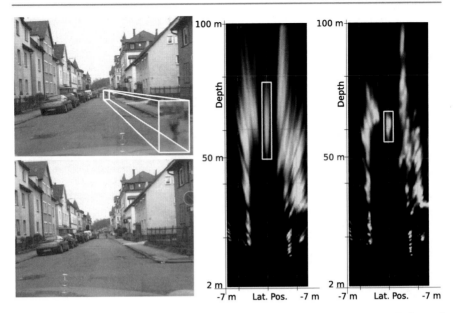

Fig. 9.25 The *left images* are a stereo pair also showing a moving cyclist on the road in front of the ego-vehicle. The *right-hand grid* shows the bird's-eye view of the depth map (i.e. the disparity projected into 3D coordinates); the *left-hand grid* shows the results using no Kalman integration; the *right-hand grid* shows the results using the iconic filters

9.4.2 Non-programming Exercises

Exercise 9.7 At the end of Sect. 9.1.2 there is a proposal how to detect keypoints at subpixel accuracy. Assume values a_N, a_E, a_S, a_W (for the 4-adjacent pixel locations) and a_p (at the detected keypoint pixel) for function g and provide a general solution for subpixel accuracy.

Exercise 9.8 The algorithm in Fig. 9.8 lists two procedures `ransacFitPlane` and `ransacRefinePlaneModel`. Specify such two procedures for initial and refined plane fitting following the general RANSAC idea.

Exercise 9.9 On p. 359 it is suggested to generate a bird's-eye view by using a homography, defined by four marked points being the corners of a trapezoid in the image, but actually the corners of a rectangular region on the road. Specify this homography.

Exercise 9.10 Explain the motivations behind the definitions of particle weights given in (9.36) to (9.40).

Exercise 9.11 Show that $\mathbf{F}_{\Delta t} = \mathbf{I} + \Delta t \mathbf{A} + \frac{\Delta t^2}{2} \mathbf{A}^2$ for the matrix $\mathbf{A}$ as defined in Example 9.7.

Object Detection

10

This final chapter provides an introduction into classification and learning with a detailed description of basic AdaBoost and the use of random forests. These concepts are illustrated by applications for face detection and pedestrian detection, respectively.

10.1 Localization, Classification, and Evaluation

The title of this section lists three basic steps of an object detection system. *Object candidates* are localized within a rectangular *bounding box*. A bounding box is a special example for a *region of interest* (RoI). See Fig. 10.1.

Localized object candidates are mapped by classification either in *detected objects* or *rejected candidates*. Classification results should be evaluated within the system or by a subsequent performance analysis of the system. Figure 10.2 illustrates face detection.

A *true-positive*, also called a *hit* or a *detection*, is a correctly detected object. A *false-positive*, also called a *miss* or a *false detection*, occurs if we detect an object where there is none. A *false-negative* denotes a case where we miss an object, and a *true-negative* describes the cases where non-object regions are correctly identified as non-object regions. Figure 10.2 contains one false-positive (the largest square) and two false-negatives (a man in the middle and a girl on the right of the image). A head seen from the side (one case in the figure) does not define a face.

10.1.1 Descriptors, Classifiers, and Learning

Classification is defined by membership in constructed pairwise-disjoint *classes* being subsets of $\mathbb{R}^n$ for a given value $n > 0$. In other words, classes define a partitioning of the space $\mathbb{R}^n$. Time-efficiency is an important issue when performing classification. This subsection only provides a few brief basic explanations for the extensive area of classification algorithms.

R. Klette, *Concise Computer Vision*, Undergraduate Topics in Computer Science,
DOI 10.1007/978-1-4471-6320-6_10, © Springer-Verlag London 2014

Fig. 10.1 Localized bounding boxes aiming at detecting vehicles and people

Fig. 10.2 Face detection with one false-positive and two false-negatives (not counting the side-view of a face)

Descriptors   A *descriptor* $\mathbf{x} = (x_1, \dots, x_n)$ is a point in an n-dimensional real space $\mathbb{R}^n$, called *descriptor space*, representing measured or calculated property values in a given order (e.g. a SIFT descriptor is of length $n = 128$).[1] See Fig. 10.3 for

---

[1] In classification theory, a descriptor is usually also called a *feature*. A feature in an image that, as commonly used in image analysis, combines a keypoint and a descriptor. Thus, we continue to use "descriptor" rather than "feature" for avoiding confusion.

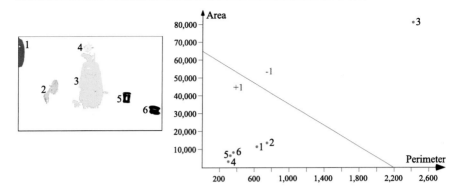

Fig. 10.3 *Left*: Six regions in an image. *Right*: Corresponding descriptors in a 2D descriptor space defined by the properties "perimeter" and "area" for image regions. The *blue line* defines a binary classifier; it subdivides the descriptor space into two half-planes such that the descriptors in one half-plane have the value +1 assigned and −1 in the other

an illustration for $n = 2$. For example, we have a descriptor $\mathbf{x}_1 = (621.605, 10940)$ for Segment 1 in this descriptor space defined by the properties "perimeter" and "area".

Classifiers   A *classifier* assigns class numbers to descriptors, typically, first, to a given set $\{\mathbf{x}_1, \ldots, \mathbf{x}_m\}$ of already-classified descriptors for *training* (the *learning set*), and then to the descriptors generated for recorded image or video data while being applied:

1. A (general) classifier assigns class numbers $1, 2, \ldots, k$ for $k > 1$ classes and 0 for 'not classified'.
2. A binary classifier assigns class numbers −1 and +1 in the cases where we are only interested whether a particular event (e.g. 'driver has closed eyes') occurs, specified by output +1.

   A classifier is *weak* if it does not perform up to expectations (e.g. it might be just a bit better than random guessing); multiple weak classifiers can be mapped into a *strong classifier*, aiming at a satisfactory solution of a classification problem. A statistical combination of multiple weak classifiers into one strong classifier is discussed in Sect. 10.2. Weak or strong classifiers can be general-case (i.e. multi-class) classifiers or just binary classifiers; just being "binary" does not define "weak".

Example 10.1 (Binary Classifier by Linear Separation)   A binary classifier may be defined by constructing a hyperplane $\Pi : \mathbf{w}^\top \mathbf{x} + b = 0$ in $\mathbb{R}^n$ for $n \geq 1$. Vector $\mathbf{w} \in \mathbb{R}^n$ is the *weight vector*, and the real $b \in \mathbb{R}$ is the *bias* of Π. For $n = 2$ or $n = 3$, $\mathbf{w}$ is the gradient or normal orthogonal to the defined line or plane, respectively.

One side of the hyperplane (including the plane itself) defines the value "+1", and the other side (not including the plane itself) the value "−1". See Fig. 10.3 for an example for $n = 2$; the hyperplane is a straight line in this case, and for $n = 1$, it

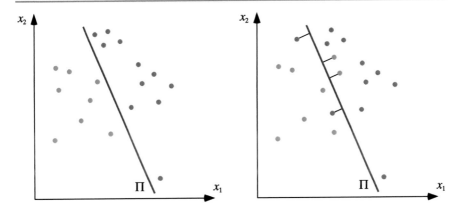

Fig. 10.4 *Left*: A linear-separable distribution of descriptors pre-classified to be either in class "+1" (*green descriptors*) or "−1" (*red descriptors*). *Right*: This distribution is not linear separable; the sum of the shown distances (*black line segments*) of four misclassified descriptors defines the total error for the shown separation line Π

is just a point separating $\mathbb{R}^1$. Formally, let

$$h(\mathbf{x}) = \mathbf{w}^\top \mathbf{x} + b \tag{10.1}$$

The cases $h(\mathbf{x}) > 0$ or $h(\mathbf{x}) < 0$ then define the class values "+1" or "−1" for one side of the hyperplane Π.

Such a linear classifier (i.e. defined by the weight vector $\mathbf{w}$ and bias b) can be calculated for a distribution of (pre-classified) training descriptors in the nD descriptor space *if* the given distribution is *linear separable*. See Fig. 10.4, left. If this is not the case, then we define the *error* for a misclassified descriptor $\mathbf{x}$ by its perpendicular distance[2]

$$d_2(\mathbf{x}, \Pi) = \frac{|\mathbf{w}^\top \mathbf{x} + b|}{\|\mathbf{w}\|_2} \tag{10.2}$$

to the hyperplane Π, and then the task is to calculate a hyperplane Π such that the total error for all misclassified training descriptors is minimized. See Fig. 10.4, right.

Example 10.2 (Classification by Using a Binary Decision Tree) A classifier can also be defined by binary decisions at *split nodes* in a tree (i.e. "yes" or "no"). Each decision is formalized by a *rule*, and given input data can be tested whether they satisfy the rule or not. Accordingly, we proceed with the identified successor node in the tree. Each *leaf node* of the tree defines finally an assignment of data arriving at this node into classes. For example, each leaf node can identify exactly one class in $\mathbb{R}^n$. See Fig. 10.5.

---

[2]This is the error defined in margin-based classifiers such as support vector machines. This error is (usually) not explicitly used in AdaBoost.

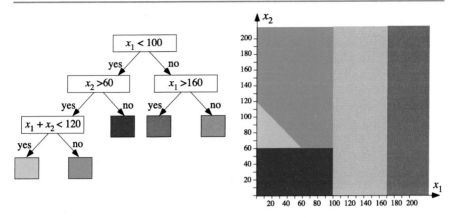

Fig. 10.5 *Left*: A decision tree. *Right*: A resulting subdivision in 2D descriptor space

The tested rules in the shown tree define straight lines in the 2D descriptor space. Descriptors arriving at one of the leaf nodes are then in one of the shown subsets of $\mathbb{R}^2$.

A single decision tree, or just one split node in such a tree, can be considered to be an example for a weak classifier; a set of decision trees (called a *forest*) is needed for being able to define a strong classifier.

Observation 10.1 *A single decision tree provides a way to partition a descriptor space in multiple regions (i.e. classes); when applying binary classifiers defined by linear separation, we need to combine several of those to achieve a similar partitioning of a descriptor space in multiple regions.*

Learning   *Learning* is the process of defining or training a classifier based on a set of descriptors; *classification* is then the actual application of the classifier. During classification, we may also identify some mis-behaviour (e.g. "assumed" mis-classifications), and this again can lead to another phase of learning. The set of descriptors used for learning may be pre-classified or not.

Supervised Learning   In *supervised learning* we assign class numbers to descriptors "manually" based on expertise (e.g. "yes, the driver does have closed eyes in this image"). As a result, we can define a classifier by locating optimized separating manifolds in $\mathbb{R}^n$ for the training set of descriptors. A hyperplane Π is the simplest case of an optimized separating manifold; see Example 10.1. An alternative use of expert knowledge for supervised learning is the specification of rules at nodes in a decision tree; see Example 10.2. This requires knowledge about possible sequences of decisions.

Unsupervised Learning   In *unsupervised learning* we do not have prior knowledge about class memberships of descriptors. When aiming at separations in the descriptor space (similar to Example 10.1), we may apply a clustering algorithm for a

Fig. 10.6 *Top left*: Two positive samples of bounding boxes for pedestrians. *Top right*: Two negative samples of bounding boxes for pedestrians. *Bottom left*: Positive patches, which possibly belong to a pedestrian. *Bottom right*: Negative patches for pedestrians

given set of descriptors for identifying a separation of $\mathbb{R}^n$ into classes. For example, we may analyse the density of the distribution of given descriptors in $\mathbb{R}^n$; a region having a dense distribution defines a *seed point* of one class, and then we assign all descriptors to identified seed points by applying, for example, the nearest-neighbour rule.

When aiming at defining decision trees for partitioning the descriptor space (similar to Example 10.2), we can learn decisions at nodes of a decision tree based on some general data analysis rules. (This will be detailed later for random decision forests.) The data distribution then "decides" about the generated rules.

Combined Learning Approaches   There are also cases where we may combine supervised learning with strategies known from unsupervised learning. For example, we can decide whether a given image window, also called a *bounding box*, shows a pedestrian; this defines the supervised part in learning. See Fig. 10.6. We can also decide for a *patch*, being a subwindow of a bounding box, whether it *possibly* belongs to a pedestrian. For example, in Fig. 10.6, the head of the cyclist is also considered to belong possibly to a pedestrian.

When we generate descriptors for bounding boxes or patches (e.g. measured image intensities at selected pixel locations), then we cannot decide anymore manually for each individual descriptor whether it is characteristic for a pedestrian or not.

For example, for a set of given image windows, we know that they are all parts of pedestrians, and the algorithm designed for generating a classifier decides at some point to use a particular feature of those windows for processing them further; but this particular feature might not be generic in the sense that it separates any window showing a part of a pedestrian from any window showing no part of a pedestrian.

Such an "internal" mechanism in a program that generates a classifier defines an unsupervised part in learning. The overall task is to combine available supervision with unsupervised data analysis when generating a classifier.

10.1.2 Performance of Object Detectors

An *object detector* is defined by applying a classifier for an object detection problem. We assume that any made decision can be evaluated as being either correct or false. For example, see Fig. 10.2.

Evaluations of designed object detectors are required to compare their performance under particular conditions. There are common *measures* in pattern recognition or information retrieval for performance evaluation of classifiers.

Let tp or fp denote the numbers of true-positives or false-positives, respectively. Analogously, we define tn and fn for the negatives. In Fig. 10.2 we have $tp = 12$, $fp = 1$, and $fn = 2$. Just the image in this figure does not indicate how many non-object regions have been analysed (and correctly identified as being no faces); thus, we cannot specify the number tn; we need to analyse the applied classifier for obtaining tn. Thus, tn is not a common entry for performance measures.

Precision (PR) Versus Recall (RC) The *precision* is the ratio of true-positives compared to all detections. The *recall* (or *sensitivity*) is the ratio of true-positives compared to all potentially possible detections (i.e. to the number of all visible objects). Formally,

$$PR = \frac{tp}{tp+fp} \quad \text{and} \quad RC = \frac{tp}{tp+fn} \tag{10.3}$$

$PR = 1$, termed *1-precision*, means that no false-positive is detected. $RC = 1$ means that all the visible objects in an image are detected and that there is no false-negative.

Miss Rate (MR) Versus False-Positives per Image (FPPI) The *miss rate* is the ratio of false-negatives compared to all objects in an image. False-positives per image is the ratio of false-positives compared to all detected objects. Formally,

$$MR = \frac{fn}{tp+fn} \quad \text{and} \quad FPPI = \frac{fp}{tp+fp} \tag{10.4}$$

MR = 0 means that all the visible objects in the image are detected, which is equivalent to RC = 1. FPPI = 0 means that all the detected objects are correctly classified, which is equivalent to 1-precision.

True-Negative Rate (TNR) Versus Accuracy (AC)   These measures also use the number tn. The *true-negative rate* (or *specificity*) is the ratio of true-negatives compared to all decisions in "no-object" regions. The *accuracy* is the ratio of correct decisions compared to all decisions. Formally,

$$\text{TNR} = \frac{tn}{tn + fp} \quad \text{and} \quad \text{AC} = \frac{tp + tn}{tp + tn + fp + fn} \tag{10.5}$$

As we are usually not interested in numbers of true-negatives, these two measures have less significance in performance evaluation studies.

Detected?   How to decide whether a detected object is a true-positive? Assume that objects in images have been locally identified manually by bounding boxes, serving as the ground truth. All detected objects are matched with these *ground-truth boxes* by calculating ratios of areas of overlapping regions

$$a_o = \frac{\mathscr{A}(D \cap T)}{\mathscr{A}(D \cup T)} \tag{10.6}$$

where $\mathscr{A}$ denotes the area of a region in an image (see Sect. 3.2.1), D is the detected bounding box of the object, and T is the area of the bounding box of the matched ground-truth box. If a_o is larger than a threshold T, say $T = 0.5$, the detected object is taken as a true-positive. But there might be more than one possible matching this way for a detected bounding box. In this case, the one with the largest a_o-value is the one used for deciding about true-positive, while the others are considered to be false-positive.

10.1.3 Histogram of Oriented Gradients

The *histogram of oriented gradients* (HoG) is a common way to derive a descriptor for a *bounding box* for an object candidate. For example, a window of the size of the expected bounding box can move through an image, and the scan stops at potential object candidates, possibly guided by the results provided by stereo vision (e.g. the expected size of an object at a given distance) or by a feature detector. After a potential bounding box has been identified, a process for descriptor calculation starts, and we explain here for the case of HoG descriptors.

Figure 10.7 illustrates a subdivision of a bounding box (of a pedestrian) into larger blocks and smaller cells for calculating the HoG.

Algorithm for Calculating the HoG Descriptor   We briefly outline an example of a possible algorithm for calculating HoG descriptors from a selected bounding box:

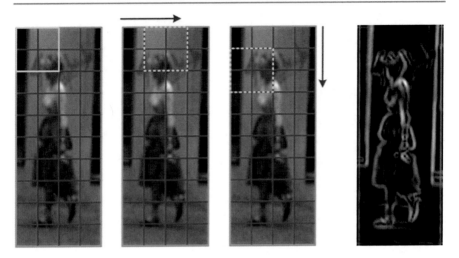

Fig. 10.7 Blocks and cells when calculating an HoG descriptor in a bounding box (the *blue rectangle*). *Yellow solid* or *dashed rectangles* denote blocks, which are subdivided into *red rectangles* (i.e. the cells). The three windows on the *left* show how a block moves *left* to *right*, *top down*, through a bounding box, when generating the descriptor. The window on the *right illustrates* magnitudes of estimated gradient vectors

1. *Preprocessing.* Apply intensity normalization (e.g. see conditional scaling in Sect. 2.1.1) and a smoothing filter on the given image window I.
2. *Calculate an edge map.* Estimate directional derivatives in the x- and y-directions, and derive the gradient magnitudes and gradient angles for each pixel, generating a magnitude map I_m (see Fig. 10.7, right) and an angle map I_a.
3. *Spatial binning.* Perform the following two steps:
   (a) Group pixels in non-overlapping *cells* (e.g. 8×8); see Fig. 10.7, left.
   (b) Use maps I_m and I_a to accumulate magnitude values into *direction bins* (e.g., nine bins for intervals of $20°$ each, for covering a full $180°$ range) to obtain a *voting vector* (e.g. of length 9) for each cell; see Fig. 10.8. Integral images can be used for a time-efficient calculation of these sums.
4. *Normalize voting values for generating a descriptor.* Perform two steps:
   (a) Group cells (e.g., 2×2) into one block.
   (b) Normalize voting vectors over each block and combine them into one *block vector* (e.g. four cell vectors into a block vector of length 36).
5. Augment all block vectors consecutively; this produces the final *HoG descriptor.* For example, if a block consists of four cells and the bounding box size is 64×128, the HoG descriptor has 3,780 elements; it might be convenient to rearrange this descriptor vector into one *descriptor matrix* **B** (e.g. of size 420×9).

Bounding boxes used for training or applying a classifier for pedestrian detection or classification are usually normalized to an identical size (e.g. 64×192, both multiples of 32, just to give an idea about numbers). Different cell sizes (e.g. 8×8, 16×16, and 32×32) can be adopted to generate HoG descriptor vectors.

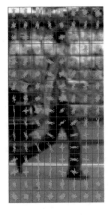

Fig. 10.8 The length of vectors in nine different directions in each cell represents the accumulated magnitude of gradient vectors into one of those nine directions

Insert 10.1 (Origin of the Use of HoG Descriptors) *Histograms of oriented gradients have been proposed in* [N. Dalal and B. Triggs. Histograms of oriented gradients for human detection. In Proc. Computer Vision Pattern Recognition, 886–893, 2005] *for detecting pedestrians in static images.*

10.1.4 Haar Wavelets and Haar Features

We describe a general appearance-based object-detection method, which utilizes integral images (see Sect. 2.2.1) for time-efficient object detection.

Haar Wavelets   Consider simple binary patterns as illustrated in Fig. 10.9, left and middle. These are called *Haar wavelets* (see Insert 10.2 for the historic background of this name). A white pixel in such a wavelet defines weight +1, and a black pixel weight −1. These wavelets are used for testing "rough brightness similarity" with such a pattern in an image.

See Fig. 10.9, right, for positioning individual Haar wavelets in an image. For example, consider a Haar wavelet $\psi = [W_1, W_2, B]$ defined by two white regions W_1 and W_2 and one black region B. Assume that each Haar wavelet comes with a reference point, for example, its lower-left corner. We translate this wavelet in an image I and position its reference point at a pixel location p. At this moment we have a placed Haar wavelet ψ_p (we consider image I as being fixed and do not include it into the notation), where W_1 occupies a rectangular image region $W_1(p) \subset \Omega$, W_2 covers $W_2(p) \subset \Omega$, and B is now a subset $B(p) \subset \Omega$. Let

$$S_W = \sum_{p \in W} I(p) \tag{10.7}$$

be the sum of all image values within the set $W \subset \Omega$.

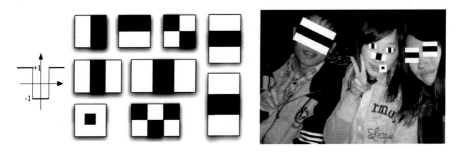

Fig. 10.9 *Left*: A 1D profile for a Haar wavelet; this wavelet is shown right of this profile. *Middle*: A few samples of isothetic Haar wavelets. *Right*: Locations in human faces where the shown Haar wavelets "roughly" match brightness distributions, with "*Black*" matches darker regions and "*White*" brighter regions. See Fig. 5.2, top left, for the original image AnnieYukiTim

Value of a Haar Wavelet The *value* of a Haar wavelet ψ at a reference pixel p might be defined by a sum such as

$$\mathscr{V}(\psi_p) = S_{W_1} + S_{W_2} - S_B \tag{10.8}$$

Figure 10.9, right, illustrates that image intensities in regions at forehead, eyes, and below eyes in a human face correspond to the (slightly rotated) pattern shown for the face on the left, the left-to-right distribution of intensities at a human eye, across the nose, and the intensity distribution at the corner of the mouth are illustrated for the face in the middle and individual eye brightness patterns for the face on the right. In all those cases, the black regions of the placed Haar wavelets are on top of darker regions in the image, and the white regions on top of brighter regions in the image. Thus, we add in (10.8) high values (i.e. close to G_{max}) in S_{W_1} and S_{W_2} and subtract only small values (i.e. close to 0) with S_B.

The size of the white or black regions in a Haar wavelet ψ also needs to be considered for "balancing" out values $\mathscr{V}(\psi_p)$ (e.g. the possible impact of values in two large white regions or in one small black region in one Haar wavelet should be "fairly" split by increasing the weight of the small black region). Thus, it is appropriate to use *weights* $\omega_i > 0$ for adjusting those values. Instead of sums as in (10.8), we will actually use weighted sums such as

$$\mathscr{V}(\psi_p) = \omega_1 \cdot S_{W_1} + \omega_2 \cdot S_{W_2} - \omega_3 \cdot S_B \tag{10.9}$$

when combining sums defined by regions in a placed Haar wavelet. The weights ω_i need to be specified when defining a Haar wavelet.

Insert 10.2 (Haar, Hadamard, Rademacher, Walsh, and the Origin of the Viola-Jones Technique) *The Hungarian mathematician A. Haar* (1885–1933) *introduced in* [A. Haar. Zur Theorie der orthogonalen Funktionensysteme, Mathematische Annalen, 69:331–371, 1910] *a very simple wavelet transform. Simplicity is de-*

fined by its base functions. Analogously to the 2D Fourier transform, the 2D Haar transform calculates a representation of a given matrix (in our context, of an image) with respect to a set of 2D base functions representing 2D wave patterns of different wavelengths and directions. The Haar transform "stays in the real domain", it does not use or generate non-real complex numbers.

In case of 2D discrete data we can apply the discrete Haar transform where base functions are given by recursively defined matrices with only a few different values, such as $0, 1, -1, \sqrt{2}$, or 2. Due to having integral image values only, the discrete Haar transform of an image can even be implemented using integer arithmetic only. When transforming $N \times N$ images, with $N = 2^n$, the 2D wave patterns are $N \times N$ matrices.

The Hadamard–Rademacher–Walsh transform is of similar simplicity with respect to used base functions; it is named after the French mathematician J. Hadamard (1865–1963), the German mathematician H. Rademacher (1892–1969), and the US-American mathematician J.L. Walsh (1895–1973).

For deriving Haar wavelets, the 2D wave patterns used by either discrete Haar or discrete Hadamard–Rademacher–Walsh transform, are simplified having values "+1" (represented by "White") or "−1" (represented by "Black") only. Haar wavelets can be seen as rectangular subwindows of general Haar or Hadamard–Rademacher–Walsh 2D wave patterns.

The use of Haar wavelets for object detection has been proposed in the paper [P. Viola and M. Jones. Rapid object detection using a boosted cascade of simple features. In Proc. Conf. Computer Vision Pattern Recognition, 8 pp., 2001], *together with a complete proposal of an object-detection technique. This paper defines a "landmark" for having today time-efficient and accurate face detection available.*

Value Calculation by Using Integral Images As discussed in Sect. 2.2.1, the calculation of a sum S_W can be done time-efficiently by generating an integral image I_{int} first for the given input image I. See (2.12). By providing (2.13) we only specified sums for isothetic rectangular regions.

This can be generalized to rotated rectangular regions. For selected rotation angles φ with respect to the x-axis, we also calculate the rotated integral images. For example, for $\varphi = \pi/4$, the calculation of the integral image I_φ is simply given by

$$I_{\pi/4}(x, y) = \sum_{|x-i| \leq y-j \wedge 1 \leq j \leq y} I(i, j) \qquad (10.10)$$

Here, (x, y) can be any point in the real isothetic rectangle defined by the corner points $(1, 1)$ and (N_{cols}, N_{rows}), and (i, j) is a pixel location in the image carrier Ω. See Fig. 10.10, left.

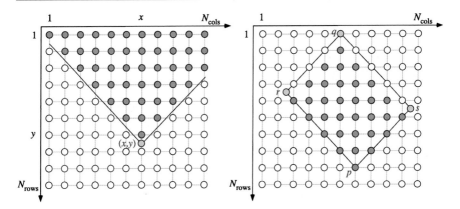

Fig. 10.10 *Left*: An area for point location (x, y) for taking the sum of image values for $I_{\pi/4}$. *Right*: A rectangular region defined by four corner points, where p and q are the defining grid points, and the corner points r and s follow from those two grid points when using $\varphi = \pi/4$ as the defining angle for the rectangle

For angles not equal to zero or $\pi/4$, the calculation formula is not as simple, but follows the same ideas. For a rectangular region W, rotated by an angle φ with respect to the x-axis and defined by the corner pixel locations p and q, and the calculated corner points r and s (see Fig. 10.10, right), we obtain that

$$S_W = I_\varphi(p) - I_\varphi(r) - I_\varphi(s) + I_\varphi(q) \qquad (10.11)$$

The calculation of any $N_{rows} \times N_{cols}$ integral image I_φ only takes $\mathcal{O}(N_{rows}N_{cols})$ time. A selection of a few angles ϕ is typically sufficient.

Haar Features The value of a placed Haar wavelet ψ_p is now used to decide whether we have a *Haar feature* at this location in the image I. For deciding, we use a parity $\rho \in \{-1, +1\}$ and a threshold θ:

$$\mathcal{F}(\psi_p) = \begin{cases} +1 & \text{if } \mathcal{V}(\psi_p) \le \rho \cdot \theta \\ -1 & \text{otherwise} \end{cases} \qquad (10.12)$$

If $\mathcal{F}(\psi_p) = 1$, then we have a Haar feature detected at p. If black regions in the Haar wavelet are supposed to correspond to dark pixels (and, thus, white regions to bright pixels), then we use parity $\rho = -1$.

10.1.5 Viola–Jones Technique

A *mask* is a window that contains a small number of Haar wavelets, such as two or three. Figure 10.11 illustrates the positioning of three different (here non-square) masks of the same size at the same location in an image.

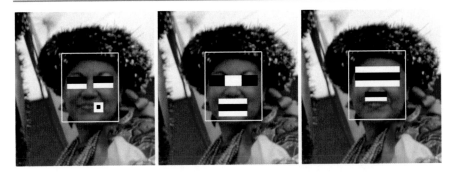

Fig. 10.11 Three non-square masks of identical size are positioned at the same location in an image; each mask contains two or three Haar wavelets in this example. The Haar descriptor calculated for one mask defines one weak classifier; a set of such masks (i.e. a set of weak classifiers) is used to decide whether there is a face in that window occupied by the masks. A detail in the image Michoacan; see Fig. 10.12 for the image

Haar Descriptors Assume a mask $M = [\psi_1, \psi_2, \psi_3]$ that contains, for example, three Haar-wavelets. This mask has a reference point, say, at its lower left corner. We position the mask in image I by moving this reference point into a pixel location p, and, for simplicity, we take p also as reference pixel for the three involved Haar wavelets. This defines now a *Haar descriptor*

$$\mathscr{D}(M_p) = \mathscr{F}(\psi_{1,p}) + \mathscr{F}(\psi_{2,p}) + \mathscr{F}(\psi_{3,p}) \qquad (10.13)$$

which is just an integer (thus a 1D descriptor only).

Weak Classifier A threshold $\tau > 0$ is now finally used to assign a binary value

$$h(M_p) = \begin{cases} +1 & \text{if } \mathscr{D}(M_p) \geq \tau \\ -1 & \text{otherwise} \end{cases} \qquad (10.14)$$

For example, Fig. 10.11 illustrates a case where three different placed masks $M_{1,p}$, $M_{2,p}$, and $M_{3,p}$ (of the same size) are used at the same reference pixel p, defining three weak classifiers $h(M_{1,p})$, $h(M_{2,p})$, and $h(M_{3,p})$ for the same window W_p, also denoted by

$$h_j = h(M_{j,p}) \quad \text{for } j = 1, 2, 3 \qquad (10.15)$$

A *strong classifier* is then needed to combine those values of weak classifiers into a final object detection result.

Sliding Masks The goal of the applied *sliding search* is to detect an object in a sliding window that defines the size of the applied masks. We have two options:
1. Generate an image pyramid (see Sect. 2.2.2) first and then slide masks of constant size in different layers of the pyramid.
2. Use the input image only at the given size but vary the size of the sliding masks.

Fig. 10.12 Variation in sizes of faces in the image Michoacan. The applied face detector detects larger faces when using larger masks and smaller faces (see the two on the *right*) by using the same masks but with reduced size. There are two false-negatives here; it appears that the used strong classifier is trained for "visible forehead"

In contrast to scale-space techniques, let us chose the second option here. We keep the image size constant, and masks of different sizes are used for detecting smaller or larger objects. See Fig. 10.12. Typically, we have an estimate for the minimum and maximum size of objects of interest.

The set of used masks is initially defined for one window size. For each window size, we scan the input image completely, top-down, left-to-right, calculating the Haar descriptors for each placed mask, thus a weak classifier, the weak classifiers are mapped into a strong classifier, and this one will tell us whether we have an object detected or not. Then we move on with the sliding window and apply again all masks in the next window position. When arriving at the lower-left corner of the image, we start again with a modified size of the search window (and thus the corresponding scaling of all masks) at the upper-left corner of the image, until finished with all the sizes of windows considered to be of relevance.

Figure 10.13 illustrates an increase of the size of a rectangular sliding window by factor $\Delta z = 1.1$.

At least 10 % increase in width and height of the sliding window ensures time efficiency. Larger percentages decrease the accuracy of the detection; this is a trade-off to be considered.

Scan Orders   The sliding search aims at detecting every visible object. An exhaustive search is the default option (as suggested above from the top-left corner

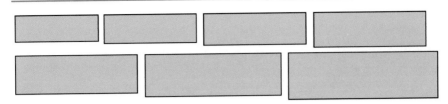

Fig. 10.13 Subsequent increases of the size of a rectangular window by factor $\Delta z = 1.1$, using a uniform scaling in the x- and y-directions. (Masks are usually square-shaped, not elongated.)

of the image to the bottom-right corner), with a scaling factor Δz in the x- and y-directions such that masks, where each contains a few Haar wavelets, go from a defined minimum size to a defined maximum size.

The Viola–Jones Object Detection Technique   The technique, proposed in 2001 (see Insert 10.2), was primarily motivated by face detection, but can also be applied to other classes of objects characterized by "typical shading patterns". The technique combines:

1. The generation of w weak classifiers h_j, $1 \leq j \leq w$, each defined by one of the w given masks; each mask contains k_j (e.g. 2 to 4) Haar wavelets; masks are systematically varied in sizes and slided through the input image.
2. The use of a statistical boosting algorithm to assemble those w weak classifiers $h_1, \ldots, h_w$ into one strong classifier H (the subject of the next section).
3. The application of the assembled cascade of weak classifiers for object detection.

There are several parameters involved in the process.

First, at the "micro-scale", for each used Haar wavelet, either isothetic or rotated by some angle φ, we have weights $\omega_i > 0$ that adjust the influence of the black or white rectangles, a parity $\rho \in \{-1, +1\}$ defining whether "black–white" should match either "dark–bright" or "bright–dark", and a threshold $\theta > 0$ defining the sensitivity of the Haar wavelet for detecting a Haar feature.

Second, at the "macro-scale", for each mask M_j, $1 \leq j \leq w$, we have a threshold τ_j defining when the Haar descriptor $\mathscr{D}(M_{j,p})$ defines value $h_j = +1$; in this case the weak classifier h_j *indicates* that there might be an object (e.g. a face).

Face Detection and Post-Processing   The w results of the weak classifiers $h_1, \ldots, h_w$ at a placed window are passed on to the trained strong classifier for detecting either a face or a no-face situation. If a face is detected, then we identify its position with the rectangular box of the window used at this moment.

After classification, usually there are multiple overlapping object detections at different locations and of different sizes around a visible object. Post-processing returns a single detection per object. Methods applied for post-processing are usually heuristic (e.g. taking some kind of a mean over the detected rectangular boxes). See Fig. 10.14 for an illustration of this final post-processing step.

Fig. 10.14 *Left*: Multiple detections of a face in the image Rocio. *Right*: The final result after post-processing of multiple detections

10.2 AdaBoost

AdaBoost is an adaptive machine-learning meta-algorithm. Its name is short for *adaptive boosting*. It is a *meta-algorithm* because it addresses sub-procedures, called *weak classifiers*, which may be differently specified (in the previous section we identified binary classifiers with weak classifiers). At the beginning, when starting with AdaBoost, we have $w > 1$ weak classifiers, defined by functions h_j (see the hyperplane definition in (10.1) for an example), which map the descriptor space $\mathbb{R}^n$ into $\{-1, +1\}$.

AdaBoost is *adaptive* by iteratively reducing mis-classifications: the weights of mis-classified descriptors are adjusted for the benefit of generating a combined (weighted) application of the given w weak classifiers at the end.

> **Insert 10.3** (Origin of AdaBoost) *The paper* [Y. Freud and R. Schapire. A decision-theoretic generalization of on-line learning and an application to boosting. J. Computer System Sciences, vol. 55, pp. 119–139, 1995] *initiated extensive work on AdaBoost algorithms. Today there are many variants available, and we only discuss the basic AdaBoost strategy in this chapter.*

10.2.1 Algorithm

We assume a case of supervised learning. We have a set of $m > 1$ pre-classified descriptors $\mathbf{x}_1, \ldots, \mathbf{x}_m$ in $\mathbb{R}^n$, already classified by having assigned values $y_i \in \{-1, +1\}$ for $i = 1, \ldots, m$.

Fig. 10.15 Five examples of descriptors in 2D descriptor space

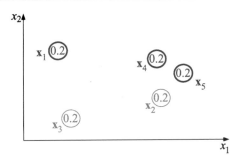

For example, for using AdaBoost for training a strong classifier for face detection, we use a large dataset of face and no-face images. Assume that we have $n > 0$ measurements in an image window showing a human face, such as the values $\mathscr{V}(\psi_p)$ for a set of placed Haar wavelets ψ_p. Those n values define a point in $\mathbb{R}^n$. For a shown face, we can also classify it 'manually' into "forward looking" $(+1)$ or "not forward looking" (-1) if the object detection task is more specific than just detecting a face.

Example 10.3 (A Five-Descriptor and Two-Weak-Classifier Example) We consider five descriptors $\mathbf{x_1}$ to $\mathbf{x_5}$ in a 2D descriptor space. See Fig. 10.15. We have $m = 5$. Each point is shown by a disk labelled with weight $1/5$, uniformly for all the five points. At the beginning in AdaBoost, each descriptor $\mathbf{x_i}$ is weighted uniformly by $\omega(i) = 1/m$ for $i = 1, \ldots, m$.

Corresponding events (e.g. images showing a human face), leading to those descriptors, have been classified. A bold blue circular line indicates the class number $+1$ and the thin red line class number -1.

We assume two weak classifiers (i.e. $w = 2$), denoted by h_1 and h_2. The classifier h_1 assigns the class number "$+1$" to any of the five descriptors, and the classifier h_2 only to $\mathbf{x}_1$ and $\mathbf{x}_5$, otherwise "-1". Let

$$W_j = \sum_{i=1}^{m} \omega(i) \cdot [\![y_i \neq h_j(\mathbf{x}_i)]\!] \tag{10.16}$$

where $[\![\mathscr{R}]\!]$ equals 1 if $\mathscr{R}$ is true and 0 otherwise.

It follows that $W_1 = 0.4$ and $W_2 = 0.2$. The classifier h_2 is more consistent with the given classification, $W_2 < 0.5$. In conclusion, we give h_2 control about modifying the weights of the data. A weight $\omega(i)$ can be interpreted as the cost of misclassification of an observation. Thus, W_j is the average misclassification cost for the classifier h_j because all weights sum up to 1. To be continued in Example 10.4.

AdaBoost Iteration Calculations as in Example 10.3 define the start of an iteration. Weights $\omega(i)$ are modified in iterations for $i = 1, \ldots, m$. This leads then to new accumulated weights W_j for $j = 1, \ldots, w$. For the new accumulated weights W_j, we look again for the classifier h_j that defines the minimum. If this minimum is greater than or equal to 0.5, then we stop.

Iteration Index Iterations run from $t = 1$ to $t = T$ defined by the case that the minimum of the accumulated weights was greater than or equal to 0.5.

Initialization of the Iteration Let $\omega_1(i) = \omega(i) = 1/m$ be the initial weights for $i = 1, \ldots, m$.

Iteration Step For $t \geq 1$, we calculate accumulated weights W_j for $j = 1, \ldots, w$:

$$W_j = \sum_{i=1}^{m} \omega_t(i) \cdot [\![y_i \neq h_j(\mathbf{x}_i)]\!] \tag{10.17}$$

with notation $[\![\ldots]\!]$ as defined in Example 10.3. Let $a(t) = \arg\min\{W_1, \ldots, W_w\}$. (We have $a(1) = 2$ in Example 10.3.) We update

$$\omega_{t+1}(i) = c_t(i) \cdot \omega_t(i) \tag{10.18}$$

where $c_t(i)$ for $i = 1, \ldots, m$, so that $\sum_{i=1}^{m} \omega_{t+1}(i) = 1$.

Iteration End Arriving at $W_{a(T)} \geq 0.5$, the output of the final classifier is

$$H(\mathbf{x}) = \text{sign}\left(\sum_{t=1}^{T} \alpha_t \cdot h_{a(t)}(\mathbf{x}) \right) \tag{10.19}$$

This is the *strong classifier* generated by AdaBoost. It may contain a weak classifier repeatedly at different positions t and with different weights α_t.

10.2.2 Parameters

In the previous subsection we specified the AdaBoost meta-algorithm; weak classifiers are free variables. We still have to explain the parameters α_t and $c_t(i)$ for $t = 1, \ldots, T$ and $i = 1, \ldots, m$.

Parameters α_t and $c_t(i)$ At iteration t, we have $W_{a(t)}$ as the minimum total weight; $h_{a(t)}$ is the classifier with the smallest average cost or error for the given sample of m pre-classified data. Thus we "allow" $h_{a(t)}$ that it can contribute to the decision, provided that $W_{a(t)} < 0.5$, which means that the classifier is better than random guessing.

The selected weak classifier at iteration t is allowed to contribute to the total decision by $\alpha_t \cdot h_{a(t)}$. At $t = 1$ we select the strongest supporter of a correct classification. Thus, α_1 needs to be large. At any of the subsequent iterations $t = 2, 3, \ldots$ we also select the strongest supporter of a correct classification for a modified set of weights, aiming at a further refinement of the definition of the final classifier H.

The value α_t is the *quality* of (or *trust* into) the classifier $h_{a(t)}$. The values α_t tend to decrease with an increase in t (with probability 1) but are not, in general, a decreasing sequence because we change in each step the weights and thus the problem. It is not "bad" if α_t does not decrease.

The parameter α_t is used at iteration t for defining the scaling factors $c_t(i)$; those scaling factors are a function of α_t.

Those parameters need to be selected in a way to ensure a stop of the iterations and should also contribute to the performance of the finally constructed classifier H.

Common AdaBoost Parameters   We have with $a(t)$ the "winner" at iteration t, having the minimum total weight $W_{a(t)}$. The common choice of the parameter α_t is as follows (we explain later, why):

$$\alpha_t = \frac{1}{2}\log\left(\frac{1 - W_{a(t)}}{W_{a(t)}}\right) \tag{10.20}$$

where the logarithm is to the basis $e = \exp(1)$, also known as $\ln = \log_e$ in the engineering literature. The parameter α_t defines the influence of $h_{a(t)}$ on the final classifier.

For example, if there is a "total consistency" between pre-defined class numbers y_i and outputs $h_{a(t)}(i)$ (i.e. $y_i = h_{a(t)}(i)$ for all $i = 1, \ldots, m$), as it may happen at $t = 1$, then we can use the classifier $h_{a(1)}$ already as the final classifier, no further processing would be needed (i.e. AdaBoost stops). Otherwise, if $0 < W_{a(t)} < 0.5$, then $\alpha_t > 0$ increases with decrease of $W_{a(t)}$.

The common choice for $c_t(i)$ is as follows:

$$c_t(i) = \frac{1}{s_t} \cdot \exp\left(-\alpha_t\, y_i\, h_{a(t)}(\mathbf{x}_i)\right) \tag{10.21}$$

where

$$s_t = \sum_{i=1}^{m} \exp\left(-\alpha_t\, y_i\, h_{a(t)}(\mathbf{x}_i)\right) \cdot \omega_t(i) \tag{10.22}$$

and thus $\sum_{i=1}^{m} \omega_{t+1}(i) = 1$ if $\omega_{t+1}(i) = c_t(i) \cdot \omega_t(i)$ for $i = 1, \ldots, m$.

Those Formulas Are Simple   The formulas for $c_t(i)$ and s_t are actually very simple. Note that $y_i\, h_{a(t)}(\mathbf{x}_i)$ equals either $+1$ or -1.

The values y_i and $h_{a(t)}(\mathbf{x}_i)$ are both in the set $\{-1, +1\}$. Their product equals $+1$ iff $y_i = h_{a(t)}(\mathbf{x}_i)$, and it equals -1 otherwise. Thus, we have that

$$c_t(i) = \frac{1}{s_t} \cdot \left(e^{-\alpha_t}[\![y_i = h_{a(t)}(\mathbf{x}_i)]\!] + e^{\alpha_t}[\![y_i \neq h_{a(t)}(\mathbf{x}_i)]\!]\right) \tag{10.23}$$

and

$$s_t = \left(\sum_{i=1}^{m}[\![y_i = h_{a(t)}(\mathbf{x}_i)]\!] \cdot \omega_t(i)\right) e^{-\alpha_t}$$

$$+\left(\sum_{i=1}^{m}\llbracket y_i \neq h_{a(t)}(\mathbf{x}_i)\rrbracket \cdot \omega_t(i)\right)e^{\alpha_t} \tag{10.24}$$

where
1. $e^{-\alpha_t} < 1$ (i.e. a reduction of the weight) for the "already-solved" data items, and
2. $e^{\alpha_t} > 1$ (i.e. an increasing weight) for the data items that still "need a closer look in the next iteration".

Example 10.4 (Continuation of Example 10.3) We had $\mathbf{x}_1$ to $\mathbf{x}_5$ with $y_1 = +1$, $y_2 = -1$, $y_3 = -1$, $y_4 = +1$, and $y_5 = +1$. The classifier h_1 assigns the class number "+1" to any of the five descriptors, and the classifier h_2 only to $\mathbf{x}_1$ and $\mathbf{x}_5$, otherwise "−1".

At $t = 1$ we have $\omega_1(i) = 1/m$ for $i = 1, \dots, m$, $W_1 = 0.4$ and $W_2 = 0.2 < 0.5$, and thus $a(1) = 2$. This leads to

$$\alpha_1 = \frac{1}{2}\log_e\left(\frac{1 - 0.2}{0.2}\right) = \frac{1}{2}\log_e 4 = \log_e 2 \approx 0.693 \tag{10.25}$$

and

$$s_1 = \sum_{i=1}^{5}\exp\left(-\alpha_1 y_i h_2(\mathbf{x}_i)\right) \cdot \frac{1}{5}$$

$$= \frac{1}{5}\left(e^{-\alpha_1} + e^{-\alpha_1} + e^{-\alpha_1} + e^{\alpha_1} + e^{-\alpha_1}\right)$$

$$\approx \frac{1}{5}(0.500 + 0.500 + 0.500 + 2.000 + 0.500) \approx 0.800 \tag{10.26}$$

This defines $c_1(1) = 5/8$, $c_1(2) = 5/8$, $c_1(3) = 5/8$, $c_1(4) = 5/2$, and $c_1(5) = 5/8$, and thus $\omega_2(1) = 0.125$, $\omega_2(2) = 0.125$, $\omega_2(3) = 0.125$, $\omega_2(4) = 0.5$, and $\omega_2(5) = 0.125$. The sum equals 1, as it has to be.

Now we are ready to proceed to $t = 2$. The classifier h_1 continues to be wrong for $i = 2$ and $i = 3$. This gives $W_1 = 0.25$. The classifier h_2 is wrong for $i = 4$. This gives $W_2 = 0.5$. O.K., now h_1 is the winner. We have that $a(2) = 1$. Because of $W_1 < 0.5$, we continue. This leads to

$$\alpha_2 = \frac{1}{2}\log_2\left(\frac{1 - 0.25}{0.25}\right) = \frac{1}{2}\log_e 3 \approx 0.549 \tag{10.27}$$

and

$$s_2 = \sum_{i=1}^{5}\exp\left(-\alpha_2 y_i h_2(\mathbf{x}_i)\right) \cdot \omega_2(i)$$

$$= 0.125\left(e^{-\alpha_2} + e^{\alpha_2} + e^{\alpha_2} + e^{-\alpha_2}\right) + 0.5 \cdot e^{-\alpha_2}$$

$$\approx 0.125(0.578 + 1.731 + 1.731 + 0.578) + 0.5 \cdot 0.578 \approx 0.866 \tag{10.28}$$

This defines $c_2(1) \approx 0.667$, $c_2(2) \approx 1.999$, $c_2(3) \approx 1.999$, $c_2(4) \approx 0.667$, and $c_2(5) \approx 0.667$, and thus $\omega_3(1) \approx 0.083$, $\omega_3(2) \approx 0.250$, $\omega_3(3) \approx 0.250$, $\omega_3(4) \approx 0.334$, and $\omega_3(5) \approx 0.083$. The sum of those approximate values equals 1.

Now we are ready to proceed to $t = 3$. For the classifier h_1 (still wrong for $i = 2$ and $i = 3$), we have that $W_1 \approx 0.5$. For the classifier h_2, we obtain that $W_2 = 0.334$. The classifier h_2 wins for $t = 3$; thus, $a(3) = 2$. Because of $W_2 < 0.5$, we continue. This leads to

$$\alpha_3 = \frac{1}{2} \log_e \left(\frac{1 - 0.334}{0.334} \right) \approx \frac{1}{2} \log_e 1.994 \approx 0.345 \qquad (10.29)$$

Continue the calculation.

Independent n Weak Classifiers Consider descriptors in $\mathbb{R}^n$, and for each $j = 1, \ldots, n$, we do have a weak classifier $h_j(\mathbf{x})$ whose output only depends on x_j, for $\mathbf{x} = (x_1, \ldots, x_j, \ldots, x_n)$. (Here we have $n = w$, where w was the number of weak classifiers before.)

For example, we can apply a simple threshold decision:

$$h_j(\mathbf{x}) = \begin{cases} -1 & \text{if } x_j < \tau_i \\ +1 & \text{if } x_j \geq \tau_i \end{cases} \qquad (10.30)$$

for n real thresholds $\tau_1, \ldots, \tau_n$. If $n = 1$, this simply defines a lower and an upper part of the real numbers where "all" h_j are either $+1$ or "at least one" is not equal to $+1$. If $n = 2$, the location of points where both classifiers equal $+1$ defines a rectangle.

What is the geometric subspace defined for $n = 3$ by the value $+1$ for all the three weak classifiers?

For example, each of those n classifiers can be defined by one scalar measurement in a digital image. That is, we may have different image functionals Φ_i, mapping images I into reals $\Phi_j(I) \in \mathbb{R}$. For n such functionals, the descriptor space is then defined by n-tuples $(\Phi_1(I), \Phi_2(I), \ldots, \Phi_n(I))$. Face detection is an example of an application where this approach is followed.

10.2.3 Why Those Parameters?

Why the given α_t? This subsection is for the readers who are interested in mathematics.

We aim at the minimum number of cases where $H(\mathbf{x_i}) \neq y_i$ for $i = 1, \ldots, m$. Consider the iterated updates of weights $\omega_t(i)$, starting with $t = 1$. We have that

$$\omega_1(i) = 1/m \qquad (10.31)$$

$$\omega_2(i) = c_1(i) \cdot \omega_1(i) = c_1(i)/m \qquad (10.32)$$

$$\omega_3(i) = c_2(i) \cdot \omega_2(i) = \left[c_1(i) \cdot c_2(i) \right]/m \qquad (10.33)$$

$$\cdots$$

$$\omega_{T+1}(i) = \left[\prod_{t=1}^{T} c_t(i)\right] / m$$

$$= \frac{1}{m \cdot \prod_{t=1}^{T} s_t} \cdot \exp\left(-y_i \cdot \sum_{t=1}^{T} \alpha_t h_{a(t)}(\mathbf{x}_i)\right) \qquad (10.34)$$

Let $f(\mathbf{x}_i) = \sum_{t=1}^{T} \alpha_t h_{a(t)}(\mathbf{x}_i)$. Thus, we have that

$$\omega_{T+1}(i) = \frac{1}{m \cdot \prod s_t} \cdot \exp\left(-y_i \cdot f(\mathbf{x}_i)\right) \qquad (10.35)$$

If $H(\mathbf{x}_i) = \mathrm{sign}(f(\mathbf{x}_i)) \neq y_i$, then $y_i \cdot f(\mathbf{x}_i) \leq 0$. Thus, $\exp(-y_i \cdot f(\mathbf{x}_i)) > 1$:
1. If $\llbracket H(\mathbf{x}_i) \neq y_i \rrbracket = 1$, then $\exp(-y_i \cdot f(\mathbf{x}_i)) > 1$.
2. If $\llbracket H(\mathbf{x}_i) \neq y_i \rrbracket = 0$, then $0 < \exp(-y_i \cdot f(\mathbf{x}_i))$.
In both cases we have that $\llbracket H(\mathbf{x}_i) \neq y_i \rrbracket < \exp(-y_i \cdot f(\mathbf{x}_i))$. We take the mean over all data items $\mathbf{x}_i$ for $i = 1, \ldots, m$ and get that

$$\frac{1}{m} \sum_{i=1}^{m} \llbracket H(\mathbf{x}_i) \neq y_i \rrbracket \leq \frac{1}{m} \sum_{i=1}^{m} \exp\left(-y_i \cdot f(\mathbf{x}_i)\right)$$

$$= \sum_{i=1}^{m} \frac{\exp(-y_i \cdot f(\mathbf{x}_i))}{m}$$

$$= \sum_{i=1}^{m} \left(\omega_{T+1}(i) \cdot \prod_{t=1}^{T} s_t\right) \quad [\text{see } (10.35)]$$

$$= \left(\sum_{i=1}^{m} \omega_{T+1}(i)\right) \cdot \prod_{t=1}^{T} s_t$$

$$= 1 \cdot \prod_{t=1}^{T} s_t = \prod_{t=1}^{T} s_t \qquad (10.36)$$

Observation 10.2 *This result tells us that the mean of the number of mis-classifications is upper-bounded by the product of the scaling factors. This relates the error of the generated strong classifier to the errors of the contributing weak classifiers.*

Thus, we can reduce the number of mis-classifications by reducing this product. One way for doing so is to attempt to minimize every scaling factor $s_t, t = 1, \ldots, T$, as a "singular event".

The Final LSE Optimization Step   Recall (10.22) for s_t. We take the first derivative with respect to α_t, set it to zero, and calculate the resulting α_t, which defines an extremum in general. In this case it is actually a uniquely defined minimum:

$$\frac{ds_t}{d\alpha_t} = -\sum_{i=1}^{m} y_i h_{a(t)}(\mathbf{x}_i) \cdot \exp\left(-\alpha_t y_i h_{a(t)}(\mathbf{x}_i)\right) \cdot \omega_t(i)$$

$$= -\sum_{y_i = h_{a(t)}(\mathbf{x}_i)} e^{-\alpha_t} \cdot \omega_t(i) \quad + \sum_{y_i \neq h_{a(t)}(\mathbf{x}_i)} e^{\alpha_t} \cdot \omega_t(i)$$

$$= -e^{-\alpha_t} \cdot \sum_{y_i = h_{a(t)}(\mathbf{x}_i)} \omega_t(i) \quad + e^{\alpha_t} \cdot \sum_{y_i \neq h_{a(t)}(\mathbf{x}_i)} \omega_t(i)$$

$$= -e^{-\alpha_t}(1 - W_{a(t)}) + e^{\alpha_t} W_{a(t)} \quad [\text{by using (10.16)}]$$

$$= 0 \tag{10.37}$$

It follows that

$$e^{2\alpha_t} = \frac{(1 - W_{a(t)})}{W_{a(t)}} \tag{10.38}$$

and thus

$$\alpha_t = \frac{1}{2} \log \frac{(1 - W_{a(t)})}{W_{a(t)}} \tag{10.39}$$

This explains the common choice for the update parameter in AdaBoost.

10.3   Random Decision Forests

Example 10.2 introduced decision trees as an option for subdividing a descriptor space, alternatively to binary classifiers. A finite set of randomly generated decision trees forms a *forest*, called a *random decision forest* (RDF). This section describes two possible ways how to use such forests for object detection. The general approach is illustrated by examples from the pedestrian-detection area.

10.3.1 Entropy and Information Gain

While generating our trees, we will make use of information-theoretic arguments for optimizing the distribution of input data along the paths in the generated trees.

Entropy   Consider a finite alphabet $S = \{a_1, \ldots, a_m\}$ with given symbol probabilities $p_j = P(X = a_j)$, $j = 1, \ldots, m$, for a random variable X taking values from S. We are interested in a lower bound for the average number of bits needed for representing the symbols in S with respect to the modelled random process. The *entropy*

$$H(S) = -\sum_{j=1}^{m} p_j \cdot \log_2 p_j \qquad (10.40)$$

defines such a lower bound; if m is a power of 2, then we have exactly the average number of bits needed.

Insert 10.4 (Shannon and Entropy) *C.E. Shannon (1916–2001), an US-American mathematician, electronic engineer, and cryptographer, founded information theory in 1937 with his Master's thesis "A Symbolic Analysis of Relay and Switching Circuits" (MS Thesis, MIT). That thesis was never formally published, but it is widely regarded as the most influential Master's thesis ever written. His ideas were expounded in his famous paper* [C. E. Shannon. A mathematical theory of communication. The Bell System Technical Journal, vol. 27, pp. 623–656, 1948]. *Entropy and conditional entropy are the central subjects in this paper. We use both in this Section in a very specific context.*

For a given set S, the maximum entropy is given if we have a uniform distribution (i.e. $p_j = 1/m$ for $j = 1, \ldots, m$), defining

$$H(S) = \log_2 m - \log_2 1 = \log_2 m \qquad (10.41)$$

Lower entropies correspond to cases where the distribution of probabilities varies over S.

Example 10.5 (Entropy Calculations) Let X be a random variable that takes values A, B, C, D, or E with uniform probability $1/5$. The alphabet is $S = \{A, B, C, D, E\}$. By (10.41) we have $H(S) = \log_2 5 \approx 2.32$ in this case. A Huffman code (see Exercise 10.8) for this example has 2.4 bits on average per symbol.

Now consider the same alphabet $S = \{A, B, C, D, E\}$ but with probabilities $P(X = A) = 1/2$, $P(X = B) = 1/4$, $P(X = C) = 1/8$, $P(X = D) = 1/16$, and $P(X = E) = 1/16$. Now we have

$$H(S) = -0.5(-1) - 0.25(-2) - 0.125(-3) - 2 \cdot 0.0625(-4) = 1.875 \quad (10.42)$$

A Huffman code has 1.875 bits on average for the five symbols in S for this probability distribution.

Observation 10.3 *Maximum entropy is given if all the events occur equally often.*

Dividing an entropy $H(S)$, defined by some probability distribution on S, by the maximum possible entropy given in (10.41) defines the *normalized entropy*

$$H_{norm}(S) = \frac{H(S)}{\log_2 m} \qquad (10.43)$$

which is in the interval $(0, 1]$ for $|S| = m$.

Conditional Entropy The *conditional entropy* $H(Y|X)$ is a lower bound for the expected number of bits that is needed to transmit Y if the value of X is known as a precondition. In other words, Y is extra information to be communicated, under the assumption that X is already known.

The capitals X and Y are variables for classes of individual events. Small letters x or y denote individual events, which are in sets S or T, respectively. For discrete random variables X and Y, let

$$p(x, y) = P(X = x, Y = y) \tag{10.44}$$

$$p(y|x) = P(X = x|Y = y) \tag{10.45}$$

be the values of *joint* or *conditional probabilities*, respectively. By

$$H(Y|X) = -\sum_{x \in S} \sum_{y \in T} p(x, y) \log_2 p(y|x) \tag{10.46}$$

we define the conditional entropy of Y over the set T, given X over the set S. Analogously,

$$H(X|Y) = -\sum_{x \in S} \sum_{y \in T} p(x, y) \log_2 p(x|y) \tag{10.47}$$

is the conditional entropy of X over set S, given Y over set T.[3]

Example 10.6 (Illustration of Conditional Entropy) We consider a hypothetical example that we recorded stereo sequences in a vehicle and had an automated adaptive process, which decided to use either iSGM or BPM for stereo matching on a given sequence.

We have an input X (our manual brief characterization of the traffic scene), and we want to predict the event Y (to prefer iSGM over BPM or not).

Let $S = \{c, h, r\}$, where c stands for recording in CBD area, h for "recording on a highway", and r denotes the event "the scene was recorded on rural road".

Let $T = \{y, n\}$, where y denotes the event "run iSGM", and n denotes the event "run BPM".

All observed cases are summarized in Table 10.1. Accordingly, we have that $P(X = r) = 5/14$, $P(X = c) = 4/14$, $P(X = h) = 5/14$, $P(Y = y) = 9/14$, $P(Y = n) = 5/14$, and

$$H(Y) = -(9/14) \cdot \log_2(9/14) - (5/14) \cdot \log_2(5/14) \approx 0.940 \tag{10.48}$$

This entropy $H(Y)$ expresses that we need 0.940 bits at least to transfer the information whether analysis is done by iSGM or BPM.

---

[3]Shannon's entropy corresponds to minus the entropy used in thermodynamics.

Table 10.1 Table of adaptive decisions for using either iSGM or BPM for stereo matching on 14 recorded stereo sequences. Sequences of the recorded traffic scene are briefly manually characterized for understanding the adaptive decisions

Sequence	Situation	Decision was for use of iSGM
1	Highway	No
2	Highway	No
3	CBD	Yes
4	Rural road	Yes
5	Rural road	Yes
6	Rural road	No
7	CBD	Yes
8	Highway	No
9	Highway	Yes
10	Rural road	Yes
11	Highway	Yes
12	CBD	Yes
13	CBD	Yes
14	Rural road	No

We want to predict whether the system will decide for iSGM or BPM, based on our rough scene characterization. For example,

$$p(y|r) = P(Y = y|X = r) = 3/5 \tag{10.49}$$

$$p(n|r) = P(Y = n|X = r) = 2/5 \tag{10.50}$$

$$H(Y|r) = -(3/5) \cdot \log_2(3/5) - (2/5) \cdot \log_2(2/5) \approx 0.971 \tag{10.51}$$

Thus, the conditional entropy for "rural road" is $H(Y|X = r) = 0.971$. The conditional entropy for using iSGM based on the input X as scene characterization is

$$H(Y = y|X) = \frac{5}{14} \cdot 0.971 + \frac{4}{14} \cdot 0 + \frac{5}{14} \cdot 0.971 \approx 0.694 \tag{10.52}$$

(see Exercise 10.9). Having the characterization of the scene, we can save approximately $0.940 - 0.694 = 0.246$ bits on each message when communicating that iSGM has been used.

Information Gain   The *information gain* $G(Y|X) = H(Y) - H(Y|X)$ is the number of bits saved on average, obtained by comparing the entropy for the unconditional case with that of the conditional case.

10.3.2 Applying a Forest

Assume that we have a trained random forest for a given classification problem that consists of w trees $T_1, \ldots, T_w$. In given image data, we segment a rectangular window W (e.g. a bounding box or a patch), and we use that as input for any of the w trees.

Passing a Window Down in a Forest   We use a window W as an input for the tree T_j. At each split node of the tree, we apply a split function $h_\phi(I)$, defined by parameters ϕ, using a defined descriptor vector $\mathbf{x}(I)$ for uniformly defined functions h_ϕ, for coming to a decision either "yes" or "no". As a result, we pass the window W either to the left or to the right child node. See Fig. 10.16.[4] The shown image is from the *TUD Multiview Pedestrians* database.[5]

Classifying the Window in One Tree   Finally, the window W arrives at a leaf node L of tree T_j. In this leaf node we have probabilities for class memberships. In tree T_j, leaf node L specifies the class probabilities to be assigned to window W. For example, for a particular class d, $1 \le d \le k$, we assign the class probability $p(d) = a$ to W if a leaf L has this value a stored for the class d.

The Strong Classifier Generated by the Forest   A window W ends at one leaf node in each of the w trees of the given random forest. Thus, it collects one value a_d at each of those w leaf nodes for membership in the class d. Altogether, a window w is assigned a sum of w values a_d, one value from each tree.

The defined strong classifier compares now the accumulated sums for the different class numbers $d = 1, \ldots, k$ and also the sum for case 0 (i.e., no object), and classifies W to the class d or to case 0 whenever we have a maximum sum.

Insert 10.5 (Breiman and Random Decision Forests) *The work by the US-American statistician L. Breiman (1928–2005) has been essential for establishing random decision forests as a technique for ensemble learning; see, for example, his paper* [L. Breiman. Random forests. Machine Learning, vol. 45, pp. 5–32, 2001]. *The technique has its roots in tree construction methods and related classifiers, with related pioneering publications by various authors, dating back to about the early 1980s.*

---

[4]The tree diagram has its root at the top (as is customary). For people who complain that it is misleading to depict a tree with its root at the top, here are two examples: Inside the large Rikoriko Cave in The Poor Knights Islands (New Zealand) some trees are growing down from the roof, and on coastal cliffs around northern New Zealand many large Pohutukawa trees are rooted at the edge of a cliff, with almost all of the tree sprawlings down the cliff, lower than its root.

[5]The *TUD Multiview Pedestrians* database is available at www.d2.mpi-inf.mpg.de/node/428 for free download.

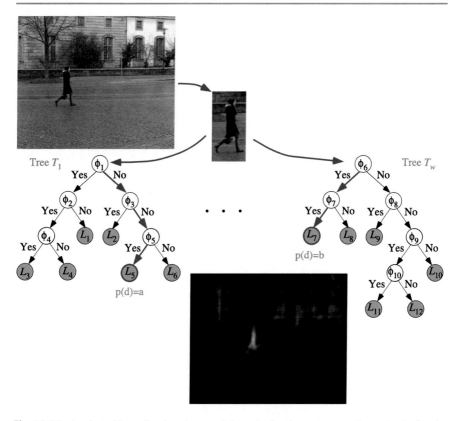

Fig. 10.16 A selected bounding box is passed down in the shown trees, ends up at a leaf node L_5 in the tree on the *left*, and at a leaf node L_7 in the tree on the *right*. Those leaf nodes assign probabilities a and b, respectively, to the bounding box for being in class d. The shown image at the *bottom* is for the particular case of a Hough forest only: Probabilities for being the centre pixel of an object can be shown here in the image carrier visualized by grey levels

10.3.3 Training a Forest

We apply supervised learning for generating a random decision forest. We have a set S of *samples*, i.e. pre-classified image data. A sample $P = [I, d]$ or $P = [I, 0]$ combines an image window I (e.g. a bounding box or a patch) with a class number d, $1 \le d \le k$, or value 0 for "no object". In a binary classification scenario we have just positive or negative bounding boxes, or positive or negative patches (i.e. of pedestrians or of no-pedestrians); see Fig. 10.6.

Cases of More Than Just Two Classes   In general we have more than two classes; see the general case in Sect. 10.1.1 with class numbers $1, 2, \ldots, k$, and 0 for 'not classified'. Figure 10.17 illustrates pedestrians in four different viewing directions (i.e. here we have $k = 4$ and 0 for "no pedestrian"). Such pre-classified data are available, for example, on the TUD Multiview Pedestrians; see also Fig. 10.16 for

Fig. 10.17 Samples of bounding boxes for pedestrians (actually here also sorted, *left* to *right*, for viewing the directions N, E, S, and W)

an example. Let

$$S = S_0 \cup \bigcup_{d=1}^{k} S_d \tag{10.53}$$

be the set of *samples*, i.e. available pre-classified data, where S_0 contains all the samples being "not an object", and S_d all the samples being classified into the class d, $1 \le d \le k$. For the presented RDF approach, this set should have a large cardinality, for example $|S| = 50{,}000$.

Randomly Trained Trees   During supervised learning, we build multiple-decision trees forming an RDF. In those trees we need to define rules for split nodes. The goal for any created split node is to define its decision rule such that the resulting split for the training data set S maximizes the information gain. Following Observation 10.3, we basically aim (ignoring the actual conditional context) at transferring about half of the data arriving at the considered node along each of the two possible ways. If doing so, the generated trees are *balanced*, i.e. of minimized depth, thus supporting time-efficiency of the classification process.

We assume that the RDF consists of a set of w randomly trained decision trees T_j, $1 \le j \le w$. Each tree is considered as being a weak classifier; and the whole forest is used for defining a strong classifier. For example, you may think about using $w = 100$ or a similar number.

Split Functions   The applied rule at a split node v is also called a *split function*. A unary split function h_ϕ decides which node (left or right) comes next:

$$S_L(\phi) = \{I \in S_v : h_\phi(I) = 0\} \tag{10.54}$$

$$S_R(\phi) = \{I \in S_v : h_\phi(I) = 1\} \tag{10.55}$$

where S_v is the set of samples arriving at node v. (To be precise, a sample is a pair $[I, d]$ or $[I, 0]$, but we identify for simplified notation "sample" with the pre-classified window I.) We provide examples of split functions h_ϕ and parameter sets ϕ below.

Outline for Growing a Tree   During training, a randomly selected subset

$$S_j = S_{j,0} \cup \bigcup_{d=1}^{k} S_{j,d} \subset S \tag{10.56}$$

of all the available pre-classified samples is employed for growing a tree T_j of the forest for $1 \leq j \leq w$. Each tree grows randomly and independently to the others. Randomness is important when training a tree. This ensures a variety in the forest, or, in other words, trees are less correlated this way to each-other. For a forest, it would be meaningless to assemble "similar" trees. For the cardinality of S_j, imagine a number such as 5,000 or 10,000.

Sketch of the Tree-Growing Procedure   We start just with a single root node, being the only *active node*. Recursively, we decide for each active node whether it should turn into a split node (with selecting a suitable split function h_ϕ) or whether it should become a leaf node (defined by a *stop criterion*). After having processed an active node, it becomes *passive*, and newly created split nodes become *active*.

Sketch of the Leaf-Definition Procedure   In a created decision tree, samples $I \in S_j$ have been passed down via split nodes to leaf nodes. In general, we not only assign one class to one leaf node (as in the simplifying Example 10.2). For the samples arriving at a leaf node, we need to analyse the distribution of classes represented by those samples.

At a leaf node L we estimate the classification probability $p(c = 0|L)$ (i.e. the probability that arriving samples have been assigned value 0) and the class probabilities

$$p(c \neq 0, d|L) = \left[1 - p(c = 0|L)\right] \cdot p(d|L) \tag{10.57}$$

for $d \in \{1, \ldots, k\}$. For example, Fig. 10.17 illustrates samples to be classified into the classes N, E, S, W (i.e. $k = 4$); such bounding boxes can also be classified into "no pedestrian" (value 0).

Compensate for Sample Bias   There will be a bias in the set $S_j \subset S$ defined by different cardinalities of randomly selected samples for generating a tree T_j, $1 \leq j \leq w$. The classification probabilities $p(c|L)$ and $p(d|L)$ are estimated based on the numbers of samples from sets $S_{j,0}$ or $S_{j,d}$, $1 \leq d \leq k$, arriving at the node L. Let

$$S_j^L = S_{j,0}^L \cup \bigcup_{d=1}^{k} S_{j,d}^L \subset S_j \tag{10.58}$$

be the set of all training samples arriving at the node L. Without compensation, we would use

$$p(c = 0|L) = \frac{|S_{j,0}^L|}{|S_j^L|} \tag{10.59}$$

$$p(d|L) = \frac{|S_{j,d}^L|}{|\bigcup_{d=1}^{k} S_{j,d}^L|} \tag{10.60}$$

which satisfies that $p(c = 0|L) + \sum_{d=1}^{k} p(c \neq 0, d|L) = 1$. The use of these probability estimates would assume that ratios

$$r_{j,0} = \frac{|S_{j,0}|}{|S_j|} \quad \text{and} \quad r_{j,d} = \frac{|S_{j,d}|}{|S_j|} \tag{10.61}$$

with $1 \leq d \leq k$, for the randomly generated training set S_j, are about the same as the ratios

$$r_0 = \frac{|S_0|}{|S|} \quad \text{and} \quad r_d = \frac{|S_d|}{|S|} \tag{10.62}$$

for the full training set S. To compensate for an expected bias, we can use

$$p(c = 0|L) = \frac{|S_{j,0}^L|}{|S_j^L|} \cdot \frac{r_0}{r_{j,0}} \tag{10.63}$$

$$p(d|L) = \frac{|S_{j,d}^L|}{|\bigcup_{d=1}^{k} S_{j,d}^L|} \cdot \frac{r_d}{r_{j,d}} \tag{10.64}$$

as probability estimates instead. For example, if $r_{j,0} < r_0$, then the factor $r_0/r_{j,0} > 1$ increases the probability estimate accordingly.

Features and Split Functions   The definition of split functions is in general based on image features (i.e. locations and descriptors). For time-efficiency reasons, split functions need to be simple but should also be designed for maximizing the information gain.

Due to having two successor nodes, the split function h_ϕ has to produce a binary result, such as a value in $\{0, 1\}$. A common choice is to compare two feature values that are easily calculable for any input image I (e.g. I may represent a bounding box or a patch). For example, a very simple option is given by

$$h_\phi(I) = \begin{cases} 0 & \text{if } I_{loc}(p) - I_{loc}(q) > \tau \\ 1 & \text{otherwise} \end{cases} \tag{10.65}$$

where $I_{loc}(p)$ denotes a value of a specified local operator at pixel location p in the image I. The parameters $\phi = \{p, q, \tau\}$ denote two different pixel locations in I, and $\tau > 0$ is a threshold. More parameters increase the chance of over-fitting. An even simpler option is

$$h_\phi(I) = \begin{cases} 0 & \text{if } I_{loc}(p) > \tau \\ 1 & \text{otherwise} \end{cases} \tag{10.66}$$

Parameters such as $\phi = \{p, q, \tau\}$ or $\phi = \{p, \tau\}$ are *learned* for maximizing the information gain. There might be also other *targets* defined for learning a "good" split function.

Learn a Split Node   Starting with the first split node (the root node), samples are split to the left or right child node according to the value of the split function. As the split function is supposed to split different classes, suitable parameters ϕ are learned from samples.

For ensuring a variety of trees and time efficiency, the parameters ϕ are selected randomly. For example, for the parameters p and τ in (10.66), the set of pixel locations in the input image I and an interval $[\tau_{min}, \tau_{max}]$ can be used for choosing randomly, say, 1,000 pairs $[p, \tau]$ of a location p and a threshold τ. Then, we choose the pair $[p, \tau]$ of parameters that maximizes the information gain within the given set of 1,000 pairs.

Stop Growing   If a stop criterion becomes true at the current node, then this node stops splitting. Examples for a stop criterion are the depth of the node in the tree (i.e. the depth is limited by a maximum value) or the number of samples reaching this node is below a threshold. A tree of large depth can lead to over-fitting, and if there are only a few samples reaching a leaf node, then this might create a bias in the classification.

Algorithm   Algorithm 10.1 specifies training of an RDF (Fig. 10.18). By Algorithm 10.1, we generate a tree of the RDF. The algorithm needs to be called repeatedly for generating the forest. The random selection of S_j and the random selections of the parameter vector ϕ_s aim at ensuring independence of trees. The way how to define a split function h_ϕ is fixed for the whole approach.

10.3.4 Hough Forests

Instead of dealing with larger bounding boxes, we can also consider smaller rectangular *patches* within one bounding box for training. This allows us to use also only "small" patches when applying the classifier. Positive patches need to "collaborate

Algorithm 10.1 (Training a tree of an RDF)

Input: Index j of the tree to be created, a randomly selected set $S_j \subset S$ of thousands of samples $P = [I, d], 1 \leq d \leq k$, or $P = [I, 0]$, with corresponding descriptors **x**.

Output: A trained tree T_j.

1: Let $T_j = \emptyset$, $\mathcal{S} = S_j$, $num = |\mathcal{S}|$, $dep = 0$, stop criterion thresholds (e.g.) $t_{num} = 20$ and $t_{dep} = 15$.
2: **if** $num < t_{num} \parallel dep > t_{dep}$ **then**
3:     Calculate $p(0|L)$ and $p(c \neq 0, d|L)$ with $\mathcal{S}$, according to (10.63), (10.64), and (10.57);
4:     Add leaf L to tree T_j;
5:     return T_j;
6: **else**
7:     $dep = dep + 1$;
8:     **for** $s = 1, \ldots, 1,000$ {1,000 is just given as an example} **do**
9:        Randomly select a parameter vector ϕ_s in the defined range;
10:       Apply split function h_{ϕ_s} on $\mathcal{S}$;
11:       Split $\mathcal{S}$ into $\mathcal{S}_L$ and $\mathcal{S}_R$, for example according to (10.66);
12:       Select that $\phi* = \phi_s$ which optimizes the split;
13:    **end for**
14:    Expand tree T_j by new split node defined by split function $h_{\phi*}$;
15:    Split $\mathcal{S}$ into $\mathcal{S}_L$ and $\mathcal{S}_R$ as defined $h_{\phi*}$;
16:    Case 1: $num = |\mathcal{S}_L|$, $\mathcal{S} = \mathcal{S}_L$; go to line 2;
17:    Case 2: $num = |\mathcal{S}_R|$, $\mathcal{S} = \mathcal{S}_R$; go to line 2;
18: **end if**

Fig. 10.18   A training algorithm for generating a tree in an RDF

somehow" to detect an object. Hough forests do not fit into the general framework of three subsequent steps of localization, classification, and evaluation, as outlined at the beginning of this chapter; they combine localization and classification within one integrated process.

The basic idea of the Hough transform (see Sect. 3.4.1) is that objects are described by parameters, and repeated occurrences (or clusters) of parameters point to the existence of the parameterized object.

Centroid Parameterization   For example, we can take the centroid of an object (for centroid, see Sect. 3.3.2) as a parametric description of an object, and relate centre points of patches to the object's centroid (i.e. this defines a vector). See Fig. 10.19.

Samples in the training set S are now triples $P = [I, d, \mathbf{a}]$ or pairs $p = [I, 0]$, where I is now a "small" patch only, d the class number, with $1 \leq d \leq k$, and **a** the vector going from the centre of the patch to the centroid of the object of class d from which the patch was sampled from. In case of "no object" (i.e. value 0), there are no vectors.

The RDF is now trained with such patches, and there are 2D class probabilities at leaf nodes, defined by the probability values at locations that are pointed to by the vectors **a**. If training patches, arriving at the same leaf node, are sampled from the same bounding box, then they will all point to the same centroid, thus contributing all probabilities to the same point in the 2D probability diagram.

Fig. 10.19 *Centre points* of patches (as shown in Fig. 10.6) are connected to the centroid of a shown object (twice pedestrian, once a cyclist). The "no-object" window does not have a centroid of an object

Insert 10.6 (Origin of Implicit Shape Models and Hough Forests) *Object categorization based on segments, showing only object details, has been introduced in* [B. Leibe and B. Schiele. Interleaved object categorization and segmentation. In Proc. British Machine Vision Conference, 759–768, 2003.]. *This use of* implicit shape models (*IMS*) *has been further developed in* [J. Gall and V. Lempitsky. Class-specific Hough forests for object detection. In Proc. Computer Vision Pattern Recognition, 8 pp., 2009] *by defining object-centroid-based Hough forests.*

Hough forests combine, within one framework, a classification by RDFs with an object localization based on object's centroids.

10.4   Pedestrian Detection

For a localized bounding box, which possibly contains a pedestrian, we use HoG descriptors as defined in Sect. 10.1.3. This section describes a way how to localize such an object candidate (i.e. a rectangular RoI to be tested in the RDF), provides specific split functions as discussed in the previous section at a general level, and outlines a post-processing step (i.e. a step contributing to the evaluation of results provided by the RDF).

Table 10.2 Relationships between distances, heights in recorded images, and disparity range for recorded stereo images where a person was assumed to be 2-m tall

Distance (metres)	10–17	15–22	20–32	30–42	40–52
Height (pixels)	260–153	173–118	130–81	87–62	65–50
Disparity	26–15	17–12	13–8	9–6	7–5

Localizing Regions of Interest   For applying an RDF classifier, at first we need to identify potential candidates for bounding boxes, to be processed by passing them through the trees of the RDF. (A benefit of patch-based Hough forests is that we can replace this search for bounding boxes by, say, a random selection of patches in image regions where pedestrians are likely to appear.)

Use of Stereo Analysis Results   An exhaustive search, i.e. passing windows of expected bounding-box sizes through the image at all the relevant places, is time-consuming. Instead, we can use disparity maps produced by a stereo matcher (as described in Chap. 8).

For example, we can assume that a person is about 2-m tall, and we estimate then in available disparity maps (where values depend on camera parameters such as the length b of baseline and the focal length f used) relationships between the distances between a camera and a person, the height in the image (in pixels), and the corresponding disparity range. See Table 10.2 for an example. In this example, a person, standing 10 metres away from the camera, appears to be about 260 pixels tall in the image plane.

For selecting an ROI, a calculated disparity map is then used to produce a series of maps showing only values for the identified depth ranges. Those partial disparity maps (also called *layers* of a disparity map) are than analysed for occurrences of objects being about of the height as estimated for a person within this disparity range: Scan through one layer of a disparity map with correspondingly sized windows and process further only those windows that have a sufficient number of valid disparities in their area.

Depth ranges for defining layers are defined to be overlapping; we need to ensure that a person can appear completely in one layer, without having, say, different body parts separated in two adjacent layers.

Split Functions   Instead of using the generated (very long) vectors as a whole for training and when applying the classifier, only a few components (possibly, even just one randomly selected component) of descriptor vectors are used for defining a split function. Based on the defined subdivision of bounding boxes and the derived HoG descriptors, a possible choice for split functions is, for example, as follows:

$$h_\phi(I) = \begin{cases} 0 & \text{if } B(a,i) - B(b,j) > \tau \\ 1 & \text{otherwise} \end{cases} \tag{10.67}$$

Fig. 10.20 *Red rectangles* represent combined results; *cyan circles* are centres where the classifier detected a pedestrian. The *few circles* in the *middle* (at a car in a distance) are not merged

where the parameters $\phi = \{a, b, i, j, \tau\}$ denote two block numbers a and b, bin numbers i and j, and a threshold τ; $B(a, i)$ and $B(b, j)$ are the accumulated magnitude values in two specified direction bins.

Non-maximum Suppression   Often, classification detects more than one window around a person in an image. For subsequent tracking or pose estimation, it is meaningful to merge them into one window. See Fig. 10.20.

Each positive window has the corresponding probability assigned by the strong classifier generated by the RDF used. The one with the highest probability in a defined neighbourhood is chosen. Alternatively, having window centres and probabilities, a *mean-shift mode-seeking* procedure could also be applied to specify the final detection of an object.

The rejection of all the false-positives can be based on analysing a recorded image sequence, using failure in tracking or repeated detection for rejecting a detection.

10.5   Exercises

10.5.1 Programming Exercises

Exercise 10.1 (HoG Descriptors, Pedestrian Detection, and Training of an RDF) Implement the calculation of HoG descriptors for rectangular bounding boxes. Allow that parameters (i.e. the size of boxes or cells, the numbers of directional bins) can be chosen differently.

For training and applying an RDF, you may use the sources provided by J. Tao on the website accompanying this book (or implement your own program, for example based on OpenCV).

Apply your HoG descriptors for pre-classified images showing pedestrians, train your RDF, and apply the RDF for classifying manually identified (positive and negative) bounding boxes. Discuss impacts when selecting different parameters in your HoG descriptor program.

Characterize the quality of your pedestrian detector by measures as given in Sect. 10.1.2.

Exercise 10.2 (Eye Detection) Write a program for detecting eyes in images that show frontal views of human faces. You can select any of the approaches listed below.

Eye detection can be done after having already a face detected or by analysing a given image without any prior face detection.

In the first case, by knowing the region of the face, we can locate eyes faster and easier. The rate of false detections decreases; however, the face detector plays a very crucial role. If face detection fails for any reason, then eye detection fails as well.

In the second case, we search for eyes in the whole image without considering a face location. The percentage of true-positive detections with this method can be higher than for the first method, but it takes more time, and the false-positive rate is expected to increase.

Regardless of the followed approach, there are also different image processing techniques to deal with eye detection.

Similar to face detection, you can design weak classifiers using Haar wavelets and a cascade of such classifiers for defining a strong classifier. The basic differences to face detection are defined by the range of sizes of sliding masks and selected training parameters.

As an example of a totally different method, eyes can also be modelled by vertical ellipses, and a Hough-transform for ellipses could be used for eye detection (e.g., after histogram equalization, edge detection, or some kind of image binarization).

Characterize the quality of your eye detector by measures as given in Sect. 10.1.2.

Exercise 10.3 (Training and Applying a Hough Forest) Write a program that allows you to collect interactively a training data set for pedestrian detection using a Hough forest defined by centroids of bounding boxes of pedestrians. See Fig. 10.19 for a related illustration.

For a given image, the program defines interactively bounding boxes (for pedestrians) and patches. If a patch is in a bounding box, then the program identifies it as an "object" and also stores the vector from the centroid of the patch to the centroid of the bounding box. If a patch is not in a bounding box (i.e. not part of a pedestrian), then the program only identifies it as "no object".

After having generated this way a few hundreds of positive and negative samples (i.e. patches), you also write a second program for training a Hough forest. For training an individual tree, you select randomly a subset of your generated samples and start generating a tree with its root. You identify split nodes, leaf nodes, and split functions as described in Sect. 10.3.3.

Finally, you write a third program for applying the generated trees. An input patch, sampled from an input image I, travels down in each of the generated trees using the learned split functions. It ends at a leaf node with a given distribution of centroid locations for object patches versus a likelihood of being no object patch. All the leaf nodes, one for each tree, define the final distribution for the given patch. In the input I you indicate this distribution at the location of the sampled patch. After having many patches processed, you have the accumulated distributions as illustrated in the lower image in Fig. 10.16. Here you may stop with this exercise.

10.5.2 Non-programming Exercises

Exercise 10.4 Continue the calculations (at least one more iteration step) as requested at the end of Example 10.4.

Exercise 10.5 Do manually AdaBoost iterations for six descriptors x_1 to x_6 when having three weak classifiers (i.e. $w = 3$), denoted by h_1, h_2, and h_3, where h_1 assigns the class number "+1" to any of the six descriptors, the classifier h_2 assigns the class number "−1" to any of the six descriptors, and the classifier h_3 assigns the class number "+1" to x_1 to x_3 and class number "−1" to x_4 to x_6.

Exercise 10.6 Let $S = \{1, 2, 3, 4, 5, 6\}$, and X and Y be random variables defined on S, with $X = 1$ if the number is even, and $Y = 1$ if the number is prime (i.e. 2, 3, or 5). Let $p(x, y)$ and $p(y|x)$ be defined as in (10.44) and (10.45). Give the values for all possible combinations, such as for $p(0, 0)$ or $p(0|1)$.

Exercise 10.7 Consider a finite alphabet $S = \{a_1, \ldots, a_m\}$ and two different random variables X and Y taking values from S with $p_j = P(X = a_j)$ and $q_j = P(Y = a_j)$. The *relative entropy* of discrete probability p with respect to discrete probability q is then defined as

$$H(p|q) = -\sum_{j=1}^{m} p_j \cdot \log_2 \frac{p_j}{q_j}$$

Show that
1. $H(p|q) \geq 0$
2. There are cases where $H(p|q) \neq H(q|p)$.
3. $H(p|q) = 0$ iff $p = q$ (i.e. $p_j = q_j$ for $j = 1, \ldots, m$).

Exercise 10.8 Calculate the Huffman codes (not explained in this book; check other sources if needed) for the two probability distributions assumed in Example 10.5.

Exercise 10.9 Verify that $H(Y|c) = 0$ in Example 10.6.

Name Index

A
Akhtar, M.W., 126
Alempijevic, A., 358
Appel, K., 189
Atiquzzaman, M., 126

B
Badino, H., 374
Baker, H.H., 306
Bay, H., 343
Bayer, B., 219
Bayes, T., 190
Bellman, R., 302
Benham, C., 33
Betti, E., 248
Binford, T.O., 306
Bolles, R.C., 337
Borgefors, G., 109
Bouget, J.-Y., 232
Bradski, G., 182, 345
Breiman, L., 402
Brouwer, L.E.J., 94, 249
Brox, T., 156
Bruhn, A., 156
Burr, D.C., 26
Burt, P.J., 75

C
Calonder, M., 345
Canny, J., 64
Chellappa, R., 279
Cheng, Y., 177
Comaniciu, D., 177
Cooley, J.M., 19
Crow, F.C., 52
Crowley, J.L., 75

D
Da Vinci, L., 39
Dalal, N., 384
Dalton, J., 32
Daniilidis, K., 227
Davies, M.E., 2
Descartes, R., 16
Destefanis, E., 335
Dissanayake, G., 358
Drummond, T., 69
Duda, R.O., 93, 123

E
Epanechnikov, V.A., 180
Euclid of Alexandria, 55
Euler, L., 16, 158, 247, 254

F
Felzenszwalb, P.F., 317
Feynman, R.P., 32
Fischler, M.A., 337
Fourier, J.B.J., 15
Frankot, R.T., 279
Frenet, J.F., 106
Freud, Y., 391
Fua, P., 345
Fukunaga, K., 177

G
Gabor, D., 81
Gall, J., 409
Gauss, C.F., 19, 57, 199, 252, 253
Gawehn, I., 248
Gehrig, S., 374
Georgescu, B., 76
Gerling, C.L., 199
Gibbs, J.W., 190

R. Klette, *Concise Computer Vision*, Undergraduate Topics in Computer Science,
DOI 10.1007/978-1-4471-6320-6, © Springer-Verlag London 2014

Index

Made in the USA
Middletown, DE
30 August 2023

37609344R00250